THE ART OF THE DANCE IN THE U.S.S.R.

THE ART OF THE DANCE
IN THE U.S.S.R.
BY MARY GRACE SWIFT
UNIVERSITY OF NOTRE DAME PRESS   1968

Grateful acknowledgement is made to the Embassy of the Union of Soviet Socialist Republics and to the Novosti Press Agency (APN) for permission to use the photographs which face pages 132, 141, 248, 249, 296, and 297.

Acknowledgement is also made to the following Soviet publications in which the remaining photographs appeared:
page 4: top, Akademiia Nauk SSSR, *Istoriia Russkogo Iskusstva,* Vol. I, 1953; bottom, *Istoricheskii Viestnik,* 1888;
page 5: Adam Olearius, *Puteshestvie v Moskoviiu,* 1868;
page 24: Dmitri A. Rovinskii, *Russkiia Narodnyia Kartinki,* Atlas, Vol. I, 1881;
pages 26, 72 (top), and 155: Mikhail M. Mikhailov, *Zhizn' v Balete,* 1966;
page 27: Yuri Slonimsky, *The Bolshoi Ballet,* 1960;
page 32: A. Lunacharsky, *On Literature and Art,* 1965;
page 33: Ol'ga Martynova, *Ekaterina Gel'tser,* 1965;
pages 44 and 154: G. Kremshevskaia, *Nataliia Dudinskaia,* 1964;
page 45: V. Vsevolodskii Gerngross, *Istoriia Russkogo Teatra,* Vol. II, 1929;
pages 50 and 51: M. Chudnovskii, *Viktorina Kriger,* 1964;
page 72: bottom, *Bol'shoi Teatr SSSR. Opera, Balet,* 1958;
page 73: A. Ruleva, *Boris Bregvadze,* 1965;
page 106: *Svetlyi Ruchei* (program), 1935;
page 107: *Radziwill Chronicle;*
page 133: B. L'vov Anokhin, *Alla Shelest.*

CONTENTS

ACKNOWLEDGEMENTS

GRADUATE study leading to the writing of the doctoral dissertation which grew into this book was financed through a National Defense Education Act Fellowship, Title IV. To those who were responsible for this assistance, I am very grateful. The Committee on International Relations and its chairman, Dr. Stephen Kertesz of Notre Dame University assisted in providing travel funds for gathering research materials. A grant from Loyola University, New Orleans, also was helpful in gathering photos and preparing the work for final publication.

I would especially like to thank Dr. George Brinkley, who served as advisor during my work on the dissertation, and who provided much needed help and encouragement. I am also grateful to Dr. Stephen D. Kertesz, Dr. James Bogle and Dr. Eugene J. Leahy for serving as readers. In translating certain phrases, I had the assistance of numerous native speakers of the languages involved. For the cordial help of all of them, I am very grateful. Though it is impossible to name all of them, many other people in the academic and dance world have also given generously of their time in answering my questions. Their willing assistance has always evoked my wonder and gratitude.

I am grateful for the kind aid and forbearance of librarians in the Slavic Section of the Library of Congress and the New York Public Library; the Dance Collection of Lincoln Center; Columbia University and its Russian Archives; the University of Michigan; the University of Chicago and the University of Notre Dame.

Many friends aided my work in countless unrecordable instances. I remember with gratitude not only their priceless assistance, but also the friendships which grew from our mutual addiction to ballet. I wish to express my thanks also to the editors of Notre Dame Press for assistance in preparing the manuscripts for publication. Any errors which remain in it are my responsibility. I would like to make it absolutely clear that the opinions, inferences, conclusions and points chosen for emphasis are my own, and do not necessarily reflect the opinion of my readers, friends, or anyone who assisted me in this project.

In the bibliography and footnotes, the Library of Congress system of transliteration without diacritical markings was used. In the body of the text, names have been spelled to conform to popular usage.

Mary Grace Swift
New Orleans, Louisiana

May, 1968

INTRODUCTION

The Art itself seems unfortunately to have incurred the Imputation of being only an amusing
Trifle, incapable and unworthy of being cultivated by Writing.

—JOHN WEAVER, 1712 [1]

THE use of the stage for political and social purposes is not a new phenom- enon. The chorus of Aristophanes' *Frogs* in 405 B.C. barred entrance to "the sacred dance of the Mystic choir" to such a man who "takes, in office, his gifts and bribes, while the city is tossed on the stormy deep" or to "the knave who tries to procure sup- plies for the use of the enemy's armaments."[2] Though not a new prac- tice, in the twentieth century the Soviet government's use and control of art has excited the curiosity of many Western scholars. Literature has rightly received the most attention,[3] for in the development of Soviet culture, a Party pronouncement on literature has been under- stood by practitioners of all other arts as a warning to rectify any pres- ent deviations from the Party line in their specific art. Soviet policy towards music has been discussed,[4] while drama,[5] film,[6] graphic art and architecture[7] have all received varying degrees of attention. In every study, it has become evident that the Communist Party has officially imposed upon artists the ephemeral, yet all-pervasive doctrine of "so- cialist realism," though in such an art form as music, the application requires much ingenuity and wide imagination by Party artistic dictators.

Yet the fate under the Soviet regime of ballet, the art which many Westerners consider most typically Russian, has not been the subject of any detailed Western studies. Until 1966, with the appearance of the *Era of the Russian Ballet* by Soviet author Natalia Roslavleva,[8] no detailed history of the Soviet period was available. Such has been the dearth of information that reputable scholars have been led to make conclusions similar to the following:

> The only realm in the U.S.S.R. which permits a free development of the artist's genius and an unfettered schooling of public taste is that of the performing arts, and consequently, it is there that Soviet culture has achieved its highest and most deserved triumphs. . . . Perhaps nothing tells more about the realities of a so-called proletarian society than the fact that Soviet culture has attained unsurpassed perfection in such an art as the classical ballet.[9]

In a dancing journal, a broad generalization such as the following might be found: "The ballet is to the Slav what stained glass windows were to the illiterate medieval Christian. Both tell their stories without need for interpreters, without possibility of censorship."[10]

American audiences have become acquainted with Soviet ballet through tours of the Moscow Bolshoi and Leningrad Kirov companies, added to occasional movies of troupes from the Union Republics which appear in American theatres. Through such talented masters as Igor Moiseyev, they have witnessed the thrilling product of the fusion of classical ballet training with folk dance. In the early samples of Soviet ballet seen by the West, occasionally a moralistic or political work crept into the tour repertoire, only to meet such universal rejection or ridicule from Western critics that the 1966 tour of the Bolshoi included chiefly the seemingly innocuous, universally-loved classics: *Swan Lake, Nutcracker, Don Quixote, Giselle, Chopiniana,* and others. Well, indeed, might scholars be led to think that classical ballet occupied so sacrosanct a position in Soviet society that the tentacles of Party control, which have so gripped and stifled the creativity of writers, painters, and musicians, might have left uncensored and unsullied this one glorious art. The author examines whether such a conclusion is justified.

In 1917, during the days when Alexander Kerensky's government tried to hold the Kremlin from the Bolsheviks, one American witness in Moscow, Oliver Sayler, reported that while anarchy, pillage, and murder stained the snow scarlet with blood, while German armies advanced forebodingly, the theatre continued to operate in Moscow. "To the Russian," he explained, "the theatre is not a refuge for idle amusement . . . the theatre is rather a microcosmos, a concentration and explanation of life."[11]

A general love for the theatre is coupled with a particular love of the dance. Russia without dancers would be as incomplete as Italy without singers. Professional dancing companies exist in every town in the Soviet Union large enough to support them; amateur groups exist in thousands of collective farm and factory "houses of culture" where competitions between the groups generate an interest comparable to the American love for baseball. A Western visitor to the village of Saburova in the militant 1930's recounted an amusing village incident whereby one Soviet apostle tried to be "all things to all men" to spread the gospel of Marx. A visitor to the village, an engineering student from Saratov, Alexei Grigorievich, found the Saburova youths were too engrossed in pastimes like dancing, thus shunning their Communist social obligations. Alexei Grigorievich decided he must beat the lads at their game to win their respect, so he challenged the local champion, a steely-sinewed shepherd lad, to a dance contest. To the accompaniment of accordians and balalaikas played by members of the local gang, the two combatants endured the muscle-searing exertion of male Russian folk dance for two hours, when Alexei wearily ceded to the shepherd. But Alexei, though losing, had made his point. "He too was lifted up and carried round amid the plaudits of the crowd. The next night began his discussions upon economics and the future of Russia. Through the dance to Communism!"[12]

Western visitors have never ceased to express wonderment at the unabashed ardor of Soviet ballet audiences.[13] However, any final doubt about the matter disappears at the account of a British reporter in Leningrad in the winter of 1944. After two years of blockade, while much of the city was still a formless heap of rubble and the surviving populace was still weak and sick from long months of stark hunger, while their own homes lacked window panes and heating facilities, the rebuilding of the Leningrad Kirov Opera and Ballet Theatre was given a first priority. The director explained:

> We're due to open May 1 and there's a lot to be done. The army has lent us 200 men to help and we've got priority over everything else. . . . if we can't open May 1 I don't know what the people will say. . . . It makes us feel when the theatre is open that life has begun again.[14]

The Soviet government understands the national passion for dance, and has indeed nourished the art as probably no other government in history has ever done. But the question at hand is whether the story is complete with a knowledge only of the coddling. An examination of the relationship of the art of ballet to the Soviet government and a scrutiny of the librettos of many of the ballets performed would seem to cast more light on the question of whether Soviet ballet has truly permitted "a free development of the artist's genius" and a performing art "without possibility of censorship."

MARY GRACE SWIFT

THE ART OF THE DANCE IN THE U.S.S.R.

CHAPTER ONE

Ballet and the Tsars

What a fascinating field—the history of art . . .
How much work here for a Communist.

—V. I. LENIN[1]

PREVIOUS to the 1917 March Revolution which deprived the Romanov
dynasty of its throne, the addiction to
ballet among the ruling circles of Russia cast many of them into the exclusive
class of balletomanes, whose family place at the imperial theatres was
passed guardedly from father to son.[2] For an understanding of the
paths of development of ballet under the Soviet government, it is in-
dispensable to probe the history of the art under the tsars.

Upon examining the origins of ballet in Russia, a cardinal term
must be understood from the outset. Officially guided by the philosophy of Marxism-Leninism, the writings of a Soviet author must be
mindful of the principle of *narodnost'*. "Narod" means "nation" or
"folk" in Russian, so the word sometimes means a conscious attention
to the nation and its heritage, while at other times the word could simply be translated as "folkness." In the early years after the Revolution,
Soviet historians could write in accordance with the internationally-
minded principles of Karl Marx, who wanted a worldwide rule by the
proletariat and the abolition of national boundaries, thus precluding
nationalism. During the years when Joseph Stalin was consolidating
his power and facing growing German strength, in order to reinforce
the patriotism of the Russian people, historians were officially charged
with the task of exalting the national past.[3] Further, all cultural efforts, in accordance with a Stalinist slogan, had to be "socialist in con-

3

tent and national in form."[4] The application of these principles has constrained Soviet historians to exalt the accomplishments of the Fatherland in all spheres of cultural and scientific activity, concomitantly minimizing foreign accomplishments.[5] It is not surprising, then, that some divergence of opinion is noticeable regarding the question of the origin of ballet in Russia. Foreign and prerevolutionary Russian writers tend to emphasize foreign influences, while Soviet art historians minimize the foreign influences and make desperate efforts to emphasize the folk roots of ballet.

Galina Ulanova, after being asked once whether she thought links existed between folk and classical dance, firmly answered that she could not agree with dance historians who made such assertions, since folk dance was a primitive, natural means of expression and classical dance was more artificial.[6]

Valerian Svetlov, a prerevolutionary balletomane and dance historian, declared that folk choreography, which had a rough character in heathenish times, was condemned when Russia was Christianized, and therefore remained apart from the development of choreographic art in Russia, which received its greatest stimuli from the West.[7]

One of the most venerated figures in Soviet ballet, Agrippina Vaganova, once declared:

> All that we have on our stage is a product of the assimilation of two schools—French and Italian. The knowledge, experience, and fame of these two schools were passed on successively to us, and artistic and technical improvement reached an unprecedented degree.[8]

Present Soviet authors are obliged to promote an opposite opinion. In assuming power in Russia, the Bolshevik Party promised that the power of the aristocracy would be crushed, and that the country would then be in the hands of the workers and peasants. In their contempt for the old regime and in their attempts to glorify "the masses," art historians now point to the folk origins of all art, urging, almost fanatically, a return to folk idioms, a study of folk forms, and the inclusion

4

Silver figures of the sixth century found near Kiev, *above*. Artist's reconstruction of eleventh-century frescoes from the Cathedral of St. Sophia in Kiev, showing *skomorokhi* performing folk dances, *below*.

Russian folk dance at Ladoga as depicted in a travel account of 1634 by the German Adam Olearius.

of folk melodies into compositions. "Classic dance is so-called because it utilizes certain poses and gestures characteristic of ancient statues and figures on ancient vases . . . at the basis of it lie also the movements of folk dance," explains one author.[9] A noted choreographer declared, "The highest form of stage dancing is classic ballet. It sprang up on the basis of folk dance and in the course of its development absorbed into itself all the best that was found in world choreography."[10] Bourgeois dance historians and "vulgar sociologists" have incorrectly pointed out that ballet was only a *pridvornoe*, "court," art, cultivated only by palace ladies and cavaliers. They err who have customarily traced the origin of ballet to spectacles such as the *Ballet Comique de la Reine,* produced by Baltazarini in 1581 at the court of Catherine de Médicis.[11] Such a view is "antihistorical" to the Soviet author.

However, it is difficult to avoid the fact that classical ballet developed in Russia in the wake of the teaching of great French, Italian, Danish, and Swedish teachers who came to the tsarist court. Ballet became a plaything of the ruling class, adding unprecedented glamour to festivities. In florid Renaissance style it extolled the merits of the gods and goddesses sitting on the Russian Olympus or danced the praises of their armies and fleets in battle.

It is true that some form of dancing has existed in Russia since the most ancient times. In the area of Kiev, there have been found small silver figures dating from the sixth century, which seem to represent male dancers with well turned-out feet, executing squatting steps. The frescoed walls of Kiev Cathedral of St. Sophia (1073) preserved figures of *skomorokhi*—clownish entertainers who played folk instruments, sang, and did Russian folk dances called *pliaska*.[12] Their dances, which stemmed partly from heathen religious rites, consisted of traditional folk steps as well as acrobatics and juggling.[13] As early as 1629, a rope dancer named Ivan Lodygin was giving lessons in his art.[14] Adam Olearius, who travelled to Muscovy as secretary to the Holstein ambassador, on July 23, 1634, described entertainers at Ladoga who played "Country Musick, which consisted of a Lute and Violin, with some voices singing aires to the honour of their Czar, Michael Federouits [Mikhail Federovich], and perceiving they were permitted, they fell a-dancing after a strange manner."[15] In 1635, emissaries to Poland from Muscovy saw a court spectacle telling the story of Judith and Holofernes, while in 1660 Likhachev, sent to the court of Ferdinand de' Medici, reported such marvelous performances there of music and dance[16] that the ruler of Muscovy, Alexei Mikhailovich (1645–1676), could well conclude that such events had become a monarchical status symbol. According, he sent out a "talent scout," Nicholas Von Staden, to Courland to recruit entertainers.[17] Meanwhile, Alexei also had a close co-worker, Artemon Matveyev, who helped bring the first theatrical performance to the Russian court. There was living at that time in the German settlement near Moscow a certain Lutheran pastor, Johann Gottfried Gregory, whose theatrical interests seemingly equalled his ministerial inclinations. Alexei saw a production of Gregory's performing company at Matveyev's personal theatre and was delighted with it, but when Gregory sought permission to stage a "comedy" at court, the tsar wavered, for he knew the Orthodox Church might question such displays there. Alexei then turned the matter over to his *dukhovnik,* his "spiritual adviser," who based his judgment on the practices of the Byzantine court which did allow similar amusements. The first court performance, *Ahasuerus and Esther,* was then given by the *nemtsi* (Germans) with the *dukhovnik's* permission.[18] Such early productions were a mixture of dance, drama, and music.

The fertile imagination of Gregory next produced a version of *Orpheus,* which was a closer approach to ballet than the previous pageant. In the performance, Orpheus first moved down the stage accompanied by two moving pyramids at his sides. Down stage Orpheus bowed low three times to the tsar, then sang the German verses:

Ist nun der gewünschte Tag	Has now the desired day
Dermahl eins erschienen	Finally appeared
Das man dir nun Freude mag,	So that we may have the joy
Grosser Zare dienen.	Of serving you, great Tsar?

Turning to the pyramids, he said:

Drumb wohlan meyn seytenwerck [*sic*]	So, then, my stringed instrument
Las dich leiblich singen	Pour forth your lovely sounds
Und du pyramidenberg	And your pyramids
Hüpfe nach dem singen.[19]	Leap to the singing.

Orpheus and the pyramids then performed a *pas de trois,* after which the whole troupe entered the stage, where they amused the court for several hours.[20] The tsar, fascinated, awarded presents to the *nemtsi,* and Gregory obtained permission from Alexei to form a theatrical school with twenty-six young pupils. The project was not well administered, for the students later sent a petition to the tsar complaining that they were starved, ragged, and shoeless. However, the significant fact seems to be that there was a theatrical school in Moscow before there was a Greek and Latin academy.[21] Subsequently, theatrical affairs were guided by A. S. Matveyev, who assiduously looked after them as if he were charged with a chief post. After Alexei's death, Matveyev was sent into exile, and for the remainder of the century, news of theatrical activity is rarer.[22]

Peter the Great, noted for his attempt to "westernize" Russia, was impressed with European dance on his first voyage abroad when he saw the ballet *Cupidon* at Amsterdam.[23] In a Soviet description, during Peter's reign, art was converted from an amusement into a means of confirming dominant political ideas, and thus acquired a social significance.[24] Music and *pliaski* were used in street festivals, and in 1710, to celebrate the victory over the Swedes at the battle of Poltava, a performance was given in Moscow with the formidable title: *The Lord's Humiliation of the Proud in the City of Israel, the Humiliation Acting through the Humble David about the Humiliated Goliath and*

The Righteous (Godly) Father Cursing Absalom with Punishment.[25]
After returning from a visit to Paris in 1717, Peter introduced into
Russian society the unprecedented phenomena of balls attended by
both sexes. He personally issued directions for their staging, and few
would have been foolhardy enough to refuse to cooperate. At one such
gathering, Peter reportedly executed one cabriole after another, and
insisted that very old men should imitate him. When they balked, he
said they would then have to suffer the standard penalty of draining a
large goblet. At this threat, the older men imitated Peter until they
could scarcely stand, but before they had time to rest a bit after one
round of such activity, Peter began a polka which they were again
forced to join.[26]

The reign of Anna Ivanovna (1730–1740) brought most significant
developments to Russian ballet. Anna's interest in dance was encouraged by her favorite, Ernest Johann Biron, though she herself was
noted for a love of coarse jokes, horseplay, and Russian folk dance.
Each year at Shrovetide she invited the noncommissioned officers of
the guards to court because they were adept at folk dancing, and members of the court and imperial family gaily joined them in the strenu-
ous activity.[27] In 1731, dance training was introduced regularly into
the program of the Shliakhetny Corps for noblemen cadets. The earliest teachers were not noteworthy, but at the arrival of Jean Baptiste
Landé on August 1, 1734, Anna's wish for a proficient master was
fulfilled. Landé worked with a group of Italian opera performers, and
at times the cadets of the Shliakhetny Corps would grace the operas
with dance interludes.[28] Landé's successes pleased Anna, and in 1737
he appealed formally for permission to establish a school of dance, asking a recompense of 1,500 rubles a year, plus a flat, firewood, and
candles. Anna signed the necessary ukase on May 4, 1738.[29] This school,
which first met in the Winter Palace, was the direct ancestor of the
present Vaganova Choreographic Institute, the seedbed for the training of dancers who in later times would circle the globe with teachers
and performers of Russian ballet.

With an output of native performers assured, the imperial court could rest assured of continued amusement, but foreign masters continued to arrive. In 1735, Antonio Rinaldo, nicknamed Fusano, came to Russia and achieved sufficient reputation to be given responsibility for gala festivities in Moscow to honor the succession of Elizabeth Petrovna to the throne in 1742. The first production was entitled *The Joy of the People at the Appearance of the Morning Star on the Russian Horizon,* and later in the same evening was given *The Golden Apple at the Banquet of the Gods or the Judgment of Paris,* depicting three rival goddesses who represented three Russian empresses: Catherine I, Anna Ivanovna, and Elizabeth Petrovna.[30] Elizabeth herself was reported to be "a true artist" of the dance, unrivalled anywhere. She especially loved to attend masked balls, dressed as a man.[31]

A significant event in the eighteenth-century cultural exchanges took place when there came to Russia from the court of the Empress Maria Theresa of Austria a balletmaster named Franz Hilferding van Wewen. In 1759, he mounted a ballet, *The Refuge of Virtue,* which bears interesting parallels to Soviet works written on "national liberation" themes. The production depicted an American Indian oppressed by European tyrants. His beloved stabbed herself in order not to fall to the enemy, and the Indian followed her example. The Russian autocrat was allegorically praised as the refuge of persecuted virtue. The entire production was crowned with another device commonly occurring in Soviet productions: a dance of the nations of Europe, America, Asia, and Africa.[32]

Many members of the nobility became involved in Hilferding's ballets. In 1764 in St. Petersburg, Peter, the Prince of Courland, danced the role of the shepherd, Acis. His lover, the nymph Galatea, was played by the Countess Sivers, daughter of the *oberhofmarschall,* the Lord High Steward of the court. In the final act, the two lovers were united in the presence of the god Hymen, which was so brilliantly danced by the Tsarevich Paul Petrovich that the applause was sufficiently great to overpower the orchestra.[33]

Soviet historians emphasize that the purpose of many of the spectacles was to glorify the power of the Russian state.[34] Such a ballet was mounted in 1768, commemorating Catherine II's truly heroic act of being inoculated against smallpox. On the stage of the ballet, called *Prejudice Overcome*, there were temples of Aesculapius and of Ignorance. The character Ruthenia, the allegorical personification of Russia, went about the stage torn between hope and fear of death. The Genie Science tried to impart courage to her, in vain. Then, from the temple of Aesculapius marched forth the Russian Minerva (a title given Catherine by admirers such as Voltaire). For the good of her people, she submitted to inoculation. Ruthenia and the Genie then also submitted to it and began a gay dance.[35]

Another production which "served the aim of political propaganda"[36] was *The Early Reign of Oleg* (1791). It depicted an episode of ninth- and tenth-century Russian history when Prince Oleg attacked Constantinople. Having portrayed Oleg's adventures, the producer "quite transparently alluded to the inheritor of his work—the Russian tsarina,"[37] who indeed at that time had dreams of her "Greek Project" of gaining Constantinople.

ORGANIZATION OF THEATRICAL DIRECTION

The quite nebulous direction of the imperial theatres was stabilized in the reign of Catherine II. She empowered Ivan P. Yelagin to bring all theatrical business under his domain, including drama, ballet, and music. In the decree of December 21, 1766, confirming the position, Catherine made it clear that all the money and everything connected with the position should be empowered to Yelagin, the Director of the Imperial Theatres.[38] From this time, the St. Petersburg Ballet School was under the authority of the director of theatres or of a committee substituting for him. Many of the private theatres of the country eventually came under the jurisdiction of the Ministry of the Interior, but the Imperial Theatres came under the power of the *Ministerstvo Dvora,* the Ministry of the Court. Theatrical administrators also had to deal with the *Kabinet Ego Velichestva,* the Cabinet of His Majesty, which acted somewhat in the capacity of a Ministry of Finance within the Ministry of the Court. The Ministry of the Court had charge of other royal amusements also, such as the stables and hunting grounds.[39]

At special times ballet was presented for the immediate imperial family in small theatres, such as the Hermitage Theatre, which was actually part of the Winter Palace in St. Petersburg; the theatre in Pavlovsk, which was the center of the summer camps of the guard regiments stationed in St. Petersburg; and the theatre of Tsarskoe Selo, the summer residence of the Russian tsars of the nineteenth century. Ordinarily, however, ballet could be seen by large audiences only in three theatres in the days of tsarist domination: the Maryinsky Theatre in St. Petersburg, the Bolshoi Theatre in Moscow, or the Wielki Theatre in Warsaw.[40]

Poland had developed its own ballet as early as 1765, while still an independent nation. After a Polish revolt in 1830, the city of Warsaw and parts of Poland became dominated by Russia. The Wielki Theatre came under the direction of the Russian Ministry of the Interior and hence was subject to budgetary complications.[41] However, even when the Russian Duma was established after the Revolution of 1905, those theatres under the aegis of the Ministry of the Court were not subject to any financial control by that body. The usual deficit for the Imperial Theatres was over two million gold rubles a year. In those days, there existed three varieties of crown properties: state property; *udely,* meaning property held jointly by the House of Romanov and the state; and the Privy Purse—property of the reigning monarch only, coming from such holdings as the whole Altai district of Siberia[42] and his civil list. The ballet deficit was paid from the funds of the Privy Purse.

In 1809, the theatrical mechanism was juridically normalized. A committee of three members was established, one member to direct Moscow theatres and two others to direct the repertoire and financial part of the St. Petersburg theatres.[43] Such jobs were to be taken seriously: an imperial ukase of January 3, 1835, placed the Director of the St. Petersburg theatres in the second rank of the Russian civil government—equalling the rank of a major general in the Russian army.[44]

In Soviet opinion, the Moscow ballet theatre had an advantage over the St. Petersburg establishment, since the latter was more closely attached to the court. Catering to a wider city population, the Moscow theatre was allowed a freer, more democratic development.[45] The actual history of public ballet performances in Moscow can be traced back to 1759, when an Italian named Giovanni Battista Locatelli built a private theatre in Moscow for opera and ballet performances. However, in 1776 the Moscow governor-procurator, Prince P. V. Urusov, was granted the privilege of being proprietor of Moscow theatres.[46] In 1780 an edifice called the Petrovsky Theatre was built on the spot of the present Bolshoi, but it burned in October, 1805. In August, 1806, on the petition of A. L. Naryshkin, Tsar Alexander I officially established the Moscow ballet and opera theatre as an Imperial Theatre, with M. B. Volkonsky as first director.[47] In January, 1823, the Moscow crown theatre was separated from the jurisdiction of St. Petersburg and put under the surveillance of the military governor-general, A. V. Golitsyn.[48] The old Petrovsky building had suffered disaster from fire and war, so that in 1825, a new structure had to be built on the site of the old Petrovsky. It was henceforth called the Bolshoi Theatre.

The first ballet school in Moscow came into existence in 1773, when the Italian Filippo Beccaria and his wife began dance instruction in a Moscow orphanage, the *Vospitatel'nyi Dom*. In 1784, the guardian council of the orphanage contracted to turn over the ballet school to the Petrovsky Theatre, then under the English entrepreneur, Michael Maddox.[49]

Imperial theatre directors were always faced with personnel problems. During the directorship of A. L. Naryshkin (1799–1819), a young dancer named Bolina married soon after graduation without obtaining the necessary permission of the superintendent. Naryshkin then asked the tsar to ratify a decree whereby graduates could not leave the service for ten years after graduation without giving financial recompense sufficient to support ten foster children in the theatrical school for five years, with an annual cost reckoned at 500 rubles. Girl students, sometimes of serf origin, were at times sold for 25,000 rubles in cash.[50]

Simultaneously with the growth of the imperial ballet, there had grown a multitude of theatres owned by rich landowners called *pomeschiki*. At times these served as fountainheads of talent to populate the larger theatres. In Moscow and its suburbs there were twenty such serf theatres, and those who could afford it had their own orchestras and ballet troupes. Standard productions were given, with the repertoire of the theatre of Prince Nikolai Grigorievich Shakhovsky including *Bluebeard* and *Vain Precautions*.[51]

Sometimes the serf ballerina might be as carefully guarded as a jewel. Such was the fate of Tatiana Vasilevna Shlykova-Granatova (1773–1863). At an early age she was taken to the theatrical school of Count N. P. Sheremetev. There, she was taught French, Italian, music, and dancing, excelling especially in the last. The talented woman lived to an old age in the Sheremetev mansion, although by 1800 the serf theatre was rapidly declining.[52] All the serf ballerinas did not share such a distinguished lot. Prince Nikolai B. Yusupov had a signal system in his theatre whereby he could command his serf ballerinas to stop the performance and take part in orgies with his guests.[53]

At one time, prices were high for serf dancers. In order to obtain a dancer named Kravchenkova and her parents for his Orel city theatre, Count S. M. Kamensky gave 250 other serfs.[54] Gradually, serf owners found it economically disadvantageous to maintain their large troupes and sold them to the imperial theatres. In 1824, Prince Golitsyn appealed to the committee of ministers to free the serfs attached to the Bolshoi, and the request was granted.[55] Gradually, the serf dancer passed into oblivion, but her memory has been melodramatically revived in such Soviet ballets as *Serf Ballerina,* staged in 1927 at the Leningrad Theatre of Opera and Ballet.

As the decades passed, the St. Petersburg Academy produced graduates capable of choreography. One of them, Ivan Ivanovich Valberkh, is praised in the U.S.S.R. for his incorporation of *narodnost'* as well as *sovremennost'* in his ballets. The latter term, equally as important as the first, means "contemporaneity." The theme of a ballet, for example, would have this highly desirable quality if it dealt with problems and people of the present age. At one of the many gala events celebrating the coronation of Alexander I (1801–1825), Valberkh staged an allegorical ballet called *Virtue Crowned*. During the Napoleonic Wars, in August, 1812, he produced *The Militia, or Love to the Fatherland*. In the Soviet view, this was an unprecedented event in the history of the imperial theatres, an occasion of great social and political significance. There, where formerly only the gods of mythology had reigned, "the spectator saw living Russian *sovremennost'*."[56] On May 19, 1813, he staged *The Russian in Germany; or the Consequence of Love to the Fatherland*. In this ballet a group of Russian peasants went to Germany in search of their children, who as soldiers had gone westward with the army. There they met Germans who had happily been freed from the French by the Russians. At the end of the ballet, an enemy fort blew up and the hero of the Russian regiment received a citation from the commanding general, with the action taking place against a background displaying signs that proclaimed "For the Fatherland!" and "Freedom of Europe!"[57]

As Napoleon's fortune grew worse, Valberkh's ideas became ever more fertile. On August 30, 1813, he produced *Celebration in the Camp of the Allied Armies at Montmartre,* a festival consisting of songs and dances of the nations which united against the Corsican. While conceding that it is now difficult to read the librettos of these ballets without smiling, a chief Soviet ballet historian, Yuri Slonimsky, affirms that "such presentations stirred the spectators, awakened in them feelings of patriotic duty and the will to struggle with the enemies of the fatherland."[58] A final toast came on July 3, 1814, with *The Triumph of Russia, or The Russians in Paris.* This work, unlike others of Valberkh, is flatly rejected by some Soviet authors for obvious reasons. They say that it falsely portrayed Russian aims in the war, and that Tsar Alexander was erroneously portrayed as the hero instead of the Russian people. In the ballet, the Genie of Russia, representing Alexander, descended on a cloud toward France, who was dressed in mourning clothes, bewailing her grief. Since she manifested repentance, France was forgiven, to the accompaniment of cracking thunder. Then suddenly the mourning maiden appeared in festive garments bestrewed with the *fleur de lis* of the Bourbon dynasty. She and the Genie of Russia, her new friend, were sped along on clouds to Paris, where the French people celebrated the return of the Bourbons. Russian soldiers stood about, looking with distrust on the tricolored scarves of the French Republic, but the Russians fraternized with their old enemies when they replaced the Republican symbol with the white cockade of the monarchy.[59] This monument to reaction by Valberkh scarcely demands any comment.

TSARIST DOMINATION OF BALLET

Considering the vast reaches of the tsarist empire, it seems incredible that the autocrat of Russia would have had time to exercise strict supervision over his ballet in the manner it was done. The story is told of a rehearsal of the ballet *Revolt in the Seraglio*. For the scene in which harem girls rise against their sultan and execute a military march-dance, a noncommissioned officer of the guards was sent to drill the girls. As the story goes, when they became lackadaisical, the tsar, who was visiting the rehearsal, reprimanded them, announcing that if they didn't study well, he would command them to be put out into the freezing air in their slippers, carrying rifles for two hours.[60] After this, rehearsals became livelier.

During the reign of Nicholas I (1825–1855), rigid censorship existed in the arts. The control was exercised through the office of the

Third Department of the Ministry of the Interior, which was actually the secret political police. In 1832, the ballet *Sumbeka, or the Conquest of the Kazan Kingdom* met the heavy hand of the censor when Nicholas objected to the manner in which it portrayed Tsar Ivan IV. Prince P. M. Volkonsky, Minister of the Court, conveyed the tsar's displeasure to the Director of the Imperial Theatres, Prince Sergei S. Gagarin. Quite disturbed, Gagarin asked Volkonsky for more detailed instructions about the principles that should govern future productions, in order to spare the censor's cutting. Volkonsky answered that he should avoid matters that insulted personalities or disparaged religion, government, or morals.[61]

One great foreign balletmaster, Jules Perrot, came from France prepared to stage the repertoire which had brought him success in Western Europe. When he tried to mount his *Esmeralda*, an adaptation of Victor Hugo's *Hunchback of Notre Dame*, the Third Department scrupled over many points. For one thing, the censor said, "a prince should be portrayed as a rampart of virtue, not as its seducer." Portraying Phoebus as a scoundrel was therefore unacceptable. The theatre was supposed to be a school of morals; it must show vice penalized and virtue rewarded.[62] Therefore, Esmeralda was not allowed to die on the gallows; instead, Phoebus saved her from death. After other elements displeasing to the censor were removed, *Esmeralda* enjoyed a long life on the Russian stage. Agrippina Vaganova herself restaged it in 1935.[63] Soviet authorities appreciate qualities which the imperial censor disparaged: Claude Frollot, the Cathedral dean, incarnates the venality of the clergy of the Middle Ages. The poet, Gringoire, a man of the people, is a "hero opposing the world of evil."[64]

A fairy story of Perrot's met similar censorious screening. The censor demanded that the name of the story, originally called *La Filleule des Fées,* meaning *The Fairy Godchild,* should be changed to *Pitomitsa Fei,* meaning *Foster Child of the Fairies,* because sorceresses could not baptize.[65]

Besides the regular channels of governmental control through the

16

Third Department, theatrical authorities were at times victimized by the cult of a female personality. The great and charming ballerina Mathilde Kschessinska had an affair with the Tsarevich, later Tsar Nicholas II. After he ascended the throne, he dutifully avoided her company but never turned a deaf ear to her complaints of personal injustice. Russian ballerinas had to struggle to hold their own against the incursions of foreign talent. Once Kschessinka's part in the ballet *Vain Precautions* was assigned to Henrietta Grimaldi. Though he was away at Darmstadt at the time, the tsar interceded for his former lover, and the part was taken from the Italian.[66] For the coronation festivities of Nicholas II, she was not given a part in *La Perle,* a ballet especially staged for the occasion. Learning that Pierrina Legnani, another Italian visitor, had been given the lead, Kschessinska appealed through the tsar's uncle, the Grand Duke Vladimir Alexandrovich. After that, special music was written and incorporated into the ballet, and a special variation was choreographed by the famous master Marius Petipa just so Kschessinska could appear in the production.[67] On another famous occasion, Kschessinska did not like the hoops which were required in her costume for the ballet *Camargo.* Defying the warning of the theatre director, she went on stage without them. The director, Prince Volkonsky, not realizing the power of the woman, posted the customary notice that she was fined. Mathilde again appealed to the tsar, who forced Volkonsky to post notice of a retraction of the fine. Having suffered a complete loss of face, the director felt it necessary to resign his post.[68]

Kschessinska herself lived in sumptuous wealth, not only from her salary of 3,000 rubles,[69] but from a constant flow of rich gifts from her admirers. The lower ranks were not so fortunate. The administration graded dancers into distinct categories, including members of the *corps de ballet,* then *coryphées,* second and first dancers, ballerinas and *premiers danseurs.* When a woman danced successfully as a ballerina for several years, she might achieve the title *Prima Ballerina.* A title of highest honor was *Soloist of His Majesty. Coryphées* and members of the *corps de ballet* received only about fifty rubles a month in the later nineteenth century.[70] However, one author has noted that the mere fact that dancers were paid a salary at all was a significant step in the liberation of Russian women, for this was one of the first careers in which they took their place, along with men, as salaried professional workers.[71]

BALLET REFLECTIONS OF THE RUSSO-TURKISH WAR

The ballet, normally viewed as a hothouse art, in its quaint manner continued to reflect Russian *sovremennost'* in the late nineteenth century. In 1875 and 1876, out of sympathy for fellow Serbians in the province of Bosnia who had tried to revolt against their Turkish over-lords, the little principality of Montenegro went to war against the Turkish Ottoman Empire. Russia, envisioning herself as guardian of all the Slavic people, formally espoused the cause of the nationalities oppressed by the Ottomans and declared war against the Turkish Sultan in 1877. It was a popular war with the Russian people and hardly needed the support of rousing propaganda efforts, but just the same there appeared the ballet *Roxana, the Belle of Montenegro*. In it, a Bashibazouk makes love to Roxana, but her betrothed succeeds in throwing the villain over a moonlit waterfall. After being liberated from their hated oppressors, the Montenegran peasants celebrate by performing their lively folk dances.[72]

THE REVOLUTION OF 1905 INVADES THE BALLET WORLD

In the year 1905, when much of Russia was rent by revolt and strikes of workers demanding alleviation of their working conditions, revolution cast its spell over the ballet world. Even the young students of the Imperial School in St. Petersburg formed a committee, as they saw everyone else doing. Searching for a grievance, they finally found one. The students then solemnly paraded to the school director, asked for an increase in the cream content of their milk, and received it.[73] Other incidents were less innocuous.

In St. Petersburg, earnest meetings were held among the artists to determine just what course their revolutionary activities should take. The troupe was rent into factions over the matter. In the description of Fyodor Lopukhov, those who opposed the revolutionary activities were Mathilde Kschessinska, her father Felix Kschessinsky, Nikolai Legat, Vera Trefilova, Julie Sedova, and Agrippina Vaganova. A middle group of "waverers" enumerated by Lopukhov included Olga Preobrajenska, Leonid Leontiev, S. K. Andrianov, and Alexander M. Monakhov. In the front ranks of the "progressives" could be found Yosif Kschessinsky, a brother but no imitator of Mathilde, Anna Pavlova, Michel Fokine, Tamara Karsavina, Lydia Kiaksht, P. E. Mikhailov, and Valentin L. Presniakov. The latter two seemed to be leaders of the group. Presniakov was said at the time to be a member of the terrorizing Socialist Revolutionary Party, a rumor which attached a special aura of romance to his person in the eyes of some of the younger participants. Among this latter, younger group, Lopukhov numbers himself and his sister Yevgenia, along with Yevgenia Eduardova, Sergei Grigoriev, A. N. Maslov, A. A. Alekseyev, R. V. Matskevich, and I. N. Potapenko.[74]

On October 15, 1905, the Maryinsky ballet troupe gathered for a rehearsal, but it actually turned into a revolutionary meeting lasting until six in the evening. The artists drew up a series of demands to present to the director, Vladimir A. Teliakovsky, including: 1) the return of Marius Petipa, Alexander V. Shiriaev, and Alfred F. Bekefi to positions of authority; 2) the right to have some voice in the choice of a régisseur and his assistants; 3) the right to form a committee of thirteen from the ranks of the soloists, *coryphées,* and *corps de ballet,* which would have the right to fix artists' salaries and give raises; 4) the privilege of having one free day in the week besides Saturday; and 5) their intention to uplift their art, and to accomplish this they demanded freedom of assembly, immunity to orators, and other rights guaranteeing open discussions.[75] If the demands were not met, the troupe threatened to strike to obtain them.[76]

On October 17, at a morning presentation of the opera *Pique Dame,* the rebellious members of the company circulated around the dressing rooms of the dancers preparing for their parts, urging them to refuse to appear on the stage. Though not all the dancers were willing to take part in the strike, in the end none of them came out to perform. The same evening there was scheduled a ballet performance, but the management decided to cancel it before giving the performers another chance to strike.[77]

The revolutionary sentiment filtered through to ballet society in Moscow as well. On January 15, 1906, Teliakovsky travelled there to meet an artistic delegation and hear their complaints. In Moscow, the chief instigators were the Italian guest-artist Grimaldi, Yekaterina Geltser, Vasily Tikhomirov, and Vera Mosolova. They asked the right to form a permanent committee of artists who would have some voice in the assigning of roles and in the distribution of work. They wanted also to serve as an examination board for determining if artists should be transferred to a higher grade, demanding salary increases for some, as well as promises that promotion would be given not simply for out-standing talent, but also for honest application to work. Loans were asked for needy members of the company, as well as the use of government carriages for transportation, since there was so much danger at the time in the streets at night. In the training system, they asked for the opening of classes of character dance and dance notation, along with a general broadening of their education to include scientific classes reaching the level of normal high schools.[78]

However, the revolts were abortive, gaining little. On October 17, the manifesto creating the Duma included an amnesty for all strikers. In St. Petersburg, the directorship demanded that the artists sign a loyalty pledge to the tsar in gratitude. This caused another storm in the troupe, and according to Lopukhov the document sent to the tsar had only eighty signatures.[79] The Soviets regard the participants of the strike as heroes, but many of them were anxious to forget the whole affair, for the small revolution in the Maryinsky devoured one of its most beloved and talented children, Serge Legat. Haunted by torn loyalties to his fellows workers, this son and brother of great ballet artists cut his own throat.[80] Another artist of the company, V. Kiselev, ended in a psychiatric hospital as a result of the harassing events. Lopukhov relates that when meetings of the chosen bureau and the active revolutionary workers of the ballet were forbidden in the theatre and rehearsal hall, they gathered in the apartment of Potapenko's father, who was a writer, and there met with revolutionary-minded students.[81] In general, the government was nervous about the power of its artists to rouse the masses during the 1905 disturbances. The great opera star, Fyodor Chaliapin, learned that the Ministry of the Interior had sent advance orders to local officials to keep careful watch over his repertoire and activities during the concert tour, lest he rouse the workers by song.[82]

In spite of the revolutionary capacity of the artists, the general social and political unrest, which leavened many great literary works in late nineteenth-century Russia, found the ballet to be no outlet for the artistic expression of discontent. The ballet performance was a refuge in the land of fairy princesses, where neither striker nor revolutionary penetrated. While Marxist circles developed, the balletomanes could escape into the mythical land of Floristan XXVI,[83] the wise and benevolent monarch of *The Sleeping Beauty,* where Evil, in the person of the wicked fairy, Carabosse, was forever foiled. Yet the dance dialectic operated, for at the same time a group of artistic rebels had begun to shake off their creative chains, and would end by indeed gaining a world revolution in the art of ballet—outside Russia.

SERGE DIAGILEV—THE BALLET REVOLUTIONARY

The fate of prerevolutionary Russian ballet has been closely connected with the art of painting, and in this field a significant revolt took place in 1860, when thirteen Academy of Art students protested against the official theme which was given them to paint that year: "Odin in Valhalla." Inspired by the esthetical doctrine of realism forcefully explained in N. G. Chernyshevsky's *Esthetical Relation of Art to Reality,* they formed a fellowship of Wanderers, the *Peredvizhniki.*[84] The great master of the group was Ilya Repin, whose works depicted social evils in a very lucid, realistic style. Reacting against this realism of the *Peredvizhniki,* another group, *The World of Art,* arose. This circle started life merely as a discussion group of young intellectuals, with which nineteenth-century Russia was replete. In 1899, it published its own organ, bearing the Russian name of the group, *Mir Iskusstva.* It was edited by two men whose names were to become legends in ballet history: Serge Diagilev and Alexandre N. Benois. Past Soviet judgment has branded the group as "decadent formalists."[85] The *Mir* group, while turning to the old Russian ikons for much of their artistic inspiration, at the same time viewed contact with the exciting movements of Western Europe in general, and Paris in particular, as the great panacea for overcoming the realistic turn which Russian art was taking under the *Peredvizhniki.* Diagilev eventually edited the *Yearbook of the Imperial Theatres* and received a governmental post as Official for Special Missions.

In 1899, Prince Serge Volkonsky charged Diagilev with the production of the ballet *Sylvia,* an act which provoked a visit by a delegation of higher grade officials protesting the bestowing of such a responsible task on a junior official.[86] After personal negotiations took place between Volkonsky and the tsar, Diagilev had to surrender his position.[87]

He then spent some of his time arranging art exhibits for home and foreign showing, but his real genius was to burst forth on the world when he and his co-workers achieved a harmonious fusion of painting, music, and dance in the tours of the Ballet Russe starting in Paris in 1909. The troupe's scenery and costumes, designed by artists such as Alexandre Benois and Leon Bakst, were a distillation of all the taste and artistry that the *Mir* group had imbibed in their searchings, while for music Diagilev selected the enchanting works of such composers as Igor Stravinsky and Nicholas Tcherepnine. The *pièce de résistance* remained the dancers themselves: Paris was astounded at the technical mastery and dramatic power of such artists as Vaslav Nijinsky, Anna Pavlova, and Tamara Karsàvina, who achieved moments of unparalleled beauty in the creations of choreographer Michel Fokine.

The financing of Diagilev's venture abroad also became the subject of direct imperial action. Originally, Diagilev had been promised help from a member of the *nouveau riche,* a manufacturer of galoshes aspiring for a title of nobility, which could be obtained with proper connections. In return for his financial support Diagilev had promised the patron to use his influence with the Grand Duke Vladimir Alexandrovich to obtain the coveted patent of nobility. However, the Grand Duke died before the transaction was complete, so the impresario had to solicit funds elsewhere.[88] Undaunted, he then secured a promise of the necessary rubles from the imperial treasury. However, he soon lost the support of his most powerful intercessor, Kschessinska, by offering her only a small dancing role in the tour. Though she had originally pleaded for funds, she officially withdrew her request, and the subsidy was subsequently vetoed in the handwriting of the tsar himself. Not only was the money lost; with it vanished also the privilege of rehearsing at the Imperial Hermitage Theatre, as well as the use of costumes and decorations from the Maryinsky Theatre that had been promised him.[89] However, Diagilev did obtain the money from private sources, and in spite of setbacks, the Ballet Russe had astoundingly successful seasons both in 1909 and 1910. At first, Diagilev merely engaged the temporary services of dancers officially attached to the imperial theatres.[90] In 1911, his prize male dancer, Nijinsky, was dismissed from the Maryinsky because of a scandal over a costume he wore. This became the cue for Diagilev to form a permanent troupe of dancers who severed their connections with the imperial theatres. The new company, subsequently based at Monte Carlo, continued to exist in Western Europe until August, 1929, when Diagilev died. The significant point in studying Soviet ballet is that it *lost* Diagilev, and with him, the great choreographer Michel Fokine and a host of irreplaceable artists who could have given the leaven of their taste and creativity to an art which needed it very much at the time in Russia.

Fokine had felt keen regret that ballet, in his day, had become artistically shallow, with long fairy-tale productions of the *Swan Lake* variety as its standard accomplishments. His solution was to choreograph shorter ballets that were artistically exciting and destined to be classics, such as *Les Sylphides, Firebird, Carnaval,* and *Petrushka.* The Fokine-Diagilev reforms hardly won the approval of all Russian balletomanes. On one occasion Maurice Paléologue, the French Ambassador to Russia, and Teliakovsky were discussing the merits of Kschessinska, whom Paléologue felt to be a cold but mechanically precise dancer. Teliakovsky explained his admiration for her, saying: "Kschessinska's art represents to us . . . something that you don't perhaps see. . . . The old ballets, which were the joy of my youth . . . presented us with a very close picture of what Russian society was, and ought to be. Order, punctiliousness, symmetry, work well done everywhere. . . . Whereas these horrible modern ballets—*Russian ballets,* as you call them in Paris—a dissolute and poisoned art—why they're revolution, anarchy!"[91] Soviet opinion, in the past, has also found much to castigate in the works of Fokine. Believing, as the Soviet esthetes do, that ballet should have *soderzhanie,* meaning "content," they have accused Fokine of such errors as "absolutizing the problem of the musicality of the choreographic spectacle, abstracting the content . . . isolating it from the living idea of *sovremennost'*."[92] The Fokine reform was a "bourgeois reconstruction of ballet," and the whole Diagilev troupe had degraded itself artistically by catering to the capitalist, imperialist, bourgeois theatrical market.[93]

In actual fact, Soviet ballet became the reactionary element in world dance. Their schools, after a period of revolutionary displacement, produced a constant stream of dancers whose technique could have equalled the group of rebels who joined Diagilev. Yet, after a few early years of experimentation, they continued for many years to

24

Folk prints depicting a dancing *Petrushka,* the puppet which later became the subject of a ballet by Mikhail Fokine, *left,* and *right,* a piping *skomorokh* and a dancing gentleman.

Village folk dancing depicted in two nineteenth-century Russian prints.

cling to methods of production antedating the Diagilev-Fokine era, giving three- or four-act dramas with scenery and costumes reminiscent of the 1890's; superb productions, yes, but lacking the special magic which the Parisian audiences saw the night the curtain opened for Diagilev's troupe in the Théâtre du Châtelet on May 19, 1909.

In later decades, Western visitors familiar with the Diagilev style have never ceased to remark about the prevalence on the Soviet stage of nineteenth-century multi-act ballets, with an absence of any innovation except revolutionary themes.[94] Cultural exchanges beginning in the 1950's brought some changes in their wake, but before that day would arrive, Soviet ballet history would have to pass through an agony of intervening decades.

CHAPTER TWO

Terpsichore and the Revolution

Once Beauty danced with Strength to give the
   God his due. . . .
Play music, play; dance on you creatures of delight
what though the God has gone, preserve the
   ancient rite. . . .

—JOHN MASEFIELD[1]

ANCIENT myths recall that for certain Olympian festivities Apollo used to summon the muse of dance, Terpsichore, and her sister muses to perform their arts. The Russian poet Alexander Pushkin, entranced with the ballerina Avdotia Istomina, penned his fascination for his idol through the bemusings of *Eugene Onegin*:

> Shall I yet see you winging
> Your way in soulful flight and free
> My fair Russian Terpsichore?
> Or must I with dull glances follow
> Strange faces amid the painted set
> And having stared through my lorgnette
> At the gay spectacle turned hollow
> Observe it with a yawn at last
> And silently recall the past?[2]

As the Russian revolution of March, 1917, closed in upon the placid world of the Russian balletomane, the words of Pushkin gained a new poignancy. For the balletomanes who remained, the permanent migration abroad of many of ballet's brightest jewels indeed made the spectacle a little hollow. Two veteran Maryinsky stars, Mathilde Kschessinska and Olga Preobrajenska, eventually established studios in Paris. Some members of Diagilev's company, including Nijinsky

26

The Leningrad Choreographic Institute 1921 graduating class. The student standing at the left is George Balanchine.

Marina Semenova in *Swan Lake*.

and Anna Pavlova, were never to dance on a Soviet stage. Tamara Karsavina and Olga Spessivtseva stayed in Russia for awhile, but even though artists fared better than most of the population under the new regime, the bad conditions of life forced many westward. In 1924, a group of very hungry dancers left Russia, including George Balanchine and Alexandra Danilova. In all, the Maryinsky Theatre lost forty percent of its company.[3]

Many people justifiably wondered if the delicate art so tenderly nurtured by the tsarist government could survive. Dire predictions were voiced. *The Journal of the Beautiful Life, Stolitsa i Usad'ba,* expressed the general trepidation:

> They say that the deputies of the Worker's Soviet, visiting a ballet in the Maryinsky Theatre, were enraptured and decided to preserve the former Imperial ballet.
> Nevertheless—ballet is ruined. . . . This exotic plant can only exist in a special atmosphere, which now no longer exists.[4]

But the prophets of doom were wrong. The exotic plant needed no hothouse; the fragile ballerina continued to pirouette in her gauzy *tutu* in halls where sharp frost made her resort to wearing shirts and sweaters underneath her costume.[5] Nor did the plant wilt under the withering winds of criticism unleashed by zealots whose revolutionary scruples urged them to question justification of the very existence of the old imperial amusement.

There were capable artists left who, in the words of *Pravda,* "were not allured by the flattering proposals of foreign impressarios."[6] Yekaterina Geltser and Vasily Tikhomirov continued to star at the Bolshoi in Moscow, while in Leningrad Agrippina Vaganova attained immortality in dance history for passing on traditions of excellence through her pupils Marina Semenova and Galina Ulanova. Nonetheless, Soviet ballet would pass through perilous times before its future would be assured.

BALLET AND THE PROVISIONAL GOVERNMENT

Through the weary days of war and strife, Russia was never long without its ballet. "One might as well ask the Spanish to give up their bullfights," Ambassador Paléologue noted on October 11, 1914, after describing the brilliant audience viewing a production of *Swan Lake* at the Maryinsky.[7] On February 19, 1916, he recorded seeing *Sleeping Beauty,* adding forebodingly: "I reflected that it is on just such a mis-laden lake that the Russian barque is sailing now. But when the scene is changed I fear we shall find something very different from a dazzling palace will emerge."[8] On March 8, 1917, he noted that agitation was spreading through the streets of Petrograd, with citizens marching to the chants of "Bread and peace." Yet, at a party the same day staged by Princess Leon Radziwill, the conversation of one group centered on whether the palm for excellence at the Maryinsky should be given to Pavlova, Kschessinska, or Karsavina.[9] Kschessinska, sooner than anyone realized, was eliminated from the competition. On March 13, Paléologue recorded that her house had been sacked from top to bottom. To many of the wrathful plebians, she had become a symbol of the old imperial order. Paléologue recalled that when fuel was unobtainable even for embassies the previous winter, he and the English ambassador had seen soldiers unloading into her house sacks of coal from four loaded military lorries.[10] Kschessinska did receive a call from Alexander Kerensky, giving her his private phone number and urging her to call if she needed help, day or night.[11]

On March 15, the tsar abdicated, but *Sleeping Beauty* played on at the Maryinsky. At the performance, the "Marseillaise" was sung and greetings were given from the stage to members of the Provisional Government and to members of the Soviet of Workers and Soldiers Deputies who were present. This established a pattern which became common for the spring season of 1917, and "seldom was there a performance not interwoven with political greetings."[12] All the imperial coats of arms were removed from the decorations of the theatre, and attendants shed their former sumptuous court liveries in exchange for dirty, grey jackets.[13]

It soon became evident that the old imperial administration would be completely revamped. The director of the Imperial Theatre, A. V. Teliakovsky, was arrested by a disgruntled actor acting on his own authority. Later Teliakovsky was set free with apologies by the State Duma.[14] Several candidates were proposed as Teliakovsky's successor, including Maxim Gorky, Vladimir Nemirovich-Danchenko, Prince S. M. Volkonsky, and Serge Diagilev, but the choice fell on a professor of history, F. D. Batiushkov, who had been a member of the theatre committee of the former directing group.[15] No one knew exactly what to do with the old august title *Ministerstvo Imperatorskogo Dvora i Kabinet Ego Velichestva,* the "Ministry of the Imperial Court and Cabinet of His Majesty." The problem was solved by simply adding the Russian adjective *Byvshee,* meaning "former."[16]

One group of artists including A. N. Benois and Vsevolod Meyerhold, with the close participation of Maxim Gorky, formed a Special Conference for Affairs of Art at the Office of the Commissar of the Provisional Government over the Former Ministry of the Court. They spent endless hours discussing how to "emancipate art from tsarist guardianship" as well as planning a new Ministry of Art.[17] However, on March 12, 1917, in the Mikhailovsky Theatre, a meeting took place of art workers from ninety institutions and societies, including the Academy of Art, the Institute of History of Art, *Mir Iskusstva,* the conservatories, and main theatres. They declared that art affairs should be independent of bureaucratic institutions, including any Ministry of Fine Art. They wanted full autonomy in the artistic life of Russia and declared that all measures and proposals of the government regarding art affairs should pass through the judgment of their Union of Art Workers.[18]

The theatrical workers themselves drew together as The Autonomous Soviet of the Union of Workers of the State Theatres. A constitution entitled "A Provisional Position of the State Theatres" was formulated in May, 1917, to regularize the new methods of participation in the rule of theatrical affairs. The document specified that a director should be elected to head each troupe. In Petrograd, I. N. Ivanov, an assistant ballet régisseur, received the job, while in the Bolshoi Theatre in Moscow, the position was taken by the well-known dancer, V. D. Tikhomirov.[19]

Participants in the unstable days remember well how committees decided everything that formerly had been mandated from on high. Fokine recalled: "The people were vote-happy as an expression of their newly-found freedom. . . . There was a notable lack of discipline and too much speechmaking, connecting art with politics for no other reason than that it was the topic of the day."[20] Voting on each trifling matter was time-consuming in a profession which takes the very maximum of a dancer's strength and ambition. Tamara Karsavina was chosen president of her dancer's committee and likewise discovered that democracy demanded service:

> I tried hard to maintain my artistic work unimpaired, fitting my practice into early hours, leaving committee meetings for rehearsals, and rehearsals for a table piled with papers. Complaints poured in: the youngest dancers claimed a raise in salary and promotions on the grounds of justice and equality. The committee sat from morning until late hours. Our mild new director, contrary to etiquette, would come across to see me, presiding in tarlatans.[21]

Others, such as Fyodor Lopukhov, recall the period as a time of artistic exhilaration when "there was actual and full self-rule, in comparison with which our demands in 1905 seemed childish."[22]

Soon after the March revolt, a singer of the second roles from the Maryinsky, F. V. Bezpalov, appealed to the State Duma to be allowed to head a guard service in the State's theatres. Although all necessary guard services were already performed by *politsmeistery*, Bezpalov became officially the Commandant of State Theatres.[23]

The premières of the opera *Samson and Delilah* and the ballet *Nutcracker* took place during the October Bolshevik Revolution. At the ballet première one of the girls in the Chinese dance had to appear without her partner because traffic across the Neva River was disrupted. On October 27, the Bolsheviks made the first attempt to take over the theatres, and they appointed an actor of the Maly Dramatic Theatre, M. P. Muraviev, as commissar over all government and private theatres. Bezpalov soon forgot his officer status and the high military orders he had won and began to play an active part in the propaganda efforts for urging recognition of the Bolsheviks as the rightful government of Russia. Muraviev asserted his new authority by proclaiming that any performer shirking his job would be punished as an opponent of the new government. He had at his disposal 150 armed soldiers, and his work was aided by the fact that Commandant Bezpalov, Meyerhold, and some members of the theatrical technical staff rallied to the support of the Bolsheviks. However, the appointment provoked a general gathering of workers of the state theatres who passed a resolution to recognize only the power of Batiushkov, and as a sign of protest against the appointment of Muraviev, voted to shorten performances in certain theatres, including the Maryinsky.[24] The theatre director lived a harrowing existence. On one occasion when Batiushkov was holding a consultation with Fokine, Karsavina, and others for planning the opera and ballet season, an usher and doorkeeper rushed into the meeting and told them they did not need to deliberate any more, for the comrades now had power and would decide what was needed to be done. Another time, during the entr'acte of the performance of the ballet *Corsaire* in the Maryinsky, a stage worker came to the director's box announcing that the stage crew was weary and wanted to go home. Ordinarily, in the final act there is a thunderous storm at sea and a shipwreck. This time, the audience had to do without its shipwreck, for the comrades refused to stay on deck to brew the storm.[25]

On November 22, 1917, the Council of People's Commissars issued a decree transferring the theatres to the authority of the new State Commission for Enlightenment headed by Anatoly V. Lunacharsky, a cultured man deeply interested in the arts, but not one to deny their utilitarian potentialities. At the Maryinsky, a conference of the artists passed a resolution that art must remain apart from the political struggle, although they did not preclude the right of certain individuals to take part in the political life of the country.[26]

Batiushkov by a volley of letters tried to impress upon Lunacharsky their desire to be apolitical. Lunacharsky then sent a letter to the artistic-repertoire committee of the theatre, inviting them to send delegates to him. The letter was unanswered. In a second letter, Lunacharsky said that if they would not send delegates to him, there were other means to induce them to do so. Through the activity of a small group including Meyerhold and N. A. Malkov, a meeting was arranged at the theatre between the Commissar and the staff. Lunacharsky could have appeared wielding a petty stick of authority, but he was wise enough to dangle the carrot instead. He spoke to the artists for an hour and a half, assuring the theatre of a wide degree of autonomy and subsidization from the new government. In the face of their hostility, he concluded: "I would like to believe that if, in the midst of my political cares, I find an hour of leisure for repose, the artists of the Opera would not refuse me entrance to the theatre."[27] His words were applauded rousingly, and they melted much icy resistance, for many of the artists were moved by Lunacharsky's intelligence and sincere desire to bring art to the people.[28] For the first open encounter between a Bolshevik representative and the artists of the old imperial theatres, the Party could scarcely have found a better mediator than the new Commissar of Enlightenment.

STABILIZATION OF THE THEATRICAL ADMINISTRATION

In 1919, several former imperial theatres, including the Bolshoi and the Maryinsky, were honored by the title "Academic." A decree of the Council of People's Commissars of August 26, 1919, nationalized all theatrical property of Russia and subjected all theatres to the jurisdiction of a Central Theatre Committee, *Tsentroteatr*. Some theatres

Anatoly V. Lunacharsky, Commissar of Enlightenment after the Russian Revolution.

Yekaterina Geltser wearing a *kokoshnik,* the woman's headdress
of old Russia.

of high cultural value were to remain autonomous, but *Tsentroteatr* reserved the right to impose on these autonomous theatres certain points regarding repertoire, in order to make sure that they remained faithful to their socialistic ideal. The president of *Tsentroteatr* was to be the head of *Narkompros*, A. Lunacharsky. To guide *Tsentroteatr's* activity, a *kollegia* was established of seven members designated by *Narkompros*, along with three designated by the All-Russian Soviet of Trade Unions. Representatives of the Moscow and Petrograd Soviets and the managers of metropolitan theatrical affairs had the right to attend sessions of *Tsentroteatr* "with a deciding vote," and representatives of the Executive Committee on the provincial level had a similar right in their domains.[29]

The representation from the trades unions was just one facet of the Party's campaign to involve the workers in cultural affairs. When formulating an official Party Program, the Eighth Congress of the Russian Communist Party of Bolsheviks (March 18 to 23, 1919) spoke of "the necessity of opening and making accessible to the workers all treasures of art, created on the basis of the exploitation of their labor, and which were formerly at the exclusive disposal of the exploiters."[30]

The worker, in turn, swarmed to the theatres just as famine victims rushed for food in those terrible times. While welcoming the enthusiasm of the new spectator, theatrical directors, like school teachers, sometimes had to scold the new spectators to make them sit quietly and refrain from smoking or eating nuts in the theatres.[31]

Famine, cold, and sickness were ever-present realities to be faced by the theatrical workers, along with the whole population. Recompense for ballet performances was often made in real food, incomparably more treasured than worthless money. In these days a pound of butter and a loaf of bread were considered "luxurious payment for an appearance."[32] At one point, when rations were cut, the Bolshoi artists appealed to the singer Fyodor Chaliapin to use his influence to get more food. He appealed directly to Leon Trotsky, whose orders had reduced the rations. Trotsky answered, "Don't you think I know

33

what it is, Comrade, to be short of bread? But I can't put the soldier in the trenches on the same level with the ballerina who smiles and twirls on the boards."[33] However, in the latter part of 1919, the director of the Maryinsky made an accord with the Red Army to provide units of entertainers for the soldiers. In recompense, the artists received army rations equivalent to those given to front line soldiers. In November, 1919, wood was obtained to heat the theatre, but in the spring of 1920, the Maryinsky had to be closed for several days to disinfect it against typhus.[34]

Under such circumstances, the party and government pursued a policy of cultural-enlightenment with militaristic determination. A resolution of the Eighth Party Congress had declared unequivocally that "moving picture houses, theatres, concerts, exhibitions, etc., . . . must be utilized for communistic propaganda directly."[35] Further, the resolution insisted that there were not any forms of science and art which were not connected with the great ideas of communism and the task of creating a communistic economy. To indoctrinate the population, there were to be arranged artistic-political evenings, lectures, and concert meetings where Marxist-Leninist ideas about philosophy, economics, and political theory would be expounded.[36] Long lists of announcements in *Pravda* and *Izvestiia* in following months reveal the thoroughness with which the task was accomplished. Every day notices of scores of political and ideological lectures appeared. Sometimes, the emphasis was on the political part with the artistic performance added as a bonus. Other times, the purpose seemed chiefly the cultural uplifting of the spectator, with perhaps a speech added. Occasionally, inserted among a dozen other less tantalizing notices of meetings, there would appear one such as:

Concert in House of the Unions

On Saturday, the first of November, there will take place the fourth evening of ballet, arranged by the Council of Trade Unions of the Moscow *Guberniia*. In the program of the ballet *In the Caucasian*

Mountains will participate [Alexandra] Balashova, [Margarita] Kandaurova, [Maria] Reizen, [Leonid] Zhukov, and others.[37]

Such meetings, organized by trade unions, were part of their culture campaigns called *kul'tpokhody*. In the season of 1918–1919, Petrograd State Theatres gave seventy-five of these "special purpose performances." In 1919–1920, in the former Maryinsky alone there were more than eighty.[38]

The demands upon the artists were heavy at a time when physical strength was diminishing. Tamara Karsavina recalls: "Under the new regime artists were treated with great consideration. Maybe from motives of policy, *Panem et circenses*. If bread was scarce, shows were liberally given to the people; we were constantly commanded to perform in suburban theatres for a public of soldiers and workmen."[39] The dancing parents of Galina Ulanova, besides their regular ballet performances at the theatre, sometimes gave three recitals a night at movie theatres, as part of their effort to bring culture to the people. Ulanova recalled: "I remember mama—with badly frozen fingers removing her felt boots and tying the rosy ribbons of her ballet slippers; I remember, how in the cold cubicle behind the cinema screen she put on her glittering, light *tutu* and with a smile appeared on the stage."[40]

The pattern was the same in Moscow. In the Bolshoi Theatre, just as in the Maryinsky, the spectators disappeared in a fog of human breath, while puffs of steam came forth from brass instruments and the mouths of dancers. In the wings, the cold numbed the muscles of the artists. The *prima ballerina*, Yekaterina Geltser, during the entr'acte would don a fur coat and felt boots, drinking boiling water for want of the accustomed tea. After the regular performance, she too would go to meetings, often appearing after a talk by Lenin.[41]

FIRST BALLET REVOLUTIONARY: STENKA RAZIN

The task of staging ballets with themes appropriate to the new ideology took some time and imagination. Russia was the first place in the world where a Communist revolution had overthrown the existing government, and in Lenin's view it was the first step toward the world-wide revolution which would fulfill the predictions made by Karl Marx in his *Communist Manifesto.* Henceforth, the promotion and exaltation of revolution became one of the chief points for emphasis in Soviet art of all varieties. Ballet could not escape.

Under the spell of revolutionary ardor, the poet Alexander Blok declared in 1917: "This is the task of Russian culture: . . . to transform the violence of Stenka Razin and Yemelian Pugachev into a resolute wave of music."[42] It was fitting that Stenka should become the hero of the first of many ballets exalting revolutionaries in Soviet Ballet. A. A. Gorsky mounted *Stenka Razin* to the music of a symphonic poem by A. K. Glazunov, and it was presented at the Bolshoi Theatre for a first anniversary program of the Revolution. The ballet was shrugged aside as a *negarmonichnaia smes'*, "a disharmonious medley," arousing in the spectator a feeling of derangement.[43] Stenka was a Cossack who revolted (1667–1771) against the autocratic Tsar Alexei Mikhailovich and led a motley army to numerous victories along the Volga River before being brought to Moscow and executed. According to the folk legend, once Stenka provoked murmuring among his fellow Cossacks by riding joyfully and drunkenly in a canoe with his beloved, a Persian princess, while his comrades in revolution lacked such charming company in their boats. Rather than let brotherly unity be destroyed, Stenka lifted up the princess and tossed her into Mother Volga, "a gift from a Cossack of the Don." He was the subject in 1918 of a number of plays, including one at the Free Theatre in the Karl Marx Club at Leningrad.[44]

Except for Razin's brief and unheralded appearance, the ballet repertoire in 1918–1919 of the former imperial theatres, when they were open, continued to include chiefly the old favorites: *Sleeping Beauty, Nutcracker, Swan Lake,* and *Raymonda.* Soon enough, however, the official paper of the Communist Party, *Pravda,* edited by Nikolai Bukharin, began to prod the ballet world for being revolutionarily retarded. Complaining about a ballet performance by the troupe of the Bolshoi, *Pravda* declared in solemn tones that ballet was isolating itself from the spectator and from real life and was still dwelling in the world of children's tales. In place of sweet love stories, ballet should portray episodes of the struggle of the masses. Indeed, workers' circles were turning away from the ballet because of its remoteness from reality. Reform was necessary, *Pravda* affirmed.[45]

This was but the beginning of long arguments that would place in question the very existence of ballet in the workers' state. Lunacharsky, upon occasion, had to quiet the doubts of Lenin about the subject. In his words:

> Several times I had to demonstrate to Vladimir Ilyich that the Bolshoi Theatre was comparatively inexpensive, but at the same time, at his urgent request, a monetary advance was curtailed. Vladimir Ilyich was guided by two considerations. One of them he named right away: "It is not fitting," he said, "to support with so much money such a luxurious theatre, when we lack the means for supporting the very simplest schools in the country." The other consideration was drawn forth when at one of the sessions I argued against his assault on the Bolshoi Theatre. I pointed to the undoubted cultural significance of it. Then Vladimir Ilyich screwed up his eyes and said: "But all the same that is a piece of pure *pomeshchik* culture, and against this no one can argue."[46]

However, in the crucial moments when it truly counted, Lenin silenced the voice of his own proletarian conscience to swing the balance in favor of saving the home of Muscovite ballet. The huge Bolshoi building consumed a great deal of fuel, greatly needed for locomotives, hospitals, electric stations, and factories. With typhus bringing further misery to the land, many wondered why this luxury should be maintained. Still, in 1919, Lenin defended it against a Comrade A. V. Galkin who urged the Council of People's Commissars to close the theatre. Galkin said it was an ineffective tool for propaganda, but Lenin answered: "It seems to me that Comrade Galkin has a somewhat naive idea of the role of the significance of theatres. A theatre is necessary not so much for propaganda, as to rest hard workers after their daily work. And it is still early to file away in the archives our heritage from bourgeois art."[47] A vote was then taken by the Council, with Lenin's opinion carrying the day.

Both the Bolshoi and ballet were saved, but the arguments continued. The disputes were larger than ballet, however, and branched from roots older than the revolution. Though developments in other arts during the postrevolutionary years have been treated elsewhere, a brief glance at the total artistic life of Russia in these turbulent years is necessary for any understanding of the tribulations that ballet was to experience. With the crushing of the old regime and its patronage of arts pleasing to it, many artists felt it was the golden chance to make a wild grasp for freedom. Painters, dramatists, musicians, and sculptors held conferences, argued, printed journals, and opened experimental workshops. The revolution was regarded as a harbinger of a bright, creative artistic future, the pledge that the last requiem would be chanted over classicism, realism, and other movements that dominated artistic life in the past. Each new group seemed to feel personally commissioned to make their art the vehicle for expressing the new revolutionary age, but few groups could agree on the forms that would most suitably serve such a mission.

BOURGEOIS MODERNISTS AND *Proletkult*

The *Bol'shaia Entsiklopediia* names two archfoes against which Soviet ballet struggled in the 1920's and grew to full development in the struggle. These were the bourgeois modernists whose abstract art emphasized form at the expense of content and "the anti-Marxist theory of *Proletkult*," advocating a denial of Russia's cultural inheritance and a repudiation of a national art of the dance.[48]

Actually, the roots of much experimentation in ballet in the 1920's, both in Russia and in the West, can be traced to artistic stirrings which preceded the Revolution. As early as 1910, Diagilev's *Mir*

Iskusstva was opposed by a more radical group of futurist painters, known in Moscow as The Knaves of Diamonds, while in 1912 another group called The Donkey's Tail came into existence, comprised of men influenced by cubism, such as Vasily Tatlin, Marc Chagall, and Kasimir Malevich. Cubo-futurism found poetic expression in circles whose most noteworthy writer was Vladimir Mayakovsky. In 1912, the poets issued a literary manifesto called "A Slap in the Face of Public Taste," thoroughly disclaiming Tolstoy, Dostoevsky, Pushkin, and all the other writers in the classic tradition. In 1923, Mayakovsky and other futurists drew together in another group called LEF, Left Front.[49]

Many of the ideas of the cubo-futurists were adopted by groups called constructivists. In 1924, a group of writers formed The Literary Center of Constructivists, LTsK, and declared themselves "welded to the general aim of communist construction."[50] Enchanted with technology, the constructivists wanted their poetry to step to the rhythm of pulleys and pistons, and sing the songs of rolling mills and lathes. Music, canvas, sculpture—all should abstract the essence of modern industrial life.

They had been preceded in 1916 by a group of artists who believed that easel painting was dead, and that constructivism alone could validly express the logic of a revolutionary machine age. Such sculptors and painters as Naum Gabo, Antoine Pevsner,[51] and Vasily Tatlin became prominent in the movement. Constructivism appeared in the music of Igor Stravinsky, as well as in the works of the western Europeans Arnold Schönberg, Paul Hindemith, and Arthur Honneger.[52]

Constructivism thus penetrated the Russian musical theatre by content, scenery, music, and acting technique. Disregarding the use of traditional painted flats for scenery, constructivists used platforms, scaffolding, staircases, and mobiles. In keeping with the trend, the great play director, Meyerhold, evolved his system of "biomechanics," designating precise gestures and movements to express certain emotions and actions, which, according to a later Soviet view, converted man into a "mechanical appendage," an acrobat, a gymnast.[53] Eventually, constructivist principles brought bizarre innovations into ballet both in the U.S.S.R. and in the West with such productions as Diagilev's *La Chatte, Le Pas d'Acier,* and Adolf Bolm's *Ballet Mécanique,* staged at the Hollywood Bowl in 1932.[54]

Along with the "bourgeois modernists," Soviet sources list *Proletkult* as a force against which Soviet ballet struggled and strengthened itself. Led by Alexander Bogdanov and, for a while, by Lunacharsky, the group antedated the Revolution and bore the official name of Central Committee of the Proletarian Cultural and Educational Organization. Constructivists and Futurists wielded strong influence within the movement.

Ideologically speaking, *Proletkult* was indeed "anti-Marxist." Marx taught that "social existence determines consciousness," by which he meant that all the products of man's thought—his philosophy, religion, legal structures, political ideas, and culture—would be conditioned by the mode of production.[55] A new class art and culture would automatically arise to reflect the new economic order built by the proletariat. *Proletkult,* however, wanted to use art to organize and consolidate the power of the new class, and not simply to allow it to be a mere reflection.[56] To achieve this aim, *Proletkult* established studios and workshops involving 80,000 people throughout Russia by 1920. Though the Theatrical Section of the Commissariat of Enlightenment backed the leaders of *Proletkult* in the early years, the organization craved autonomy. They boldly proclaimed that Soviet power, issuing from the Soviet of Workers, Peasants, Soldiers, and Cossacks deputies, was derived from such heterogeneous class sources that it dared not call itself a pure dictatorship of the proletariat. Therefore, it would be a great mistake to place the development of proletarian creativity under the power of these motley representatives of the peasants, the army, Cossacks, and Lumpenproletariat.[57] At a *Prolet-*

40

kult Congress in 1920, Lenin, who could not tolerate Lunacharsky's soft attitude toward the organization, forced passage of a resolution whereby *Proletkult* was obliged to work "under the general direction of Soviet power (especially *Narkompros*) and the Russian Communist Party."[58]

In its own theatres, *Proletkult* sometimes used most extraordinary methods to make the theatre comprehensible to the proletariat. They maintained that the circus and the juggler had entertained Russians before the formal theatre, which was a Western import. Therefore, at times they abolished the stage and gave long performances composed of running, jumping, juggling, and rope dancing. Elements of cubism, futurism, the music hall, or the biomechanics of Meyerhold might be seen in their productions.[59] It was a carnival time for the innovators, and the respectable ramparts of classical dance could hardly resist their assaults.

RAPP

Almost from its inception, *Proletkult* engendered splinter groups within itself. In October, 1920, such a group was formed, calling itself at first the VAPP, All-Russian Association of Proletarian Writers.[60] By 1928, now bearing the name RAPP, Russian Association of Proletarian Writers, the organization had become the most powerful literary group in the U.S.S.R., being joined by Mayakovsky and other leaders of LEF. The members of RAPP were fanatical propagandizers, opposed to nonpolitical art, striving "to organize man's psyche" for socialist construction.[61] Like *Proletkult,* they claimed to be the only proletarian group. Members of RAPP sought to control key positions in publishing houses and the censorship apparatus, and authors not bowing to the demands of RAPP during the period 1928 to 1932 were subject to persecution and arrest. Also like *Proletkult,* their very power and assertiveness predestined them for annihilation in the Stalinist scheme. The blow fell on April 23, 1932, when the Central Committee of the Communist Party published a decree "On the Reorganization of Art and Literary Organizations," officially abolishing RAPP.[62]

RAPM AND ASM

While it might seem that Soviet literary policies would have, at most, only a fringe influence on ballet, the literary field has always been the pivot around which all other Soviet artistic life has revolved. In the musical field, no less than in literature, graphic art, and drama, composers breathed in the heady wine of revolution and showed similar symptoms of artistic intoxication. On the first anniversary of the October Revolution, their obsession for the machine and industrialization prompted a group of Moscow conservatory students to intone the "Internationale" by blowing factory whistles in the streets, while an instructor, standing on top of a building, directed them.[63]

In 1924, there was established the ASM, *Assotsiatsiia Sovremennoi Muzyki,* later condemned for being modernistic, formalistic, and inclined to admire foreign bourgeois decadent music too much. Further, contrary to the Party spirit, ASM was blamed for insisting that "music is not ideological."[64] ASM did seek contact with Western European composers, publishing in its organ, *Novaia Muzyka,* lists of their current compositions. However, the members of ASM had their own ideas about music and ideology. To them, revolutionary music meant music that defied the traditional forms, patterns, and canons, such as Vladimir Deshevov's *The Rails* (1926), which captured the noise of a moving train, or Prokofiev's *Le Pas d'Acier*.[65] In speaking of ballet music, one member of ASM lauded the ballet suite *Steel,* a part of Alexander Mosolov's *Iron Foundry* (1927), which employed the banging of a piece of sheet metal in the orchestration. He likewise praised Deshevov's ballet *Jezebel* as a work "authentically revolutionary in form as well as in content." Expressing the urban-oriented philosophy of the organization, he concluded: "What is nearer to the proletariat, Tchaikovsky or Deshevov's *Rails*? The proletariat, who grew up among city

42

buildings, who was rhythmically educated by the machine, who soaked up machine oil with his mother's milk, justly demands music of the contemporary fatherland."[66]

It is hardly surprising to find that ASM, with its western orientation, soon found an adversary officially named The Russian Association of Proletarian Musicians, RAPM. The official *History of Russian Soviet Music* makes the comment:

> Those organizations which presented themselves as proletarian, by no means were free from bourgeois influence, above all those appearing in the form of one or another variation of *Proletkult*. In literature, such organizations were the Association of Proletarian Writers (RAPP, VAPP) and analogous to this was the Association of Proletarian Musicians.[67]

Actually, for a time, RAPM was directly inspired by the Propaganda Section of the Central Committee of the Party.[68] Composed at first of a number of members of the Komsomol, Communist Union of Youth, in Moscow Conservatory, RAPM gradually overcame the power of ASM. In doing so, it became as ruthlessly dictatorial as RAPP.

In the magazine *Musical Virgin Soil*, 1924, RAPM published a platform so heavily impregnated with Marxist terminology that it would be unintelligible to an uninitiated reader. It emphasized the fact that in the Marxism schema, Western society had entered the phase of finance capitalism, the highest phase before its annihilation by the revolutionary proletariats. The music of this society characteristically expressed the decay of that dying society. Its bourgeois class was systematically poisoning the minds of the workers by supplying them with sensual, erotic music expressive of pathological moods; with mystical music, reflecting the premonitions of the bourgeoisie of their impending annihilation as a class; and with naturalistic music, echoing the rhythm and bustle of the capitalistic city. In writing such music, the decadent capitalistic society had to resort to distorted harmonies and spasmodic rhythms, resulting in constructivistic, mechanistic music.[69] The manifesto declared that the members of RAPM believed in

43

dialectical and not mechanistic laws of evolution, thus making it known that in an important philosophical struggle which was occurring in the U.S.S.R., they were on the side of a group which included A. M. Deborin and Leon Trotsky, and were opposed to the mechanistic philosophy advocated by Nikolai Bukharin and his followers.[70]

Positively, RAPM stated its aim to promote the hegemony of the proletarian class in the field of music to the detriment of the bourgeoisie's position. They intended to create a Marxist musicology and a completely new style of proletarian music. To them, this meant a fuller employment of folk music and a greater emphasis on the production of "mass songs" instead of solo numbers. Such a policy would bring a parallel emphasis of "mass dances" while also urging that dance music should lean even more heavily on folk music than in the past.

In the decree of April, 1932, officially liquidating RAPP, one phrase stated the government's intention "to promote a similar change in the sphere of other forms of art,"[71] which meant that RAPM was likewise dissolved. Even though the association was annihilated, many of the ideas of RAPM were adopted as general policies of the Communist Party toward music in the U.S.S.R., although in subsequent years, issues of *Sovetskaia Muzyka* (the official magazine of the Union of Soviet Composers) commemorated the demise of RAPM and RAPP and excoriated its principal leaders as Trotskyites.

FOREGGER'S ATELIER: DANCE REFLECTS THE MACHINE

After seeing the paths taken by art in general during the first decade of Soviet power, the developments in dance seem completely logical. According to a contemporary account, at this period, many schools were united in their negative attitude to classical ballet, and were striving to leave the closed circle of the ballet system.[72]

In harmony with the mania for expressing the rhythm of machines in poetry, graphic art, and music, a choreographer named Nikolai Foregger caused a stir in the dance world with his attempts to make the movement of human bodies represent machines. In 1920 and 1921,

44

Natalia Dudinskaya and Boris Shavrov in *Strange Illusions*.

A scene from *Machine Dance* by Nikolai Foregger.

at a *Proletkult* Studio in Moscow, Foregger taught courses of *tafia-trenazh,* the name given to his system of dance physical-culture. Later in 1921 he organized his own workshop called *Masfor,* from *Master-skaya Foreggera.* Foregger had a new mission for dance, and ridiculed the old slogans:

> "I create—as the bird sings"; "Above all, I create what my foot wishes" ... These are phrases forgotten now. The Muses have become production workers and dispersd into trade unions. The place of their meeting is not Olympus, but VTsSPS, and it is not Apollo who summons them, but Tomsky.[73]

He believed that dance did not need to be an illustration of music, and sometimes used a "noise band" for accompaniment.[74] In his view, decadent past epochs of ballet had concentrated their attention upon women, but in the era of socialist construction, the man would predominate.

As for the thematic tasks of dance, its movements should express such phenomena as struggle, defeat, passion, and victory—or else be an expression of contemporaneity.[75] In his words,

> The dances of savages made visible the songs of rich game birds, thick forests, victorious battles. Our life creates dances of the sidewalk, of rushing autos, the accuracy of machine work, the speed of the present-day crowd, the grandeur of skyscrapers. The future historian of art will call our years—years of the prophets.[76]

One of Foregger's chief creations was his unusual *Dance of Machines* (1924–1925). In it, he arranged his performers to form the parts of a giant machine, with the dance imitating the movement of a flywheel around an immobile axis.

The young Karl Marx had castigated the machine for alienating man and depriving him of his humanity in capitalist society,[77] but Soviet ideologue Nikolai Bukharin best expressed Foregger's attitude in a boast he made about socialist culture: "For the soullessness of capitalist technology we have substituted the liberating role of the socialist machine."[78] Foregger, too, viewed the machine as an instrument of redemption which would bear the drudgery of labor, thus restoring to man his power of creative and interpretative movement.[79]

Later Soviet judgment has not been kind to Foregger. *A History of the Soviet Theatre* (1933) complained that he promoted "the fetishism of the human body as an ideally trained machine."[80] Elsewhere he was linked with a certain class "who attempted to revive decadent anti-folk tendencies supposedly under the flag of revolutionary art."[81] Yet, the rhythm of machines never quite lost its fascination for choreographers in the U.S.S.R. In the 1960's, Igor Moiseyev's State Academic Folk Dance Ensemble performs a number called *A Day on Board a Ship*[82] where sailors, in beautiful synchronization, reenact the movements of wheels and pistons in the ship's engine room, imitating the rhythm and precision of engine strokes and turns. It seems that Foregger's machines have not been completely relegated to the Marxist scrap heap of history.

AMERICAN FREE-STYLE INFILTRATES SOVIET DANCE

Russia was not alone in producing dance rebels. America lent one of its most passionate dance "anarchists," Isadora Duncan, to Russia, and she proved indeed to be a "subversive" influence.

After purposeful and serious study of the images of ancient Greek figures which she found on museum pieces, the famous Isadora Duncan had developed her own unstructured, flowing dance style. She had made a prerevolutionary visit to Russia, where her innovations made an enduring impression upon such choreographers as Fokine. However, for free-living Isadora, the discipline imposed on a ballerina was worse than slavery, and she had nothing but contempt for classic ballet, with its precise five positions and a technique acquired only at the expense of arduous daily work for a lifetime.

Isadora had a wide, humanitarian outlook, which prompted her to preach often on concert tours that art should be available to all people, and not be merely the exclusive property of the rich. She also had frustrated maternal instincts and longed to establish a school where she could teach hundreds of beautiful little children her methods of free, happy, uplifting dance. Yet, she could not convince any capitalist state to support her. In the spring of 1921, the Russian government received a telegram from her asking permission to come to Russian, since she felt her dream school could best succeed there. Lunacharsky was very open to such proposals at the time, even though he could not support the existing schools and theatres.

Isadora recounts receiving a telegram from Russia, reading: "The Russian government alone can understand you. Come to us, we will make your school."[83] With her hopes high, she arrived in a Russia wounded and suffering from all the human miseries that follow revolution and civil war. After many delays, she finally received a mansion in Moscow where her school began its precarious existence. Lunacharsky asked Isadora to celebrate the fourth anniversary of the Revolution by dancing at the Bolshoi Theatre. She agreed on condition that all seats would be free, with tickets given out by workers' groups and the Red Army. Revolutionary eyebrows were raised when she began to dance to Tchaikovsky's *Marche Slav* which contains portions of the hymn, "God Save the Tsar."[84] However, the audience, paradoxically composed of Party officials and commissars, forgot the tsarist strains as she portrayed, with writhes and grimaces, the shattering of a slave's fetters and the crushing of the master. Later, draped in a red shawl, she mimed the crushing of the old regime while the musicians played the rousing strains of the "Internationale."[85]

Lunacharsky greatly admired the free and happy spirit which the children of her school radiated.[86] However, the institution still suffered from lack of fuel and government support in the days of the New Economic Policy. Isadora was thus forced to give concert tours, charging for tickets to finance her art, just as in the bourgeois West. When the discouraged Isadora left Russia, one of her protégées, Irma Duncan, carried on with the school, making ends meet by performing various dances such as *With Courage, Comrades, March in Step; One, Two, Three; The Young Guard; The Blacksmith, or Forging the Keys of Freedom; Dubinushka* (a work song); *The Varshavianka* (in memory of 1905); *March of the Young Pioneers; The Marseilles; The Carmagnole;* and *Internationale.*[87]

In 1927, after training her dancing girls with her own resources for years, Irma Duncan was told by the Ministry of Enlightenment that her school could now receive state aid, but that she would no longer be its director. The administrators would be Communist Party members, and she, as a teacher, would have to take indoctrination courses in Marxism-Leninism. Fearing that Party action would destroy the spiritual quality of her dancing and leave only gymnastics, Irma returned to the West, bringing her group of girls for a concert tour. After they gave several successful performances, an unofficial agent of Russia in Washington named Brovsky threatened the girls with dire treatment of their Russian relatives if they did not return home, thus causing all the dancers to depart for the homeland.[88]

Isadora herself thought that not only the ballet but many of the Russian peasant dances should be abolished. Once, seeing some Russian children dropping a handkerchief while dancing, a symbol of country courtship, she somehow thought it was connected with subservience to the tsar. Urging the children to stop making dance movements toward the earth like slaves, she bade them instead to dance as free people, flinging their arms skyward, while thinking of Apollo.[89] In the Soviet Union, where such an attitude toward folk dance would be shameful, it is understandable to read a remark of later years: "The study of Duncan's unhealthy decadent art, brought to our country from America, must be subjected to criticism because it is essentially alien to realistic folk art."[90]

A HARVEST OF NEW STUDIOS

In the early 1920's, however, Isadora Duncan's radical ideas fell on fertile ground in Russia. Studios mushroomed in imitation of her

48

dance style, lasted briefly, then disappeared. Among several others, a Leningrad group called the Heptachor assumed Duncanesque poses and donned Greek tunics.[91] In similar experiments to discover methods of dance expression outside the strictures of classic form, several choreographers employed plastique modes as she had used them, dancing to the music of Beethoven, Chopin, and Lizst. One group which combined such a style with elements of sheer physical-culture was the studio of Vera Maya in Moscow, whose ensemble was called The Art of Dance.

According to reports, Maya's cadres of girls went through routines of exercises that would have wearied Amazons. They were in training to be sent to dance in workmen's, peasants', and soldiers' clubs, representing the ideal physically developed womanhood of the new Russia. Her *Dance of October* portrayed the revolution and the march of Pioneers' groups, while her *Gallop* depicted the Red cavalry in action. The girls imitated factory machines and extended their talents to the farm by developing swaying movements which represented Russian wheat fields, as well as cutting motions which depicted the work of reapers and binders.[92]

Foregger's, Duncan's, Maya's, and a host of other "free schools" were merely the expression of the general surge of unorthodox artistic activity to which the Revolution gave impetus. In general, these extreme innovators were soundly rejected after the art world of the U.S.S.R. was guided into the straight and narrow paths of socialist realism by the Party in the mid-1930's. After surveying the early proponents of rhythmo-plastique dancing, acrobatics, physical-culture, machine dancing, and "the so-called free dance in the style of Isadora Duncan," a typical modern Soviet dance historian dismisses the lot of them with the comment: "In these innovations were veiled orientations of the formalistic decadent art of West Europe, experiencing stagnation and crisis, showing insulting distrust to the new spectator, as if he were unable to understand classic art, serious themes, and strict form."[93]

REVOLUTION FROM WITHIN

Besides the extreme radicals who wanted to abolish ballet completely, there were many who merely wanted to give it a very new look. One experimental group of this type, called the Young Ballet, grew up in St. Petersburg. The chief choreographer was a young graduate of the 1921 class named Georgii Balanchivadze—for many years known to the world as the head of the New York City Ballet, George Balanchine. Among the organizers of the group, Fyodor Lopukhov lists two students of the art academy, Vladimir Dmitriev and Boris M. Erbstein, as well as a university student named Yuri Slonimsky who was then only beginning a long career as a ballet critic. Among the dancers were Alexandra Danilova, Leonid Lavrovsky, Pyotr Gusev, Vasily Vainonen, Mikhail Mikhailov, Andrei Lopukhov, Lydia Ivanova, N. Mlodzinskaia, and Nina Stukolkina. Like other such groups, they displayed their art in "evenings" in whatever quarters they could acquire. The Young Ballet gave performances in the auditorium of the City Hall in 1921 and 1923. At the latter, instead of musical accompaniment, a chorus chanted Alexander Blok's poem *The Twelve*. Balanchine and several of the members left the country in 1924, but a group with the same name was revived in 1925.[94] In 1928, another "Evening of the Young Ballet" took place with many of the same dancers participating. This time some of the works of choreographer Fyodor Lopukhov were performed, such as Prokofiev's *Fugitive Visions*, which was criticized for its "grotesque erotics" which hearkened back to the time of "decadent impressionism."[95] A *Sport Dance* to the accompaniment of what the reviewer called a "suspicious" fox-trot likewise earned little praise in the press.[96]

Another group stemmed from the work of the great dancer Mikhail Mordkin, who broke with the Bolshoi Theatre after the Revolution, then took charge of ballet productions at the Theatre of the Soviet of Workmen's Deputies in Moscow, which was located in the former Zimin's Opera House.[97] Isolated in southern Russia

50

Viktorina Kriger and Mikhail Mordkin in *Salambo*.

Viktorina Kriger and Mikhail Mordkin in a waltz
by Fritz Kreisler.

by civil war, Mordkin worked in Tbilisi for a while and then chose to migrate westward, but some of the dancers in the group, including N. S. Gremina and Asaf Messerer, carried on in Moscow under the name of The Dramatic Ballet. After five years of work, the group was urged to go to Leningrad because of a lack of buildings in Moscow. Though the collaborators had fitted out the stage of their studio on Dmitrovka with their own hands, the spot was converted into a furniture store. Articles appeared intermittently in the Soviet press urging the artistic section of *Narkompros*, called *Glaviskusstvo*, to give the company a place to work. One author pointed out that there was little hope that the Bolshoi would produce the type of ballet needed by contemporary society, since, "You can't put new wine in old wineskins";[98] and the future hope of ballet lay in such new groups. Further, they had done their duty toward producing dances on agitation themes, such as *Internationale, Communist Soviet Navy March, Song of the Commune, The Blacksmith,* and *March at the Death of Ilyich.*[99] Apparently, they never received the needed support.

Another group which gained a permanent place in the ballet life of the U.S.S.R. was started by the ballerina Viktorina Kriger in 1929. In writing a preface to a short set of memoirs written by Kriger, a Comrade Pikel spoke the view of the left-wing reformers of ballet:

> There is needed in ballet and dance in the U.S.S.R. a basic severing and reevaluation of all its former foundations and principles. Ballet themes need to be given a social meaning. A critical ballet is needed; it needs to be impregnated by the new achievements in art movements (biomechanics, eccentric dance, acrobatics). A new system of preparation and education is needed—in other words, an organic correspondence between the new content and new form of the ballet.[100]

He wanted to see established "a scientific Marxist study of ballet as an art," believing "the establishment of a methodological basis of the science of ballet will accelerate the revolutionary transformation of ballet art."[101]

Kriger herself would probably not have believed in such radical innovations as Pikel seemed to be urging her art to accomplish. She remained firm in her conviction that classical training was the pivot and stronghold of all further developments in dance. However, she completely agreed that "technique must exist—only in order that there will be full expression of the inner content. Otherwise, there will be no creativity, but only machine action."[102] Kriger's company performed a number of the old classics, but she also produced such works as *Komsomol'skaia* and *Carmagnole*—the first ballet on the theme of the French Revolution.

In 1934, her company became an established part of the Musical Studio of the Moscow Art Theatre of Stanislavsky Nemirovich-Danchenko. Kriger became a Party member in 1939,[103] and in later years has engaged in much writing and criticism in the ballet field.

CHAPTER THREE

Ballet's Time of Troubles

Ballet is a dead, hackneyed genre, doomed to be scrapped.

—IVAN SOLLERTINSKY[1]

IN regard to ballet, Commissar of Enlightenment Lunacharsky faced a dilemma. While he ardently believed in the revolution, he was still irritated by fanatics who believed that the theatre was good for only one thing in Russia: to make the people view life through a Marxist lens. The cultured Lunacharsky could not renounce his own bourgeois artistic tastes, no matter what demands the revolutionary esthetic might make, so he tried to walk a tightrope between the two positions.

Lunacharsky by no means would completely free ballet from its social obligations or from the task of reforming itself so that it could better serve the revolution. In 1919, he declared:

> Ballet, as a spectacle for the people, has colossal force, but, for the present, its strength is poured into stupid melodramas and monotonous pretty steps. Ballet itself does not recognize its own power, does not want to know it; it still drags on itself the chains of past servitude to a lustful, perverted public.[2]

Yet, he could not remain quiet in the face of any hints that all the classical heritage should be destroyed or replaced by propaganda works. He fought with Nikolai Bukharin over this matter during the early years, declaring:

> We are far from the categorical program of Comrade Bukharin [who says] you must tear down the bourgeois theatre. . . . This slogan, ex-

53

tended further, would lead to the slogan: you must tear down bourgeois libraries, you must tear down bourgeois physics laboratories, you must tear down bourgeois museums. We support another opinion. We think that libraries, physics laboratories, and museums must be made worthy of the proletariat. . . . We think that the proletariat not only has the right, but even in some ways is obliged, as the inheritor of this past, to be acquainted with it. In view of this we shall preserve theatrical traditions, theatrical mastery. . . . Representatives of the workers often present different theatrical demands to me. Comrade Bukharin would wonder at the fact that not once have the workers demanded of me that I increase their accessibility to the revolutionary theatre, but they ceaselessly demand opera and ballet. Perhaps Comrade Bukharin would be distressed at that. It distresses me little.[3]

Too steady a diet of propaganda works would only bring boredom, he said, then added:

We must remember that the proletariat, having taken possession of the country, wants also a little enjoyment. He wants to admire beautiful performances. He wishes, and in this he is a thousand times correct, to live by the various aspects of his heart and soul. . . . While I remain People's Commissar of Enlightenment this work of introducing the proletariat to the possession of all human culture shall remain my first task, and no kind of alphabetical primitive communism shall turn me away from this task personally.[4]

In support of his own views, Lunacharsky said that he had seen a letter from sailors of the nearby Kronstadt naval base to the Leningrad Theatrical Department in which they had begged, "Just don't send us anything instructive."

In February, 1920, an agency for uniting all cultural-enlightenment work was formally established under *Narkompros*. Headed by Lenin's wife, Nadezhda Krupskaya, it was christened *Glavpolitprosvet*.[5] Under its vast authority came much of the activity for forming the mentality of the new proletariat, including scores of agitation-propaganda theatres. At the Tenth Party Congress, in 1921, *Glavpolitprosvet* was instructed to work with the Red Army, with the trade unions and with Komsomol units.[6] The thoroughness with which this agency accomplished its task is made patently evident by the fact that all Soviet books about even such a seemingly neutral topic as ballet bear the unmistakable, omnipresent aphorisms of Marxism-Leninism.

In the fall of 1920, an Association of Academic Theatres was formed which included the Maryinsky and the Bolshoi under its jurisdiction. Lunacharsky wished to keep the academic theatres and their great traditions out of the hands of the radical innovators and propagandizers such as Meyerhold,[7] and while *Glavpolitprosvet* gained power over much theatrical work, the position of administrator of the academic theatres remained apart and in the hands of Ivan V. Ekskuzovich. Lunacharsky believed that the academic theatres should concentrate above all on artistry, while the theatres of *Glavpolitprosvet* should concentrate mostly on the work of revolution. However, he said that he did not want the academic theatres to think that their role was that of a "museum mummy." On the contrary, he deemed it desirable that the academic theatres' repertoires should "arrive at some sort of correspondence with the experiences of our epoch."[8]

With enthusiasm for theatrical innovation at a high pitch, there had to be choices made about the distribution of scarce funds. Lunacharsky reported in 1929 that during the days of famine, Lenin preferred to concentrate all their efforts to preserve the pillars of their culture, for the proletariat would never forgive them for allowing the disintegration of their cultural heritage. Lunacharsky said:

> Lenin considered that we must first preserve from ruin the museums which enclosed inestimable treasures and prevent the flight abroad or death by famine of our great specialists. He thought that we would not commit a very great fault in making the young be patient, though they were avid for novelties.[9]

On the twenty-fifth jubilee celebration of Yekaterina Geltser, Lunacharsky declared publicly the path the Commissar of Enlightenment intended to follow. In tsarist days, such jubilees were grand events. A performance was given where the artist would receive a large part of the proceeds, and she was showered with expensive gifts. Lunacharsky was determined that this jubilee of a faithful artist who had not been lured by the blandishments of foreign impressarios would be a great occasion. After Geltser finished dancing the role of Raymonda, Lunacharsky appeared on the great Bolshoi stage and began his speech:

Comrades and Citizens:

I do not intend to dedicate this short speech to the special characteristics of this marvelous artist whose twenty-fifth jubilee we honor today. I intend to approach the characteristics of her significance from a wider point of view, which corresponds better to the role which I play as representative of the government, and perhaps, to the moment which we are experiencing. When our authentic proletarian revolution arrived, then people of culture repeated in their hearts those misgivings which, with great eloquence, the great Herzen[10] forecast: "Are they not vandals? Do they not bring the destruction of all values, those still unknown but powerful masses?"

Of course, the new working class, having entered into ownership of the old culture, is far from gathering and cherishing all of it. On the contrary, in that which interested the old public, there is much rubbish, much debris, I say much dung, which is not suitable even for fertilizing the new fields. But, in digging out that heap, by no means is the newcomer like the cock, which did not know enough to value a pearl-grain.[11] When the pearl falls to representatives of the new class, then it is carefully, lovingly laid aside and pampered, as museum property, and this new master, this new power laments nothing more than that difficult circumstances do not allow cherishing it more. And such a pearl is . . . Geltser. But my comparison limps in one respect: not only the rooster who understands only the essence of the barley-grain, but all are agreed that a pearl, this most beautiful and rare production of great nature, in comparison with a living grain is of little worth. Those pearls, among which Geltser might be numbered—they are living in the full meaning of this word and capable of wide development.

We need the old art not only because it is valuable in itself, is pleasingly and esthetically perfect. We need it because from this lamp new candles are lighted, since new generations, growing up about such artists, receive from them school traditions. Due to special social conditions, of which I will not speak now, Russia particularly was able in the field of ballet art to create marvelous traditions, to reach a degree of mastery unattained by any other country, in any other field of the theatre. All this clear, strict mastery, this possession of all the secrets of the noble art, gives full freedom of the body and grace. This is the image which Geltser presents to us. To lose this thread, to allow it to be suppressed before it can be used for the new artistic, cultured public— this would be a great misfortune, and if this depends on the will of a certain person, a great crime. Not only is it a question here of a living pearl which might give a harvest, no, here there is involved a whole complex, which must calmly, richly, beautifully, and significantly develop.

*　　*　　*

But, of course, ballet must cleanse itself of any lines of antiquated routine, it must be penetrated by higher human feelings, by a more general depth of ideas. It must be set aflame by a great union with symphonic music, it must enter into the interpretation of the very great symbols of human life.

Is it needed, or not? Maybe ballet might be abolished in Russia? Never. But we do not need to have a dilettante's ballet, but one which would be an achievement of the greatest sovereign-worker nation. If, on one hand ballet's chalice overflows and soon will strive toward new achievements, then on the other hand, it is not an accident that the people on all sides are drawn to dance. When our schools turn out leaders of quality, they are in very great demand. There is no school which does not want to teach rhythmics. We observe an unprecedented desire to study ballet.

Three or four days ago I received a telegram from the well-known priestess of the same art, from Isadora Duncan, who asks permission to come to Russia and educate not less than a thousand children, since she considers that exactly here, in Russia, she will succeed in establishing a school of free rhythm.

Comrades, if it is really predestined to be, and it will be, that the rhythm of life and democracy will merge, and, as in antiquity, art will overwhelm the peoples' masses, then they will gather in some kind of centers, where the most complicated actions, rhythms, and dances will be combined and disclosed in the highest achievements and experiences of the collective spirit in organized multinationality holidays. That is why I consider that to turn aside from ballet, to fail to understand its great cultural significance, means to be nearsighted, to fail to envision that which awaits us in the near future.

Yekaterina Vasilyevna is so young, fresh, so much in the flowering of her mastery that, having lost nothing by it, she has lived to that moment when the pearl grains are revealed, and from them will grow silver palms among the rainbow garden of people's art, which covers the Russian land. . . .

Long live, comrades, the works of the people! Long live great art! Long live our wounded, our poor homeland—though it be great in strength and beauty!

Geltser then came onto the stage and Lunacharsky spoke to her:

The Peoples Commissariat for Enlightenment . . . asks you to receive the title of merited artist of the Russian academic theatres. . . . Everything, which might depend on the government in the cause of facilitating your service to art, always will be done with the greatest willingness.[12]

Delegations from various groups then presented Geltser with gifts. No jewels were mentioned, as of old, but she did receive gifts of lace, statues, an album of chamber music, and other luxuries of the times.

Lunacharsky's task was sometimes complicated by the trade unions —artistic and otherwise. After the February Revolution, more than fifteen art unions existed in Russia, including a National Union of Musical Art Workers, a Union of Actors of the Private Ballet, a National Union of Actors, a National Union of Scenic and Arena Artists, a Union of Painters, a Union of Composers, and many others whose work influenced ballet. In more recent times, the Soviet press has declared they were never of great importance for they could never work together.[13] However, on May 7, 1919, in the movie theatre Ars, where the Moscow Stanislavsky Dramatic Theatre is now located, there was held the First All-Russian Conference of Workers of Art,

Vserabis, attended by 114 delegates. Often, the name was shortened to *Rabis.* As the organization spread, each theatre had a local committee, a primary organ of the Union, exercising the same functions as a factory committee. A pamphlet issued in 1920 made it clear that the Union admitted all, regardless of political opinion, but that the Union had a Communist faction which exercised great influence.[14] Eventually *Rabis* meetings played a significant role in instructing art workers about appropriate themes for their productions, besides providing a channel for them to air grievances.

On November 5, 1921, Lunacharsky and other Muscovite citizens read the following notice in *Izvestiia:*

Reorganization of the Bolshoi Theatre

The Presidium of the Moscow Guberniia Soviet of Trade Unions has resolved to reorganize the troupe and administration of the Bolshoi Theatre. If it turns out that the reorganization is impossible, then the Bolshoi Theatre shall be closed. The Presidium considers desirable the departure of the manager of AKTEO, Comrade Malinovskaya, and the manager of the theatre, Comrade Sobinov.[15]

Lunacharsky publicly replied that he did not consider it their business to close the theatre. An exchange of letters then took place in *Izvestiia* between him and Comrade G. Melnichansky, president of the Council of Trade Unions of the Moscow Guberniia. The administrative problem was finally referred to a committee from the All-Union Central Soviet of Trade Unions, *Rabis,* and *Narkompros.* Meanwhile, workers from a Muscovite factory wrote a letter to *Izvestiia* protesting the proposed closing of the Bolshoi.[16]

The interaction of some of these agencies can be examined in the manner in which they entered the lives of the dancers themselves. One performer, Igor Schwezoff, recorded that once he applied to a *Rabis* office for summer employment and received it. Later he was hired by the Propaganda Studio Opera, a cultural enlightenment theatre which gave performances and lecture-demonstrations in workers' clubs, factories, and committee rooms in outlying regions.

Productions had to be given, in his words, "a Communist twist," which was the task of the régisseur. Sometimes *rabkory*, correspondents from the workers of various factories to newspapers, would come to survey their theatrical work and write reports of it for their factory newspapers. When groups of such workers would come to watch rehearsals, members of the Worker's Committee of the theatre would conduct them behind the wings, where they would learn something of the mysteries of stage management and the construction of scenery and costumes. In Schwezoff's words, their theatrical life had become "intensely political."[17] The performances taxed the strength of the dancers who were expected to perform morning, afternoon, or evening. When one of the ballet dancers complained of being tired, the reply was given, "You are against us, you don't want to help us, you are a saboteur."[18]

When Schwezoff learned that Viktorina Kriger was forming a new ballet company in Moscow, he wanted to go for an audition, and used the excuse that he had to travel to Moscow to settle an inheritance. The theatrical director told him that it was contrary to Communist principles to arrange inheritance affairs from abroad. He was called before a committee of theatrical workers, as well as a special committee formed from the local chapter of *Rabis*. At the hearing, he was constantly badgered by the secretary of the Communist cell of *Rabis*.[19] The "trial" lasted from one to seven in the evening, as he was accused of being a wrecker, a saboteur, and what was more, of having a long, thin nose and face unlike those of a normal proletarian.[20]

THE ACADEMIC BALLET IN THE 1920'S

At the same time that Party propagandists made initial attempts to make art serve the revolution, the musical academic theatres continued to perform *Nutcracker, Swan Lake, Giselle,* and many of the older favorites. For the first time, Russians were able to see the classics *Petrushka,* at the Bolshoi and Maryinsky in 1920, and *Firebird,* at the Maryinsky in 1921.[21] The *History of Russian Soviet Music* points out that ASM had a rather significant influence upon the opera theatres during these years, especially in Petrograd,[22] where there was also produced Stravinsky's *Pulchinella* (1926) and *Tale of a Fox, Rooster, and Ram* (1927).[23] Nor was Diagilev alone in using the sparkling music of Prokofiev's *Chout;* the Shevchenko Opera and Ballet Theatre of Kiev mounted this ballet in 1927–1928.[24]

However, in these early years the theatre was drawn ever more tightly to the task of socialist construction. At the Twelfth Congress of the Russian Communist Party (April 17–25, 1923), a resolution was passed declaring that the way must be paved for use of the theatre for systematic mass propaganda of the idea of the struggle for communism. For this, the decree declared, it was necessary to strengthen work for the creation and selection of a corresponding revolutionary repertoire, utilizing in it heroic moments of the struggle of the working class.[25]

In 1924, through mandates of the Party, subtle changes began to appear in the ballet, a trend which has continued through the decades. Few of the new attempts at Soviet propagandistic ballets pleased anybody, for many factions—ASM, RAPM, and others— could not agree as to the role ballet should play or the form it should take.

Some thought that the ballet librettists should simply change older librettos to make them more contemporary and revolutionary. According to Slonimsky, *Proletkult* demanded the modernization of ballet plots in this manner, resulting in rather crude productions.[26] An example of one old ballet given a new "Communist twist" was *Le Roi Kandavl,* or *Tsar Kandavl* (1924). It was a product of an experimental laboratory which grew up with the Leningrad Academic Theatre, called *Mamont (Masterskaiia Monumental'nogo Teatra).* In the older ballet a queen, in love with a shepherd, poisoned her husband, King Candaulus. Tormented by his specter, she lost her mind. In the new Soviet scenario, the director, N. G. Vinogradov, converted the shepherd into a revolutionary, while the queen was made his accomplice. The plot was lost in the third act, which depicted a circus, but at the end of the ballet, the despotic Candaulus was dragged about the stage for two minutes. After he had been duly humiliated, a rainbow appeared on stage.[27]

Needless to say, this early attempt to make a revolutionary ballet did not last long in the repertoire.

FYODOR LOPUKHOV

In Leningrad, the man who produced *Firebird*, Fyodor Lopukhov, was destined to bestir Soviet ballet for many future years, earning the reputation of being one of the chief leaders of the formalist movement in the ballet world.[28] In the fall of 1922, he became artistic director of the Leningrad State Theatre of Opera and Ballet, the former Maryinsky. Contrary to those who merely wanted to put new characters in old plots, Lopukhov wanted to renew ballet by revitalizing the dance form itself while preserving what was worthy in the inheritance of the past. He reworked many classics and his productions used every conceivable device to bring ballet closer to the new spectator, including acrobatics, folklore, constructivist decor, sport, and physical-culture movements.

In 1923, Lopukhov mounted the ballet *The Greatness of Creation* to Beethoven's Fourth Symphony. The tone of it may be gleaned from the fact that in place of concrete human personages, in the ballet there was an "actively pulsating manly principle" and a "passively pulsating womanly principle," and "scholastic categories similar to that."[29] This was one of the very first ballets in Russia to veer from the organically composed system of classical dance and use acrobatic movements. Proletarian tastes were simply not yet sufficiently developed to relish such abstract works.[30]

Lopukhov was not deterred by one failure. He proceeded to produce a second one in 1924, called *Red Whirlwind*. In this work, he intended to produce a ballet similar to the well-known play, *Mystery Bouffe,* written by Vladimir Mayakovsky and produced by Meyerhold.[31] Lopukhov's revolutionary intentions were evident enough, but unsatisfactory. The ballet attempted to formulate an idealistic allegory expressing "the great events of October." The content of the prologue consisted of a repudiation of the cross, the symbol of humility and servitude, and the appearance of the red, five-cornered star, the symbol of struggle and revolution. Dancers, meant to embody the spirit of the revolution, were outfitted like flying lizards with webbed wings.[32] The prologue was followed by "processes" instead of "acts." The First Process presented the idea of socialism, its paths, schisms, and continual affirmation. The struggle of two themes was depicted: the first theme was portrayed by Viktor A. Semenov, using strong, definite, forward movements. Yelizaveta Gerdt, using steps based on evasive, soft, bodily movements symbolized the second theme.

In the Second Process, the inhabitants of a city, dreaming of their old cross, are unable to understand the revolution. Dissenters against the revolution appear as a group of robbers, drunks, licentious riffraff. Opposed to them, there appear workers and peasants. The revolution conquers, the "dark negative elements disappear," while on the scene a joyful May 1 celebration of Pioneers and Komsomols takes place. The epilogue attempted "scenically to reveal the idea of the Soviet Socialist Republic as the logical completion of the October Revolution—a living placard of the *smychka* of the city with the country."[33] According to the *History of Russian Soviet Music*, the ballet "clearly yielded to the influence of *Proletkult*,"[34] employing songs, declamations, and acrobatics. Again, according to Slonimsky, the spectators "refused to accept its absurdity." It played twice on the stage.[35]

An interesting comment on the ballet was made by the critic S. Voskresensky who, as one book explains, "forecast the forms of social control over emerging productions, which soon would be accepted in theatrical practice," proposing that if the direction of the theatre and the régisseurs would establish a rule to discuss a new production with representatives of professional and party organizations before the dress rehearsal and eve of performance, when it was too late to change it, then such unsuccessful shows might no longer be mounted.[36]

Lopukhov was also responsible for *Don Quixote* (1923), *Night on Bald Mountain* (1924), *Tale of a Fox* (1927), *Pulchinella* (1926), and *The Ice Maiden* (1927). In the judgment of one knowledgeable critic, *The Ice Maiden* was the best "fairy-tale" ballet created in the Soviet period, and only disappeared from the Soviet repertoire because Lopukhov's work as a *whole* was subjected to sharp criticism when the Communist Party in 1936 officially criticized his ballet *Bright Stream*.[37] In the ballet, many acrobatic and angular movements were used to remind the viewer of ice crystals. By this time, "splits" and "backbends" had taken their place in the language of ballet along with the older classical French terms.[38]

Night on Bald Mountain depicted a mockery of Church liturgy by the *skomorokhi*, the ancient jesters whose peculiar antics hark back to heathenish times in Russia. The *skomorokhi* and the Russian Orthodox Church had a long record of mutual antagonism toward each other. Lopukhov explained that since Christianity had been implanted forcibly on the people, many of them kept their heathen customs secretly. His ballet depicted such a secret assemblage on the Bald Mountain.[39]

Lopukhov's *Tale of a Fox* was an "incriminating satire-piece." It attempted to depict a fox, pretending to be a nun, and in her movements Lopukhov attempted to show the fox's habits. In Lopukhov's opinion, the press did not spoil him with praise of these ballets and they brought forth whistles of disapproval from the spectators. With his *Pulchinella* it was different. This was a noteworthy success. but the theatre had paid the music publisher for only ten performances and Russia had such a foreign currency shortage at the time that they could not afford to pay any further foreign royalties. Although it was one of his best works, it, too, had to be withdrawn from the repertoire.[40]

64

One of the first of many victims of social injustice and one of many plots based on "antifeudal" themes to be presented on the Soviet ballet stage appeared in Lopukhov's *Serf Ballerina*. Appearing in 1927 in Leningrad, the work was described as a "choreodrama," "dedicated to the theme of the terrible deprivation of rights of simple Russian people in the epoch of autocracy, and the tragic ruin of folk talents at the caprices of serf-holding feudal landlords."[41] The melodramatic story opens in a poor village with a dance at the wedding of the peasants Dushenka and Egor. The festivities are interrupted by men from the court of Catherine II, who come to camouflage the miseries of the village people before the arrival of the Empress. When Catherine comes the village looks rich and happy, and she stops to watch the wedding dances. Noticing Dushenka's dancing and greatly impressed, she has Dushenka and her brother sent to Italy to study ballet, so that in the future they might perform at the imperial court. The two dancers win honors in Italy, but during their absence from Russia, the Pugachev Rebellion begins. The people of their home village are aroused after a poor citizen is unjustly flogged, and the villagers join the revolutionary movement, with Egor becoming deeply involved in it.

After having completed her ballet studies and having returned to Russia, Dushenka is dancing one evening at a garden performance when she arouses Catherine's jealousy by taking the eye of a favorite of the Empress. Catherine has Dushenka dragged away to the stables, where Egor finds her and comes in to cheer her. She is flogged and is forced to dance some more, but meanwhile the peasants rise, burn the mansion, and Dushenka loses her mind; Egor then goes forth to join the forces of Pugachev again. In later years, the ballet was judged "naturalistic," a "vulgar sociological approach to the history of the Russian people."[42]

In 1928, Lopukhov produced a version of the revered classic, *Nutcracker*. The artist V. Dmitriev collaborated with Lopukhov in the production, and, under his direction, *Nutcracker* incarnated many of the constructivist principles, utilizing moving planes in the decorations, acrobatics in the dancing, and, what was worse, sacrilegiously introducing into this hallowed classic that device of Western music halls: chorus girls. The production caused an uproar; the magazine *Rabochii i Teatr*, Worker and Theatre, said that it showed both the artistic bankruptcy of the directors of the ballet and an absolute lack of understanding of the tasks facing the Soviet theatre.[43]

After *Nutcracker*, Lopukhov, like many of the artists in the U.S.S.R., took part in the established practice called *samokritika*, "self-criticism." In later years, it became common to see printed confessions of artistic mistakes by the most prominent composers and poets of the nation, especially after being publicly criticized in the party press or conferences. Later, such confessions became much more abject than this 1929 declaration of Lopukhov, who combined both confession and defense in one article in the magazine *Zhizn' Iskusstva,* Life of Art:

Declaration of Fyodor Lopukhov

In connection with all the events on the state ballet front I consider it necessary to declare the following:

1) There is need for a full, but at the same time, circumspect reconstruction of the ballet style.

2) The reconstruction must not consist alone of formalistic quests and reforms.

3) Yet it is neither advantageous nor right to await calmly the appearance of a new ballet theme.

4) In expectation of the new theme, it is unavoidable to submit the old canons of art to a most brutal, critical attack, and to experiment in those fields where the opportunity presents itself, in order to be armed to master all forms.

5) It is unavoidable to search specifically and in detail for a new language of choreographic expression of the new social, political mode, of the working processes, of physical culture, circuses, musical comedy, cinema, living newspapers, manifestations of the professional and amateur theatre in all forms.

6) The enthusiasm for acrobatics [in dance] . . . is not an end in itself, but only a step in the experiment.

7) All the aforementioned sources will give expression to a new choreography, and it will correspond to the new Soviet theme, in contrast to the old classic canon which borrowed its language of ballet from court etiquette and customs of the salon.

8) [It is necessary] to reveal and categorically to put an end to the balletomania which went underground after the revolution, and which also was based on court customs—but only in their worst aspect.

9) It is necessary to draw the worker to the choreographic performances and the choreographer-actor to production, in order to find out what they mutually wish to receive and give.

10) In my searchings there are mistakes, but I propose a) all experiments are attended by mistakes, and b) that I am not alone guilty of mistakes, but along with me are also mistaken the former social arrangement of the ballet theatre, the former system of preparation of ballet cadres, the absence of an independent experimental area, and our secluded way of life, so inimical to all experiment.[44]

Lopukhov then made the point that those who were experimenting should be able to count on the friendly help of society and press, and not be subject to persecution, constant nagging, and distortion of facts. This was not the last of Lopukhov's public humiliations, nor was he the only choreographer whose ambitious plans for the Soviet ballet went astray in the 1920's.

KASIAN GOLEIZOVSKY

Lopukhov had a Muscovite partner, Kasian Goleizovsky, who shared "formalistic" guilt with him although the work of the men was entirely different. Goleizovsky was a graduate of the St. Petersburg Imperial Academy, and like Michel Fokine believed Russian ballet was effete and needed revival. For this, he organized his own studio called the Chamber Ballet, styling himself "the leader of the new ballet."[45] Goleizovsky was considered to be the terpsichorean exponent of the Left in Soviet dance history of this period.[46]

In 1925 at the Experimental Theatre[47] he presented a new and startling production, *Joseph the Beautiful*. The work was a novelty in many ways. The scenery was clearly constructivistic, and his dancers assumed sculptured poses and made plastique movements like enlivened statues. Contrary to tsarist traditions, Goleizovsky's dancers were often scantily clad and barefoot. This ballet was the biblical story of the boy sold into Egyptian slavery and mistreated by Pharaoh's wife. In one critic's description, it was a continuation of the "fairy-tale-mythological line of musical performances."[48] Because its subject matter was "far from the interests of the Soviet audiences," they reportedly rejected it. Later the composer of its score, Sergei N. Vasilenko, "freed himself from modernistic influences"[49] and wrote more acceptable works.

In 1927, Goleizovsky attempted an allegorical ballet, which, according to the *History of Russian Soviet Music,* repeated the mistakes of *Red Whirlwind* of Lopukhov.[50] Since its name could also best be translated *Whirlwind,* it will be designated here by its Russian name, *Smerch.* As in the case of *Red Whirlwind,* the accounts give a hazy view of it. The ballet *Smerch* depicted the world of fox-trotting capitalists opposing the world of the proletariat, dancing in light blue working clothes and displaying hammers and sickles. The program remarked, "the theme of the ballet is class struggle. The activity is beneath time and space." The death of the old order and revolutionary uprising were traced by symbols and allegories. However, the emblems and symbols invented by Goleizovsky were judged to be too far from the current ideology to have the necessary character of *sovremennost'*.[51] According to reports, at a preview of it the spectators began demonstratively to abandon the auditorium, and the ballet was taken out of the repertoire.[52]

After *Smerch,* in 1928 at the Experimental Theatre, Goleizovsky mounted his *Carnaval,* which contained a procession of political masks, including Chamberlain and workers of the Yellow International.[53] In future years, Goleizovsky lived a peripatetic existence, giving *Sleeping Beauty* at Kharkov, *The Fountain of Bakhchisarai* at Minsk and L'vov, and the ballet *Two Roses* for an Armenian Festival of the arts in 1940. Undoubtedly he was very creative; an "Evening" of his Chamber Ballet inspired George Balanchine to try innovations of his own. However, he seemed to belong to that long line of prophets unappreciated in their homelands, and his work was declared to be "too impregnated with mysticism and erotics to meet with general recognition in the U.S.S.R."[54] In later decades, Goleizovsky was "rehabilitated" and the Bolshoi company has recently used some of his works, including an electrifying gypsy dance grafted onto the old ballet, *Don Quixote*.[55]

Sovnarkom DEBATES LITERACY VS. BALLET

With many of the new productions understandably turning out to be utter failures, by the mid-1920's proponents of the annihilation of ballet in Russia had effective ammunition. Writing in 1926, one critic pointed out:

> For the current season, our ballet is much closer to catastrophe than it seems to some of its apologists—to a catastrophe which our drama and opera succeeded in avoiding well. . . . It is symptomized . . . by a progressive cooling of interest to those dried up repertorial rags even on the part of the new spectators who took possession of the theatre after the revolution.[56]

He pointed out that Stravinsky's *Pulchinella* alone gathered a full house, and only at the première. His particular solution was to enliven it by putting on works such as Stravinsky's *Sacre du Printemps* and Debussy's *Jeux*, which Diagilev had used, but which had not yet been performed in Russia.[57] His words were not heeded.

The lack of success naturally did not lighten the task of Lunacharsky. On the one hundredth anniversary of the Bolshoi Theatre, in 1925, he issued an apologia for preserving the life of the institution, saying:

Comrade Communists often have expressed the thought that Russian ballet is specifically a creation of the *pomeshchik* regime, a court caprice, and that as such it bears within itself lines antipathetic to democracy and the proletariat.[58]

Further, many had objected that a nation could have ballet only if the children were instructed in the art from tender years, thus excluding the ballet schools of Moscow and Leningrad from the general system of national education. But he pointed out that no other country in the world had ballets such as Russia's, with their full-evening performances. If their traditions were once severed, it would be extremely difficult to re-create them; he declared: "I am a burning partisan of the preservation of opera and ballet, not only so much for their own value, as for the sake of that which undoubtedly must come forth from them."[59]

Lunacharsky's defense of ballet was carried even to the meetings of the Council of People's Commissars in 1926. Being in full charge of the gigantic task of making the sprawling nation literate as well as providing for its esthetic education, he had to defend the use of funds for luxuries when many citizens did not have the barest necessities. In one fiery session of the Central Executive Committee, VTsIK,[60] in 1926, after Lunacharsky delivered a progress report on the work of *Narkompros*, a certain Comrade Kartashev remarked sarcastically: "It seems to me that the chief activity [of *Narkompros*] has been to search out old church monuments and develop the art of ballet."[61]

Lunacharsky yelled from his place, "What nonsense you speak!"

A Comrade Volkov then asked, "What will the peasants and workers understand about these monuments of old if they remain illiterate?" Lunacharsky answered their objections in a long, impassioned speech:

Can it really be that you, Comrade Kartashev, a Communist, believing in the Communist Party, think that the Party would keep me nine years at a post if I gilded cupolas and revelled in ballet instead of occu-

70

pying myself with the people's education? This—is distrust of our Party. How much do we spend on art? We spend on art eight hundredths of one percent, that is, less than one thousandth part of our budget! Less than 300 thousand rubles a year we spend on all repairs of old buildings in our republic. Might you with this build the needed schools? No. You would not lift the general level a noticeable hairbreadth, but you would compel to crash down and mix with the earth things that speak of centuries and millennia, things which interest all the cultured world. . . . To all the state theatres is given a subsidy of 450 thousand rubles because, on the order of Vladimir Ilyich, it was calculated how much the maintenance of the theatrical buildings, including the Bolshoi, would cost if they did not play anywhere, if they were liquidated. And only this sum we give them. That is, in fact, we do not give them one kopek for their functioning. When it was proposed to close this unfortunate ballet, it turned out that this would bring a loss because it compensates for itself. What trifles are appearing here as serious questions, when we are discussing how to distribute two and a half billion on people's education. . . . It is necessary to put an end, comrades, to such gossip, all the more since it is an affair of such a thousandth part of the budget of NKP, which could correct nothing, but which makes us honorable before all mankind, pointing out that in ruin, in hunger, and epidemic, we can save the monuments of culture. That is our merit.[62]

At this point, Lunacharsky sorely needed a successful ballet which would justify the expense of preserving the art in the frugal workers' state. For this reason, the appearance of a scintillating new production called *Red Poppy* at the Bolshoi stirred fresh hopes for the future of Soviet ballet.

For years, Soviet composers, librettists, and choreographers had been told they should produce ballets conformable to the ideology, but various attempts such as *Tsar Kandavl, Red Whirlwind,* and *Smerch* were at most only stillborn children of the revolution. Then an artist named Mikhail Kurilko conceived an idea for a ballet about Chinese revolutionaries, and Reingold Gliere produced a vivid score for it.[63]

From the point of view of ideology, the idea was inspired; it was the first ballet to deal with the theme of imperialism. Karl Marx, writing in the mid-nineteenth century, predicted the downfall of capitalist society as a result of progressive enrichment of the exploiting class and simultaneous impoverishment of the proletarian class. By 1916, when capitalism had not collapsed as Marx predicted, Lenin wrote his book, *Imperialism, the Highest Stage of Capitalism,*[64] which gave a rationale for the failure of Marx's prediction: the capitalists had found new avenues of expansion in underdeveloped areas, establishing colonies which drained the wealth of the natives while enriching the exploiters, thus for a time warding off capitalism's inevitable downfall. The theme of imperialism, of domination and dehumanization of poor and ignorant people throughout the world by Western oppressors, has been portrayed in many art forms in the U.S.S.R., while at the same time the Soviet Union is portrayed as the great friend and champion of the abused peoples of the world.

By the end of the nineteenth century, parts of the coast of China had become spheres of influence for several foreign powers. Chinese revolutionaries, wishing to rid their nation of the hated foreigners, found that Soviet Russia was only too willing to exploit such an issue. In 1925, Stalin affirmed:

> Truth and justice are on the side of the Chinese revolution. That is why we sympathize and will continue to sympathize with the Chinese revolution and its struggle for freedom of the Chinese people from the yoke of imperialists and in the uniting of China in one government.[65]

A great shift was taking place in Sino-Soviet relations while this very ballet was being rehearsed. In December, 1927, a formal break in diplomatic relations occurred between Stalin and the Kuomintang—the Chinese Nationalist government of Chiang Kai-shek, which Russia had actively supported until the spring of 1927. The ballet was first staged on June 14, 1927, and it lasted in the repertoire of the Bolshoi Theatre until 1936. Although certain elements of the plot were frequently altered to suit changed political situations, the ballet in all its versions carried the enduring theme of struggle

A scene from the ballet *Red Whirlwind, above.* A scene from the ballet
Red Poppy at the Bolshoi Theatre, *below.*

A scene from *Red Poppy*, showing Feia Balabina as Tao-Hoa being carried away by Boris Bregvadze as Ma Li-chen. Robert Gerbeck as Li Shan-fu stands to the right.

between "good" simple Chinese and "bad" imperialistic Westerners and the Chinese "feudal" oppressors who collaborated with them. In the 1927 version, the chief enemy was Britain, dominating the port through the despicable character, Sir Hips. This, no doubt, reflected the fact that in May, 1927, the British police raided the British-Soviet firm "Arcos" in London, which had been a center of espionage, prompting Britain to break diplomatic relations with Russia.[66]

In 1949, when Chinese Communists triumphed over the Chinese Nationalists, the chief enemy became America, represented by a hook-nosed, sneering "Boss" in the port, a sympathizer of the despicable Kuomintang. The following account of this revived 1949 version is taken verbatim from a Soviet source, the magazine *Soviet Woman*:

> The action takes place in Kuomintang China in the thirties. The curtain opens on a large Chinese port, with the smooth blue surface of the bay stretching toward the horizon. Exhausted coolies, driven by overseers, are carrying packing cases bearing the labels of American firms into a warehouse.
>
> Everything seems to be tranquil in the port, but one only needs to scrutinize the faces of the Chinese dockers or intercept the looks they cast at the American and British officers, the conceited and brazen American Boss and the wealthy Chinese merchant Li Shan-fu, who kowtows to him, in order to see how the workers loathe the foreign "masters" and the rich Chinese who have betrayed their country.
>
> The dancer Tao-Hoa, who is a great popular favorite, enters the square in front of the port restaurant. Her exquisite dancing brings a ray of light into the somber lives of the toil-worn dockers, and they welcome her enthusiastically.
>
> The Boss evinces a desire to see Tao-Hoa dance, and the obliging Li Shan-fu grips the dancer roughly by the arm and takes her into the restaurant.
>
> The file of coolies, bent low under their back-breaking loads, continues to wend its way across the square. One of them falls and is crushed under a case marked "cigarettes." An overseer beats the unfortunate man to make him get up. His comrades come to his defense. The leader of the coolies, young Ma Li-chen, throws down the case he is

carrying. It breaks from the fall and to the amazement and indignation of everyone its contents prove to be not cigarettes, but American rifles!

These, then, are the "cigarettes" the American "traders" are sending to China! Forthwith, the dockers led by Ma Li-chen declare a strike.

Once again we see the square adjoining the port. A Soviet ship is moored at the dock. It has brought grain as a gift from the Soviet trade unions to the striking Chinese workers. With malicious glee the chief of the port informs the captain that the coolies are on strike and there is no one to unload the grain. A quick-spoken command from the captain and the Soviet sailors begin to empty the holds themselves. Gradually the square fills up with people until the police can no longer keep the crowd back. The multitude expresses its joy at this generous gift from the Soviet trade unions. The coolies join the sailors in unloading the ship and the work proceeds apace. From hand to hand the sacks of grain are passed by the Soviet seamen to the Chinese workers.

As she watches the proceedings, Tao-Hoa is filled with admiration for and gratitude to the people of the Soviet land, and she dances in honor of the Soviet visitors. The ship's captain presents her with a red poppy which Tao-Hoa accepts and cherishes as a symbol of freedom, a token of the bright future awaiting her people.

The dockers' strike spreads. Tao-Hoa joins the popular wave of revolutionary struggle. One night she has a fantastic dream that symbolizes the bitter past of the Chinese people and their happy future. And the talented young dancer, tender and fragile as a flower, acquires fresh inner strength and fortitude.

The principal hero in this choreographic production is the people fighting for liberation and against both native and foreign oppressors. The basic theme of the ballet—the struggle of the Chinese people— is vividly interpreted in the music of Gliere.

The port coolies' strike grows into an uprising, which gains in strength and scope. The city's foreign bosses flee in panic. The American and British officers and the police make a hasty escape, dropping their guns as they run. The square is now filled with the revolutionary people. Ma Li-chen climbs onto a barricade and addresses the assembled crowd: "We are victorious!" "The Power is in our hands!"

At the height of the general rejoicing, Tao-Hoa notices the disguised Li Shan-fu aiming his revolver from behind a corner at Ma Li-chen. She darts over to the workers' leader to shield him from the assassin.

74

The traitor's bullet hits Tao-Hoa and she dies, pressing to her breast her cherished Red Poppy. Silently, the people drop to their knees before the heroine.

Ma Li-chen swears by the name of the people's heroine to carry through to the victorious culmination the great cause of the liberation of the Chinese people.

The closing scene of the ballet is extremely moving. Years have passed. The great Chinese people have won their historic victory and liberated their native land forever from the yoke of the reactionary Kuomintang and the foreign invaders. As the scarlet national flag with its five gold stars is hoisted on the stage and the triumphant strains of the "Internationale" ring out, the spectators, their thoughts on the friendly country of China, rise from their seats deeply stirred, and in applauding the heroes of the ballet they accord a warm ovation to the liberated Chinese.[67]

In Gliere's score, the Soviet captain is represented by "The Internationale" theme. Soviet sailors dance to a civil war tune, "The Yablochko," contrasting with the "bourgeois" characters who are heralded by the "Charleston" and other jazz and waltz themes.[68]

In the original 1927 production, instead of merely falling asleep, Tao-Hoa, after hearing that a plot to kill the Soviet captain exists, becomes heavy-hearted and smokes opium. In her dreams she is at first haunted by a pageant of Chinese masked gods and their priests, representing the religious superstition of olden days. Phoenixes and Chinese acrobats cavort, sword dancers brandish their weapons, and human butterflies, grasshoppers, lotus flowers, and poppies dance.[69] Entrancing as the opium-induced dreams sound, the Chinese communist government had begun to wage a war against the vice. Opium and escapism were to be associated with capitalistic decadence, and not with the optimistic, hard-working, clear-visioned, reality-facing Communists who were building a new society. Therefore, the name of the ballet was purged of its opium association and changed to *Red Flower*.[70]

Soviet press reports after 1949 were uniformly enthusiastic at any mention of the ballet's name. Viktorina Kriger wrote at the time of its revival:

> The performance describes the arrival in a Chinese port of a Soviet ship with food for the workers. The Chinese reactionaries and foreign oppressors—American imperialists—meet the Soviet people with hostility, but the Chinese working people see the Soviet ship as a sign of the friendship between the Soviet and Chinese peoples ... And in the apotheosis when the red flag with the five golden stars waves and the solemn strains of the "Internationale" are heard, our feelings and thoughts go out to the great friendly country and to the Chinese people who have started building a new, happy life.[71]

Another author, A. Dashicheva, pointed out in 1950 that in spite of the opinion of the formalists, esthetes and *Proletkult:*

> [*Red Poppy*] disproved the old theories of the impossibility of showing contemporary heroes and subjects in ballets, showed those who said ballet was not understood and not needed by the masses that they were wrong, and confirmed the fact that classical ballet could be a basic expressive means. For the first time in ballet there was resolved the task of contemporary realistic drama, and in *Red Poppy* there was projected the path of Soviet ballet and its basic lines: Bol'shevik *ideinost', sovremennost', khudozhestvennost',* and *narodnost'* [meaning that it expresses ideology, contemporaneity, artistry, and folkness].[72]

Such was the tone of the criticisms, and in 1950 in the U.S.S.R. no one would have written about *Red Flower* in a different tone. However, the reviewers of 1927 had been far from being so agreeable. Slonimsky explained that the adverse criticism came chiefly from formalistic critics and representatives of RAPM, who "could not see the woods for the trees."[73] Contrary to the plaudits of Kriger and Dashicheva, a 1927 critic pointed out that the ballet confirmed two truths: 1) that it is impossible to put new wines in old skins, and 2) that never in any place was a revolution made by a ruling class, and in the Bolshoi Ballet the ruling class was composed of a little circle of representatives of classic ballet headed by Yekaterina Geltser (who played the part of the young Tao-Hoa, although fifty-one years old) and Vasily Tikhomirov. He added that for some reason or other on the tenth anniversary of the revolution they decided to give a "revolutionary" ballet, sardonically adding, "We acknowledge their good intentions—with which, as is well known, the road to hell is paved."[74] Another critic styled it "a piece of pseudorevolutionary French Rococo Chinoiserie."[75]

Nevertheless, the ideologues tried to make the most of it. A scholar specializing in Chinese affairs conducted preliminary lectures and discussions about it in the local workers' club and commended it for abandoning the "toy country" image of China which the usual Chinese production portrayed, and for attempting instead to reproduce the spirit of the new industrializing, contemporary China.[76] Mikhail Kalinin, president of the U.S.S.R., styled it "the beautiful, but Soviet creation, *Red Poppy*," as he was urging the Eighth Congress of the Komsomol (May, 1928) to take up the standard of cultural revolution.[77]

If many of the critics derided the ballet, it seems only fair to conclude that its robust melodies, vibrant color, and scintillating showmanship intrigued the Russian audiences. In the year 1928, at the Bolshoi, the following ballets were given:[78]

Ballet	Number of Performances	Ballet	Number of Performances
La Bayadère	3	*Swan Lake*	8
Joseph the Beautiful	1	*Raymonda*	5
Don Quixote	5	*Sleeping Beauty*	5
Little Humpbacked Horse	5	*Esmeralda*	6
Le Corsaire	6	*Red Poppy*	69

The Leningrad Theatre of Opera and Ballet, whose tastes appeared a bit more sophisticated than the Bolshoi's, was in no hurry to stage the famed ballet. However, pressure was exerted upon it to present it.

In September, 1928, concurrently with a campaign to enroll all art for propagating the Five-Year Plan of industrial development, *Narkompros* stepped up the activity of artistic councils in state theatres. Into the composition of the council, along with the theatrical direction and noted artistic workers, there were put representatives of local enlightenment organizations, Komsomols, trade unions, writers, artists, critics, and *rabkory*.[79] In August, 1928, *Izvestiia* said that the Workers and Peasants Inspection, investigating the Leningrad Academic Theatre, discovered that:

> In the course of two years, the artistic council was not able to mount *Red Poppy*. Apparently the directors of this theatre prevented its appearance. Under pressure from workers and theatrical societies, it was obliged to surrender. The new artistic council, organized for the theatre from representatives of mills, factories, the press, party, Komsomol, and trade union organizations, at the first session resolved to proceed with the presentation.[80]

Thus, on January 20, 1929, *Red Poppy* opened on the old Maryinsky stage. During the remainder of the season, it played forty-five times.[81]

ART AND THE FIVE-YEAR PLAN

Red Poppy appeared on the Soviet stage at the dawn of a new period. In December, 1927, the Fifteenth Party Congress decided to elaborate its First Five-Year Plan of industrial development. During the years of the New Economic Policy, private industries and farms had been tolerated. By 1927, emerging victoriously from a power struggle with Leon Trotsky and others, Joseph Stalin launched a campaign for state control and development of the economic life of the country. While plans were formulated for every facet of production, every conceivable resource for rallying public opinion to support the program was tapped. Nothing could escape. At meetings of RAPM, RAPP, *Rabis*, and special gatherings in theatres, artists were reminded that "in the period of socialist construction, art could not remain outside of politics."[82] They were constantly urged to engage in a closer *smychka* with industrial unions, to hold meetings to see what they could do to aid the Five-Year Plan, to engage in socialist competition, to organize brigades to go to factory clubs and other centers for the dissemination of propaganda.[83]

At this point, Lunacharsky had to fight a repertorial battle. The original decree nationalizing the theatres had given *Narkompros* the right "to give the autonomous theatres certain instructions of a repertoire nature." On February 9, 1923, there was established in *Narkompros* a Chief Repertorial Committee, *Glavrepertkom*, whose function was the scrutiny of all dramatic, musical, and cinema productions.[84] Through the intervening years, this agency had at times annoyed Lunacharsky by its arbitrariness—on occasion removing works from production as late as the dress rehearsal. In a theatrical conference called in 1927, Lunacharsky met the left-wing zealots in open battle. He declared:

> We have a theatrical policy. Theatre must become a real weapon of agitation and propaganda. This is the basic pivot of its work. It must preserve . . . the old academic traditions accumulated and worked out through the decades. We must use everything in it of worth. Having acknowledged the necessity of fortifying the cultural and agitational role of the theatre, we, however, by no means deny that theatre is a place of rest and amusement.
>
> The question of regulating the role of the censor in the theatre is a current question. . . . The policy of *Glavrepertkom* in this field is not yet the policy of *Narkompros*. . . . The censor must have a definite place. Its interference must be minimal.[85]

Speaking further, he declared: "Doubtful points lie on the conscience of the author. Let only the undoubtedly counterrevolutionary, undoubtedly pornographic, undoubtedly mystical themes be removed."[86] His words did not seem to cool any of the zeal in evidence. A resolution was formulated to support "the advancement of productions, expressing . . . the epoch of socialist construction, penetrated by the spirit of class struggle of the proletariat."[87] To aid this, it was proposed that Communist Party members should henceforth occupy certain key positions as critics and censors, and that contests offering prizes for ideas for appropriate productions should be arranged.[88]

In 1928, both *Glavpolitprosvet* and *Glavrepertkom* and the Administration of Academic Theatres came together in a new division of *Narkompros* called *Glaviskusstvo*.[89] To clarify the problem of repertoire, a *Repertoire Index* was issued in 1929 classifying hundreds of plays, operas, and ballets for the use of theatrical directors. The following classifications were used:

A   The best works ideologically; universally recommended for presentation.

B   Ideologically acceptable and permitted without hindrance.

C   Not completely supportable ideologically, but not forbidden. The actual presentation had to emphasize the socially acceptable elements of the production. A special *prosmotrovaiia repetitsia*, a rehearsal for examination purposes, was required.

D   Ideologically acceptable, but considered *agitkas*—works that were admittedly primitive in content, form, and language, usually timed to a special political campaign or historical date.

E   Forbidden.[90]

The entire classification of ballets is given in the Appendix. The classics which were deemed worthy of note were those of Shakespeare, Lope de Vega, Molière, and Gogol, while those which were apologies of monarchism, which showed antagonism to workers' classes or were "absolutely mystical ones" were excluded.[91]

As far as ballet is concerned, the list points to the fact that members of ASM might still have had some voice in the selection, for besides *Red Poppy*, the only other ballets which received an "A" were Prokofiev's *Chout* and *Pas d'Acier;* Stravinsky's *Petrushka, Pulchinella, Firebird, Tale of a Fox, L'Histoire du Soldat*, and *Les Noces*; Rimsky-Korsakov's *Coq d'Or, Capriccio Espagnole*; and Schumann's *Carnaval* and *La Sylphide*.[92] The "E" classification fell to *Fairy Doll, Smerch, The Vestal Virgin*, and *Number o, or the Wreck of the Council of Five*, by Nikulin. No current ballets were in the "D" class.

For seeing the result of new pressures on repertorial policies, a report of S. V. Aleksandrovsky, director of the Bolshoi in 1929, is instructive. In a theatrical magazine, he said that a committee for reorganization of the Bolshoi and its Filial had been working with the Bolshoi artistic council and the members of the troupe in judging the music and librettos of new operas and ballets. Further, the director had called special conferences with librettists and composers for exploring the creation of new Soviet ballets and operas, while also meeting with Party representatives and professional organizations for a conference on the theme "The Bolshoi Theatre and the Worker-Spectator." As a result of their deliberations, he said the Bolshoi was planning one new classical production, four Soviet operas and ballets, one opera representing the national minority groups, and two experimental productions from the West, one of which was *Pas d'Acier*.[93]

CLASSICISTS STRUGGLE IN THE BALLET WORLD

The pressure applied to art to serve the Five-Year Plan seemed to give new energy to those who thought that all the old theatrical establishments should be reevaluated. Article upon article repeated the same arguments: the classics, based on the affected movements and manners of the French court, were "organically foreign to our epoch."[94]

An open forum was conducted on the pages of *Zhizn' Iskusstva* in the summer of 1928, and the following questions were posed to various dancers, choreographers, and critics: 1) What themes could be used in contemporary ballets? 2) Can a contemporary choreographic spectacle be built on the basis of classic dance? 3) Can acrobatics be used? 4) How can ballet pantomime be renewed? 5) Would an experimental studio help solve the current problem?[95]

Against many replies which advocated the inclusion of more acrobatics and physical culture in ballet training, the steadfast Leningrad teacher Agrippina Vaganova held her ground. Classic dance, she affirmed, always had to be the basis of any training system. Building ballet on elements of acrobatics and physical culture made

81

no sense; they should be used elsewhere.[96] However, her self-assured answer did not daunt a continuing stream of opposing opinions. A subsequent article pointed out that classical dance could have really only one theme, with just endless modifications of it, and that was romantic love. The language of classical dance could only be the language of specters and spirits and not of contemporary people, for living people just do not dance that way. By its very nature, then, classical dance had to be abstract. The author urged that dance should portray industrial, urban themes and deal with material, concrete events. To do this, it should be filled with elements of acrobatics and physical culture, and the ethnographical material of the dance should be widened by incorporating the dances of the small ethnic groups of the Union into it.[97]

A choreographer, Emil Mei, added his bit to the arguments: the Bolshoi was a monument, not of the nineteenth, but of the eighteenth century. Its ballet was a result of modes implanted from on high, in no way expressing the demands of the wide mass. The basis of future teaching must be an all-sided development of the body. At the same time, it was necessary to create a new ballet artist, a socially literate and cultured man.[98]

"Carthage must be destroyed, classical ballet must be annihilated," cried another. No pseudorevolutionary work such as *Red Poppy* would satisfy the need for reform. A truly new dance must be built, with the form flowing from the content. The *corps de ballet* must not degenerate into a chorus line, but must be a vibrant mass, the bearers of ideas, capable of infecting and seizing the spectator, producing "grand presentations, worthy of the heroic pathos of our day." Elements of cinematography and the circus might be used profitably in it, and training of the artist must be based in great part on physical culture. The turning out of the foot as an essential element was questionable practice, as well as the use of such basic steps as *pirouettes, tours* and *entrechats.* The special attention formerly given to foot technique should be given in the future to the whole body. For this reason, physical-culture training, sports, games and light athletics should occupy an important place in training of the dancer.[99]

The choreographer Leonid Yacobson joined the chorus of dissidents. "The theatre in the reconstruction period has the task of activization of the masses, of organizing its will, reeducating its psyche," he affirmed.

> [There was needed the] dialectical-Marxist régisseur, revealing forms in the process of their development, in their contradictions, taking themes from surrounding Soviet reality, resolving class-proletarian problems, exciting and activizing, breaking with the rule-encircled and helpless dance art of the past, and by every means trying to create a theatre of the great proletarian culture.[100]

He would grant that some ballets should be preserved as historical pieces, such as *Sleeping Beauty* and *Swan Lake,* but such works as *La Bayadère, Don Quixote, Le Corsaire, Esmeralda,* and *Little Humpbacked Horse* did not deserve preservation either from the historic or artistic point of view. He said that "they educated vulgar tastes and propagandized abstract esthetics." Yacobson wanted to change the dance system by incorporating more mime drama, by using gestures that were real, concrete movements flowing from the content itself, instead of the former stereotyped ones.

During the quarrels, Fyodor Lopukhov seemed the most available whipping boy. Yacobson judged that Lopukhov's chief mistake was that he never really understood the unity of content and form; he simply adopted acrobatics from the circus. Content, to him, was something simply added onto form.[101]

A certain Yuri Brodersen bemoaned the fact that while RAPP was influencing the dramatic theatre, RAPM was exercising its influence in the musical field, and ARRK was uniting the workers of the revolutionary cinematography, "the ballet theatre, to its shame, has not made up to this time attempts at class consolidation." On the contrary, it "continued to be boiled in its own sanctified-by-the-centuries juice."[102]

As if announcing a prizefight, the author V. Vsevolodsky summarized the quarrel: on one side there stood Fyodor Lopukhov, Olga P. Mungalova, Pyotr Gusev, and perhaps even Yelizaveta Gerdt; on the other side stood Agrippina Vaganova and Marina Semenova. It was not simply a struggle between certain members of the troupe, he said, but "it is a struggle of the leaders of two artistic tendencies, of two ideologies." The attacks upon Lopukhov were well calculated by the reactionary group; to get rid of him would mean at one blow to discredit progressive leadership and be rid of his administrative-artistic rulership. Further, fate had dealt a kind turn to the conservatives. As if to taunt the progressives, the conservative wing turned out from the Leningrad Ballet School one of its choice products of a decade: Marina Semenova. Vsevolodsky had to admit that "her appearance made possible the rousing of a dying trend. The drowning grasp at her, as at a straw. They strive to turn a postponement into a salvation."[103] Semenova's debut was doubly significant because she was entirely the product of Soviet training schools. Her "points of steel" were quite effective in stifling doubts about whether the tender plant could indeed be raised in the new atmosphere.

What was more, though A. V. Lunacharsky had been replaced in 1929 as head of *Glaviskusstvo*, his voice still effectively reinforced the advocates of conservation of the art. On May 12, 1930, he read a speech at the Bolshoi Theatre answering the strident voices of the opposition :

> . . . Perhaps opera and ballet have quite outlived themselves? . . . If they had outlived themselves, then the Bolshoi Theatre would be empty. And we know, that it is always full and that the proletarian spectator with great pleasure cherishes a ticket to these opera and ballet performances. . . . If they draw the attention of our mass spectators, then this witnesses to the fact that any one who says that this theatre is not needed speaks against life; he speaks in quite an un-Marxian manner.
>
> No, the matter is clear . . . opera and ballet are needed. They will still be incomparably more needed, if we succeed in leading them to actual correspondence with the demands of our time. . . . We have people who

say that the classic ballet is an outgrowth of the distant past, and that it is not needed by us in the present day, since we shall chiefly need forms of dance imitating authentic reality, mime drama, or in a real sense, folk dancing. Artistic "classics" are not needed. But in the course of my activity as director of theatres and of artistic formation, everyone feared to sever the traditional lines, because having lost them, never more could we pick them up. If Russian classical dance would be killed, standing at such an unusual height, against which no one in the world dares compete, then not only the lovers of ballet will weep bitter tears, but, perhaps, proletarian youth, when he begins to build the palace of his life, will ask: "Where do you have it?"—and then we will say to him: "That is something imperial; we annihilated it"; and they will stigmatize us with a black word. For that reason I prefer now to make a mistake, not in the opinion of the proletarian mass, but of those who are prepared to break the porcelain in our museums, because aristocrats drank from those cups.[104]

He added, however, that he expected changes in it:

In the new ballet there must be sufficient attention to reality. This reality must be captivating, dealing with present stories, and not of silly fairy tales which we can not read without tedium.

A LIBRETTO CONTEST

As it was proposed at the 1927 meeting of theatrical workers, a contest was actually initiated in Leningrad in 1929, when ideas for new, contemporary ballets were scarce. The announcement, printed on a full page of *Zhizn' Iskusstva*, is significant because it concisely formulated many of the features the government and Party considered desirable in the new Soviet ballet at the time.

Stipulations of the Competition on
the Creation of a Libretto for Soviet Ballet

Having announced a contest on the composition of librettos for Soviet ballet, the State Academic Theatre of Opera and Ballet is directed by the following considerations:

Choreography, until recent times an art preeminently of the court aristocracy, now must become, thematically and formally, Soviet art.

The old ballets have outlived themselves and have ceased to satisfy the mass of spectators. The new spectator demands that the choreographic theatre bring meaning to scenic activity taken from events near to us. The libretto of contemporary ballet is not just an accidental frame for the display of dance which lacks inner cohesion and does not issue from the basic activity—but the libretto is a choreographic drama, obligated to satisfy all the demands laid upon Soviet dramaturgy in general.

To write a really contemporary scenario for ballet is to take a first step along the way in the path of creating a Soviet choreographic theatre.

A libretto presented to the contest must satisfy the following demands:

1) Revolutionary theme, primarily oriented toward contemporary events: the years of the Civil War, or of our construction. Historical subjects are less desirable. It would be interesting for the librettos to include not only the village, but themes of the city (urbanism, industrial culture). There are possibilities for scenarios built on true-to-life material, in particular on *ethnographical material of the mode of life of nationalities* populating the U.S.S.R. While not objecting to the introduction into the activity of elements of the fantastic (especially healthy, "scientific" fantasy, in the spirit of Jules Verne, for example), the State Academic Theatre of Opera and Ballet categorically rejects all attempts at mystical themes.

2) Themes must be developed on the level of a concrete perception of reality, and not by constructing abstract dance forms loaded with symbolic or allegorical meaning (as, for example, it happened in *Smerch* and in the first act of *Red Whirlwind*).

3) It is desirable to build a spectacle on mass movements (meetings, demonstrations, battles, train station crowds, street scenes).

4) It is necessary that intrigue in the scenario be sufficiently uncomplicated for it to be understood as a whole from pantomime, without the abuse of clarifying superscriptions or word cues, or conventional gestures. . . .

5) It is necessary that the librettist take into account the achievements of contemporary theatrical technique (quick changes of decorations, the use of radio, movies, lighting apparatus, and so forth).

6) Not presenting any kind of categorical demands concerning the genre of the scenario, the State Academic Theatre of Opera and Ballet

86

points to the possibilities of use of the following genres: contemporary reviews (Soviet revue, lyric-heroic poems, choreographic comedies and satires, contemporary fairy-plays).

7) It is desirable that the scenario of the ballet give the balletmaster material for pantomime—choreographic experiment, i.e., that for the scenic fulfillment of it, there would be necessary not only the old pantomimes and classics, but also new forms of dance: acrobatics, physical culture and others—and new pantomime gestures.

8) The scenario of the ballet must be calculated as a whole evening performance (two or three hours of pure activity).

The date of presentation of the scenario: not later than March 1, 1929.

Prizes: 300, 200, 100 rubles.

Direct the scenario to the Artistic Council of the Ballet of the Leningrad State Theatre.[105]

The result of the contest was a scenario written by a cinema producer, A. V. Ivanovsky. At first the ballet was to be called *Dinamida*, but later it was changed to *Golden Age*, the name of an industrial exhibit that takes place in a capitalist city. There, a Fascist delegation is welcomed and wheeled around to the booths, while a Soviet football team, invited by labor organizations, is scarcely noticed. In the first act, a boxing glove firm supports a match between a Fascist and a Negro. A secret Fascist agent bribes the referee, who ignored the white's foul play in downing the Negro. The workers are furious, and a local Western Communist woman slaps the referee.[106]

In the second scene, in a cabaret, a diva, a Fascist dancer, makes a pass at the Soviet football captain. Negro boxers and two Soviet citizens do a dance symbolizing good comradeship. Then the diva invites the Soviet captain to drink wine. He refuses, enraging the Fascists standing about. The Soviet captain lifts his football, which they think is a bomb, and all Fascists sink to the floor in terror while the Soviet lads leave.

In the third scene, the Soviet football captain, a Soviet Komsomol woman, and a Negro walk about the city. Police shadow them, slip counterfeit notes into the captain's pockets, and then arrest the three. The Negro escapes from the police and rescues the girl.

In a new scene, there is a procession of workers to the stadium, while pioneers play the game "Find the Fascist." A movie is shown where the police are seen chasing a Negro and the Komsomol woman, who run toward the stadium. The incensed workers form a Red Front, and the police give up their chase.

Another scene takes place at a music hall near the exhibition *Golden Age.* A tap dance is given to advertise Superfine Boot Polish. A polka is rendered, called "Once Upon a Time in Geneva," parodying the Geneva Disarmament Conference. Then there is a "Dance of the Reconciliation of All Classes," and the diva dances with a Fascist partner who is disguising himself as the Soviet football captain. A cancan, "a bacchanalian orgy," is followed by a film showing the freeing and rescuing of prisoners by the Red Front. The Red Front surrounds the music hall, a Western European Communist girl reveals the diva's partner to be a Fascist, and the ballet is ended by a dance symbolizing the cooperation of workers of Western Europe and the Soviet football team, while also symbolizing the joy of labor.[107]

Golden Age was given in the season of 1930–1931 in the Kiev Theatre of Opera and Ballet as well as in Leningrad.[108] The RAPM journal, *Proletarskii Muzykant*, declared that "such a coarse alloy of nauseating fox-trots and other decadent dances . . . is insufferable on the academic stage," and "the ideological harm of such productions is evident."[109] However, the ballet had one feature which made the production good for more than just laughs: the sparkling music of Dmitri Shostakovich.

An equally inane attempt at a Soviet scenario was staged also in 1931 at the Bolshoi entitled *Footballist.* Its chief title to fame is that one of its choreographers was the man who has charmed the world with his State Academic Folk Dance Group: Igor Moiseyev, working, at this time, in conjunction with L. A. Lashchilin. It was the standard fare. The ballet had two sets of opposing characters:

88

Frant, meaning "dandy," and Dame, representatives of the bourgeois NEPmen, opposed to a Soviet woman Streetsweeper and a Football Player, representing Soviet youth. At the end of the first act there was a football contest, where Dame was fascinated by the Football Player, and Frant by the Sweeper.

In the second act, the flirtations continued. The third act was described as "some kind of a pathetic finale, dedicated to our construction."[110] A tractor came on the scene, driven by four men, clearly visible from the orchestra seats, then a waterfall appeared. Different dances represented harvest, oil, coal, and water. A physical-culture dance was staged, followed by a dance signifying the removal of the *yashmak*, the face veil worn by Central-Asiatic women. This symbolized their emancipation from feudal customs by the Soviet regime.

For portraying the positive heroes in it, the composer V. A. Oransky used melodies of revolutionary and workers' songs, while the native characters were connected with the music of jazz dances.[111] The critics severely criticized the ballet, pointing out that its physical-culture movements, built upon classical principles, were completely unsuccessful, and it seemed a little naive to see women dancing on toe shoes while holding tennis rackets. However, the critics gave it credit for trying to portray a revolutionary theme, and for "crossing the thematic Rubicon."[112] Lunacharsky commented that he did not approve of bringing games onto the stage as such, but would not object to ballet being influenced by "the moral beauty" of physical-culture.[113]

In 1931 there also appeared in Leningrad "the first industrial ballet" in the Soviet Union, produced by Fyodor Lopukhov, and called *Bolt*. In it, Lopukhov attempted to show by satire the contrast between shock workers building socialism and the world of the petty bourgeoisie. Lopukhov tells that at the time, they had before them the famous example of The Blue Blouses and the Theatre of the Working Young People, TRAM, and dreamed of presenting something similar to their work.[114] The result turned out to be a "primitive agitation approach to art."[115] In it, a slacker and drunkard, Lenka Tulba, and his boon companions wreck production by their drinking bouts. In revenge for being discharged they try to sabotage the mill by placing a bolt in it. A member of the Komsomol discovers the treachery, and Tulba finds himself in the hands of the factory guard. In it, a group of textile workers imitate in dance the movement of spinning machines; a dance of blacksmiths made sport of the industrial theme; a group of horsemen, *Budënnovtsy*,[116] made galloping movements on stools, seemingly mocking the Soviet cavalry, and the dancers distorted the folk dances of the Caucasus.[117] Later, the *History of Russian Soviet Music* criticized the fact that "the positive heroes in *Bolt* were primitive, negative persons with a naturalistic, deformed, grotesque delineation."

Further "the music only underlined the vices of the libretto," and was composed of "vulgar-commonplace melodic material presented through the prism of the grotesque."[118] One commentator quite prophetically wrote:

> Here allow me to ask, for how long a time will our ballet experiment blindly and flounder in swaddling clothes? . . . *Bolt* is not simply a failure of one theatrical appearance. . . . It is a failure witnessing the depravity of that method which continues to rule in ballet theatre and which graphically points out that its path, up to the present, lies hopelessly far from the general path of Soviet theatre. It seems . . . that *Bolt* —is a last warning.[119]

The critic's words were truer than he realized for in 1932, with the dissolution of RAPP, the Party increased its drive to steer all art on the path of socialist realism. In the process, elements from *Bolt* would meet the heavy hand of outright Party condemnation. As far as choreographer Lopukhov was concerned, for the present the failure of *Bolt* brought the termination of his position at the State Academic Theatre. He affirms there remained nothing for him to do but turn over the reins of government to his assistant, Agrippina Vaganova. However, in the winter of 1930–1931, he was summoned to the headquarters of the second secretary of the oblast unit of the Communist Party, whose office was in the Smolny Institute. The Secretary told Lopukhov that ballet enjoyed great success in Leningrad, and for that reason they had decided to form a second ballet group in the city at the Maly Opera Theatre—formerly the Mikhailovsky Theatre. Lopukhov was given the chance to form and head the new company.[120]

CHAPTER FOUR

Socialist Realism vs. "Ballet Fraud"

. . . [In Egypt] it has actually proved possible. . . to canonize melodies which exhibit an intrinsic rightness permanently by law. That must have been the doing of a god, or a godlike man.

—PLATO'S *LAWS*[1]

IN 1932, the Soviet government and Communist Party issued a monumental decree, "On the Reorganization of Art and Literary Organizations," abolishing RAPP and RAPM. Artistic hegemony in their respective fields eventually passed into the hands of two new groups: the Union of Soviet Writers and the Union of Soviet Composers. On October 26, 1932, another significant event reportedly occurred in the apartment of Maxim Gorky.[2] There Joseph Stalin coined one of the most artistically lethal terms of all times: "socialist realism."

In the Soviet definition, "socialist realism" means "a comprehensive and truthful portrayal of life in art." Further, in their view, "Socialist realism implies an art imbued with communist ideology, that is to say, its very core is a deliberate purposeful struggle for the victory of communism, an evaluation of life in the light of communist ideals."[3]

The term was not just a new "ism" destined to march triumphantly for a while in the wake of impressionism, futurism, constructivism, and then, as they, to lie down to a peaceful rest. Socialist realism became an officially imposed esthetic standard which every art in the U.S.S.R., without a single exception, was forced to follow.

The Soviet ballet world soon learned that socialist realism was meant for them, for the Party has continually enforced the policy that literary dicta must be heeded in other arts. The idea is expressed in many Soviet writings about ballet that "the historic decrees of the Central Committee of April 23, 1932, 'On the Reorganization of Art and Literary Organizations,' was a mighty influence on all Soviet artistic culture, including ballet."[4]

In the 1930's the artistic director was faced with the task of trying to produce a ballet embodying the principles of socialist realism. By studying the decrees of the Party and reading literature then being published, he would notice that a literary work which passed the test of socialist realism portrayed Soviet life in an optimistic manner, showing "positive heroes,"[5]—miners overfilling their production quotas, military heroes, or stalwart Soviet women heroically and literally laying the brick and mortar of a new society. Ballet, too, was to embody the ideals of heroism, duty, honor, comradeship, and other virtues of the new Soviet citizen.

On the musical plane, a composer creating a ballet score learned that his work would find acceptance if it, too, fulfilled the tenets of socialist realism. This meant that it must avoid strange rhythms or unusual dissonances, especially if they evoked erotic, dismal, or introspective moods. Positively, a composition was supposed to incorporate folk music, or be made up of similar tuneful melodies.[6] Actually, in Russia, the birthplace of Stravinsky and Prokofiev, the musical clock was turned back to the ninteenth-century romanticism of Tchaikovsky.

In the scenic formulation of a ballet, the artist came to understand that anything resembling the fantastic avant-garde sets of Diagilev was not acceptable. Models for socialist realism in painting were unearthed in 1922, when an exhibition was held in Moscow to celebrate the fifth anniversary of the revolution.There, members of the new regime with the money and power to commission paintings were struck by the works of the Wanderers which were displayed at the exhibit.[7] When the drive for socialist construction began, their realistic style was most suitable for portraying happy farmers tilling fields, workers building new dams, or Stalin benevolently addressing such workers. Just as Tchaikovsky became the model for musicians, Ilya Repin became the new guide for painters.

Transferred to the ballet stage, this style brought a reversion to the kind of scenery common in the nineteenth century. In those days, Russian ballet had seen marvelous displays of realism. To portray the storm in the third act of the ballet *Le Corsaire*, members of a tall Guards regiment had been loaned to the theatre and covered with a huge cloth, painted to represent the sea. At periodic intervals, each guard rose and lowered himself beneath the cloth to give the effect of wildly churning waves, and incidentally made the cost of the production 500,000 gold rubles.[8] In 1820, a ballet called *The Virgin of the Sun* displayed a mechanical sunrise and sunset, as well as an earthquake and an active volcano.[9] With such a heritage, it is not surprising to read the uncanny skill of Soviet technicians in reproducing a flood on the Neva River for the ballet *The Bronze Horseman*, where wind visibly blows the performers hair, rocks trees, and makes boats on the stage heave in the stormy waters. Startlingly real fires, even to the hissing of the smoke, are lit by Tatar invaders of a Polish castle in the ballet *The Fountain of Bakhchisarai*,[10] while the spectator watching the heroine burn in *Joan of Arc* feared for the life of the ballerina.[11] In the meantime, Chagall, Pevsner, Kandinsky, Burliuk, and other artistic revolutionaries had permanently migrated West.

As far as ballet itself was concerned, it seemed that the 1932 decree of the Party, bringing a general reversion to nineteenth-century styles, considerably lessened the legitimacy of attacking classical ballet as a product of the past. In 1932, when Agrippina Vaganova became artistic director at the Leningrad State Theatre of Opera and Ballet, a check was placed upon the proponents of physical culture, acrobatics, and the bizarre productions which the previous decade had produced at the Maryinsky. Her direction offered an assurance that the classical tradition would be preserved at its unsullied best, and

94

Vaganova herself proceeded to stage the old favorite, *Esmeralda.*[12]

With these basic canons in mind in the 1930's, the Soviet ballet world steadfastly tried to do its socialist and revolutionary duties. The trials and errors of the 1920's had given directors many examples of what not to do, along with one example in *Red Poppy* of what might be acceptable. Fortified by past experience, the Bolshoi Theatre emerged with another victory in 1933: *The Flames of Paris.* Yuri Slonimsky declared, "Work on this ballet became a significant step in mastering the method of socialist realism for all its authors."[13]

The uninitiated reader might be curious to know how it deserved this Soviet-style compliment. First of all, *The Flames of Paris* possessed a full-blooded revolutionary theme. It was not the first ballet based upon the French Revolution. The company of Viktorina Kriger had given *Carmagnole* in 1932, which one reviewer described, dispensing with sentences:

> Its theme—the French Revolution. The struggle of sansculottes with the aristocracy and coarse bourgeoisie. The corruption of the monarchical class. Officers' "administration of justice." Hypocrisy of the Church. Petty bourgeois demagoguery of "democrats." Stratification of revolutionary forces.[14]

From the report, the reader could well conclude that the ballet proceeded in a manner comparable to the reviewer's style. Though it was commended for the fact that "the antireligious moments in it were well-developed," real praise was saved for its more successful cousin, *The Flames of Paris*, which first went by the name *Triumph of the Republic.*[15] *Carmagnole* had used a score by V. Femilidi, but *The Flames of Paris* had a new one written by Boris Asafiev, formerly a pillar of ASM, but sufficiently ductile to become one of the most important composers of acceptable ballets in the U.S.S.R.

The plot of the ballet becomes quite complicated, but a simplified version of it is sufficient for grasping its *ideinost'*. As the curtain opens, a French peasant named Gaspar and his children, Jeanne and Pierre, gather wood. A horn sounds and the local aristocrat arrives on a hunt.

The noble's son tries to embrace Jeanne, who runs to her father for protection, whereupon the hunters accompanying the party beat the father unmercifully for shielding his daughter, and he is sent to jail.

The next scene takes place in a square in Marseilles. After Jeanne tells the crowd why her father was imprisoned, they storm the prison and set old Gaspar free. Jeanne and Pierre are then swept away by royal enlistment officers. In the next scene the voluptuous life of the nobility at Versailles is shown. A counterplot is being brewed by the king and his henchmen against the revolution the people are planning. The plot is unmasked by a court actress, Mirelle de Poitiers, who discovers a scroll telling of the king's treachery.

The scene switches then to Paris, where a revolutionary crowd is roused by the playing of the "Carmagnole," the orations of a Jacobin, and the incriminating scroll which Mirelle shows them. They then attack the Tuileries to the accompaniment of the song "Ça Ira." The defenders of the old regime are swept away and the people celebrate victory.[16]

The Flames of Paris reportedly "opened a new chapter in the history of Soviet choreographic art."[17] Musically it satisfied one of the primary demands of socialist realism by incorporating folk melodies into the lively score. Visually, its decorations by V. Dmitriev left little to be desired from a realistic point of view. Thematically it was beyond reproach: the "people" were the "real heroes" in the production, and the story allowed "the masses" to be a moving force in the drama. Choreographically, it gave ample play for a heroic style. Slonimsky remarked that in it, "the dance grows into a power symbol. It is the spark that sets Paris aflame."[18]

In 1966, American audiences had a taste of what this meant when a *pas de deux* from the ballet was performed by Yuri Vladimirov and Nina Sorokina. The force of Vladimirov's style defies description: his bold leaps, defiantly clenched fist, and self-assertive manner would have made any Bourbon cringe; his dance was indeed that of a "positive hero." However, when snatches of the balletic drama were shown in the West as part of a Soviet movie on ballet, a typical reviewer commented about the aimless running about of a woman who waved a tricolor flag and struck poses which appeared ludicrous and melodramatic to Western viewers.[19] Understandably, the whole ballet has never been brought to America.

The Flames of Paris, from the standpoint of the Soviet state, was a success. But it did deal with Paris, and in 1933 Joseph Stalin's biggest problem was not with Paris, but with food production in Russia. In the two previous years, the U.S.S.R. had suffered from a mass famine which eventually took the lives of perhaps ten million people.[20] Following the introduction of the First Five-Year Plan, the government had begun to collectivize all farm lands which middle-class peasants, *kulaks*, had held privately during the days of NEP. This action produced furious, stubborn, desperate countermeasures by the kulaks, who hid or burned grain to keep it from collection agents, and slaughtered their livestock rather than surrender it. Stalin, in turn, coolly proceeded with his declared policy to "eliminate the kulaks as a class."[21]

The appearance of the ballet *Fadetta* at a graduation performance of the Leningrad Choreographic Institute in March, 1932, would seem to portend nothing extraordinary. For music, the ballet used the score of an older work, *Sylvia*, by L. Delibes. The new scenario was an adaptation of one chapter of George Sand's work, *La Petite Fadette*, and took place in the south of France, where, in the words of the choreographer Leonid Lavrovsky, "the influence of the reactionary Catholic clergy existed strongest of all."[22] *Fadetta* is an example of how librettists used themes dealing with "poor versus rich" while equating the rich with the class upon which the state wished at this point to show the most opprobrium, the kulaks.

It told the story of a boy, Andrei, who defies his father and forsakes the class in which he lives to marry Fadetta, a very poor little lass who lives in the woods. *Fadetta* was a bit more subtle than the usual Soviet ballet with a message, but the moral was there: it

97

contained a new theme, the theme of struggles for free feelings against an egotistic petty middle class environment. In battling against his enemies, Andrei "found within himself the strength to rise above the coarse, cruel kulak inhabitants of the country."[23]

The first appearance of *Fadetta* was followed by several significant ballets a few months later. Although the wellsprings of Russian national literature had scarcely been touched as bases for ballets in the internationally-oriented 1920's, the appearance of the ballet *The Fountain of Bakhchisarai*, based upon a poem by Alexander Pushkin, was the beginning of a new, abiding trend. The ballet, which first appeared in Leningrad in September, 1934, portrays the story of a gentle Polish woman, Maria, captured by Khan Girei, who falls in love with her. Though he abjectly courts her, the Khan arouses only revulsion in the woman, who is later stabbed by another harem woman. Its lush, oriental settings were heavily realistic, and, as if to justify the existence of the production, a program issued at a revival of the ballet in 1951 assured the spectator that "it assisted the formation of realism on the Soviet ballet scene."[24] Just before the war, Maria was found to be Western Ukrainian instead of Polish; and the ballet was taken briefly from the Moscow stage in the mid-thirties when the Party passed through one of its more Puritanistic phases, and the costumes were found wanting.[25]

In succeeding years, numerous ballets appeared based on Russian literary works, particularly those of Pushkin, whose realistic style and clashes with tsarist censors endeared him to the Soviet government. The list includes Pushkin's *Prisoner of the Caucasus, Mistress into Maid, Tale of a Priest and His Workman Balda, The Stone Guest, The Stationmaster, Tale of the Dead Tsarevna and the Family of Bogatyrs, Gypsies,* and *Cleopatra,* based upon his poem *Egyptian Nights.* M. Lermontov's *Bela, Ashik Kerib, Demon,* and *Masquerade* have been used as bases for librettos, as well as I. Turgenev's *On the Eve,* N. Leshkov's *Levsha,* and N. Gogol's *Taras Bulba, Fair at Sorochinsk,* and *Christmas Night.* One knowledgeable American explained that by giving such attention to the classics, Soviet leaders strive to convey the idea of a cultural continuum with Pushkin, Lermontov, and other great literary artists of a previous age.[26] Undoubtedly the timing was important, for at a time when the state was making every effort to exalt national patriotism, many ballets on the national classic themes started to appear.

On the stage of the Bolshoi, in March, 1935, a new ballet was produced by Igor Moiseyev, based upon the story *Three Fat Men* by a well known Soviet author, Yuri Olesha. In a land ruled by three tyrannical, aristocratic, capitalistic fat men, a revolutionist named Prospero agitated the workers to attack the royal palace, and he is thrown into the dungeon of the Three Fat Men. Within the palace, the royal heir, Prince Tutti, is disconsolate because a puppet he loves is broken. A travelling actress named Suok resembles the puppet enough to replace it and is taken to the palace. There she secures the keys to the dungeon and frees her lover, Prospero. Her hero then leads the workers to a victory against the Fat Men.[27] The theme, combining a spoof of capitalists along with a tribute to the honest toiler, was an acceptable one anytime.

THE ALIENATED ARTIST

With the hindsight of history, it would seem that those responsible for deciding to stage the ballet *Lost Illusions* in December, 1935, at the Leningrad Kirov Theatre possessed some eerie powers of divination. As if to fortify inwardly the people of the artistic world against a series of onslaughts by the Party which threatened on the horizon, there appeared a ballet designedly calculated "to unmask the imaginary freedom of creativity in the capitalistic world."[28] To convey this lesson, the novel of Balzac, *Les Illusions Perdues*, was adopted. As Slonimsky notes, the authors of the libretto dreamed of creating a choreographic illustration of the undying lines of the *Communist Manifesto:*

99

The bourgeoisie, wherever it has got the upper hand, has put an end to all feudal, patriarchal, idyllic relations . . . and has left no other nexus between man and man than naked self-interest, than callous "cash payment." It has drowned the most heavenly ecstasies of religious fervor, of chivalrous enthusiasm, of Philistine sentimentalism in the icy water of egotistical calculations. It has resolved personal worth into exchange value.[29]

Ideologically, the ballet was important, for it was an incarnation of the concept of artistic freedom which has been voiced through many decades of communist writings. Their doctrine teaches that in a society based on the power of money, real freedom is impossible. Lenin once asked the question, "Are you free from your bourgeois publisher, Mr. Writer? Are you free from your bourgeois public, which demands pornography from you. . . ?"[30] Such freedom to Lenin was simply masked dependence on the moneybag, and this was the fundamental idea which the librettist emphasized in Balzac's story.

The Soviet literary world has manifested esteem for Balzac on many occasions, but the greatest recommendation came from Engels himself in a well-known letter to Margaret Harkness, in which he called Balzac a great master of realism.[31] The plot of this ballet makes little pretense at authenticity in copying Balzac's story. In the ballet a talented French musician, Lucien, composes great music but remains unsuccessful until a dancer he loves, named Coralie, persuades a rich patron to help stage one of his ballets. Intoxicated by the success of his ballet, Lucien abandons Coralie for her rival, Florine, who works to prevent his ballet from being a success. She then forces him to write trivial music which will sell, but which is beneath his talent.[32] The "lost illusion" was the illusion of the Western artist who thought he was free, but really was at the mercy of cash payments by capitalist patrons. The theme was emphasized that the purpose of the ballet was "to lay bare the myth of free creativity claimed by bourgeois historians."[33]

Barely two months had passed after the première of this ballet, when the Soviet musical world was faced with the Central Committee of the Communist Party's outright condemnation of the ballet *Bright Stream* and the opera *Lady Macbeth of the Mtsensk District*. The artists involved learned that commissars could be as artistically dictatorial as the capitalists portrayed in *Lost Illusions*.

In the 1930's, Joseph Stalin effected what his defeated archenemy, Leon Trotsky, called "a betrayal of the revolution." Trotsky affirmed that in the early years after the revolution when the enthusiasm of the masses for world revolution was at its highest, there was no fear of experiments in the U.S.S.R., and opposing schools of artistic thought could flourish. However, as Stalin struggled to overcome his political enemies, literary schools were successively strangled. Anonymous directives governing such diverse fields as natural science and ballet emanated from the central Party powers, and they had to be received like military orders.[34]

On January 17, 1936, a vast reorganization took place in the agencies for artistic control in the U.S.S.R. By decree, the Central Executive Committee and the Council of People's Commissars established an All-Union Committee for Affairs of the Arts in the Council of People's Commissars. Under the authority of this group came all theatrical productions, the cinema industry, and all institutions fostering music, painting, sculpture, or any other form of art. The Committee was divided into administrative branches which dealt with theatres, musical institutions, circuses, and other phases of cultural life.[35]

Under this system, the theatrical director and his artistic director prepared a yearly repertoire plan of all productions and submitted it to the Committee for ratification. The music to be used along with the full text of all songs was attached to the plan. The Committee critically evaluated each new production after dress rehearsal. In order to avoid bottlenecks created by a change in political climate, the directors had to develop intuitions about what would be politically safe by the time the première of the production would be ready.[36] Sometimes a theme, chosen with the most docile intention, would encounter disaster simply because it did not fit into the *exact* groove which was currently to be followed.

To try to understand why any particular incident occurred in the history of Soviet artistic policies is to step into quicksand. More often than not, a web of causes dealing with foreign and domestic policies needs to be untangled. At best, after probing and assessing the possibilities, any conclusions drawn are only calculated guesses.

There were many changes taking place in the lives of citizens of the U.S.S.R. in the 1930's. In August, 1935, a miner named Alexei Stakhanov increased his productive output fourteen times and immediately became the leader of a great army of Stakhanovites, who performed similar feats around the nation.[37] Emphasis on increase of production had existed for years even in the ballet world. According to reports in *Rabochii i Teatr*, the Leningrad ballet company was engaging in "socialist competition" with Moscow's Bolshoi company as early as 1929.[38] In such competitions, a company would strive to stage more new ballets than the other company while keeping within a low budget.

Simultaneously attitudes toward the individual's moral life were changing. After the Bolshevik rise to power, family bonds were greatly weakened by legislation in 1917 and 1918 which made divorce possible by mere application of one partner. The second partner would be notified by postcard of the transaction. Adultery and abortion were no longer punishable. By 1935, these policies had produced such a decline in the birth rate and such a breakdown in family structure that the government had begun to envision serious effects upon its economic plans as well as its military potential for checking Germany's evident aspiration for *Lebensraum*. In September, 1935, divorce laws were tightened, and, in addition, laws were passed against homosexuality and abortion. Parents were held responsible for the delinquency of their children.[39] The state would tolerate no nonsense in these matters.

It was at this time that the Soviet government initiated a program of mass purges involving the lives of millions. A calculated, government-induced terror was instituted and the law-abiding, peaceful citizens kept bags packed in fearful expectation of the knock at the door by secret police, who would whisk them away to a concentration camp.

On December 1, 1934, the assassination of the prominent leader of the Leningrad Party District, Sergei M. Kirov, produced new waves of purges. In the theatrical world, the purge took the lives of Vsevolod Meyerhold and his wife after Meyerhold protested openly against governmental art policies. Lev M. Karakhan, the husband of Marina Semenova, fell in the tide of executions, as well as top Party figures such as Nikolai Bukharin. Death and banishment were not the only weapons for cowing the population. Both the artistic and scientific world were subjected to the more refined methods of coercion.

In the midst of this terrifying decade, a young composer named Dmitri Shostakovich scored a triumph with a new opera called *Lady Macbeth of the Mtsensk District,* which later went by the name of its chief character, Katerina Izmailova. The music for it was undoubtedly brilliant, and in 1934 the opera was eulogized as a bright product of the solicitude of the Party, as manifested in the decree of April, 1932, and was hailed as a herald of the rich growth of Soviet art that would come in the future.[40] In the space of two years, it was produced in Cleveland, New York, Prague, Lublin, London, Copenhagen, and Zurich.[41] The plot, based on a story by Nikolai S. Leshkov, veered far from the rosy-visioned view demanded by socialist realism. It portrayed the despairing downfall of a bored provincial merchant's wife who passionately turns to the love of another man, only to be spurned by him in the end for a prostitute's love. Murders, rape, and suicide form the structure of the plot.

On January 28, 1936, the official paper of the Communist Party, *Pravda,* carried an article entitled: *"Sumbur Vmesto Muzyki,"* "Confusion Instead of Music." The opera was castigated at length for its "clamorous, neurasthenic music," and for transferring "Meyerhold-ism" to opera. Acknowledging that the opera had been a foreign success, *Pravda* attributed this to the fact that it tickled the perverted tastes of the West, where it was liked for being confused and absolutely apolitical. *Pravda,* however, objected to more than the music: "The merchant's double bed occupies a central spot in the mounting of it; . . . the author tries to evoke sympathy for the crude and vulgar ardor and behavior of Katerina. . . ." In it, Katerina's illicit lover is beaten by her father-in-law, who is in turn poisoned by Katerina. Its portrayal of the poisoning and beating were judged to be too naturalistic.[42]

The condemnation was a supreme humiliation for the young composer, and he had no redress, since this criticism was from the highest power in the land. Along with the condemnation of *Lady Macbeth,* the Party singled out as a model opera *Quiet Flows the Don* by Ivan Dzerzhinsky. He had used the novel by the future Nobel prize winner, Mikhail Sholokhov, as basis for the libretto, and the opera contained no discordant music in the style of Shostakovich. Musically, it was on a much lower plan, but it was high in *narodnost',* being replete with Cossack folklore and music.[43] This point, however, has further ramifications.

FATHERLAND AND "BALLET FRAUD"

At the time that the new policy toward the family was being instituted by the government, other fundamental changes were occurring in the dogmatic foundations of Marxism itself. Marx once said: "The working men have no country."[44] During the early years of Soviet power, in conformity with Marx's idea, it had been a governmental policy to de-emphasize nationalism and patriotism. While speaking about the teaching of history, Lunacharsky himself had said in 1918: "We socialists above all must place teaching on the basis of international principles." He scorned those educators who were striving to inculcate "a healthy love for the homeland," and declared that such education had been necessary only when Russians had to fight

104

Germans or other soldiers.[45] Stalin knew, however, that some concessions to the national pride of the minority groups would be necessary, and he began a controlled policy of recognizing their aspirations. Added to this was the growing power of Germany which undoubtedly aided in stamping out the remains of Marxist internationalism. On June 9, 1934, *Pravda* issued a monumental statement summoning the patriotism of the nation under the title "For Our Fatherland."[46] Under this new policy, the government began to grant to national groups concessions which had been denied them in past decades. Various nationalities subject to Soviet power had not always found official encouragement for their national art; for example, the Belorussian theatre was told to abandon its native repertoire, which was called "bourgeois nationalist," and to start emphasizing Soviet productions.[47] In the 1920's, Ukrainian historical songs had been ruled out of the repertoire of a Ukrainian musical group, and gradually even the works of most Ukrainian composers were not to be played.[48] However, in 1934 and 1935, the Soviet government became much more conscious that various ethnic groups in the Union had richer traditions of folk song and dance than had been acknowledged in the past.

There was one powerful group in the U.S.S.R. which the regime especially wished to win over: the Cossacks. These men, fabled in literature and song, were the descendants of freebooters who had fled in past centuries to uncontrolled regions on the fringe of Russia, there setting up their own governing councils. Pressed by the needs of survival, through the centuries the Cossacks had become some of the world's most fabulous fighters and horsemen. In the years of civil war (1918 to 1920) some of them fought with White Russian forces or with German troops which attacked Russia at the time. In the 1920's, they had been denied the right to wear their colorful, traditional uniforms, which included the squat fur cap (*kubanka*), and a voluminous black cape (*burka*), and a flashing dagger. Possibly nowhere in Russia did the policy of collectivization provoke such rage as in the Cossack regions. Often urged on by the village priest, various Cossack villages had rioted against Communist officials, who were at times lucky to live through the ordeal. In 1930, Viacheslav Molotov personally made a trip to the Kuban region to pacify the Cossacks there. Before the region was subdued, whole villages had to be removed to more distant points, such as Central Asia.[49] In the mid-thirties, where coercion had proved to be unsuccessful, the regime decided to change its tactics.

After the civil war, the Cossacks had not been allowed to form their own military units within the Red Army; understandably their allegiance had been considered questionable, but if their loyalty to the Soviet government could be assured, their verve, their courage, and their colorful ways could raise Red Army morale considerably. On April 20, 1936, the Central Executive Committee issued a decree which allowed them to form units within the Red Army and to don once more their colorful garb.[50]

In 1935, groups of Don, Terek, and Kuban Cossacks were given official sanction to form their own songs and dance groups. Their repertoire could consist of some of their old songs which were not politically offensive, plus a few new ones such as *"Kazach'ia Pesnia o Staline,"* "The Cossack Song about Stalin." In the Don River region in 1935 there began to be held contests among folk dance and song groups, with the winners being invited to perform in the opera *Quiet Flows the Don* in Moscow.[51]

It was about these same Kuban Cossacks that Dmitri Shostakovich wrote a ballet called *Bright Stream.* An early reference to the ballet calls it simply *Kuban,*[52] but later it was called *Bright Stream,* the name of a collective farm upon which the Cossacks lived. Unlike *Lady Macbeth,* with its tragic air of despair, *Bright Stream* was a comedy, written with mischievous mockery—a type for which Shostakovich had great aptitude. Before its debut in Moscow, a Theatrical Criticism Circle from the Kaganovich Ball-Bearing Plant attended the dress rehearsal and made suggestions regarding its theme, as well as its dances and costumes.[53]

In the zany libretto of the ballet, visiting city entertainers come

Artist's sketch for the set of the Shostakovich ballet *Bright Stream,* condemned in 1936 by Party decree.

Folk dancing pictured in the fifteenth-century "Radziwill or Koenigsberg Chronicle," a copy of which is in the New York Public Library.

to the kolkhoz Bright Stream. A farm worker named Zina is an old school friend of a visiting ballerina. Zina is crushed when Pyotr, her husband, is bedazzled by her friend. In the complicated plot that unfolds, the farm husbands and wives hold farcical rendezvous with members of the entertainment company, which leads to a comically fought mock duel. However, the rural husbands and wives become reconciled to each other and beg forgiveness for their temporary streak of unfaithfulness and pursuit of the city visitors.

During the course of the ballet, some Kuban Cossacks dance, but apparently neither wearing their native costumes nor performing their native dances.[54]

The program issued at the time of the performance quite innocently remarked that *Bright Stream* was an important and essential link in those attempts to renew and reform ballet.[55] The artists responsible for it were attempting to reveal in the language of ballet "the joy of living, the gaiety and lyricism of our reality, our youth, our festive, sparkling life."[56] This was their affirmation of the Stalinist catchphrase of November, 1935: "Life has improved, comrades. Life has become more joyous."[57]

Another point noted in the ballet program is worth considering further. The ballet depicted city youths in contrast to country youths, with a farm girl's husband ready to cast her aside for a more sophisticated city dancer. The teachings of Marxism-Leninism point to the elimination of differences between city and country life. In a speech of November 16, 1935, Molotov affirmed to the First All-Union Conference of Stakhanovites that "the old contrast between town and country is beginning to be obliterated."[58] For fear that the production might have pointed up too sharply the differences existing between the class of city visitors and the kolkhoz people, the program cautiously assured the spectators that "between the Soviet youth in the city and in the country there are no principal differences. These are not different people."[59] As if trying to reassure themselves further, the program repeated that they were all the children of one great country building one culture in the city and in the country and that those who thought otherwise were mistaken.

As far as the audience was concerned, "The performance enjoyed great, tumultuous success."[60] The choreographer, Fyodor Lopukhov, was invited to go to Moscow to stage it for the Bolshoi Theatre. There the performance brought a holiday mood to the audience. Although the people seemed to like it, the critics were not agreed about *Bright Stream*. Ivan Sollertinsky criticized it from the point of view of its dramatic action,[61] though later he defended the music of Shostakovich. Yuri Brodersen applauded it. It was, he declared: "A realistic scenic fulfillment of a Soviet theme. For the first time on the ballet stage there was shown with great persuasiveness of new, happy people of our country and a bit of the joy of kolkhoz life. The force and fascination of the performance lies in this very sunny joy, in its unlimited optimism."[62] He singled out for special commendation the work of Lopukhov:

> The merit of Lopukhov is all the more significant, since not long ago, he, more than anyone, was on the formalistic plane. . . . There was a time when each new presentation of Lopukhov's on the stage of the Theatre of Opera and Ballet was accompanied by whistles in the audience . . . however Lopukhov decisively overcame his mistakes and irrevocably rose to the level of realistic theatre.[63]

He added that the music by Shostakovich was "provocatively gay, tempermental, sharply danceable in rhythm and instrumentation." While it was true that the composer had incorporated whole pieces into it from his old ballet productions, especially from *Bolt*, this is in no way detracted from its quality. It is interesting to speculate how Brodersen felt on February 6, 1935, if he picked up an issue of *Pravda*. There, with large headlines, on the third page appeared a four-column article, entitled *"Baletnaia Fal'sh'."* Since it was unsigned, this meant that it came from the highest echelons of the Party, and its judgments were more binding than law. It began:

Socialist Realism vs. "Ballet Fraud"

Ballet Fraud

(Ballet *Bright Stream,* libretto F. Lopukhov and A. I. Piotrovsky, music of Dmitri Shostakovich. Production of the Bolshoi Theatre.)

Bright Stream—this is a so-called kolkhoz. The libretto obligingly indicated the precise address of this kolkhoz: the Kuban. Before us is a new ballet, whose entire action the authors and performers tried to borrow from present-day kolkhoz life. They portrayed in music and dance the completion of harvest work and a harvest holiday. According to the design of the author of the ballet, all hardships were past. On the stage all is happy, gay, joyful. The ballet must be permeated by light, by festive enthusiasm, by youth.

This is not to object against an attempt to join ballet and kolkhoz life. Ballet—this is one of our most conservative forms of art and finds it more difficult than any other to break with those traditions which shaped the tastes of the prerevolutionary audiences. The oldest of these traditions is that of a doll-like, unreal attitude toward life. Ballets prompted by such tendencies do not portray people, but dolls. Their feelings are those of a doll. The basic difficulty in Soviet ballet is that dolls are impossible here. Their falsity would be glaring and unbearable. This imposes serious obligations on the author of the ballet, the producer, and the theatre as a whole. If they wish to present a kolkhoz on the stage, it is necessary to study a kolkhoz, its people, its mode of life. If they decide to present a Kuban kolkhoz, they should became acquainted with that which is charactertistic of the Kuban kolkhoz. A serious theme demands a serious attitude, with great and honest work. The rich sources of creativity in folk songs, in folk *pliaski,* in games should be explored by the authors of the ballet.

The life of a kolkhoz, with its new customs and festivities still in the process of formation, is indeed a very important, great theme which must not be handled lightmindedly, without sufficient knowledge—be it in drama, opera, or ballet. One who is really near and dear to the new attitudes, to the new people in the kolkhoz, will not allow it to be converted into a game with dolls. No one pushes our ballet and musical art. If you do not know a kolkhoz, if you do not know in particular a kolkhoz in the Kuban, do not rush, but work a bit; do not convert our art into a mockery before the public. Do not vulgarize life, which is full of the joy of creative work.

According to the libretto of Lopukhov and Piotrovsky, a kolkhoz on the Kuban is depicted. But in reality, there is neither Kuban nor collective farm. Here, there are tinsel "paysans,"[64] coming off a prerevolutionary candybox, who depict joy, but having nothing in common with the folk dances of the Kuban or elsewhere. On the same stage of the Bolshoi Theatre, where dolls were imitating kolkhozniks, real kolkhozniks from the Northern Caucasus recently showed the amazing art of folk dance. These were characteristic of the individuality of the people of the Northern Caucasus. It is not necessary to reproduce these dances and games directly in the art of ballet, but only after having taken them as a base is it possible to build a folk, kolkhoz ballet.

The librettists, least of all, thought of the real thing. In the first act doll-kolkhozniks play. In the other acts, allow me to say, there disappears all trace of the kolkhoz. There is no kind of intelligent content. The ballet dancers execute nothing but disconnected numbers. Some kinds of people in clothes having nothing in common with the clothes of the Kuban Cossacks spring onto the stage like insane people. Ballet foolishness in the worst sense of the word rules on the stage. Under the form of a kolkhoz ballet there is presented a mixture, contrary to nature, of false folk *pliaski* along with numbers by dancers in *tutus.*

More than once, paysans have appeared in ballets at different times. Dressed up doll-like men and women serfs came forth as shepherds and shepherdesses, executing dances which were called "folk." This was only a fraud in the literal sense. It was doll art of its time. Sometimes these ballet serfs tried to preserve ethnographic veracity in their costumes. Nekrasov wrote ironically in 1866:[65]

> But out came in a peasant shirt
> Petipa—and the theatre roared! . . .
> Everything, to the white gussets in the shirt—
> Was correct: flowers on the hat,
> Russian swagger in every sweep . . .

In this, indeed was the unbearable perversion of the ballet, and Nekrasov addressed himself to the ballerina:

> . . . Houri of paradise!
> You are fair, you are light as air,
> So dance then, "Daughter of the Danube,"
> And leave alone the peasant of Russia!

110

Socialist Realism vs. "Ballet Fraud"

Our artists, masters of dance, masters of music, undoubtedly might show in realistic, artistic form the contemporary life of Soviet people, utilizing their creativity, songs, folk dances, and games. But for this, it is necessary to work persistently, and conscientiously study the new way of life of the people of our country, avoiding naturalism and esthetical formalism in productions and presentations.

The music of D. Shostakovich exactly matches the ballet. In *Bright Stream,* it is true, there are fewer tricks, fewer strange and wild harmonies than in *Lady Macbeth of the Mtsensk District.* In the ballet, the music is simpler, but it decisively has nothing in common with the kolkhoz or the Kuban. The composer has the same devil-may-care attitude toward the folk songs of the Kuban as the librettists and producers have toward its folk dances. For that reason, the music is characterless. It strums along and expresses nothing. From the libretto we learn that it was partly transferred into the kolkhoz ballet from the industrial ballet *Bolt.* It is clear what happens when one and the same music must express different scenes. Actually, it expresses only the composer's indifferent attitude to the theme.

The authors of the ballet—both the producer and the composer—apparently consider that our public has simple tastes, that it accepts everything which clever and indifferent people concoct.

Actually only our musical and artistic critics are undemanding. They often overload with praises productions which do not deserve them.

In subsequent weeks, after the criticisms of Shostakovich, *Pravda* printed articles entitled "Against Formalism and Naturalism in Painting," and "Cacophony in Architecture," leveling charges along the same vein against these arts. In November, 1936, "A Very Serious Lesson" condemned a play given by the Kamerny Theatre, *The Bogatyrs.* Other decrees appeared dealing with such subjects as history, legal theories, and even biology.[66]

Such articles in *Pravda* were followed by long speeches and open discussions at meetings which took place so frequently in theatres and professional societies that this became a routine feature of the life of artistic workers. The pattern for these meetings was quite uniform: a Party member in the theatre, often a stage crew member, would read aloud the newest Party pronouncement in *Pravda* on art. Then he would elaborate on it and describe in great detail the lessons the theatrical workers should learn from these edicts. One who attended such meetings in the Vakhtangov Theatre recorded his reactions:

> I remember the puzzled and sardonic mood in which we attended the first meeting following the appearance of the editorials in *Pravda*. Shostakovich was admired and respected in our theatre, and we listened in silence while the secretary of our Party organization, the barber Ivan Baranov, heatedly denounced and execrated the unfortunate composer.[67]

The attacks brought an end to many of the brilliant innovations in theatrical methods introduced by men such as Meyerhold, and the acting methods of Konstantin Stanislavsky, used to enforce realism on the stage, became obligatory in Soviet theatrical schools.[68] For choreographer Fyodor Lopukhov, it spelled the end of his career at that time in the Maly and Bolshoi Theatres. Lopukhov was now completely vulnerable to any enemy with a grievance, and in the ensuing discussions of his work, even his very good ballet, *The Ice Maiden*, was removed. In later, less terrible times Lopukhov referred to the incident rather cryptically:

> In the end, I scarcely am able to explain everything that took place, although I now see rather well my mistakes and weaknesses in this performance. . . . I do not wish either to justify myself or to allude to any kind of objective causes. But one thing I must say. The thirties were a turning point not only for my personal fate, but in the life of Soviet ballet.[69]

He exonerated the composer Shostakovich from all blame for the incident, affirming that the score was clear, melodic, with great humor and lyricism. It was still heard in the 1960's on the Soviet radio and was used in other productions. However, the attack on Shostakovich still aided the removal in the 1930's of works of all foreign contemporary composers from concert programs, including Hindemith,

112

Stravinsky, Bartok, Cassela, Schönberg, and many others.[70] The new emphasis placed on Dzerzhinsky's work made it completely clear to those capable of reading the signs that socialist realism in music, now more than ever, meant that bold and unusual harmonies had to give way to a simple diatonic idiom.[71] Further, any music which was inclined toward the erotic, or which probed the human psyche too deeply, would be bypassed for straightforward, wholesome tunes, preferably based upon folk music.

An official record of discussion by the Union of Soviet Composers about the Shostakovich decrees is contained in the magazine *Sovet-skaia Muzyka* for March and May, 1936. There, it is revealed that the Muscovite U.S.C. spent three days discussing and analyzing Shostakovich's work in the light of the Party's criticisms, as well as thirteen evenings analyzing and criticizing new productions. However, the president of the society complained that the discussions did not have "that incisiveness which is completely necessary for defining the paths of future development of Soviet musical creativity."[72] He reaffirmed the viewpoint that folk creativity was the authentic source of everything significant that art had produced in the course of its history, and that deep folk roots lay at the basis of the great creativity of masters such as Vivaldi, Bach, Handel, Haydn, Glinka, Beethoven, and many others. Former members of RAPM condemned Shostakovich for being too influenced by "Western" composers such as Hindemith, Stravinsky and Křenek.[73] At the meetings, members of ASM were accused of taciturn sabotage.[74] Many of the participants articulated the clichés which they knew were expected of them, such as the declaration of composer Vladimir Fere: "We composers are still in a significant degree isolated from the reality surrounding us. Visits to the army, to the kolkhoz, to Pioneers' camps must be organized so that we may become deeply acquainted with our reality."[75]

In Leningrad, a widened plenum of the board of administration of the Leningrad Union of Soviet Composers, after acknowledging its debt to the Leningrad City Party Committee, made a resolution in support of the opera *Quiet Flows the Don,* along with a few other works, including Asafiev's *Fountain of Bakhchisaria.*[76] Remarks were recorded by dozens of composers, critics, and conductors, dutifully confessing their own past false evaluation of the works of Shostakovich, or promising in the future to produce works reflecting Soviet society more faithfully.

Comrade Chernetskaya, the secretary of the Party committee of *Rabis,* declared: "The Union of Soviet Composers must convert the articles of *Pravda* into a militant Bolshevik program of activity. We need to organize systematic hearings of new productions being discussed in mass lecture halls, in the presence of composers, critics, and the best people of our country—Stakhanovites, who love art and music."[77] The slogan was immediately taken up by Comrade Chulaki: "Stakhanovites—the best people of our country—lay claim to their right in the field of music. They have demanded that music express the authentic heroism of socialist construction."[78] Boris Asafiev, the former leader of ASM, in the May issue dutifully commented that Shostakovich had resorted to the use of "Lumpen-Musik" in his depiction of the kolkhoz.[79]

The attacks on Shostakovich jarred the whole world of the Soviet intelligentsia. Comments upon the opera and ballet appeared in many journals dedicated to the arts, including the literary journal, *Red Virgin Soil,* which carried the usual assailments upon the ballet's lack of *narodnost'.*[80] Elsewhere, Yuri Olesha, the author of *Three Fat Men,* ruminated in a manner much like Rubashov in Arthur Koestler's *Darkness at Noon:*

> I had always been fond of Shostakovich's music. I had heard his symphony, his ballet suite *Bolt,* his pianoforte, and liked them.
> I know Shostakovich personally. His is a personality that attracts one, whose attention one wishes to win.
> The article in *Pravda* deals with a question of principle. It is the opinion of the Communist Party; either I am wrong or the Party is wrong. . . . If I do not agree with the Party in a single point, the whole

114

picture of life must be dimmed for me, because all parts, all details of this picture are bound together and arise one out of the other; therefore, there must not be a single false line anywhere.

That is why I agree and say that in this matter, the matter of art, the Party is always right. . . .[81]

The tragic resemblance to Rubashov went even further: Olesha, like Rubashov, fell victim to the Stalinist purges when hints of Fascist ideology were found in a movie scenario he had written.[82]

REALISTIC COSSACKS IN BALLET

For the twentieth anniversary of the revolution the Kirov Theatre produced a new ballet, with the collaboration of the men who had successfully produced *The Flames of Paris* for its fifteenth anniversary: the composer Asafiev, artist V. Dmitriev, and choreographer V. I. Vainonen.[83] The ballet dealt with Cossacks living in the Northern Caucasus during the civil war and was called *Partisan Days*. In the opening scene, a Cossack woman named Nastia is betrothed to Andrei, the son of a rich Cossack. In the crowd of celebrating people, there is a Bolshevik named Grigory and his "right arm," the mountaineer Kerim. A group of White Guards enter the village, trying to enlist help for their side. The rich people do go to their side, but Grigory calls upon the worker Cossacks to enlist against the White Guards, whereupon the rich people arrest him.

Later, Nastia is being led unwillingly to the altar to marry Andrei. Drunk kulaks jeer at a poor peasant, Fyodor. Nastia stands up for him, but Andrei maliciously pushes her away from helping the poor man, which encourages the Cossacks to mock Fyodor all the more. All this strengthens Nastia's determination to break with the hateful people. She tears off her bridal veil and throws her wedding ring at Andrei. The Cossacks threaten Fyodor for inciting her to do this, but the Red partisans rush into the village, led by Kerim. They free Fyodor, let Grigory out of captivity, and then flee. In the last scene, the partisans gallop off, with Nastia joining them.

The second act takes place in an *aul*, a mountain village. Partisans arrive there in order to enlist the aid of sympathetic mountaineers. The mountaineers fraternize with the partisans, swearing to fight for victory. That night, a lyrical scene between Nastia and Kerim is interrupted by an alarm. Detachments of Cossacks and mountaineers leave the aul.

A health resort which the White Guards have captured is the scene of the third act. They lead in for questioning the partisan Fyodor, whom they have caught, and then sentence him to be shot. Scenes of White Guard revelry are broken up by the appearance of partisans. A wounded Red Army man arrives bringing news that the Red Army is near. Grigory sends Kerim with a sailor to the staff of the Red Army. Nastia goes with them and they are surrounded on the way by White Guard Cossacks who are led by Andrei. The next scene is in a *stanitsa*, a Cossack village. The libretto relates the dissatisfaction among the population with the White regime. The partisan captives are led in to be executed, but a detachment of partisans led by Grigory bursts into the stanitsa just in time. Final rejoicing comes when units of the Red Army arrive, marching into the village with banners flying.[84]

As a ballet, the critics did not find *Partisan Days* to be too successful. The attempt to tell its story involved a great deal of activity on the stage other than dancing. However, though it has no connection to this ballet, one of the most successful numbers ever given by the Moiseyev Folk Dance Ensemble is their depiction of the Partisans. Moiseyev's dancers enter a stage that is lighted only by moving, eerie spotlights. Covered with long burkas, the dancers give a completely realistic illusion of riding horses. They then throw off their great cloaks and burst into a display of marvelously wild folk dances. After the display of such fireworks, they again put on their burkas and slowly "gallop" off into the distance, while one lazily lights a cigarette, another scans the horizon with his field glasses, or a couple converse.

Minus the attempt to show the evil of rich White Guards, *Partisans* has thrilled audiences throughout the world, who always want to see it on a return engagement of the company.

BALLET FOR PIONEERS

With ballet set firmly on the rails of socialist realism by the mid-thirties, the ingenuity of choreographers and composers became quite amazing. Ballet took its place as an instrument for teaching Soviet virtues to the younger generation in a ballet called *Little Stork*, first presented by the Choreographic Institute in the Filial of the Bolshoi Theatre. It was adapted from an opera of the same name by Dmitri L. Klebanov, a Ukrainian composer.[85]

The curtain opens to reveal a scene in a Pioneer camp. A little girl, Olia, rises from sleep and does her morning exercises. On the roof of their camp house, a stork has built a nest. A mischievous boy, Vasia, throws a rock at the mother stork and wounds its leg. The Pioneers carry the wounded mother stork inside and doctor it. Fall comes and the birds all fly away except the wounded mother's baby stork. Since he does not know how to fly, the Pioneers teach the Little Stork. He then flies to Africa for the winter.

There, he makes friends with all the African animals, but their games are interrupted by a planter and overseer who come pursuing a family of Negroes. The Negro father hides his son in the overgrowth to save him. The overseer then goes after the other Negroes while the planter attempts to get the little boy. However, the animals who have befriended the boy help him, and the planter is trapped by a great crocodile. When night falls, the animals lullaby the child, and then the overseer returns. After deciding it is too dangerous to stay, the animals suddenly see a Soviet ship sailing in the distance and the Little Stork proposes to his friends to go into the land of the Soviets, whereupon these clever animals build a raft and set out for the vessel, taking the little boy with them.

117

In the U.S.S.R., it is spring and the Pioneers are decorating the nest, hoping the Little Stork will return. They see birds flying by, among them their Little Stork, so they raise a great flag to attract his attention. The Little Stork lands and brings his animal friends with him. An elephant appears with the little Negro in a basket on his back. In the Soviet description: "Seeing the people, he is afraid. Indeed, in Africa a meeting with white people always brought misfortune. But the Soviet children regard him as a brother and receive him into their Pioneer detachment."[86] The official program issued with the production stated:

> Before Soviet children, sitting in the auditorium, there was revealed that terrible world, where exploiters order the lives and oppress millions of people working for them. This world seems especially terrible after the bright and joyful picture of the first act. For childish spectators there remains no doubt that only in the Soviet Union where there is no social and national inequality; only here will the little lonely Negro boy find shelter, love, and kindness.[87]

In Moscow, this ballet was shown upon the suggestion of the All-Union Central Soviet of Trades Unions. It was staged in Leningrad in 1939 at the Palace of Culture, where amateur arts were performed. In 1948, it was again presented at the Bolshoi Filial. This time, according to the program, the idea of renewing it came from the Komsomol unit of the Bolshoi, the chief participants in it. They gave their free time to its production, and it was shown at the thirtieth anniversary of the founding of Komsomol.[88]

Other companies have employed Pioneers in ballets for educating young Soviet citizens. In Gorky in 1957, a work was staged called *Timur and His Command*. The activity of this ballet took place in a Pioneer camp near Moscow where the hero was Timur, the nephew of a young engineer. Timur went about doing good deeds by carrying water to the house of an old milk-woman, taking care of the families of Soviet soldiers, and preserving an orchard from thieves. The antagonists were groups of hooligans, but Timur triumphed in the end.[89]

ACCEPTABLE CLASSICS

Even a classic Soviet ballet has to justify its existence. For an established favorite such as *Swan Lake,* it seems sufficient for their critics to point to the fact that it shows the triumph of good over evil. There have been a few delightful ballets which have been perennially popular in the Soviet Union, and were ideologically acceptable because they have emphasized ideas which the government strives to see included in new productions. Such points would include ridicule of the rich, the nobility, or the monarchy, while peasants and workers would be made to look wise in comparison. Some of these ballets were enjoyed throughout the world during tsarist days and continue to be popular in the present age. One such favorite is *Vain Precautions,* in which an ambitious mother tries to match her daughter to the witless son of a vineyard owner, while daughter prefers a charming, clever peasant lad instead. In the end, the mother's precautions to keep the two lovers apart are vain, and the two become happily matched, while the rich boy goes his doddering way. *Vain Precautions* was staged at the Bolshoi in 1916 with Yekaterina Geltser playing the role of Liza in the manner of a graceful French girl from a Watteau painting. After the revolution, she democratized the heroine, making her appear as a sturdy farm girl, able to reap and spin.[90] It has since been produced repeatedly in the U.S.S.R.

One noteworthy ballet containing Russian folklore was produced in Russia during tsarist times. It was mounted by Artur Saint-Léon, a Frenchman who visited Russia, and was called *Little Humpbacked Horse.* The plot, based on a tale by P. Ershov, described the trials of the simple Ivan the Peasant who is charged with impossible feats by the foolish old tsar, who extracts this price for Ivan's gaining the hand of a beautiful tsar maiden. As everyone knows, the innate good sense of the peasant will triumph, and in the end, the stupid tsar jumps into a pot of boiling hot water after seeing Ivan do the same and emerge as a handsome and noble prince. Of course, the tsar did not know that the Little Humpbacked Horse had executed a bit of magic to make Ivan's dip innocuous. It has been staged numerous times in the Soviet period, using both an older score by Cesar Pugni and a new one by Rodion Shchedrin, husband of Maya Plisetskaya.

In searching for new ballet themes in the 1930's, the treasures of Spanish dance were explored twice on the ballet stage. In 1931, the ballet *Komedianty* was staged in the Bolshoi Theatre, using a score by Reingold Gliere. The great Spanish author Lope de Vega's *Fuente Ovejuna* provided a basis for this libretto and also for the ballet *Laurencia*. De Vega's work was long a favorite with Russians inclined toward a revolutionary mentality. The actress Maria Yermolova used *Fuente Ovejuna* for her first benefit performance in 1876, sufficiently arousing the audience to worry tsarist officials.[91] In the first two decades of Soviet rule, the play was staged as a dramatic production in over twenty theatres.

Although the story attempted to portray a revolt of the Spanish people against a noble, when first presented *Komedianty* was scourged by the RAPM journal, *Proletarskii Muzykant*, which said that it presented a typical petty-bourgeois treatment of class struggle. They said that while in Spain there was occurring a cruel class war, while the Spanish were experiencing Russia's 1917, while workers and toilers and masses were leading a struggle with the Spanish Kerensky and Kornilov—to portray Spain on the stage in such a manner as this would be the last measure of tactlessness.[92]

A casual glance at the issues of *Sovetskaia Muzyka* for the last half of the 1930's leaves no doubt that Soviet musicians were frequently reminded of this Spanish struggle. In an open Party meeting in the Union of Soviet Composers there was selected a commission for work on the creation of new mass songs dedicated to the struggle of the Spanish people against fascism,[93] and at the meeting a collection of money was taken up among the members to send to the aid of their Spanish brethren. Links existed between the U.S.C. and the Barcelona Musical Section of the Commissariat of Propaganda of the Republic

Government of Catalonia. With all the exchanges of friendly greetings between Spanish composers and the U.S.C. which were printed in *Sovetskaia Muzyka,* along with the many articles on Spanish revolutionary songs,[94] it comes as no surprise to read that the composer A. Krein wrote a new score for the revolutionary story of de Vega. Futher, there was a skillful choreographer interested in the matter. In November, 1937, Vakhtang Chabukiani declared to the press:

> The thought captivates me of doing some work on a performance about the new Spain, of the struggle of the Spanish people for their freedom and independence. In such a ballet, not only the rich Spanish local color draws me, which might be brilliantly used in the show, but especially the contemporary experiences of the Spanish people—their thoughts, expectations, heroic struggle, and selfless devotion to the native land.[95]

The ballet which resulted came to be called *Laurencia,* and was first presented at the Kirov Theatre on March 22, 1939. In 1940, it was presented in Moscow on an *Island of Dance* in the Central Park of Culture and Rest.[96]

Laurencia was the fifteenth-century heroine of the story by de Vega; Fuente Ovejuno was the name of the village where she lived. The story depicted the cruelty of a Spanish Comendador in the village who covets the beautiful Laurencia. She resists his advances, however, and marries the man she loves, Frondozo. Upon coming to the wedding party of Laurencia, the Comendador insists upon his ancient *Droit de Seigneur* toward the girl and has her taken forcibly to his castle. The local peasants are incensed, but do nothing at the time. In the end, Laurencia, having been raped, is thrust out of the castle and walks slowly downstage on the lane leading to the village. In a Soviet description,

> She can hardly move, her hair is dishevelled, her wedding dress has been torn and hangs about her in shreds. The crowd watches her in dumb horror. And now the outraged woman rails and ridicules them. Swaying and wringing her hands in despair, the ballerina goes through

a sequence of motions so eloquent that the spectator can almost hear the words of the famous monologue in Lope de Vega's tragedy. Her rage arouses the peasants from their stupor.[97]

The villagers then arm themselves with axes, knives, and clubs and burn the lord's castle.

In the course of the action, Laurencia's brother kills the Comendador. Everyone knows who did it, but when the King's representatives come to the village to ask who committed the murder, each villager only gives the reply, "Fuente Ovejuna, Señor." *Laurencia* achieved far more success than its predecessor, *Komedianty*. It still plays occasionally on the Soviet stage. One of its dances, lifted from the melodramatic plot, was presented by the British Royal Ballet after Rudolf Nureyev joined the company.

BALLET PORTRAYS THE NEW SOVIET WOMAN

It was inevitable that the advent of war clouds on the horizon would call forth reverberations on the ballet scene. In the summer of 1938, on the border between the U.S.S.R. and Manchuria, fighting erupted near Lake Khassan between Soviet forces and Japanese troops. Japanese incursions into Manchuria brought more encounters between the two armies in May, 1939.[98] On December 9, 1939, at the Bolshoi Filial Theatre, there appeared a contemporary ballet named *Svetlana*—which just happened also to be the name of Stalin's daughter. The score was written by Dmitri Klebanov. The ballet opens with a prologue somewhere in a forest where conspirators with Japanese features are operating. Among them is a man who looks like a Russian. They hand documents over to him and acquaint him with one of the Japanese men. After a careful survey of the locality, the Russian and Japanese go off into the depths of the forest.

The next scene takes place deep in the taiga, where the heroine Svetlana lives with her father. At her first appearance, she is dressed in high boots suitable for a hunt. Later, for *adagios*, she appears in ballet slippers. Some Komsomols come to the spot where they live, hoping to build a new city. Svetlana falls in love with one of the company named Ilko. When the Komsomols leave, a carpenter named Stepan, who has suddenly appeared, goes with them, charming all by his sociability. However, the spectator can surmise that this fellow is really the crafty enemy seen in the prologue.

The building project proceeds successfully, but Ilko and Svetlana quarrel and she runs away to her home in the forest. A man appears on the scene disguised as a Chinese conjurer and distracts the attention of some of the young builders while his accomplice blows up a power station in the new project. The conjurer is caught, but the second saboteur runs into the forest where he meets Svetlana. He wrestles with her to get her father's weapons, stuns her and runs away. Coming to her senses and in order to draw the frontier guards to the right place, Svetlana sets fire to her own house. The saboteur is caught, and a celebration takes place where Ukrainian, Russian, Gypsy, Tatar, Azerbaidzhani, and Kazakh dances are performed.[99]

In the annals of Soviet ballet history, *Svetlana* is remembered for being the first time that ballet showed satisfactorily the theme of socialist construction. Further, it was the first time that a real, contemporary Soviet girl appeared as the positive heroine of a ballet. The dancer portraying the part was Olga Lepeshinskaya, a ballerina with a flashing stage presence who became a member of the Communist Party in 1943.[100] At one time she was married to Leonid Federovich Reichman, a Lieutenant General in the State Security system and a supporter of Lavrenty Beria. In August, 1951, at the time of a temporary purge of Beria's henchmen, Lepeshinskaya divorced him, explaining that she would have no enemy of the people for a husband. Later, he was released and she remarried him. When Beria was finally executed in 1953, Reichman was again arrested and she divorced him a second time.[101]

CHAPTER FIVE

Hot and Cold War Ballets

For the artist who truly serves his people, the question of whether or not he is free in his creative work does not exist under the conditions of a socialist society.

—NIKITA KHRUSHCHEV[1]

THE year 1940 showed promise for Soviet ballet, for on January 11, the Leningrad Kirov Theatre presented one of its greatest achievements of the Soviet period: *Romeo and Juliet*. Part of the time and talent of Soviet theatrical workers has always been diverted into utilitarian productions, which scarcely fail to irritate the sensibilities of true artists. No one questions their innate artistry, and perhaps this is one reason why the ageless classics are so well produced in the U.S.S.R.; when a Soviet artist can leave behind the world of revolutionary uprisings, production quotas, and wicked imperialists to produce *Swan Lake, Giselle,* or *Romeo and Juliet,* he does it exceedingly well. A moral can be found in *Romeo and Juliet,* for in the Soviet view it paints a black picture of the petty warring that took place in the last stages of feudal society, but the work was still artistically conceived and executed. Twenty-six years later, *Romeo and Juliet* was still fine enough to show Charles de Gaulle in his visit to Moscow in June, 1966—long after most of the works described in this chapter had been laid to an inglorious rest.

The end of 1940 brought forth another production based upon a classic. In September, 1939, after an agreement for partition of Polish lands was made between Hitler and Stalin, the Red Army entered and took possession of territories known as the Western Ukraine and Western Belorussia, which at that time were under Polish control.

124

These areas had proud nationalistic traditions of their own. One great Ukrainian-born author, Nikolai Gogol, in his novel, *Taras Bulba,* had immortalized the spirit of the Cossack inhabitants of the Ukraine. Taras was the father of two young sons whom he initiated into the Cossack brotherhood. On one occasion when the Cossacks besieged a Polish town, Taras' son Andry gave bread to the local Polish governor's daughter, whom he loved madly. Further, he betrayed the Cossacks and fought on the Polish side. Learning this, Taras arranged to be in a position to meet his son in battle and shoot him. When the Cossacks made peace with the Poles, Taras, who had seen his faithful son Ostap tortured and executed by them, gathered a band of followers and continued his raids on Polish towns. The ballet première appeared on December 12, 1940, at the Leningrad Kirov Theatre. On March 24, 1941, it was presented at the Bolshoi Theatre, the last new production staged by that company before German armies invaded Russia in June.[2]

After war came to the Soviet Union, the Bolshoi troupe was evacuated to the town of Kuibyshev. However, its work did not stop. In 1940, the company gave 112 performances on its main stage and Filial. In 1941, the number was reduced to 56, but in 1942 they gave 89 performances in Kuibyshev and 126 at the Filial in Moscow. In 1943, due to the process of resettling in Moscow, the number was reduced to 120, but rose in 1944 to 144 productions. Galina Ulanova recalls performing for Churchill when he visited Moscow in wartime.[3]

The Leningrad Kirov Company was evacuated to the city of Molotov in the Ural Mountains. A few artists who did not go kept on performing and teaching in the besieged city. Led by the ballerina Olga Jordan they presented the ballets *Esmeralda* and *Chopiniana,* though they were often weak with hunger. The Kirov Theatre was actually hit by a bomb and riddled by artillery fire, thus demanding extensive repairs after the war.[4]

For the twenty-fifth anniversary of the Revolution the Bolshoi and the Kirov theatres signed a contract to engage in socialist competition in 1942, obliging themselves to create two new Soviet productions, to give one thousand concerts, and to form five brigades for service at the military front and industrial centers—while lowering production expenditures by ten percent.[5]

In 1946, when the people of the U.S.S.R. were still trying to build a normal life after the wide destruction of war, the Party saw fit to begin another cultural purge similar to the one which began in 1936 with the condemnation of *Lady Macbeth*. During wartime, many Soviet writers and artists had experienced a certain respite from Party control agencies, whose energies were diverted to other channels.[6] Further, there were historical precedents for thinking that the population itself might profit by having the ideological and political reins tightened. The Soviet government could not afford to forget that when Russian armies had travelled westward in the Napoleonic Wars, they had noted comparisons between their life and that of the West, and had imbibed sufficient liberalistic ideas to prompt them to stage their own small, unsuccessful revolt against tsarist authority. In history, the event is known as the Decembrist Revolt of 1825.

Thus in August, 1946, the Central Committee of the Party decided that an ideological chastening was in order, and decreed that the curriculum and organization of Party schools was to be reexamined and tightened thoroughly.[7]

The first step toward eliminating all traces of ideological laxness in the arts came with the publication on August 14 of an accusation against two literary magazines called *Zvezda,* "Star," and *Leningrad.* The author of the condemnation was the same man who reportedly wrote their counterparts of 1936: Andrei Zhdanov, an associate of Stalin. Zhdanov complained that the magazines had published undesirable works of two writers, Mikhail Zoschenko and Anna Akhmatova. Zoschenko was accused of a "maliciously hooliganish portrayal of our reality, accompanied by anti-Soviet thrusts." Akhmatova was an advocate of art for art's sake, and was out of step with Soviet reality.[8] Her poetry was said to be weighted with moods of sorrow, death, desperate yearning, mysticism, and an aura of foreboding doom.[9] Such poetry could only perpetuate bad attitudes in youth, Zhdanov declared. It would inculcate in them inclination to turn aside from action on burning social questions of the day and thus become introverted in their own narrow little world of petty, personal experiences.[10] Zhdanov affirmed that if Soviet youth had been brought up in such a spirit previously, they would have lost the war.

This decree was only the beginning. August 25 brought "On the Repertoire of the Dramatic Theatres," followed by the condemnation of a movie, *The Great Life* on September 4, 1947. In 1948, an opera by Vano Muradeli called *The Great Friendship* met treatment similar to Shostakovich's *Lady Macbeth* in 1936. However, this time the condemnation not only included the particular work of Muradeli, but also such composers as Prokofiev, Khachaturian, and Shostakovich again. They were guilty of the cult of atonality, and had transformed music into cacophony, resulting in works reeking of modernistic, bourgeois European and American music which was only a reflection of a decaying bourgeois culture. The Central Committee declared that in recent years the tastes of the Soviet audience had improved, and that they had come to expect "works of high quality and ideological content in all categories—in operas, in symphonic music, in song writing, in choral and dance music."[11]

While calling upon composers themselves to correct the matter, Zhdanov also declared that the matter was going to be referred to the Department of Propaganda and Agitation of the Central Committee of the Communist Party and the State Committee on Art Affairs. The pattern that followed was the same as in the 1930's. World-famous composers sent in humble apologies to the press for their individual artistic failures, and the Union of Soviet Composers wrote a group apology to Stalin of which the following is an excerpt:

Dear Joseph Vissarionovich:

*   *   *

For us, Soviet musicians, yet more painful is the consciousness that we have been unable to draw true and consistent conclusions from those warnings, which our Party has made more than once whenever Soviet musical art has strayed from the true realistic path. The articles "Confusion instead of Music," and "Ballet Fraud," published in *Pravda* twelve years ago, the resolutions of the Central Committee of the All-Union Communist Party "On the Journals *Zvezda* and *Leningrad*," on the moving picture *The Great Life*, and "On the Repertoire of Dramatic Theatres and Measures for Its Improvement" did not call forth, as it states with profound truth in the resolution of the Central Committee of the Party, any reform of Soviet music.

*   *   *

We give to you and to all the Soviet people our oath to direct our creativity in the path of socialist realism, to labor untiringly for the creation of modes worthy of our great epoch in all branches of music.[12]

Rounds of meetings again took place in theatres and theatrical trade unions where Zhdanov spoke and leading artists confessed their mistakes. In one of the talks, Zhdanov again complained about compositions "so saturated with naturalistic sounds that they make one think of a dentist's drill . . . or a musical murder van."[13] This time, no particular ballet was condemned, but it was understood from the very first pronouncement from Zhdanov that his esthetical principles were meant for ballet as well. In a discussion of the new documents at the All-Russian Theatrical Society in October, 1946, the dancer Mikhail Gabovich declared that: "In these decrees there is nothing said directly about musical theatre, and in particular, about ballet. But the main thought, lodged in them, belongs to all forms of theatrical art, including, of course, ballet."[14]

From December 19 to 21, 1946, an All-Union Conference on Questions of Opera and Ballet took place under the aegis of the Moscow All-Union Committee on Affairs of the Arts. There, the main workers in the ballet field revealed their production plans for more new ballets on contemporary themes, in accordance with Zhdanov's demands, and restated their zeal to produce operas and ballets reflecting contemporary life. Fyodor Bondarenko, the head of the Bolshoi

Theatre, pointed out that they were producing *Life,* which Ulanova later danced, and all the participants followed suit in affirming their zeal for fulfilling the new commands. Boris Khaikin, artistic director of the Kirov, declared that "a composer must be a flaming agitator, speaking seriously from the heart." Pyotr Gusev declared: "All of us who are active in the field of Soviet ballet must regard, and we do regard, ballet as a part of the ideological front. We also take part in the formation of the consciousness of the Soviet viewer."[15] As it happened in 1936, meetings took place in far-flung outposts of the U.S.S.R. to probe and evaluate whether various theatres were complying with the new directives. The results of this newly reinforced zeal became very apparent in the succeeding years.

"MYSTICISM" IN BALLET

It is possible to glean samples of the manner in which works were finecombed for ideological deficiencies in future months. In 1942, the Bolshoi Theatre had produced on the stage of the House of Culture in Kuibyshev the ballet *Crimson Sails.* The ballet begins amid a violent thunderstorm on a seashore. Suddenly, there appears a distraught woman looking for someone. She sees a figure in an oilskin coat and thinks it is the one she is seeking, but this stranger tries to embrace her and carry her away, and she dies from her exhaustive efforts to resist him. Soon another oilskin clad figure appears and a little girl named Assol runs out of a nearby cottage. After embracing his daughter, the man lifts up his dead wife.

In a new scene the little girl has grown up to be a sad, pensive maiden, and her retired father makes little models of sailing ships. Assol especially likes one that has red sails. An old wandering musician promises her that someday a ship with crimson sails will come and a strong seaman will step out of it and lead her to a faraway happy land. "It is only necessary to wait, to believe, and the dream will become reality," he assured her.[16]

In the next scene, members of many nationalities are gathered in

129

the harbor to do their native dances. Assol comes to the quay where certain rough elements scorn her, but a charming Captain Grey, who has seen her and loved her, takes one of the little ships with red sails, leaves a ring, and disappears. Eventually he comes back again in a big ship with red sails to take her to their dream land.

The ballet, on the surface, would not seem to be especially dangerous to the Communist Party or Soviet government. However, it could not stand in the light cast by the Zhdanov decrees. Here was balletic Akhmatovism, clearly akin to the old type of forbidden romanticism which portrayed nonexistent life and nonexistent heroes, thus leading the reader to disregard the struggles and oppression of reality and take refuge in a world of impossible dreams.[17] Eventually, someone was bound to awaken to the fact.

In 1950, an article appeared in *Sovetskaia Muzyka* which pointed out all the faults of the production. The author of the story on which the libretto had been based was Alexander Green, whom a Soviet literary magazine, *Novyi Mir,* had labelled a writer without a country, a prophet of cosmopolitanism. The greatest criticism of the ballet was that it centered about the passive fulfillment of a dream; in the story, happiness was reached by a chance confluence of circumstances. The tale had a spectral, mystical, unreal character. The author of the article declared, "Here there is no place for the idea of struggle, of real activity, overcoming living obstacles." The old story teller had told the girl to dream, to be patient and wait. This was a depraved, reactionary philosophy. The author labeled one scene expressionistic in which grimacing American thugs in top hats beat Assol on the feet with whips, forcing her to dance. Another number in which a Negro danced was declared to be politically tactless, since it portrayed the Negro as some kind of an obtuse buffoon. The dances of the second act were like a bacchanal.[18]

A discussion about the article took place in the Bolshoi Theatre, attended by leading masters of ballet, régisseurs, and artists of the orchestra. Most of them agreed with the article. Mikhail Chulaki declared that the ballet was formalistic, and Vainonen, Lavrovsky, and Ulanova criticized it. The director of the Bolshoi Party organization, A. Tomsky, supported the condemnation, saying: "This production is typically idealistic in content. Many American films are built on such a basis. . . . You live, you dream, and there will come some kind of a hero who will create a better life for you." This was not a true conception, he affirmed. "The best life is reached in struggle, not in passive expectation."[19] In the end, the director of the Bolshoi formed a creative brigade to rework the ballet. *Crimson Sails,* like the poems of Akhmatova, had not preached anything subversive or defied any ideological tenet. The problem was that the Party wanted art to portray positively a happy, hard-working, optimistic life with confidence in a rosy future won by this enduring labor.

In this case, the loss to world ballet was probably not great. It could have been otherwise with the old favorite, *Giselle,* which had come under fire for "mysticism" even before Zhdanov began his attacks. It was the first new ballet to be staged at the Bolshoi after the troupe returned from Kuibyshev, though it had been presented at the Bolshoi in new versions in 1922 and 1934. After the war, the *prima ballerina* of the Kirov Company, Galina Ulanova, had transferred her services to the Bolshoi, beginning there to dance the part of *Giselle* most gloriously. The ballet is the story of a peasant girl who falls madly in love with a visiting nobleman in disguise. When she learns his true identity and realizes that she can never marry him, she loses her mind and dies. Giselle had a peasant suitor, Hilarion, who discovered the sword of his rival and tried in vain to warn Giselle about him. In the second act, she has joined a spiritual crew of Wilis, maidens who died before they were wed, and who, according to legend, come alive at night to dance to death any males who strayed into their orbit. The vengeful Wilis manage to force Hilarion to the edge of an abyss and push him over the precipice; however, Giselle manages to save her equally threatened nobleman by love. In ordinary productions, Giselle's grave was marked by a rather prominent cross.

Even before Zhdanov wrote after the war, someone in the inner circles began to be jittery about *Giselle* because it was felt to be mystical.[20] In a lengthy article on "Contemporaneity and Fantasy" in the magazine *Teatr,* the theatrical critic V. Golubov-Potapov poked fun at their scruples as he said:

> Let us return to the question of mysticism. Several years ago comrades of the Leningrad repertoire committee suspected *Giselle* of it. Poor, meritorious Giselle, who in the spring of next year will celebrate her centenary. They rummaged about and tried to find something, apparently with a view to fighting superstition, and decided to abolish the cross on Giselle's grave. Let her rest in peace without religious emblems, like the usual, civil burial. Now instead of a cross stands some kind of block, not quite a tombstone and not quite a tree stump. Such anxiety for the spiritual purity of the spectator, the attempts to guard them from the noxious influence of the mystic leads to fantastic consequences. The graveyard—that is mysticism; the cross—that signifies the temptations of religiosity. This indeed is some kind of fetishism. You don't understand who is more inclined to superstition, the wards or the guardians.[21]

Somehow, *Giselle* survived the onslaughts of the antimystics. An interesting feature of the Soviet production is their portrayal of Hilarion. In Western productions, Giselle's local lover is a villain, sometimes a black-moustached one, who is selfishly jealous of the noble lover, and tries to wreck their happiness. The Soviet esthetical creed could not allow this man of the people to be portrayed villainously. Instead, he is pictured as an honest, stalwart, fearless peasant, deeply and genuinely in love with Giselle, and his chief interest is in shielding her from the deceptive philanderer.

Soon after Zhdanov issued his injunctions against the literary journals and in one of the meetings called for the purpose of discussing the Party position, he told the authors what they were expected to produce in a positive vein:

Scene from the ballet *Giselle* at the Bolshoi Theatre, with Bessmertnova as Giselle and Lavrovsky as Albert.

Alla Shelest in *Tatiana, left,* and *Gayane, right.*

> Our people are waiting for Soviet authors to comprehend and general-
> ize the tremendous experiences gained by the people in the Great Patri-
> otic War, for them to portray and generalize the heroism with which
> the people now work on the restoration of the national economy of the
> country after the expulsion of the enemy.[22]

Zhdanov's mandates were followed by a series of ballets on war themes,
one of which was called *Tatiana, or Daughter of the People*.

The ballet begins by depicting the demobilization of forces after
the war. Three people who have just been released from service—
Tatiana, Andrei, and Nikolai—knock at the house of one of their
relatives. The scene of joyful reunion is overshadowed by the bitter-
ness of Tatiana, who lost her lover Igor. On the following morning,
a holiday is arranged for them, but the general gaiety only aggravates
the sadness of Tatiana. She recalls a terrible scene in which Igor,
though mutilated, remained true to his military oath to his last
breath. An old sailor then tells the story of the death of Igor to those
at the celebration, and his narration forms the second act of the ballet.

Igor and Tatiana were once stationed with a detachment on the
shore of the Finnish Bay. The commander interrupts their rest and
orders Tatiana and Igor to make their way into the headquarters of
the Germans and blow it up, to give the Soviet detachment a chance
to pursue the dispersed opponents. Tatiana and Igor do penetrate into
the Nazi camp and carry off the explosion successfully, but the couple
are seriously wounded and taken captive. In vain the Nazis torture
Igor to extract some information, but he loses consciousness without
saying a word. Tatiana is also questioned, but she too is loyal to her
native land in spite of threats and torture. The Soviets seize the Nazi
headquarters and Tatiana is saved, but not her Igor.

The activity of the third act takes place in winter outside the
home of Tatiana. Some youths have decorated a New Year's tree there,
but Tatiana's thoughts keep returning to Igor, in spite of the fact
that Andrei has confessed his love for her. Suddenly Igor inexplicably

appears in the garden, alive. Tatiana does not believe her eyes. In a new scene, spring arrives and the two of them visit the former battle scene where the Nazi headquarters stood. The place has been completely changed by the creative work of the Soviet people. From the ashes there now rises up that undying creation of Russian architecture —Petrodvorets. The young cadets at the Nakhimov Naval School come out and stand at attention for the two courageous warriors —true sons of the Fatherland who triumphed over the Fascist oppressors.[23]

In November, 1948, the Stanislavsky Nemirovich-Danchenko Musical Theatre produced another ballet following Zhdanov's mandates. Called *Shore of Happiness*, it was later shown in Paris. In the first scene, a girl named Natasha waters her flowers at a Pioneer camp named Artek, but three boys named Petia, Kostia, and Tolia crush her little garden during their game of football. They try to make up to her, but she will not talk to them, so they secretly fix the flower bed at night. Later, they are all walking along the seashore, and when Natasha is caught up in the waves, Petia saves her.

Years pass, and Natasha lives in the suburb of Sevastopol. One day, into her yard come three sailors named Petia, Kostia, and Tolia. There is great joy in the meeting, and they walk along the wharf and dance. All three of the boys seek her hand, but she loves Petia. Later, she bids them goodbye as they board ships in the harbor. A new scene shows detachments of marines under the command of Petia. The enemy draws near, and those Black Sea heroes defend the native shores. An enemy tank appears on the stage, and Kostia, who knows Natasha does not love him, picks up a box of dynamite, walks toward the tank, and it falls to pieces in a sheet of red flame, taking Kostia's life. Natasha arrives with a group of other women to help the wounded and finds that Petia has also been wounded. Tolia later perishes in battle.

Many months later, Natasha has dedicated herself to the education of future workers. Young naturalists, sportsmen and soldiers flock around her at Camp Artek. Natasha is lonely at times, but one day Petia shows up. The children enlist him, Hero of the Soviet Union Lieutenant Pyotr Volkov, as an honorary member of their detachment. Petia takes out his own Pioneer tie which he has preserved from childhood and which he even took into battle with him.[24]

In 1949, Ulanova appeared in the promised ballet *Life,* which depicts a contemporary Soviet woman named Jeiran. The young heroine, a woman from a fishing village in the Caucasus, has to see her husband off to battle and then shoulder his work on the collective farm. The husband is killed, but Jeiran's burning patriotism, motherly love, steadfast work, and kindness to her neighbors assist the heroine to face her own grievous loss.[25]

In 1959, the Bolshoi Theatre staged a ballet called *We Stalingraders.* As the curtain opened, a group of five Soviet Army men held aloft a red flag, typifying the spirit of Stalingrad at the climax of the German siege. By dance, they then depicted their advances, setbacks, and losses in combat. Finally, although bloodstained, wounded, and fatigued, they advanced to victory.[26] Related to this was a ballet given by the Kirov company in 1961 to the music of Shostakovich's Seventh Symphony, which he wrote at the time of the siege of Leningrad. In the ballet of the same name, the choreographer first shows a scene where happy youths dance on the beach at Leningrad. Then the music resounds with a menacing beat as brown-clad figures with German helmets come goose-stepping in. The Russian boys then make military formations and the girls bid them farewell as they go off to war. The main hero is killed and the last scene of the ballet shows a solemn requiem procession by his lover and other sympathetic women. As the scene ends, the heroine stretches her hand toward the auditorium figuratively asking, "Will this ever be repeated?"[27]

Another short ballet with an antiwar appeal was called *Mother.* The ballet portrays war time, and in the distance, the flash of an explosion is seen. On the smoldering ruins a woman searches for her child, but he is nowhere to be found. Then she becomes deranged, and she begins to see her son standing beside her. She plays with him, nurses him, then suddenly realizes that all this is only imaginary. Despair possesses her, she curses the war, and like the heroine of Leningrad, she turns to the audience as if to say, "This must not be repeated."[28]

Lessons of courage and endurance are taught in a ballet called *Stronger Than Death*. The ballet brings to life a piece of sculpture with the same name, made by F. Fiveisky. The ballet begins as a prisoner is pushed out from an enemy torture chamber. He is exhausted by the ordeal, but his will is not broken. They throw out a second prisoner behind him. A third prisoner appears, but his steps are unsure; he is blind. All three are led to execution. They warmly embrace each other, lift their heads, and bravely come forward. Death already looks them in the eyes, but they are not frightened by it. Each struggles to defend his comrade with his body, and without quavering, they hurl challenges at their enemies. They smile in the face of their murderers as shots resound. The prisoners are killed but they do not fall; the three remain standing, supporting each other. Their will to victory is stronger than death.[29]

Another patriotic ballet which appeared in 1949 was called *Youth,* and was based on Nikolai Ostrovsky's novel, *How the Steel Was Tempered*. The action takes place in a southern Russian city in the years of the Civil War. Under pressure from White Armies, part of the Red Army has to leave the city. As a detachment of Whites comes to the city, the local bourgeoisie festively greet them. However, one boy named Petia has received news that his father, a member of Budënny's forces, died at the front defending Soviet power, and the boy then receives his father's sword. He makes friends with Dasha and Dima, young people of the city who are sympathetic to the revolution and are against the White forces. Dasha and Dima are playing on the shore one day when Petia arrives and tells them that they should no longer play with wooden swords, but should take an active part in the present struggle. They break their wooden sabres, and over the sword of Petia's father, declare their loyalty to the cause. Childhood has ended and youth has begun for them. The little group aids two revolutionary workers named Semen and Matvei accomplish heroic deeds in the city, and after many trials and difficulties, help the people overcome the Whites. As a sign of triumph, the villagers hang a red flag over the bell tower of the village.[30]

Another ballet on a war theme appeared in the Sverdlovsk Theatre of Opera and Ballet, where it was called *To the Heart of Marika*. It was meant to be a lyric poem of youth, of friendship and happiness. In the prologue, which takes place during the Great Patriotic War, the Soviet Army is freeing Hungary from the Fascists. Thirteen-year-old Marika is the daughter of an army officer named Sandor, who had served Admiral Horthy, the Regent of Hungary, after an attempt at communist rule in 1919 failed. Fulfilling the order of Sandor, Marika tells Soviet soldiers that there is no one at home, although her father is really hiding there. Sandor shoots the Soviet officer in the back, then sets fire to the house in which Marika remains. He carries his son Ferko along with him, however, and flees. Marika does not die because the gravely wounded Soviet officer carries her from the burning house. When grown, Marika goes to the Sixth All-World Festival of Youth in Moscow and falls in love with a Soviet boy named Oleg. Later, she meets his father and recognizes him as the Soviet soldier who saved her life. Ferko and Sandor come to the U.S.S.R. as tourists and try to tear her away from her friendship with the Soviet people, but they naturally do not succeed in doing so.[31]

In 1950, the Bolshoi Theatre was planning to produce several ballets which never made it to an opening night on their stage. One of them by Mikhail Chulaki was called *For the Power of the Soviets*, which speaks for itself. A ballet called *Ruby Stars* by the composer Andrei Balanchivadze seemed to be in the advanced stages of production and was said to be dedicated to the happy life of the Soviet people and their outstanding achievements during the Great Patriotic War. However, it fell a victim to the general wave of fear and criticism that followed Zhdanov's action. The third one of the group, *Under Italian Skies,* was eventually staged, not in Moscow, but in the Kiev Theatre of Opera and Ballet.[32]

It must be remembered that this was the time when the Soviet Union was very hostile to the United States for pouring millions of American dollars into the countries of Western Europe in the form of Marshall Plan aid. It is also probably no coincidence that an Italian election of 1948, which could have resulted in a Communist government being installed in Italy, did not turn out that way. The setting of the ballet *Under Italian Skies* is an Italian port dominated by American occupation forces. An American steamship brings tanks and airplanes to be unloaded, and the American soldiers make life miserable for the population. At the call of a Communist named Valentino, regular dock workers refuse to unload the ship, and they are all thrown in jail. Then Valentino's friend Lucia places herself at the head of a struggle for freedom for the strikers and leads to the port a march of strikers carrying signs saying "Yankee Go Home." When they arrive there, they throw American weapons into the sea. At this time, the Soviet steamship *Timiriazev* arrives in the port with food for Italian people who have just suffered from a flood. Thereupon the villagers welcome the Soviet envoys warmheartedly with a song about Stalin. In Soviet words, this is a ballet "dedicated to the stirring theme of the struggle for peace. . . . Its heroes are simple people, authentic patriots standing up to the struggle with oppressors of the Italian people—American occupation forces."[33] Interestingly enough, when Galina Ulanova made a trip to Italy in 1949 as a delegate of a Soviet Women's Anti-Fascist Committee, one of her observations, recorded in the Soviet press, was of Italian men and women striking in order not to have to unload American weapons.[34]

Another ballet was presented by the Leningrad Kirov Company in 1962, using Italy as a background. The name of it was *Into the Port Came* Russia—referring to a boat of that name which arrived in an Italian harbor. It is the story of an Italian street dancer, Pepelina, who encounters sailors from the Soviet vessel *Russia* on the shore of her native city. She knows that one of them named Andrei was formerly a participant in the Italian Resistance during the war, and that he was the hero who saved her from a fire when she was only a tiny girl. The meeting produces a strong impression on the girl, and later, when she becomes the star in a variety show, she cannot forget the man who saved her life. She sees him once in the hall at the time of the show, and overcome with shame, tears off her adornments, throws them to Mauricio, her millionaire patron, and turns to Andrei. She then decides to leave with him and his wife Peppo in order to attend an international youth festival in Moscow. The final scene of the ballet, which represents the festival, is composed of a suite of dances of many nations.[35]

In content, this ballet carried the same message that *Lost Illusions* preached in 1936—the fact that a Western artist has to degrade himself and cater to the rich to make a living. Soviet artists are prone to point up this fact, and to compare their security as artists under a state-supported system to the vicissitudes of life for artists in some Western nations. After Ulanova's trip of 1949, she also remarked how it had astonished her to see real artists passing their hats in Italian cafes after singing there marvelously. She said that having seen these singers so demean themselves, she could play with more understanding the part of Tao-Hao, the little Chinese cafe dancer of *The Red Poppy*.[36]

A ballet which was a bit more subtle than the usual propagandistic type was *Shore of Hope* (June, 1959). This work depicted a stormy sea which divided two worlds, two different shores. On one of the shores, there was friendly solidarity and a mutual sharing of joys and grief among the people. The ballet showed how the girls would go to see their fishermen off to sea. One day one of the men was lost during a storm and ended up on the forbidden foreign shore. On this side of the sea, there was no friendly solidarity. When the shipwrecked fisherman landed on the unfriendly shore, the local fishermen tried to protect him, but he was taken away by soldiers clad in black suits and white belts. The fisherman languished in detention, where the enemies questioned him and tried to woo him with promises of glory, riches, and delights. Some redheaded enticers were even sent in to beguile him but he remained steadfast to his people.[37]

In postwar years, there has been a periodical recurrence of rebels in Soviet ballets, following in the dainty but rebellious footsteps of the heroes and heroines of *The Flames of Paris, Laurencia,* and their countless counterparts. One of these heroines, named Lola, appeared during the war years at the Stanislavsky Musical Theatre in Moscow. The ballet depicts a holiday in a Spanish mountain village in which Lola, her beloved, and a jealous rival are participating. Festivities stop as French troops of Napoleon draw near, and the inhabitants flee to the mountains to form partisan detachments.

The sinister rival of Lola's lover betrays Spain and becomes a French scout, aiding the French to penetrate into the partisan camp and to take many prisoners. In the end, Lola drinks poisoned wine because she has offered it to a French officer and he asks her to sip it before he does. In the final scene, the partisans find her body and carry it in solemn procession. One author remarked that in viewing *Lola,* the Soviet people saw their own war heroines, such as Zoia Kosmodemianskaya, a young Russian girl killed by the Nazis for her work in partisan warfare.[38]

The durable, melodramatic revolutionaries of the 1930's again appeared in the 1950's with equal vigor as in their youth. In these years, many dance students from Soviet satellites came to the U.S.S.R. and returned home ready to perform Soviet revolutionary hero and heroine roles. Starting in 1950, *The Flames of Paris* was mounted within a few years in nine Soviet and satellite cities. *Laurencia* was restaged at the Bolshoi in 1956. Further, between 1950 and 1961, it was produced in at least twenty other cities of the U.S.S.R. or its satellites.[39]

The motley crew of balletic revolutionaries also came to include

Recent postage stamps from the U.S.S.R. and Bulgaria.

Scene from the fourth act of Khachaturian's ballet *Spartacus*, produced by the Kirov Opera and Ballet Theatre in Leningrad with Makarov in the center playing Spartacus.

a member of the Italian revolutionary sect of Carbonari, which was active in the struggle to establish a republican form of government in Italy in the nineteenth century. The ballet was called *Vanina Vanini,* after an Italian princess in a novel of that name by Stendhal. She finds a wounded member of Carbonari hiding in her father's house, nurses him back to health, and falls in love with him. In spite of the great risks she takes to win him as a lover, his devotion to the cause constrains him to forsake her love in order to be able to carry on his struggle for freedom.[40]

A Parisian gamin, stepping out of the pages of Victor Hugo's novel *Les Misérables,* became the basis for another revolutionary ballet. It was named *Gavroshe* after the winsome hero of the story, a young revolutionary who was the friend of the children and the downcast of Paris, and who in Hugo's novel died in action on Parisian street barricades in 1832.[41]

A truly monumental attempt to portray a theme of revolt was made in 1956. Karl Marx once listed Spartacus, the rebel slave hero of ancient Roman days, as one of his favorite characters.[42] To reproduce in ballet the story of his famous uprising, a fabulous sum of money was spent, especially for presentation during the Bolshoi American tour of 1962. In attempting to depict the ponderous grandeur of ancient Rome, the production lacked nothing in realism, but lacked much in good taste. In one critic's opinion, *Spartacus* "out De Milled De Mille,"[43] and subsequently it was withdrawn from the American repertoire. Its life in the Soviet Union was somewhat longer. In 1957, during a period when the Party wished to stifle complaints from a liberal faction that said their artistic freedom was being impaired, an article striving to prove the beneficial effects of Soviet guardianship of the arts pointed out *Spartacus,* boasting that its score was the direct result of applying Party directives, and that it will certainly go down in the treasury of Soviet music.[44] The composer of the score, Aram Khachaturian, was reported to have commented about it:

The epoch of Spartacus was an exciting historical epoch in the life of mankind. Now, when many oppressed peoples of the world are struggling for their freedom and national independence, the immortal form of Spartacus acquires special fascination. . . . I have always sensed the spiritual closeness of Spartacus to our epoch, our struggle against all tyranny, the struggle of oppressed peoples against imperialist aggressors.[45]

In a much lighter vein, one recent ballet depicts only a paper revolt against the tsar by his own bureaucracy. *Lieutenant Kizhe* is a story of the mad Tsar Paul I as depicted in a tale by Yuri Tynianov. In it, a dancer costumed to represent a pen writes out a military order and makes a blot. Hurriedly rewriting the order, the pen mistakenly writes an extra name to the list, that of Lieutenant Kizhe. The deranged tsar signs the order and this brings to life the nonexistent Lieutenant, who then receives military honors and is married to a lady of the court. When troops go to battle under his command, they kill the nonexistent Kizhe to get out of a strange, confused situation. Thereupon Kizhe is given a state funeral, and when the tsar goes by night to see Kizhe, he finds only an empty coffin. As the ballet concludes, the tsar is barraged by pens and soldiers with imaginary orders, and finally is stabbed by one of the pens. A Soviet author styled it a biting satire on stupidity and servility.[46]

SOVIET HEROES TAME NATURE IN BALLET

One of the most abiding and aggravating problems the Soviet government has had to face has been a constant shortage of agricultural products. To motivate the people to work hard on the collective farms, there have been instituted numerous titles and rewards, such as Hero of Socialist Labor and the Order of the Red Banner. In times when strong efforts were being made to increase agricultural output in some crucial area, ballets dealing with the subject would appear.

On the boards of the former Maryinsky, in 1953 a ballet appeared called *Native Fields*. It portrays a great village surrounded by the spacious Don Steppes, where a gay celebration is taking place to honor the engagement of the tractor driver Fyodor and the collective farm girl Stasha. After the solemn congratulations of the young folks by Ivan Romanovich, the president of the kolkhoz, they all begin to dance. Among the many guests is Andrei, the nephew of Ivan Romanovich. He had recently returned from the front and is attracted to Galia, sister of Fyodor. Andrei is preparing to go to Moscow to study, and Galia promises to wait for him. The kolkhoz girls are all distressed about the harvest, because the sun is drying the fields, ruining all their hard work. Only Ivan Romanovich looks optimistically to the future, for he dreams of a time when the streams will run full, giving water to the fields and electric current to the homes. All are carried away by Ivan's dreams except Andrei, who only thinks of his own future in a Moscow institute. Galia reproaches him for his indifference, so Andrei promises to come back to build a hydrostation for them.

Several years pass, and his studies come to an end. He successfully defends his dissertation and the professors congratulate the young engineer. He then writes to Galia to come to Moscow. In the meantime she has become a brigadier of the Komsomol brigade, and decides not to leave the farm. All the kolkhozniks are awarded the title Hero of Socialist Labor, so they ride to Moscow to receive their honor from the government. Decorated by gold stars, they go to see Andrei in the Institute. He talks of future life in Moscow, but Galia tells him how much she loves her native fields, especially now that the government prizes her work so highly. All the kolkhoz people remind Andrei of his promise, but he does not understand his social duties and wants to stay and work at the Institute. One of his friends named Sandro goes to the kolkhoz instead.

Work progresses on the hydrostation with the help of Sandro. One day Andrei unexpectedly arrives, since he has been tormented by repentance and now understands that he was completely wrong. Galia coldly listens to him. Then a terrible *sukhovei,* a dry desert wind,

143

blows in. Galia runs to her brigade, but the fierceness of the gusts of wind knocks her down unconscious. Andrei seeks her and carries her to the kolkhoz shelter, but the sukhovei has ruined the fruits of their labor. Galia calms her comrades and reminds them of their plan of subjugating nature. Andrei and Sandro both work to save the situation, but in the meantime something wonderful has happened. The government has passed a decision to build the Volga-Don Canal, and the regions of the Don Steppes served by it will receive water to irrigate the land.

The day arrives when the kolkhozniks celebrate the opening of this dam. There Galia meets Andrei, one of the engineers of the great construction. He asks her forgiveness and speaks of his love. Then, the Soviet account declares, the orchestra solemnly sounds, proclaiming the victory of Soviet man over nature.[47]

Actually, the Council of Ministers did publish a decision on December 28, 1950, to build the Volga-Don Canal, and it was opened on May 31, 1952. The ballet has other real factors involved in it. In 1950, *Pravda* complained of a shortage of engineers in the Donbass region and suggested stripping research institutes to fill the needed cadres.[48] However, the ballet was criticized in the Soviet press; the comment was made that while Andrei was dressed in contemporary garments, he danced like the Prince in *Swan Lake*. The reviewer asked, "How, in fact, can you believe in a hero if, when he defends a dissertation draft or receives a good mark from a professor, he pirouettes and makes little. leaps, using the movements of classical variations?"[49]

Another ballet was produced in 1953 which also emphasized work themes. Undoubtedly, it was more subtle and artistic than *Native Fields*, but there was still too much moralizing in it for the tastes of Western audiences. With a score by Prokofiev, the ballet came to be called *Tale of a Stone Flower*. It was said that the central theme of the ballet is the joy of creative work for the welfare of the people, the spiritual beauty of Russian man, and the true love of Katerina and Danila overcoming serious trials.[50] As the ballet opens, Danila, a skilled stone craftsman of the Ural Mountains, is carving a stone vessel called a *chasha* for a demanding landowner. He is disgusted with its design and wishes to carve one more perfectly. His wicked overseer Severian forces himself on Katerina, Danila's beloved. Eventually, Danila makes his way to the realm of the fantastic Mistress of the Copper Mountain who unlocks the secret of how to carve a perfect piece of work. Katerina finds him there, but the Queen tests her love by turning Danila into stone, which Katerina melts with her tears.[51] The ballet, while containing many beautiful scenes, brought reproaches from Western critics for its Victorian melodrama and its blatant socialist realism. However, the ballet was in accord with the Soviet policy of honoring folk art in its many forms. Speaking of the real stone carvers of the Urals, one Soviet article pointed out: "The art of the Urals carvers has made great strides since the October Revolution. . . . This is due largely to the great concern the State has shown for the development of all forms of applied folk art."[52]

In another ballet staged by the Bolshoi Theatre, there is depicted a long exploratory journey into the endless tracts of Siberia, an area which the Soviet government is taking great care to develop at present. In *Heroic Poem of Geologists,* the heroes are two boys and a girl who carry imaginary knapsacks on their backs. Following the musical pattern, the action portrays eight episodes: the Taiga, Wind, Exhaustion, the Discovery and Joy, Relaxation, Fire, Lament for the Dead Hero, Meeting with the Yakuts. After being harassed by winds, two of the explorers are ready to quit and return home, but the third encourages them with his steadfastness. Suddenly their hopes are raised as he finds some of the mineral they are seeking. Fire takes the life of this brave boy and seriously burns the other, but the girl's character grows through the episode and she experiences the satisfaction of fulfilling her duty. She drags the injured boy through the

145

taiga, and, just as she is about to succumb, members of a Siberian tribe, the Yakuts, find them.[53]

One of the more famous examples of socialist realism to emerge in balletic form was based upon Alexander Pushkin's poem, "The Bronze Horseman." Its appearance was probably a direct result of Zhdanov's action against Muradeli on February 10, 1948, for this ballet was said to have been composed by Reingold Gliere between September, 1948, and March, 1949.[54] Its inspiration was the 150th anniversary of the birth of Pushkin and the tremendous celebrations planned for it. The poem dealt first with the building of the city of St. Petersburg by Peter the Great (1689–1725), who is noted for his attempts to westernize Russia and to build up its naval and military might. In Pushkin's poem, Peter gloats over the fact that the new city would help him to utilize his new navy to harass his Swedish enemies, although the building of the city on so ill-chosen a site was costing an untold number of human lives. Pushkin's poem describes a flood which in 1824 threatened to ruin Peter's creation. In the poem, a poor clerk named Yevgeny has a fiancée named Parasha, whose house with all its inhabitants is swept into the sea. The poem focuses upon the conflict between the rights of Yevgeny, representing the individual, and the rights of the mighty state, for whose glory the city was built on this geographically unfavorable spot. The Bronze Horseman is a statue of Peter in the city. It comes alive, pursues Yevgeny in a nightmare, and defeats him. The Soviet description of the ballet pointed out that the Bronze Horseman personified the tsarist state, based upon noble classes and serfs, which exercised a fateful and complete power over man.[55]

The resulting ballet placed this work in the ranks of such monumental productions as *The Flames of Paris* and *Spartacus,* which are unique to Soviet ballet. According to one Western viewer, this production achieved its message by its staging, light effects, tricks, and rousing music. He said:

146

> One came away . . . over-awed by the use of color, by the technicians'
> ability to stage a roaring flood without spilling a drop of gauze water,
> by electrical storm devices, by the orchestra's rising tribute to the Soviet
> state, and by the audience's total absorption in their own individual
> identification with the music of state communism. The dancing was
> irrelevant.[56]

Another Pushkin poem whose ballet version was supposed to carry
a message was "Tale of the Priest and His Workman Balda." Since
Pushkin's works were subjected to imperial censorship, this poem was
only published posthumously, and then with changes in it. It is a
piece ridiculing a Russian Orthodox priest who engages the services
of a seemingly simple peasant named Balda, "Blockhead." His wages
are low: after working diligently for the priest, Balda can give him
three blows. After he has performed all kinds of jobs, Balda extracts
his price and sends the priest heavenward with his fist. The ballet
seemed to have some interesting episodes, for in it, to show Balda's
capacity for work, he makes dishes and other inanimate objects come
alive and dance. However, the Soviet critic cannot concentrate upon
levity. One of them affirmed that the ballet *Balda* had "great political
acuteness," showing the idea of the people's retribution against exploitation, as well as having "a militantly antireligious character."
Further, "the tone of political agitation penetrates *Tale of the Priest
and His Workman Balda* from beginning to end."[57]

The attempts to insert antireligious elements in Soviet theatre
have been made at the insistence of party and government forces. In
1930, for example, the Militant League of the Godless, the very active
Soviet agency for promoting atheism, at a Moscow meeting openly
criticized the theatrical world for not taking its proper part in antireligious work, and urged theatres to create an antireligious repertoire; to form artistic shock brigades to work actively in antireligious
propaganda; and to send such shock brigades into kolkhozy for the
presentation of antireligious evenings and concerts.[58] While such

antireligious campaigns abated during the war years in order to pacify the people, the trend continued in full force in later years. This attitude is reflected in countless minute ways, such as having a knavish character make an ostentatious Sign of the Cross or obeisance before an ikon before performing some foul deed.

While promoting such a policy, many Soviet theatrical productions have designedly promoted anticlericalism by making religious characters appear a little foolish in the manner of Pushkin's priest, or else by portraying them in an equally hilarious manner by an exaggerated overemphasis of their black and sinister villainy. Such a treatment could be found in their version of *Joan of Arc*.

Galina Ulanova had long wanted to portray in ballet the story of the romantic French heroine. The role finally fell instead to Violetta Bovt, whose career has been tied to the Stanislavsky Nemirovich-Danchenko Musical Theatre. The well-known story of Joan had several points to interest the ideologues. It glorified patriotism, and contrasted the bravery of a peasant girl to the stupidity of the nobility. When Joan and the peasants arrived at the court of the Dauphin, the courtiers all hid in a cowardly way behind available pillars, fearing that a revolt was taking place.

Further, it afforded another chance for portraying the clergy as the incarnation of the "forces of evil"—on an equal level with Rothbart and Carabosse.[59] The most perfidious character in the ballet was called the Black Monk, the spiritual guide of the Dauphin, under whose tutelage the heir to the throne pursues the paths of indolence. Even the veteran critic Valerian Bogdanov-Berezovsky complained about the portrayal of this Black Monk, saying that he was not in the original scenario of B. Pletnev and that he did not harmonize with the rest of the *dramatis personae*, who were living people. The monk was only an abstract, impersonal being "symbolizing in some sort of generalized plane the reactionary forces of Catholicism."[60] Whether well- or ill-drawn, the villainous Black Monk was on hand whenever there was treachery afoot; he popped up in the Ardennes forest, for

148

instance, leading the English forces to capture Joan as she hid there.[61]

The same type of emphasis is seen in the Soviet version of the ballet *Paganini*. When originally produced by Fokine in 1939, Paganini was characterized as a tormented artist who sold himself to the devil in exchange for perfection in the art of violin-playing. Choreographer Leonid Lavrovsky related that in a new version, he purposely shifted emphasis to make the true forces of evil in the plot to be the Catholic Church, represented by black-clad hooded figures who pierce Paganini with their violin bows while a cardinal stands in the background, wielding a huge cross.[62]

The production of a ballet is a complicated process involving coordination between a composer, librettist, choreographer, and artistic director. In the U.S.S.R., sometimes years of preparation are required before the opening night. Therefore, official changes in artistic policy, which could be reflected readily and dramatically in the production of a single painting or literary work, are not evident immediately in ballets. There have been vast changes wrought in artistic policies since the critical days of Stalinism. With his death in 1953, a phase began which in literary history is called "The Thaw," after a novel of that name by Ilya Ehrenburg. During this time, books were published which never would have seen a printing shop in the days of Stalin. In February, 1956, Nikita Khrushchev soundly denounced the terrorism of Stalin in a speech to the Twentieth Party Congress. With the gates thus unbolted for denunciation of the past, criticism erupted. In June, 1956, Dmitri Shostakovich spoke out from the depth of his humiliations, declaring that an arbitrary use of the word "formalism" could often hamper or ruin the work of creative young people, sometimes turning composers into "cautious old men."[63] However, the outbreak of the Hungarian revolt in the fall of that year, fermented by the Petöfi literary circle of Budapest, brought a relative curtailment of the artistic freedom of "The Thaw."

The scapegoat this time became Dmitri Shepilov, a high-ranking Party official who had assumed control over cultural affairs in 1956–

1957, advocating a relatively liberal course. Shepilov became involved in a faction called the "Anti-Party Group," along with Viacheslav Molotov, Lazar Kaganovich, and Georgi Malenkov. In a power struggle of June, 1957, Khrushchev triumphed over these opponents, and Shepilov was blamed in the magazine *Kommunist* for the spread of inordinately liberal ideas among the artists and intelligentsia of the U.S.S.R. *Kommunist* declared that the events in Hungary had proved the folly of disregarding the Leninist principles of guidance of literature and art which Shepilov had so flouted.[64]

However, in 1958, the Central Committee of the Party saw fit to print an official retraction of their condemnation of several theatrical works, including Muradeli's *The Great Friendship*.[65] The opening years of the 1960's brought increased signs of a more permissive attitude, which was reflected in various ways in the dance world. The once unappreciated Kasian Goleizovsky seemed to be vindicated, since he again gave concerts in Moscow of his one-act ballets to the music of Scriabin, Tcherepnine, Ravel, and Rachmaninoff. Moreover, he was commended for remaining true to his artistic principles through the years.[66]

In 1962, a peak of artistic unrest beset the U.S.S.R. In the early part of that year, there was manifested much permissiveness in the arts. A poem called "Stalin's Heirs" by Yevgeny Yevtushenko was printed, boldly asking how Stalinism could be rooted out of Soviet life. Shostakovich's formerly condemned opera, *Katerina Izmailova*, was again presented in December, 1962, in its homeland. However, perhaps the most dramatic manifestation of permissiveness appeared in late 1962 with the publication of the novel *One Day in the Life of Ivan Denisovich* by Alexander Solzhenitsyn, which described as never before the depth of human degradation experienced in Stalin's labor camps.

However, many factors made it necessary to restrain this trend toward de-Stalinization and artistic liberalism. The Soviet Union suffered an international humiliation in the Cuban crisis of October,

1962, and internally had to cope with a rise in food prices and unfulfilled economic promises. Conservative forces within the Party saw a need to halt the new permissiveness, and their views carried the day. On December 1, 1962, Khrushchev voiced the new line in his remarks at an exhibit of abstract art, which he judged to be "art for donkeys." He likewise expressed his disgust for some modern music, saying, "When I hear jazz, it's as if I had gas on the stomach." Rambling on, he complained:

> Or take these new dances which are so fashionable now. Some of them are completely improper. You wiggle a certain section of the anatomy, if you'll pardon the expression. It's indecent. . . . Jazz comes from the Negroes. They've had it for a long time, and here it's treated as a novelty. I understand our own Russian dances a lot better—Georgian and Armenian ones, too. They are wonderful dances. . . .[67]

Leonid F. Ilyichev, head of the Ideological Commission of the Central Committee of the Party, then called a meeting of art workers on December 17 where he denounced recent attempts to show that Lunacharsky and Lenin were advocates of abstract art, and he decried the new "infatuation with the wild howling of different foreign (and not only foreign) jazz orchestras."[68] The campaign gained force in March when Khrushchev felt compelled to denounce Ilya Ehrenburg for intimating that Lenin stood for "coexistence" of various artistic creeds in the U.S.S.R., and to castigate the poet Yevtushenko for his defense of abstract art.[69] As had become customary in such times of artistic stress, the usual rounds of meetings of artistic workers and unions took place, with Ilyichev cautioning further about "the inordinate preoccupation with jazz and vulgar dances."[70]

Although this period in 1962 was quite serious, never since the death of Stalin have artists been subjected to such marked and intense persecution as in 1936 and 1946. But the condemnation to ten years of penal servitude given to the writers Andrei Siniavsky and Yuri Daniel in the spring of 1966 shows that there are definite limits to the present regime's toleration. Since the ever-vacillating artistic policies depend upon a complex network of international and domestic factors, the individual innovator can never be sure that a work accepted or rejected in one era will be equally treated in the next. For an excellent case study of this ambivalence, no better example can be given than that of Igor Stravinsky.

The first wildly creative postrevolutionary years had seen the production of Stravinsky's ballet *Firebird* and *Petrushka* in Russia, along with his *Renard* and *Pulchinella*. Further, without benefit of the accompanying dancing, his *Les Noces* was sung in 1927 by a State Choral Society,[71] and his *Rite of Spring* was given by the Bolshoi orchestra in a concert in 1926.[72] But, when the ring of socialist realism closed about the arts in the 1930's, Stravinsky's works did not measure up to its canons, and his works disappeared from public performances. According to the *History of Russian Soviet Music*, "his stay in Paris and the United States led to a break from Russian tradition. Stravinsky became one of the acknowledged leaders of cosmopolitan, formalistic musical art."[73] A "cosmopolitan" in the stock Soviet vocabulary was one who did not produce works imbued with Russian patriotism, or who tried too many new forms in his works. At the height of the campaign against Muradeli, it was said that Stravinsky's *Rite of Spring, Petrushka, Les Noces,* and *Mavra* manifested "a deliberate search for musical barbarism, startling sound effects or mystic harmonies."[74] In 1951, an article entitled "Dollar Cacophony" appeared in *Izvestiia* which voiced various complaints. It castigated American business men who were corrupting the Marshall Plan countries by selling American records there, and it denounced cosmopolitans like Stravinsky, who supposedly had said that "the wide masses bring nothing to art. They are not able to raise its level."[75]

However, with the general amelioration of official attitudes which took place after Stalin's death, the situation gradually grew more favorable for Stravinsky in his homeland. Finally, someone became courageous enough to stage his ballets again. The task of sending up the trial balloon was handled by the Maly Theatre in Leningrad, which has often been a citadel for experimentation. In 1961, *Petrushka* was produced, followed by *Firebird* and *Orpheus* in 1962.[76] Further, in 1962, a delegation of Soviet composers came to the United States, headed by the chief of the Union of Soviet Composers, Tikhon Khrennikov, an indefatigable Party member, who assured Stravinsky that *Petrushka* and *Firebird* were staged in the U.S.S.R.[77] The composers declared a state of musical coexistence, with Stravinsky receiving an invitation to Russia. He accepted it and in October, 1962, was received personally by Khrushchev.[78] In 1963, the music of Stravinsky's *L'Histoire du Soldat* was played in Estonia for a special Soviet version of the ballet. Later in 1964, it appeared at the Bolshoi. The following year the first performance of his famous *Rite of Spring* appeared in Moscow. Since Russia had been deprived of the work for thirty years, *Rite* was probably afforded the best reception of its history in Moscow. Produced in Paris in 1913, the music itself was such an innovation that it was at first received with catcalls and jeers. As conceived then, the ballet was a celebration of a wildly primitive pagan rite in ancient Slavdom, with no particular story or moral attached. In the Soviet version of 1965, it became the story of a primitive young shepherd who fell madly in love with a maiden chosen to be the sacrificial victim to an ugly god, Dazh-Bog. Before the shepherd's eyes, the maiden is murdered and consumed by red flames on the stage, thus impelling the enraged youth to plunge his knife with violent hatred into the totemlike god for whom she was sacrificed. The population stands in dumb horror at his action, expecting the retribution of the gods to rain disaster upon them, but nothing happens. As portrayed at the Bolshoi, it was a dramatic blow against religious superstition.[79]

It is noteworthy that as Stravinsky became acceptable in the U.S.S.R., Michel Fokine also seems to have been reinstated. In 1962, his book of memoirs, *Protiv Techeniia*, appeared in print in Russia, and his ballets *Egyptian Nights* and *Carnaval* appeared on Soviet stages.

153

NATIONAL LIBERATION AND RACIAL THEMES

The Soviet Union's portrayal of its own role as the friend and guide of colonial nations was sharpened after World War II when many nations, subjugated in the past, sought to sever the ties that bound them to their colonial masters. The National Liberation Movement, as the Soviet Union has termed it, became a major theme particularly in the years after Stalin's death. The policy was a long-standing one, but it received more concrete expression in the words of the Party Programme of 1962 which said: "The C.P.S.U. regards it as a duty to assist the peoples who have set out to win and strengthen their national independence and who are fighting for the complete abolition of the colonial system."[80] In line with this, the official text, *Fundamentals of Marxism-Leninism,* states that "the most important condition for the future success of the national liberation movement in this part of the world is the establishment and utmost strengthening of the *solidarity of the African peoples* [sic] both those already liberated and those still oppressed by imperialism."[81]

In recent years, the Soviet Union has given much attention to African dance. Groups of native African performers are shown in Soviet journals after performing at Youth Festivals, and Soviet choreographers have tried their hands at expressing the spirit of the new Africa in dance.

One of the most dramatic portrayals of this new interest emerged in the ballet *The Path of Thunder,* based upon a book by the South African author Peter Abrahams. However, the librettist, Yuri Slonimsky, made many subtle changes in Abrahams' story, reducing a quite complicated plot to the level of a struggle of good native Africans against bad colonials.

In Slonimsky's version, the action begins in a little African city. A group of students are in a cafe and Lenny, a mulatto, joins them, visibly proud of himself in the gown and hood of a university graduate, since he has just received his diploma. Lenny starts to return

Konstantin Sergeyev as Lenny and Natalia
Dudinskaya as Sari in *Path of Thunder*.

Alla Shelest in the title role of *Katerina* and
Mikhail Mikhailov as the *pomeshchik,* a landowner.

to his native village with some other students, but as they board the train, the railway conductor strikes them to remind them that they cannot enter the car for whites. Back in his native village, Lenny's mother hardly recognizes him, but tenderly strokes his head when she does. They all go to the village square, since his mother wants to display her son in his academic robes to her friends. Just then, the white landowner, Gert, appears on the square with his overseer, BillJohn [sic] and his assistant, Smith. The villagers bow low, and Lenny alone looks Gert straight in the eye. Smith then knocks Lenny's hood off, but Lenny puts it right back on again.

Out in the African veld, Lenny is alone, dreaming of the school he will open, when Smith and BillJohn come and beat him on the head, hoping thereby to teach him a lesson. Steps are heard and Sari, the daughter of the landowner, enters and finds Lenny lying senseless. Preparing to aid him, she puts light to his face and discovers that he is colored. She steps back in horror as Lenny awakens. He starts up in anger, but falls back again exhausted. Sari is then moved by compassion and binds one of his wounds with her own scarf.

Lenny manages to found a little school in which to teach. One day, Sari comes to the school and meets him, but he tells her to leave the black settlement for if she were seen with him, it would be her ruin. Lenny is troubled by her attention, and his mother beseeches him to put thoughts of Sari from his mind, but he cannot. One day a white recruiter for workers comes into the village, treating the people to a holiday and making them big promises. At the same time, he manages to stir up the rancor which exists between the mulattoes and the black people; many of them have become intoxicated with liquor supplied by the recruiter, and a scuffle breaks out in which several are killed.

Sari and Lenny meet in the veld, and their rendezvous is seen by a black friend, who in turn is beaten by some drunk whites who pass through the area. In a subsequent scene, a Christmas celebration is taking place at the home of Sari. She has planned to run away with

Lenny, but BillJohn notices her preparations, warns Gert of the matter, and the two pursue her as she tries to flee. Lenny is in the garden of the house, when Smith arrives to prevent him from leaving. Gert and BillJohn come out of the house and her father hits Sari on the face. The guests run out of the house and look contemptuously on Sari, and the men want to kill Lenny. But Gert stops the men and turns on Lenny himself. The two men fight. Sari, trying to defend Lenny, is hurled by her father into a crowd of colored people. Gert kills Lenny, and the mulattoes and blacks forget their own animosities to unite in a funeral procession for him.[82]

The ballet fulfilled Soviet musical canons, for it contained elements of folklore from the tribes of the Zulus and Kafirs, old Negro hymns, and a great deal of percussive rhythms. Its composer, Kara Karaev, has been a member of the Communist Party since 1949.[83]

When Aneurin Bevin visited Leningrad, he publicly criticized the ballet. It portrays the whites in typical sun helmets and costumes usually associated with British colonials. Bevin tried in vain to explain that the British no longer believed in colonialism.[84] An American scholar in the U.S.S.R. remarked that some Americans who had seen the ballet in Leningrad felt embarrassment at the implied comparison to the American South.[85]

Another ballet on the racial theme was produced in Latvia and was called *Rigonda*. The name comes from the setting, a small isle in the Pacific. As the ballet begins, islanders named Ako and Nelima express their love for each other on the peaceful seashore. They then go to tell other islanders of their desire to marry, but their little gathering is disturbed as a boat filled with white men pulls forebodingly up to the shore. The armed whites take island men, including Ako, as prisoners.

In the next scene, Ako's ship has come to a European port where there is much commotion because of a strike. He manages to escape from the ship and is befriended by the leader of the strikers. After becoming a seaman himself, Ako earnestly desires to return home, but

156

does not know even the latitude and longitude of his small island home. Only one white man knows—the wicked Planter who formerly enslaved Ako. By chance, Ako meets him in a port bar and forces him to reveal the location.

Ako goes there by serving on a millionaire's yacht, where the depravity of the rich is carefully portrayed. In Rigonda he finds his people all enslaved by the wicked Planter, but Ako kindles within them the will to struggle. When the Planter finds Ako stirring the people to revolt, he orders his bodyguard to shoot him, but the shot kills the beloved Nelima. Ako's grief further inspires the people to fight until they are delivered from slavery to the white exploiters.[86]

A recent theme which has appeared in more than one Soviet ballet is that of the conquering of space by Soviet man. In 1961, a ballet called *Dream* depicted space travelers *sur les pointes*.[87] In 1962, the I. Franko Theatre of Opera and Ballet in L'vov staged the ballet called *Holiday Suite in Honor of the Cosmonauts, or Praise to the Cosmonauts*.[88] Another one called *Cosmos* appeared in Moscow in 1962 at the Stanislavsky Musical Theatre.[89] The most successful attempt was probably *Distant Planet*, produced by the Kirov Theatre in 1963. Its chief advantage was the superb dancing of Yuri Soloviev in portraying the part of the spaceman. The composer of the score, B. Maizel, dutifully declared that the thought for the ballet came to him after the launching of the first Soviet sputnik, and he finished the last measure of it on the historical date of the flight of Yuri Gagarin.[90] The libretto of the production merely describes Man, dreaming of being able to conquer space, and finally achieving it, even though Earth beckons to her son to stay. In the finale, an apotheosis is "dedicated to the victory of the virility, intelligence, and will of man."[91]

CHAPTER SIX

Ballets of Mountains, Steppes, and Deserts:

The Soviet Nationalities

How many times have we contented ourselves with the obvious deficiencies of a production only because of its title which spoke of the great and stirring themes of love to the homeland, the struggle for peace and the friendship of peoples.
—ARAM KHACHATURIAN, 1953[1]

IN 1936, the U.S.S.R. adopted a new constitution. By an earlier constitution effective in 1924 a multinational federation was formed. In 1936, a rearrangement of older political divisions took place, so that the new nation emerged as a federal union composed of eleven Soviet republics: the R.S.F.S.R. (Russian Socialist Federated Soviet Republic, often referred to as Great Russia), the Ukrainian, White Russian (Belorussian), Georgian, Armenian, Azerbaidzhan, Kazakh, Kirghiz, Uzbek, Turkmen, and Tadzhik Soviet Socialist Republics. The new constitution granted "equality of rights to citizens of the U.S.S.R. irrespective of their nationality or race, in all spheres of economic, governmental, cultural, political, and other public activity."[2] It was understood, however, that the culture was to be developed according to the pattern advocated by Stalin in 1930: "Socialist in content, national in form."

In seeking to influence smaller nations, the Kremlin ceaselessly points out that the nationalities subject to the U.S.S.R. have found warm encouragement for their self-development. A cardinal point emphasized in Soviet propaganda is that Russia, in contrast to the nations of the West, has nourished and encouraged the most ancient folk art of less developed peoples—a point readily appreciated by

158

African and Asian audiences.[3] Again and again the assertion is made that:

> The first socialist state [the U.S.S.R.] became an inexhaustible source of moral and political support for the oppressed peoples of the world. In particular they saw the inspiring example of the Central Asian republics of the Soviet Union, which in a very short period of history passed from colonial backwardness to the all-around flowering of their national economy and culture.[4]

Beginning in 1936, one of the devices used by the Soviet government to show its encouragement of national and folk art was the initiation of a series of national *dekady*—ten days set aside when each republic would display its art in Moscow. Stimuli for producing the *dekada* came directly from the Committee on Affairs of the Arts, which informed a republic that by a certain date they must organize such a festival.[5] Preferably, they were to present plays, ballets, and operas based upon national or folk themes.

Some of the regions of the U.S.S.R. have ancient, proud cultures. Armenia, for example, had experienced a Golden Age of literature when the site of present-day Moscow was still a forest. Certain other republics, however, had reached only the cultural level of nomads, and to expect that they would produce a national opera or ballet was highly optimistic. Consequently, the Soviet government initiated a program to help these backward regions create their own national art. A composer was sent from Moscow or Leningrad to study local folklore. He would then write a national opera or ballet, and, when the music was written, performers from Moscow or Leningrad would be sent, not always willingly, to work with whatever local talent could be found to produce the "national" opera and ballet.[6] Starting in 1935, a drive was begun to send a number of talented youths to Moscow and Leningrad to study ballet at the main choreographic institutes. In this way, a national opera and ballet theatre was gradually built in each republic. Some of the resulting works have interested worldwide audiences, such as the ballet version of *Othello*, choreo-

159

graphed by Vakhtang Chabukiani for the Georgian Theatre of Opera and Ballet. Others would like to be forgotten even by Soviet dance historians, but regardless of the repertoire they produced, the existence of these groups of well-trained ballet dancers in Frunze, Ulan-Ude, Ufa, and hosts of towns whose names most Westerners have never heard is a source of justifiable pride to the people of the area.

The national *dekady* were carefully planned by the Chairman of the Committee on Art Affairs of the U.S.S.R., or after 1952, the Minister of Culture, who worked in conjunction with top officials of the republic, such as the Secretary of the Communist Party, the Chairman of Art Affairs, the leading officials of the Union of Artists, and a specially appointed artistic director of the *dekada*. Local officials responsible for the success of the festival approached the task with trepidation, knowing well that *kritika* and *samokritika* would abound during the ten days. A responsible official might nervously issue the following appeal to his artistic performers: "Our *dekada* performances must be a worthy answer to the summons of the native Communist Party—to strengthen the bonds of the people, to express deeply and truthfully the life of Soviet society, the heroic work of our contemporaries."[7]

No preparation was too great. In 1936, when the U.S.S.R. was in the process of building its industrial potential at the frenzied level of Stakhanovism, special railway cars were still allocated by the government just to transport scenery and costumes to Moscow. Participants were well paid; an announcement in *Pravda* revealed that each performer was given two months' salary for appearing in the Ukrainian *dekada*.

The performers would be met at the railway station with honors and formal greetings such as:

We are happy to greet you, emissaries of the talented and work-loving Georgian people, on Moscow soil. The exhibition of art, the achievement of Georgian culture will be united to the future development of our art, socialist in content, national in form, and still more strongly fortify the bonds of brotherly friendship of the Soviet people.[8]

Large exhibits of pictures of the *dekada* performances would be on display in public places in Moscow, and during its course the newspaper coverage given the *dekada* would outspace almost all other national or domestic issues. *Pravda* gave the Azerbaidzhan festival in May, 1959, approximately twice the coverage it gave to sports during the *dekada*. Further articles would appear in the leading magazines of the country. Obviously the regime wished to impress the people with the importance of the festival.

In the first round of *dekady* which began in 1936, only a few republics had a national ballet to present. However, on the second round, beginning in the 1950's, most republics had not only a national ballet, but national operas and national plays. In addition, many of them proudly performed Shakespearean classics. Besides the regular stage performances in the main theatres, members of the delegation would perform in neighboring factories and collective farms. After performances, discussions of the production would be held with interested parties such as the Union of Soviet Writers, the Union of Soviet Artists, or the All-Russian Theatrical Society.

The closing night of the *dekada* would be a monumental affair where all members of the ballet, opera, and drama companies would perform, ending with an assembly of all participants on the stage in such a setting as that described for the Uzbek festival:

Solemnly and resoundingly reverberates the finale of the concert: a choreographical tableau, "Cotton," showed the gathering of the "white gold." High over the heads of the participants of the dance there is raised a tremendous boll of cotton. A combined chorus appears, there is heard the song "Stalin—Great Standard-bearer of Peace." Before the eyes of the spectators appear endless sunlit fields of cotton and deep blue mountains in the distance. Against the background of the Uzbek landscape towers the sculptured figure of the great Stalin.[9]

161

It became the custom to have a reception after the final performance in the headquarters of the Ministry of Culture. Some of the participants would return home with newly won Stalin medals as rewards for faithful service to the cause of socialist art.

Since many of the national ballets of the republics of the U.S.S.R. were produced specifically for performance at these *dekady*, they afford a convenient focal point from which to examine the type of original ballet that the government and Party encouraged among these national groups. There is no intention here to deny that other ballets were produced in the republics. On the contrary, the local company would usually first produce a standard Russian work, such as *Swan Lake, Red Poppy,* or *Fountain of Bakhchisarai.* This chapter only proposes to examine some of the ballet themes which the Soviet government had a special interest in cultivating in the particular time and place in which they were produced.

Broadly surveying these special national ballets, it can be seen that certain themes recur repeatedly. In many outlying parts of the U.S.S.R. the government forced collectivization of agriculture upon unwilling peasants or upon nomads whose personal wealth and well-being depended on their herds. Therefore, in many cases the ballets depict the inhabitants of these regions happily building a communist society by working on collective farms and at the same time developing hydroelectric projects to aid irrigation of the crops.

Again and again the element of revolution occurs. An incident from the history of the area will portray the poor being oppressed by the rich, thus equating poor with good and rich with evil. The point is repeatedly emphasized that all the common man wants is to be left free to *work* in peace.

In these ballets, there is also continually present an "antifeudal" theme where "feudal oppressors" take various forms: Polish Pans, Turkish Beys and Caliphs, Teutonic Knights, and Knights of the Sword. Closely linked with this element, an antireligious strain appears which tries to make religion look either silly or sinister, whether dealing with Moslems or Christians. Figures representing religion—knights, monks, or characters enforcing Moslem customs—are depicted as instruments of oppression against a heroine who stands for all the bright, patriotic virtues of her particular national group.

A third theme, intimately related to both "antifeudal" and "antireligious" themes is that of the emancipation of women. It takes only a brief survey of such publications as *Soviet Woman* to see that this theme has been very carefully cultivated in many art forms in the U.S.S.R. In describing one of her trips to neighboring Iran, ballerina Irina Tikhomirnova typically commented:

> Iranian actors lead a hard, pitiful existence. The private owners of the few theatres think only of box office returns, and completely ignore the creative mission of art. Women in Iran are treated as despised inferior creatures. Looking at these unhappy women who never dare to remove the veil in public, I thought of our free and happy Soviet women. . . . Vera Davydova, the opera singer, is a deputy to the Supreme Soviet of the Russian Federation; Olga Lepeshinskaya, the ballerina, has been elected to the Moscow Soviet three times; and the young singer, Yevgenia Smolenskaya, is likewise a deputy to the Moscow Soviet.[10]

One more brief comment seems in order before investigating the national ballets. It would be a great mistake to infer that some of these ballets are any measure of the artistry, the sentiments, or the political convictions of some of the composers, choreographers, or dancers involved in their production. In the U.S.S.R., the state has the means to control the production of every ballet and every other stage performance, not only by negatively condemning some, but also by positively commissioning others to be done. If a composer, for example, does not feel greatly stirred to write a new ballet encouraging greater corn production, he can refuse to write it. However, his royalties come from works which the state wishes to see staged.

NATIONAL BALLET: THE UKRAINE

Ballet had been seen in Kiev as early as 1823,[11] and Ukrainian folk dance has long charmed the world. In the late 1920's and early 1930's, the Kiev Theatre of Opera and Ballet staged works which were avant-garde for their day, but this brief phase was soon curtailed. Several other cities besides Kiev within the boundaries of Soviet Ukraine have their own theatres of opera and ballet, including Kharkov, Odessa, Donetsk, and L'vov. The ballets described below have originated in these various cities.

In 1930, the ballet *Ferendzhi* was first given in Kharkov, then the capital of the Ukraine. The Ukrainian composer B. Yanovsky may have been influenced by *Red Poppy,* for the Soviet account says that *Ferendzhi* is the name given to foreign oppressors by natives of India. The basic theme of the story was the revolutionary struggle of the workers of India against English colonizers, fully in line with the anti-British sentiment rampant in the U.S.S.R. at the time. The hero of the ballet was an Indian worker, Dako-Das, while the villains were the English governor Seymour and the shady enterpriser Major Campbell, betrothed to the governor's daughter, Effie.

Since Nikolai Foregger had made his way to Kharkov and was in charge of choreography, something unusual could be expected. In one scene, the spectator saw only the feet of the oppressors mechanically performing the same uniform walking movements. With this technique Foregger strove to show that the imperialists were interested only in the well-trained feet of soldiers walking on foreign lands, since feet could neither question the politics nor policies of their owners. *Ferendzhi* was later performed by many companies, including theatres of Kiev, Sverdlovsk, Odessa, Tbilisi, and Donetsk.[12]

A year later, the first ballet on a Ukrainian theme was presented in Kharkov and it was called *Pan Kaniowski.* Its heroine was a proud daughter of the Ukrainian people, memorialized in the "Song about Bondarivna," which told her sad tale. The archvillain of the story,

Count Kaniowski, made advances against Bondarivna, but she heroically slapped the powerful man's face. The story took place in the seventeenth century, when numerous uprisings against magnates and landowners took place on the Right Bank of the Dneiper River. At the end of the story, the heroine dies of a bullet wound from the magnate's gun as she flees his castle to meet the peasant insurgents who have rebelled against him. According to the Soviet account, a real Polish count, Nicholas Potocki, was known in the region as Pan Kaniowski, and on his numerous estates in the Ukraine he reputedly performed horrible and inhuman acts.[13]

One of the novellas from Boccaccio's *Decameron* became the subject of a Ukrainian ballet called *Petty Bourgeois from Tuscany*. The story centered about the lust of an ease-loving and cunning abbot for the wife of a rich peasant, Ferondo. The abbot put Ferondo to sleep with pills, then imprisoned him in an underground monastery where he convinced him he was in Purgatory. The abbot then broadcast the death of Ferondo to the townsfolk while making merry with his wife. This ballet was produced in 1936, and voicing the Party edict against *Bright Stream,* a critic declared that its greatest service was in overcoming the routine traditions of the old ballet art with its "doll-like, false attitude toward life."[14]

The Ukraine has produced great artists in the literary field, such as the nineteenth-century author, Taras Shevchenko. One ballet named *Lilea* is based upon one of his works, and though it centers about another serf ballerina, the result seems more poetical than the earlier attempts to portray her. Lilea is the name of the dancer who is forced into the baron's serf theatre. At the same time, her new husband, Stefan, is forced into the baron's police force, his *haiduks.* In fleeing from the baron's men, Stefan is caught by the Tatars and blinded. He comes back to the village disguised as a bandura player, and by his songs excites the village people against his former cruel master.

In 1951 a popular legendary figure of the Carpathian region named Oleska Dovbush became the hero of the ballet *Khustka Dov-*

busha. According to the Soviet account,[15] it told the struggle of the West Ukrainian peasantry against foreign oppressors. In 1959, the steppes became the scene of the ballet *Tavria.* Here, a rich landowner named Voldemar begins to love a beautiful hired girl named Ganna. When his mother and rich friends attempt to prevent their marriage, Voldemar tries to rape Ganna. However, she escapes to the steppes and her peasant friends are incensed at her fate. In the epilogue, an uprising takes place, led by Bolshevik sailors.[16]

In 1961, the ballet *Last Ball* told the story of Kati, the daughter of a Petersburg worker-revolutionary. She loves a Junker named Gleb, who traitorously murders Kati's father, the leader of a gathering of revolutionary workers. Kati then takes part in the storming of the Winter Palace in Petersburg and kills her former lover, the Junker, the enemy of the revolution.[17]

The Ukraine was the first republic to give a *dekada* in Moscow in 1936. No ballet appeared in the first *dekada,* although dancers took part in the opera *Zaporozhets za Dynaem.* At the second Ukrainian *dekada,* the national ballet *Marusia Boguslavka* appeared, and in 1960, *dekada* spectators saw the lovely *Song of the Forest* and the less-than-lovely *Black Gold.*

Marusia Boguslavka is based upon a Ukrainian ballad. In it, as Marusia's friends help prepare for her wedding to the Cossack Sofron, Turks raid Boguslav, her village, and carry off Marusia and her brother Stepan. From her window in the palace of the pasha, she sees fellow Ukrainians worn out by their forced labor. She is given a chance to escape, but does not take it until her brother and friends can escape with her. The ballet, blending folk and classical dance, was said to be "full of optimism, lyricism, and spirit."[18]

Many dancers of the Ukraine follow the refined technique of the Leningrad Kirov Theatre, and many émigré teachers have enriched the art of dance in the West by passing on these traditions. Ukrainian ballet stars have won prizes of their own at international competitions.[19] For this reason, it becomes even more painful to read about such a production as *Black Gold*. This is a ballet telling the story of Transcarpathian Komsomols who go to the Donbass coal region to work. Among the Komsomols, there is a couple who love each other—Vasily and Maria. But in their new way of life, "their feelings undergo a trial and she becomes the victim of egoism and deceit."[20] However, her comrades, teachers, and contemporaries come to her aid. Vasily is the "positive hero" who "struggles against the evil force of nature." The second heroic character is a girl named Varia, who by her inspiring tales of the Donbass region awakens within the Komsomols the desire to work there. There are many lessons taught in the ballet. In one version, a scene shows a character named Mikhail on his way to the mine. He is stopped by two friends who invite him to have a drink and Mikhail gives in to them, thus missing a day of work.[21] It is clearly an "agitka," a propaganda-agitation work, but it has one unique title to fame. Where else would the costume of a ballerina include a coal miner's helmet?

Another Ukrainian ballet called *Festival of Love* tells the story of the worker Taras and a physical education teacher named Oksana. They are separated from each other, but conveniently manage to meet at points such as the Far East where an appropriate dance is presented. Taras later transferred to the polar region where he is building new roads. This locale affords a chance to stage an attractive stage display of Northern Lights.[22]

A final sample of Ukrainian ballet is called *On the Blue Sea*. It takes place in a Dneiper village in the seventeenth century where the peasants live a hard and uneventful life. There is a shortage of salt in the village, preventing the fishermen from preserving their fish. A rich peasant named Karpo suggests that they go to sea for it, though they risk capture and enslavement by the Turks. The Cossacks embark on their trip, and while at sea they storm a Turk boat and free Ukrainians, Russians, Czechs, Moldavians, Bulgars, and Poles who are captives on it. Among those liberated are two friends, Kuzma and Yarema, who on the ship find gold which the Turks had stolen.

They disguise themselves and go to the Turkish slave market to buy their enslaved countrymen. Kuzma won the love of Zuleika, the daughter of the Turk shipowner, and their love is tried both by a Polish count and by the rich peasant Karpo, whose advances finally drive Zuleika to jump off a cliff to save herself from him. In the end, the true friends Kuzma and Yarema go from village to village in search of freedom and truth.[23]

The name of this ballet is taken from a line of a well-known Cossack song entitled "Cried the Grey Cuckoo." The work was mounted in 1954, in the Soviet description, to commemorate the 300th anniversary of the union of the Ukraine with Russia. Its picture of the friendship of the Russian and Ukrainian people, with their common concern in the seventeenth century for all their fellow Slavs, would scarcely be considered a valid theme by a good many Ukrainians.

BELORUSSIA

The Belorussian Theatre of Opera and Ballet was opened in Minsk in 1933 with the production of *Red Poppy*. By the time of their first *dekada* in June, 1940, Belorussia was ready to present the ballet *Nightingale*. It was so named because in it, a serf shepherd named Simon has a remarkable ability to imitate the bird's song. The action takes place in a Belorussian village at the beginning of the nineteenth century. By a whim of the Pan (the Polish landowner), Simon and his beloved Zoska are made actors in his serf ballet. The Pan will not agree to the marriage of the lovers, and instead wants to give Zoska as wife to his satrap, the haiduk Makar. Simon knows about it, but fearing persecution, he has to hide in the forest. The serfs, enraged by heavy extortions imposed upon them by the Pan, under the leadership of Simon rebel and set fire to his castle. However, the success of their venture is darkened by a sad event; Zoska, worn out by mockery, loses her reason.[24]

In the ballet *Substitute Bride* again a rich landowner named

168

Gonor Sniusevich is involved. He takes a fancy to a young girl named Nastia, the bride of the blacksmith Andrei, but the girl resists the importunate lovemaking of the Pan. A cunning friend of the couple named Matei manages to marry the villain to a substitute bride who long dreamed of an advantageous marriage.[25]

Another Belorussian ballet dwelt upon the festivities connected with the holiday *Ivan Kupala,* while also demonstrating a successful method of dealing with "feudal oppressors." The ballet, called *Prince-Lake,* told the story of how the oppressed people of one region drowned their prince in the lake, and the waves rushing to the shore washed away all traces of his castle. Like the previous ballets, *Prince-Lake* was supposed to depict the struggle of the Belorussian people against social injustice, that is, to show the good progressive forces triumphing over evil, feudal regressive elements.[26]

In 1963, the Belorussian National Ballet produced a work called *Light and Shade.* In it, a father, a sectary, decides to dedicate his daughter Anezhka to Christ, giving her over to a group of Women in Black—religious fanatics. However, a Belorussian lad named Ales and his comrades, among whom are Russians, Lithuanians, and Latvians, help her to break loose from the religious group. Angered with Anezhka, her father wounds her, so she turns again to her friends for aid.

In one ghastly scene of the ballet, the curtain rises to show a group of ridiculous figures moving unnaturally. These are the members of the religious group on their way to pray. A great cemetery cross seems to pull the praying figures toward it. The musical background has an almost uninterrupted bass ostinato which charges the atmosphere, producing "a mood of repulsive ecstasy." Anezhka, shocked at the scene, faints at the feet of one of the Black Women, and immediately in the sky there blazes up the monstrous face of a saint. Then the bursting flame illuminates the white dress of the young girl amidst the surrounding darkness, made all the more sinister by the black whirlwind of ominous dancing figures. The reviewer remarked that "something of a Gogolesque *Viy* is in this horrible picture."[27] The ballet was admittedly designed to express an antireligious theme.[28] Specifically it strove to show the mutilating influence of religion on the soul of man and the gradual disentangling of his psyche from the clutches of religion through the dual influence of "the collective" and the blossoming of youthful love.[29]

The first Belorussian ballet on a contemporary theme was called *Dream,* and it was another variation of the *Lost Illusions* theme. In it, a Belorussian girl finds herself exiled from her homeland and has to become a nightclub dancer. Her art is not appreciated in the decadent West, and she dreams of her faraway native land where an artist is truly revered and treated decently. Back again in her homeland she finds authentic happiness in creative labor. In the third act, having fulfilled her dream, she takes part in a great choreographic presentation, called "To the Star," which depicts cosmonauts. The ballet tried to show "the corruption of bourgeois society, the moral degradation of bourgeois youth, and the different fate of Soviet artists from those abroad."[30]

LITHUANIA

In 1940, Soviet control was established in the Baltic Sea lands of Lithuania, Latvia, and Estonia, and these countries were promptly incorporated into the ranks of the Union Republics. The Lithuanian Opera Theatre had been established in 1920. An accompanying choreographic school was established in the following year, so that by 1925, *Swan Lake, Coppélia,* and *Nutcracker* were playing in Kaunas, the capital of Lithuania.[31]

It is easy to forget that Lithuania, now only a tiny Union-Republic, was once the vast Grand Duchy of Lithuania, covering a great part of what is now western Russia and Poland. To gather and unite the lands of the Grand Duchy, in the thirteenth century a prince named Mindovg (Mindaugas) began to struggle against the opposition of many local rulers. Further, in the Baltic Sea area, Lithuanian princes had to resist Germanic invaders known as Teutonic Knights. This order, formed for the purpose of undertaking a crusade, ended by staging its own drive to the East nearer home. In 1237, the Teutonic Knights joined forces with another group, the Order of Swordbearing Knights, later know as Livonian Knights. These knights became a convenient symbol for the hated German aggressor in the 1930's, when the Soviet regime was particularly interested in portraying Germans in just such a light. American audiences became familiar with this characterization in the well-known movie of Sergei Eisenstein, *Alexander Nevsky,* depicting the Russian hero defeating the Teutonic Knights in 1239 at Lake Peipus. Similarly portrayed, the knights appeared in ballets such as *Audrone,* staged in the newer capital at the Vilnius Academic Theatre of Opera and Ballet in 1959.

According to the description, the ballet hearkens back to the thirteenth century when the region in the area of the Nieman River was divided, and Prince Mindaugas, partisan of a united and strong Lithuania, had to struggle with inner opposition of petty lords, as well as with the insidious crusaders trying to enslave the Lithuanian people.

In the beginning of the production, a conversation takes place on the shore of the Niemen River between Ugnius, a Lithuanian warrior, and several others who desire Audrone, the daughter of a noble Gurinis. Their conversation is disturbed by the report of an enemy invasion by Germanic crusaders. After the enemy is routed, the first to return home is a Prince Kunotas who tells Audrone and her father the false news that Ugnius, the one she really loves, has fallen in battle against the crusaders. Gurinis, completely against the will of Audrone, gives her as bride to Kunotas. After some time, Ugnius himself comes to the castle of Kunotas, and since he is a conquering hero, by custom has a right to Audrone, but she is already unhappily wed. Audrone then realizes how Kunotas has deceived her. At this point, a spy for the crusaders penetrates the castle and proposes a method for Ugnius to get rid of his rival, to which Ugnius acquiesces.

Meanwhile, a civil war has developed among the Lithuanians. Ugnius, conspiring with the crusaders, manages to burst into the room of Kunotas and murder him. However, Audrone, seeing the vengeance of Ugnius complete, repulses him as a betrayer of the fatherland and lights a fire on top of the castle as a sign of alarm. Understanding his guilt. Ugnius turns against his fellow crusaders, bars their way of escape and perishes at their hands. As a price for saving the homeland, Audrone dies as well, but in the end, united Lithuanian warriors free the castle.[32]

Another Lithuanian ballet first went by the name of *The Betrothed* (1943), but later was called *The Rising Dawn*. It depicts a peasant movement which opposed the landlord exploiters, who were in turn protected by the tsarist government. An account of the libretto points out that it shows that the ideas of the Russian revolutionary democrats of the nineteenth century had a vast influence upon the working people of Lithuania.[33]

In the ballet, there are preparations being made for the wedding of two serfs, Antanas and Maryte. However, the local landlord, Daugela, is holding a feast and demands that Maryte and other girls be brought to entertain his guests. Antanas intends to go to the palace and liberate the girls, but a liberal university student on vacation in the village tells him that it would be more expedient to rouse the working people against the landlord and not try to conquer him alone. The "rottenness and moral depravity" of the nobility are shown by revellings which are pictured in Daugela's palace. Antanas breaks into the party, but alone he is ineffective and is beaten and bound. Then the student arrives with a group of aroused peasants for the purpose of liberating Antanas and Maryte. Thereupon the peasants stage a thorough uprising, set fire to the lord's castle, and the ballet ends with a big celebration of their victory.

In spite of its obvious *ideinost'*, the ballet was criticized on several points. For one thing, the critic said, it did not sufficiently emphasize the role of the student in rousing the people. Further, when the landlord took the girls away, the peasants simply went on with their celebration as if nothing had happened. The work of the *corps de ballet* did not meet the reviewer's standards, and he ended his article by saying that the Committee on Affairs of the Arts should "give serious support to the ballet collective in order to help it raise its artistic and ideological level."[34]

The national ballet which was shown at the Lithuanian *dekada* of art in May, 1954, was called *On the Sea Shore*. In the words of the reviewer:

> The creative success of the ballet's composers and producers was first of all determined by the fact that they have based their efforts on social- ist realism, depicting by artistic means all that is new and advanced, showing life in all its variety and the development and movement toward the victory of communism.[35]

The ballet centers about a fishing collective by the Baltic Sea. Marius, a soldier released from military duty, returns to his native village. The collective actively supports this Soviet patriot, and he starts a project for harbor construction. However, there is jealousy in the village. Kaste, the lover of Marius who had faithfully waited for him during the war, is also sought by a young brigade leader named Jonis. When the construction project is finished, the villagers are going to celebrate the opening of the lighthouse connected with it, and Jonis is jealous. A former kulak named Krezas takes advantage of Jonis' ill humor and convinces him he should refuse to go to sea. During a sea storm he extinguishes the lighthouse while the village fishermen are still on the raging waters, but Jonis soon realizes he has fallen into the kulak's wicked plan. To make up for his villainous act, he succeeds in saving the fishermen. The pleased reviewer re- marked further: "The motives of class struggle are clearly seen in the ballet. In emphasizing this aspect the director and producer have chosen the right path. They have raised the ballet's ideological level and educated the working people in the spirit of political vigilance."[36]

LATVIAN NATIONAL BALLETS

Latvia could boast of a well-established ballet company long before Soviet domination in 1940. The founding of serious ballet was the work of Valdemars Komisars, a student of Mikhail Mordkin. However, the growth of the art was aided by émigré Russians such as Alexandra Feodorova, who taught in Riga until 1937, and Michel Fokine, who gave temporary aid, and Soviet guest balletmasters Asaf Messerer and Vasily Tikhomirov. By 1924, the ballet school at Riga had 120 pupils, many of whom were state subsidized. At the Latvian National Opera House in Riga, the ballets of Glazunov, Chopin, Tchaikovsky, and Delibes were all seen as early as 1925 and 1926.[37] By 1937, Latvia had even devised a patriotic ballet in the manner of its Soviet neighbors. The ballet *Ilga* was the story of a battalion of Latvians stationed in Vladivostok in 1917 and 1918, who wished to return to Latvia to serve their country. A lieutenant named Lauva loves the heroine Ilga, but he has to leave her when his ship sails for home. In the end they manage to be united and have a grand wedding with various folk dancers taking part in the festivities.[38]

At their *dekada* in December, 1955, the Latvians performed two ballets, *Amulet of Freedom* and *Laima*. *Laima* again depicts the struggle of the people against their oppressors, the Teutonic Knights. In it, the crusading knights arrive at the celebration of a folk holiday and demand that the people stop the heathenish rites. One of the knights abducts Laima, and there is a ghastly scene in his castle where she is held captive and an attempt is made to force her to accept the faith of the knight. A group of monks in black soutanes stand impassively at first while carrying lighted candles in their hands. Among them, as a symbol of the unconquerable human will, stands Laima. Suddenly, the monks fling down their black garments and engage in wild revelry, while in their midst Laima appears as a symbol of purity and chastity. Just as it seems there is no end to her trials, Laima's

174

betrothed, Austris, and his Russian warrior friend Nikita burst into the castle with their comrades to free her from the dark forces of evil. The basic idea of *Laima,* in the words of the reviewer, was "the great, strong friendship of the Latvian people and Russian people."[39]

Amulet of Freedom is another ballet which "was dedicated to the theme of the heroic struggle of the Lettish people with their well-known enemies—the German barons."[40] In it, a sparkling gem, the amulet, symbolizes freedom. When the gem is in the hands of the people, it is lit by marvelous fires, but it goes out when the enemy appears. The action of the ballet begins at a festival honoring the nuptials of a peasant girl named Lelde and her beloved, Zemgysa. But a baron comes to the festival, and aided by a local elder, a traitor, carries away the amulet. A village musician named Totam inspires the people to storm the castle of the hated baron, and in the end they recover the charmed jewel.[41]

ESTONIA

The third Baltic republic, Estonia, began to develop ballet as an art in the first decade of the twentieth century. Its growth was influenced both by the Russian classical school and by the free dance style of Isadora Duncan, perpetuated in Estonia by one of her followers named E. Ilbak.[42]

A composer, Eugen Kapp, in Soviet Estonia has produced several operas and ballets deemed worthy of Stalin prizes. One of these was the ballet *Kalevipoeg,* first given in 1948 at the Theatre of Opera and Ballet "Estonia" in Tallin, the capital.

In this ballet, Sorts, an evil ruler of a subterranean kingdom, wants to wed a widow named Linda, the mother of the warrior hero Kalevipoeg. Rather than yield to Sorts, Linda begs the help of lightning, which turns her into a rock statue. Kalevipoeg, out to avenge his mother's misfortune, is chosen ruler, but Sorts manages to steal the golden lance and shield which are the emblems of his power.

175

Undaunted, Kalevipoeg goes to Sorts' dark kingdom and struggles with the "beast men." There, the hero succeeds in tying Sorts to a rock with an iron chain which will shackle him forever. The score is built upon Estonian folk melodies, and like many others, could simply be passed by as a folk heroic tale. However, in Soviet hands the *narodnost'* is emphasized, and Kalevipoeg is "the people's hero," who symbolizes a "healthy optimistic perception of life, courage in the struggle against the gloomy survivals of the past, and the bright joy of work and creation."[43]

For their first national *dekada* in December, 1956, Estonia presented a ballet called *Tiina,* based upon a tale of August Kitzberg's. *Tiina* serves the purpose of showing the insidiousness of the feudal system and of religious characters. When Tiina is a little girl, she sees her mother dragged before the village church. There the pastor throws a wolf's skin over her shoulders—a sign that she is guilty of being a witch, a werewolf, and must be executed. The people look upon the scene with horror and then take her little daughter to be raised by Gammaru, the master of an outlying farm. Years later, the family of Gammaru is coming out of church one day. Tiina and Gammaru's son, Margus, have grown up together and now love each other dearly. But there also emerges from the church a girl named Mari, whose parents have arranged her marriage with Margus.

In a later scene a wicked overseer enters with a group of peasants from the local baron's estate. The peasants have let a wolf kill one of the baron's sheep. Tiina begs the overseer to free the herdsmen and not punish them. He refuses and tries to make advances toward Tiina, who resists, which infuriates him. The overseer then gets Mari to take an oath on a prayer book that she has evidence that Tiina is a werewolf, and that she was the one who killed the sheep. Later, Tiina again meets the overseer and some of his friends in a wooded spot. He tries again to embrace her and she bites his arm, drawing blood, thus giving him more evidence for accusing her of being a werewolf. The baron and pastor enter the scene after learning that

176

Mari has testified that Tiina is a werewolf, and they exile her to live in the forest.

Later Margus finds her there, and she begs him to live with her in the woods, but he lacks the courage. Finally, on the wedding day of Margus and Mari, preparations are interrupted by a wolf's howl resounding in the nearby forest. Margus takes his rifle and shoots out of the open door of their hut. A cry comes from the darkness, which makes Margus run out to discover that instead of the supposed wolf, he has shot his beloved Tiina, who dies in his arms, a victim of superstition, of religious beliefs, of mores that subjugated women to cruel, unfeeling barons and their henchmen.[44]

KOMI AND KARELO-FINNISH NATIONAL BALLETS

The Komi Autonomous Soviet Socialist Republic is a far northern region specializing in such economic enterprises as fur trapping and salmon fishing. But Komi was not to be outdone in ballet accomplishments. They, too, produced a national ballet called *Iag-Mort,* named after an evil forest inhabitant who causes trouble by abducting women and tearing up fish nets. Typically, the ballet is described as "an expression of the agelong theme of the struggle of good and evil, of light and darkness," a theme of "great social significance."[45] It was praised for incorporating into the ballet their national folk games in which reindeers are imitated.

The Karelo-Finnish Soviet Socialist Republic was added to the original eleven republics in 1940 and returned to the status of an autonomous republic of the R.S.F.S.R. in 1956. Their national ballet is called *Sampo.* It is based upon a story of a miracle mill, forged by the blacksmith Ilmarinen and his tribe members. The mill was taken away by an evil woman magician named Loukhi, but was again returned to the people. According to the reviewer, *Sampo* was more than a fairy tale to the people of Karelia; it was one of the episodes of the epic *Kalevala,* a poem of work-loving people and their struggle for happiness and freedom.[46]

MOLDAVIA

The Moldavian Soviet Socialist Republic was formed in 1940 after the Red Army marched into Bessarabia, an area which had been the subject of long-standing territorial disputes between Rumania and Russia. A Moldavian Theatre of Opera and Ballet opened in 1955 in Kishinev, based upon an older Musical-Dramatic Theatre which had existed in the town of Tiraspol since 1933. Several ballets have been produced by the company. One of them which particularly follows the established pattern is *The Sisters*. In the Soviet description, it was dedicated to the theme of the overcoming of old, long outlived prejudices amidst the toilers of Soviet Moldavia, the formation of Communist morals, and the triumph of the new over the old.[47]

In the ballet, a girl named Iliana finishes her studies in an agricultural technicum and returns to her native fields and her fiancé, Leontii. Their friends receive Leontii right away into the family of Komsomol, but Iliana's oldest sister Dokiia and her relatives oppose their marriage. According to the old custom, any younger sister may not marry earlier than the oldest, so her family forbids Iliana even to meet with Leontii. This causes the girl to defy parental objections, leave home, and marry her lover anyway. The village then festively celebrates their marriage, and on this day a timid lad named Ionashku declares his love for the proud beauty Dokiia, and general gaiety then rules for the wedding of the two couples.

Another ballet, called *Dawn,* "tells of the heroic struggle of the workers of Bessarabia for reunion with the Soviet Union in 1940." The ballet depicts a concentration camp with all its gloominess and barbed wire, where chainclad prisoners despairingly, realistically enact their exhaustion and misery. In the story a boy named Iona escapes from the camp and meets peasants who shelter him. Together with a young boy from the village, he then takes up his gun to fight for the cause of freedom. The ballet is "concluded by a joyful scene of the freeing of Bessarabia by the Soviet Army."[48]

178

CENTRAL ASIAN NATIONAL BALLETS

UZBEKISTAN

In Central Asia, the villains for ballets are provided by forces which opposed the establishment of Soviet power in this region. Much of Central Asia was annexed by the tsars in the nineteenth century, and after the revolution, many groups inhabiting the area snatched at the opportunity to secure freedom. In opposition to Bolshevik power, there began in the Ferghana Valley of Central Asia a wide, successful resistance movement called the Basmachestvo. Before the revolution, a Basmach was just an ordinary bandit, highly successful in evading tsarist officials. When Bolshevik power threatened to envelop Central Asia, many citizens joined the Basmachi, whom the population now regarded as liberators. Operating as partisans from 1918 to 1924, they made life miserable for Soviet commanders in the area by their uncanny ability to dissolve into a village in the face of pursuers. In 1921, the movement acquired the leadership of the famous Enver Pasha, but he was killed in 1922. Soviet sources like to say that the Basmachi rebellion ended in 1924, but their leader Ibrahim Beck Lakai was not captured and executed until 1931.[49] There are reports that outbreaks of Basmachi fury continued sporadically until the start of World War II. Numerous Basmachi have turned up in the ballets of Central Asia, naturally as vile perpetrators of base and ignoble actions.

Throughout Central Asia, many ethnic groups had a strong bond in their common Moslem faith. According to the ancient Moslem law of the Holy Shariat, women were not to appear in public without being covered by their face veil, the parandja or yashmak, often woven of horsehair. At the time of the Russian revolution, many Moslem intellectuals with a Western, liberal orientation were involved in a movement to secularize their life. At a First All-Russian Moslem Congress held in Moscow in May, 1917, two hundred women were present, an unprecedented occurrence that jarred delegates from Turkestan and the Northern Caucasus. In spite of opposition, the westernized wing of the congress succeeded in passing laws to give women the right to remove their veils in public and to have equal inheritance rights. There were also laws passed prohibiting bigamy and child marriage.[50] However, neither the Moslem Congress nor Soviet power could bring about an immediate change in these customs of inherently conservative people. Economic as well as religious motives were involved, for the government wanted to utilize the labor of women in projects other than the care of their own hearths. In the end, Soviet power won the battle, but not without struggle. In Uzbekistan, for example, the veils were not removed until 1928.

The trials of one real Uzbek dancer named Tamara Khanum (Tamara Artemyevna Petrosian) form an interesting chapter in the struggle. In her youth, women were never allowed to speak to strangers, much less to sing or dance in front of them. If a woman had such talents, they would be displayed only within the walls of her husband's home. Instead, scores of boy dancers performed at local teahouses. Thus, to subjugated women in many parts of Asia and Africa, Tamara Khanum's story provides a compelling drawing card for the Soviet Union. In her, Soviet authorities can point to a Central Asian woman sufficiently liberated under the new regime to become a performing dancer who has earned the highest artistic honors of her country, while being elected to the Supreme Soviet of her native Uzbekistan.

As a little girl, Tamara Khanum left her native village to follow wandering actors. Later, in Tashkent, she went to a local high school where she sang and danced at school functions. Then one day, according to the Soviet accounts, the young women did a courageous and bold act. At a celebration of a victory of the Red Army over some Basmachi, she appeared on a city square and danced with her face unveiled. When her performance was over, Basmachi in the crowd were plotting to seize her, but she merged with the people and slipped away from their snare. In 1923, she appeared in a public theatre, completely breaking the laws, and for several years Tamara Khanum was the only woman actress in Uzbekistan, taking all the roles in a local dance ensemble. Once she did engage three women from the Ferghana silk mills to dance with her. However, one of the dancers named Khalchakhan was killed along with her husband. Their relatives murdered the woman for her dancing, and the man for allowing his wife to do it. After that, Tamara Khanum's other two dancers deserted the group out of fear. It was reported that some Central Asian women, upon seeing her dance without her yashmak, would go home and throw their own veils into the fire, in spite of reactionary males around the household.

Eventually, Tamara Khanum received the opportunity to study dance at the studio of Vera Maya in Moscow. In 1924, she was sent to perform in Paris at a World Exhibition of Decorative Arts. Her dances have always been done in the voluminous, chaste garments and heavy jewelry of Central Asian women, and she had no use for the unclothed "eastern" dancers plying their trade in the Paris music halls. She danced again in 1934 at a world international dance festival in London.[51]

Tamara Khanum has been a tireless performer and teacher, one of the pillars in the growth of the native Uzbek ballet and folk dance groups. One of the early ballets staged by the Uzbek company which she helped establish was named *Shakhida* after the first girl in her village who threw off her veil. One of the most successful scenes in the ballet was reported to be "The Dance of the Removal of the Veil." This ballet was also one of a number of them which dealt with the struggle against the Basmachi.[52]

In the first Uzbek *dekada* of May, 1937, Tamara Khanum danced in a musical drama called *Farkhad i Shirin*. In 1940, she aided in the choreography of the ballet *Guliandom*, depicting a heroic uprising of the workers of Khorezm against the khan.[53] In the second *dekada*, November, 1951, the Uzbek ballet company performed two ballets,

Dream and *Masquerade*. The former was "dedicated to the toilers of a kolkhoz village,"[54] and the latter was based upon a story by the Russian author Lermontov.

In 1951, the Uzbek Alisher Navoi Theatre of Opera and Ballet was verbally chastised on several counts in the wake of the Party condemnation of the opera *Great Friendship* in 1948. For one thing, the accuser, Sh. Rashidov, complained that there were grave deficiencies in the training of musicians and ballet masters for the republic. Serious blame for such an unsatisfactory state lay with the leadership of the administration of the Committee on Affairs of the Arts of the Republic, which did not make efficient use of a wide *aktiv*, a trained and dedicated nucleus of active workers, in their work, and consequently had no really firm supervision of the work of professional organizations and theatres in the republic. Neither had the Union of Soviet Composers nor the Department of Propaganda and Agitation of the Party Central Committee of Uzbekistan been doing their jobs well, in his view. The theatre had violated the direct injunctions of the Party Central Committee by presenting too many pseudohistorical legendary fairy tales which idealized the feudal past to the neglect of contemporary themes. Rashidov said the matter had been a subject of discussion at the Party Central Committee of Uzbekistan, and measures were being formulated to alleviate the situation.[55]

The next year, an Uzbek ballet appeared with the name *Ballerina*, which was a reworking of an older one named *Giulnara*. To understand this ballet it is useful to know that when Stalin imposed collectivization upon the lands of the people of Uzbekistan, the Uzbeks were made to produce great quantities of cotton and other technical, industrial products, at times to the detriment of the food crops. In 1947, the Central Committee of the All-Union Communist Party issued a decree demanding increased production of cotton in the country. It complained that some areas, including regions of Uzbekistan, had notably failed to meet state plans for cotton production in the past.[56] These economic sidelights had much bearing on Giulnara, the heroine of the ballet called *Ballerina,* for the lass was not only a talented dancer, but a fine, happy worker on a cotton-growing Uzbek collective farm as well.

Giulnara loved dancing with a passion and performed in local amateur shows during her spare time. One day students from a choreographic institute came to help celebrate a collective farm holiday, and they were attracted by Giulnara's dancing. Though they thought she had talent that should be developed in a ballet school, Giulnara's father would never hear of her leaving the cotton fields of the kolkhoz. Giulnara, of course, disobeyed him and went to the ballet school anyway. There her progress was so great that she was sent as part of a Soviet youth delegation to perform at an international festival in one of the People's Democracies. When they heard of this back on the farm, her father's heart was softened and he realized that "in the land of the Soviets the work and calling of the ballerina is as important to the state as that of a cotton grower."[57] So, he rejoiced with his daughter instead of condemning her and went to the airport to send the delegation on its way. The final scene is at the international festival, where many young citizens "form an indissoluble union to struggle for peace, rallying around the advanced young people of the Soviet Union."

TADZHIKSTAN

In describing the cultural progress of Tadzhikstan, Soviet sources like to point out that before the revolution there were not even any words in the Tadzhik language for "theatre," "cinema," "opera," "ballet," or "ensemble."[58] However, Tadzhikstan was one of the first republics to have a national ballet ready for its first *dekada* in April, 1941, due perhaps, to their securing the talented services of the stormy petrel, Kasian Goleizovsky.

The ballet which emerged was called *Two Roses,* and it dealt with the period in which the Basmachi tried to rule Tadzhikstan. The "two roses" are Nozgul and Zarragul, the two beautiful daughters of a poor blind Tadzhik peasant woman. Both girls are engaged, but unknown to them, Zarragul's fiancé, Sanghine, is a Basmach. Although they are engaged, a rich bey named Abdurasul decides to abduct the two girls. A detachment of the Red Army comes to arrest Abdurasul, but he manages to get away, carrying the girls with him. Then Sanghine becomes disgusted with the drinking and looting of his fellow Basmachi and joins forces with Nozgul's fiancé, Zamon, who helps the Red Army capture Abdurasul and free the two sisters. As the girls return home, a festive celebration is held in their honor.[59]

Another Tadzhik ballet, named *Dilbar,* seems to be a first cousin to the Uzbek's *Ballerina.* It is another story of the struggle of the people with the "feudal-bey survivals" and like Giulnara, Dilbar is a talented dancer who in spite of her father's protests becomes a successful ballerina.[60]

One of the most successful ballets based upon Central Asian themes started its musical theatrical life as an opera in Azerbaidzhan in 1908, but was adapted for a Tadzhik ballet in 1947. *Leili and Mejnun* is the story of a simple, poetical nomad named Kais, who loves the daughter of the cruel ruler of the town. Because of class and tribal animosities, Leili cannot marry Kais, but is forced instead to marry the distinguished Ibn-Salom. Kais, heartbroken, does nothing but wander around the countryside and the people call him Mejnun, a name referring to one madly in love. A warrior named Nofal and his men help Kais to attack the palace of Ibn-Salom and take him prisoner, but Leili's father will still not let his daughter break her marriage vows and wed Kais. She is locked in a golden cage, and there stabs herself with a golden dagger that Kais had given her. Kais, who secretly penetrated into her cage, finds her dead and falls dead of grief beside her. The production of *Leili and Mejnun* might well be no different from the staging of *West Side Story* or *Romeo and Juliet* in another country. However, it happens to fit well into the Soviet pattern for emphasizing the hard lot of women in pre-Soviet

Central Asia. Its tender poetry has made it popular, and the story was also made into a full movie.[61] In 1964, the Bolshoi Company staged the ballet with the aid of Kasian Goleizovsky. The part of Leili provided an outlet for the unforgettably poetic dancing of one of the rising great young Soviet dance artists, Natalia Bessmertnova.

KIRGIZIA

Kirgizia is another area which the Soviet government can claim lacked a dance tradition before the establishment of Soviet power. This mountainous land was peopled with nomads, and until 1936 it had no musical theatre. In March, 1935, a decree of the Council of People's Commissars of Kirgizia ordered that steps be taken to prepare personnel to establish a musical theatre.[62] In 1937, a ballet troupe began to function in Frunze at a former dramatic theatre. The Uzbek ballet heroine Giulnara and the Tadzhik ballet heroine Dilbar have a strikingly beautiful living Kirgiz prototype in Biubiusara Beishenalieva. In the summer of 1936, talent scouts from the Leningrad Choreographic School came to Kirgizia and saw Biubiusara, then a nine-year-old daughter of a shepherd from Tash-Tyube kolkhoz. Her parents did not want her to go to dancing school, but the Kirgiz government urged them to submit. Beishenalieva, like Tamara Khanum, became a teacher in her republic choreographic school and later was elected a deputy to the Supreme Soviet of the Republic. She also earned honors for the U.S.S.R. at the World Youth Festival in Bucharest. Like many Central Asian dancers, Beishenalieva has given performances for shepherds and road builders on the green mountainsides of her native land. Typically reporting on one of these concerts, an author pointed out that in Kirgizia:

> . . . The dance was once taboo among them. Even simple rhythmic movements in time to music were frowned upon. The appearance of a woman dancer on the stage three decades ago would have been considered sacrilegious by the very same people who were now warmly applauding the popular ballerina.[63]

The Kirgiz people took their turn at producing a *dekada* in May and June, 1939, and in October, 1958. In summing up the achievements of the people, a review of their ballet at the 1958 *dekada* declared:

A dark shade of oppression and deprivation of right, of feudal arbitrariness, of religious prejudice and enslavement of women for a long while darkened the historical path of the talented, proud, freedom-loving people, preventing them from revealing their creative powers.

Now in the friendly family of brotherly republics, they are creating their own culture. Nineteen years ago, they were not able, in the first *dekada*, to show a national ballet. Since then they have created many. With help of the Leningrad Choreographic Institute they prepared the first Kirgiz cadres, opened in Kirgizia a choreographic school, produced talented performers, ballet masters, artists, inspired people. They then created a ballet theatrical repertoire including *Swan Lake, Sleeping Beauty, Raymonda, Anar, Cholpon,* and others.[64]

The latter were their own national ballets, presented at the 1958 *dekada. Cholpon* is a simple girl who fights against a mighty magician, Aidai, personifying the forces of evil, darkness, and destruction.[65] The ballet *Anar* is the story of a couple whose love is tried by a manap, a rich, aristocratic man of the Kirgiz area who also wielded political power. With the aid of his *dzhigitti,* "skilled horsemen," he carries Anar away, but her lover succeeds in bringing about the death of the manap on a mountain waterfall. This ballet was built on pantomime scenes, games, and folk dances—without complicated dance technique, except for the main characters. An actor took one leading part in the original production, leaving the adagios to the few trained dancers available.[66]

BASHKIRIA

In May and June, 1955, the first Bashkir *dekada* was held in Moscow. Bashkiria is not a union republic, but is officially an autonomous republic within the R.S.F.S.R. In 1955, the Bashkir Theatre of Opera

186

and Ballet of Ufa gave the tried and true ballet *Laurencia,* along with one based on native folklore called *Crane Song.* It is another struggle of good against evil, with the forces of good personified by the girl Zaitungul and the shepherd Iumagul. They dream of happiness and love, but a cunning and cruel rich man named Arslanbai stands in their way, trying to possess the girl. Love, of course, triumphs over all.[67]

One very interesting sidelight resulted from the 1955 Bashkir *dekada.* A talented young Bashkir dancer, though his training was meager, went to Moscow to take part in the *dekada.* There, he took his earnings, bought a one-way ticket to Leningrad, and asked for an audition at the famed Choreographic Institute. Though far over the usual age of admission, he was accepted. The youth suffered numerous humiliations, but managed to stay at the Institute long enough to absorb its uniquely fine training. Later, he became known to the world as Rudolf Nureyev.

In 1960, the Bashkirs produced a ballet called *Mountain Tale,* depicting an eighteenth-century uprising of Bashkir prospectors and Russian miners against a cruel tsarist functionary named Mrak-Turkhan, the foreman of the Nogai road. It was said that the ballet "expressively reveals the friendship of the Russian and Bashkir people, their love of freedom, spiritual nobility, and moral strength."[68]

Strong *narodnost'* is evident in a later Bashkir ballet called *Giulnazira,* produced in 1963. The story begins in the fall of 1909, when the inhabitants of a Bashkir village see their relatives off as soldiers. An old man sadly plays despondent music. Into the village comes a rich man. Kasymbai, together with his son Bakhtiiar. Kasymbai is cruel to the peasants, and he brings on the death of Albike, the wife of the village poor man, Shaibek. In order to get revenge on Kasymbai, Shaibek kidnaps his son.

The years pass and the Bolshevik revolution is completed. The kulaks, headed by Kasymbai, show furious resistance to the people's struggle for freedom and happiness. Bakhtiiar, now grown, struggles on the side of the revolution. In one of his skirmishes with White Guards he is taken captive. Kasymbai, fighting with the Whites, recognizes him as his son and demands that he pass to the side of the White Guards. However, Bakhtiiar refuses and dies the death of a hero. The musical score is filled with revolutionary songs, including a march of the Red Army.[69]

KAZAKHSTAN

Kazakhstan was also one of the regions where no dance tradition existed. The explanation was given that in regions such as this, where the feet would sink into desert sands, the people did not engage in dancing, but all this was changed with the development of Stalinist friendship among the Soviet peoples.[70]

In their first *dekada* in May, 1936, Kazakhstan had no national ballet to present. By 1938, *Kalkaman i Mamyr*, a ballet based upon a Kazakh legend, had been written by a Leningrad composer named Vasily Velikanov. An interesting ballet was produced for the second *dekada* in 1958, called *By the Friendship Road*. The libretto was designed to show "the friendship of the Soviet and Chinese peoples."

The ballet opens in a Kuomintang prison, where an executioner hurls about a courageous Kazakh woman named Zhamilia. After being beaten unmercifully, the Kazakh woman falls asleep. In a dream, the joyful and sad days of her life pass before her. She sees the gay holiday in her native mountain village for celebrating the engagement of her daughter to the son of a friend, then an unexpected raid of the Basmachi brings captivity. The dream reveals Zhamilia as a tender, thoughtful mother, blessing her daughter in the revolutionary struggle, while she herself fights valiantly for the cause. "Such is the modest and beautiful heroine of the Kazakh people in the performance of Rakul Tazhieva [the ballerina]," wrote the reviewer, dancer Olga Lepeshinskaya.[71]

For a time, during the years of World War II, Kazakhstan had

188

the eminent services of Galina Ulanova. Under her direction, the Kazakh ballet presented *Giselle* in 1943.[72]

In order to ameliorate his food-production problems, Nikita Khrushchev launched a project of tilling vast areas of virgin land in Kazakhstan in 1954. At this time, large groups of dancers were sent there to bring a bit of cheer to the workers in the bleak wasteland. Brigades of performers from the Bolshoi, Kirov, Stanislavsky Musical Theatre, and Maly Theatre of Leningrad were given quotas to fill each quarter of the year, with a projected plan whereby two thousand concerts would be given as morale-lifters. On one of the tours, the Bolshoi director, Mikhail Chulaki, told the press that "as envoys of the great Russian nation" each performance was for them "a holiday of friendship and brotherhood of the peoples of the one great Soviet family."[73]

Before leaving the area of Central Asia lands, two more groups should be mentioned. In 1955, a Turkmen *dekada* took place in Moscow, where the ballet *The Adventures of Aldar-Qos* was presented. This is a story of a magician who saves a young pair of lovers from interferences in their romance, including the desire of a cruel khan to have the girl, Ene.[74] In 1957, a Tatar *dekada* took place, where the ballet *Shurale* was presented.[75] Both of these ballets were successful enough for major companies to use them in their repertoires. *Shurale* was a forest sprite whose mischief the ballet enacts. When it was staged by the Leningrad Kirov Theatre in 1950, it was almost removed from production before the premiere. This time, the authorities who wished to remove the ballet were urged to let it play once to see if the people liked it before finally removing it from the stage. This was done, the people liked it, and it stayed in the repertoire.

BURIAT-MONGOLIA

The cultural accomplishments of Buriat-Mongolia were somewhat bleak at the time Soviet power was established. This region had a three percent literacy level and no dancing traditions. According to the Soviet explanation, this was due partly to the nomadic existence of its people and partly to religious taboos propagated by 44 Buddhist monasteries and 14,000 lamas in the region.[76]

In October, 1940, and November and December, 1959, the Buriat-Mongols put on their *dekady* in Moscow. No ballet was ready for the first one, but in the second, they had two to show, called *Beautiful Angara* ánd *In the Name of Love*. The former is the story of three characters, Angara, Yenisei and Baikal. They personify the rivers and lake by the same names. Though the work was choreographed by Igor Moiseyev, it brought forth the wry reviewer's comment that "its content was exhausted sooner than the curtain was lowered."[77] However, the Buriat ballerina Larissa Sakhianova is said to be among the top ten in the Soviet Union, and could bring excitement to Angara's part, with or without "content."

In the Name of Love, like dozens of others, tells of the triumph of justice, freedom, and love, involving an uprising of the people against the cruelty of an oppressor.[78]

TRANSCAUCASIAN BALLETS
AZERBAIDZHAN

Azerbaidzhan had its first *dekada* in April, 1938. The absence of a ballet in the first one was made up for in the second in May, 1959, where they performed three of them: *Seven Beauties, The Maiden's Tower* and *Giulshen*.

Maiden's Tower tells of a cruel ruler, Dzhangurkhan. Upon being told that his wife had borne him a daughter, he thinks it is an evil omen and banishes the mother and daughter from the palace. Next, the ballet shows the grown-up girl, Giulianak, being wedded to her lover, Polat. At their wedding holiday the khan suddenly appears, and seeing the beautiful Giulianak demands her for his harem. A nurse-maid vainly tries to point out to him that this is his child, proving it by a jeweled bracelet which he gave her at birth, before he knew

190

she was a girl. To make her submit to the khan's wishes, his soldiers seize Giulianak's lover. She tries to draw out the days before she will have to be the wife of the khan by asking that her marriage chamber would be in a high tower erected from the bottom of the Caspian Sea. When this is built and she is living in it, she hears quick footsteps outside her door one day, and thinking it is the khan, hurls herself from the tower into the sea, never knowing that the footsteps were those of Polat, who had come to rescue her.[79]

In the ballet *Giulshen*, the composer tried to reveal a genuine picture of the joy of labor, and to emphasize the idea of cohesion and unity of feelings of the Soviet people. Giulshen is a gay brigade leader of cotton pickers. She has a friend, Azad, who is an engineer, a builder of the Mingechaur hydroelectric station, which was a key project in the development of this area by the Soviet government at that time.[80] The builders of the dam and the toilers in the cotton fields engage in socialist competition. The two lovers become heads of competing work brigades, wherein they overcome various difficulties and reach their production victories. There is an agronomist named Akhmed who is jealous of the love of Giulshen and Azad. When an explosion takes place at the dam site, Azad hurls himself into the churning waters which have just been released, trying to save some building materials which are being washed away. Akhmed forgets his jealousy and risks his own life to save his comrade. In the finale, there is the usual festival in honor of the opening of the dam.[81]

Seven Beauties is based upon a tale by the poet Nizami Giand-zhevi, with typical additions and new slants by Yuri Slonimsky. The story tells of a young shah, Bakhram, who is lost on a hunt, and a hermit who shows him portraits of seven beauties. They come alive and entertain him, but at daybreak they vanish. The shah then comes upon a young fighter and patriot named Menzer and his simple un-spoiled sister Aisha. The area is ruled by a cruel vizier and the people are willing to support Bakhram, thinking he will be a just ruler. However, the shah connives with the vizier, who wins him over with

191

flattery, and Bakhram preoccupies himself with thoughts of his seven beauties while the vizier goes about setting fire to villages and crops. The village people finally succeed in killing the vizier, and envoys from the people come demanding the abdication of Bakhram. Aisha, who now loves him, also encourages his abdication, so angering the shah that he kills the girl. The people conquer in the end, and Bakhram goes into exile.

Seven Beauties has been relatively popular and has been adopted by the major companies. It is a ballet which could be seen and enjoyed without the viewer being overly disturbed by the weak efforts to preach. However, in case the viewer fails to comprehend the lessons he is supposed to learn, there are always reviewers to teach the desired lesson:

> *Seven Beauties* reveals the sharp and irresolvable conflict between the people—artisans and peasants—and the shah Bakhram, the vizier, and their henchmen. The ballet affirms the idea of the moral-ethical excellence of the people over the spineless government.[82]

GEORGIA

Georgia, the birthplace of Stalin, is a land which has suffered from numerous invasions through the centuries. It was Christianized in the fourth century, and in the eleventh and twelfth centuries enjoyed a period of rich cultural growth when a literary masterpiece, *Knight in a Tiger's Skin,* was written by Georgian poet Shotha Rusthveli. Georgian folk dancing mirrors this cultured past. The women perform graceful, dignified movements in long skirts, while the Georgian men are unique in their ability to dance on their toes. Georgian audiences became acquainted with classical ballet as early as 1852 in Tbilisi, the capital, when dancers from St. Petersburg performed there.[83] Under Soviet power in the 1920's and 1930's, the Paliashvili Theatre of Opera and Ballet was the scene of such works as *Chopiniana, Giselle, Cinderella,* and *Firebird.* Georgia was fortunate in producing a famed dancer, Vakhtang Chabukiani, who served both as a dancer and choreographer for many years with the Leningrad Kirov Company, where he produced *Laurencia* and other works. During World War II, Chabukiani served full time with the Tbilisi ballet, and by the time of its second *dekada*, Georgia had produced several ballets of its own.

One of the early productions, called *Maltakva*, was an attempt to depict the heroes of socialist labor, but it did not find the heartiest reception. The ballet tried to represent the draining of the marshy Colchid lowlands in Western Georgia and to show the improvements in the new collective farm life of the area. The Soviet description admits that the "dramaturgy" was built on a weak conflict basis and was too naive an attempt to agitate the Soviet people to drain the swamps. It pictured workers in the marshes going about the stage with squeaking wheelbarrows filled with gravel, while some dug with pickaxes and shovels. The program described a "Dance of the Labor Process" which reminded some viewers of Foregger's machines. Criticism was levelled at the ballet for giving too much attention to its sick heroine, Tsialy, who was seized with swamp fever. The ballet attempted to reproduce her delirious condition, and dancers entered representing serpents, infusoria, malarial mosquitoes, microbes, and other Colchid swamp inhabitants. In spite of various enemies which were disclosed—there was even a "Dance of Conspirators"—a final scene showed the triumph of the Soviet people in their struggle with nature.[84]

One of the earliest ballets based on Georgian folklore was *Heart of the Hills,* with a libretto by the Georgian poet, G. Leonidze, and the composer, Andrei Balanchivadze. As Chabukiani described it, its theme was that of "the early outbreaks of revolutionary discontent among the Georgian peasants, spontaneously rising against their feudal oppressors."[85]

In the first scene of the ballet, Manije, the daughter of the local

Prince of Eristav, meets the hero, Djardje, as she makes her way to a spring for water. In the second scene, the people are having a holiday when Mouravi, the prince's overseer, appears demanding taxes from the people for the use of the land. The peasants argue, and Djardje fights against the tax collector. Manije's father appears on the scene and hostages are taken to the castle, but Djardje manages to run away. The peasants then go to the prince to free the hostages.

Manije has been promised in marriage to a neighbor, Prince Zaal, and she seeks Djardje's help. On the wedding day, Djardje arrives with a group of peasants disguised in masks. Mouravi recognizes Djardje, and the wedding feast is turned into a battle with Djardje being wounded. Prince Zaal is in the process of dealing him the final knife blow when Manije steps between the two, and the dagger stabs her instead. In the final scene, the curtain lifts, and on a dark background there is seen the smoking castle of the prince which the peasants have burned.

The music of this ballet attempts to weave folk melodies into the score, such as one called "I Am an Old Man, Do Not Kill Me," which are linked with the burdensome past of the Georgian people. In the final scene, the orchestra plays a Georgian melody, the "Khorumi," which was used throughout the ballet as a leitmotiv to express the peasant's will to victory over despotism.[86]

A Georgian ballet named *Sinatle* comes from their word for "light." It is based upon a Georgian legend about a hero named Avtandil who, like Prometheus, conquered the forces of darkness and evil. The story is a typical fairy tale of a tsarina who has no sons until she and the tsar make a pact with the devil, Davrish, who promises them two sons if one will be given to him. The boys grow up and are ready to be betrothed when Davrish appears, claiming Avtandil. Then a big dragon surrounds the city and is devouring the people, but a good fairy gives Avtandil a magic lamp and he kills the dragon, so that "from then on the people can peacefully live and *work*."[87]

The two ballets which were chosen for presentation at the

Georgian *dekada* in 1958 were *Gorda* and *Othello*. The latter was
an adaptation of the Shakespearean play, and its chief merit was the
dancing of Chabukiani as Othello. *Gorda* was about a young sculptor
who turns into a valiant warrior to defend his country against
invaders, and to assure his countrymen the right to "a peaceful, free
working life." He loves the Tsarevna Irema and shuns the love of
Dzhavara, the daughter of a rich prince who tries to beguile him. A
nearby Arab caliph demands Irema as a wife, and her father the tsar
sends Gorda to the caliph to refuse him the hand of Irema. For this,
the caliph is going to kill Gorda, but he jumps out of the window into
the sea. When he arrives home, he marries Irema and they have a son.
Later, the country is invaded by Arabs and the people seek advice
from a fortune teller who is really Dzhavara. She says that the only
way to save the crumbling city walls is to entomb the son of Irema
and Gorda in them. Gorda, however, leads the Georgian army against
the Arabs and dispels the enemy. As can be expected, Soviet critics
said the merit of the ballet was its theme of ardent love for the homeland and willingness to defend its honor, freedom, and independence
against invaders.[88]

With so many fairy-tale ballets to its credit, Georgia had to
produce an impressive contemporary work to save its ideological face.
Among the dozens of productions which ended with an uprising or a
revolt, a few have been presented which portray the U.S.S.R. as the
proponent of world peace. Such a work was the Georgian ballet, *For
Peace*. The dramatic action is described as being admittedly "incomplete." Its hero, named Sergei Sokolov, is the epitome of "the steadfastness and beauty of character of young Soviet patriots." In one scene
in a park he makes love to his girl friend Natasha Petrova. There, in
the description of the ballet, "is depicted the degree of ideological
maturity of the group of young members of the Komsomol, for whom
his feeling for Natasha naturally implies love of the Fatherland, of
his people."[89] On a sunny morning on the shore of the Black Sea, he
and Natasha decide to unite their fates. Their friends, including the

Ukrainian Galia Goncharenko, the Georgian Zoia Rukhadze, and an Uzbek, Rakmanov, dance and celebrate. Suddenly the sky darkens, a column of water flies up from a bomb which an enemy plane dropped in the sea, thus killing Natasha's father. In the next part, the scene switches to the war. When Sergei takes part in a parachute landing, he finds himself in the same park in which he once expressed his love to Natasha, and he sees her there again in his memory. After blowing up an enemy bridge, Natasha, who is a partisan, ends up in a Fascist torture chamber where with proud dignity she somehow shields Sergei from enemy bullets. Zoia Rukhadze, like her living model, is a member of the wartime Crimean underground, and loses her life, as does her friend Galia.

In the final scene, a youth festival is shown where there is a solemn march of the nations, and in it Natasha and Sergei take their place with representatives of China, Hungary, East Germany, and other countries friendly to the U.S.S.R. in 1953. There, each nationality executes national dances praising peace and friendship of all peoples. In the last scene, airplanes fly over; this time they are not messengers of war, but of peace, and they send forth a shower of flowers. In return, the youths send skyward flocks of white doves and toss bouquets as a sign of their friendly greetings. Chabukiani explained about his ballet:

> Our new ballet production *For Peace* is dedicated to the heroic struggle waged by the Soviet people during the Great Fatherland War for the independence of their country. It also portrays the peaceful labor of the Soviet people after the war. . . . The underlying theme of the ballet is the struggle for peace and friendship among nations. In our production we strove to convey through the emotional and expressive medium of the dance those ideas, so highly cherished by the Soviet people. . . . The policy of war, of enslaving people, is something entirely alien to the Soviet people, whose thoughts and aspirations are bound up with peace and creative effort. This evidently explains the warm reception the public has given our ballet.[90]

ARMENIA

Armenia has one of the oldest theatrical traditions of all the nations that have been incorporated into the U.S.S.R. The little country reached a pinnacle of strength from 94 to 56 B.C. under a ruler named Tigranes II. In his capital, Tigranocerta, there was a Greek-type amphitheatre. Hellenistic actors and scholars found a warm reception in Tigranes' court, and his son Artavasdes III absorbed enough of his father's love for the theatre to engage personally in play-writing. Around 300 A.D., Armenia was converted to Christianity, and in the fifth century A.D. enjoyed its cultural Golden Age. The land was eventually drawn under tsarist control, but not without resistance. In 1890, there was founded an Armenian revolutionary party called the Dashnaktsutiun. With the coming of the revolution, the Dashnaks gained a ninety percent majority in the Armenian parliament. Mistrustful of their Turkish, Georgian, and Azerbaidzhani neighbors, the Dashnaks cooperated with British forces who invaded the area in 1919 during the civil war. They also willingly accepted the leadership of the White Russian General Denikin. A territorial dispute between Armenians and Turks made it possible for the Bolshevik Party and Red Army to gain control of Armenia in December, 1920. In February, 1921, the Dashnaks made an attempt to regain power, but their efforts failed, and the leaders fled abroad, carrying on their activities from Western Europe.[91] The Soviet government has never forgiven them for working for agents of imperialism and against Bolshevik power. In revenge, they made them "bad guys" in ballets.

One of these ballets was named *Sona*. Its subject was "the struggle of the people against the hated power of the bourgeois nationalist Dashnaks."[92] It portrays a village where a detachment of Dashnaks brutally attack the inhabitants. The officer Varsham lifts his nagaika against an old miller named Ogan, in whose possession they find the Red Banner. However, the grandchild of Ogan, the beautiful Sona, fearlessly takes the part of her grandfather. Varsham is conquered by Sona's beauty and recoils, but Sona is still led to prison with other peasants. Ogan then turns for help to the soldiers of the Red Army, among whom is Sona's fiancé, Levon.

In spite of threats and tortures, Sona resists the attempts of Varsham to solicit her love. She is led to execution. Varsham, jeering at the prisoners, tramples their Red Banner. The angry Sona then stabs Varsham with a kinzhal, a dagger, then grabs the Red Banner and runs toward the mountains. However, a bullet strikes her, and Sona dies. The Red Army and Levon arrive and vow to avenge the death of the young heroine.

Armenia was one of the few republics to have a ballet to present at its first *dekada* in October, 1939. This fact is credited to the enduring Armenian politician, Anastas Mikoyan, who suggested to the composer Aram Khachaturian that he should write a ballet score for the *dekada*.[93] The result was called *Happiness* in its original version, but the world knows the music as *Gayane*.

As originally given at the *dekada* in 1939, *Happiness* depicted a kolkhoz village drowned in bright sunlight and displaying flowering gardens. The kolkhoznitsas are bidding goodbye to their sons, who are being enlisted into the Red Army. Among them is Armen, who bids a warm goodbye to his beloved Karine.

The next scene shows Armen on duty at the frontier. Some trespassers try to cross the border, but Armen and his friends save the border from being violated. In the process, he is wounded. Back at the kolkhoz, Karine receives word of his wounding and is distraught, but Armen eventually comes home and they are married. At the wedding there are mass dances by the collective farmers and also by many guests who are present: Ukrainians, Georgians, and Russians. The ballet was finished by an "apotheosis-chorus of kolkhozniks and frontier guards, praising the socialist motherland."[94]

Happiness went through several transformations, with each one a little more interesting than the last one. In 1942, the ballet was

produced again under the name *Gayane*. Here, the action takes place
on an Armenian kolkhoz in the midst of the harvest of a rich crop of
cotton. Gayane and her brother are prize workers, but she is worried
about the behavior of her husband, Giko. He is the only one on the
farm who spends his time loafing and drinking. Giko protests against
Gayane's participation in community life and does not want her
working in the cotton fields, so he demands that she stay at home and
not meet with her countrymen, whom he hates. However, Gayane
firmly refuses to submit to his orders. The kolkhozniks are indignant
at Giko's behavior, and a Soviet border guard shields Gayane against
her husband's threats. Gayane's father and friends come to sympathize
with her, and her brother speaks to Giko, whereupon he makes a
confession of his mistakes, but his new humility is only a pretense.
Later, Giko is seen entering a house of saboteurs who commission
him to set fire to the harvest of cotton. Gayane tries to dissuade Giko
from doing this, since she overheard the conversation, but this only
spurs him on. He then bolts Gayane into their house and hides
himself.

Having engaged Giko to do their work, the foreign agents try to
flee the border. In seeking a mountain passage they come to a place
inhabited by a tribe of Kurds "devoted to the Socialist Fatherland."
The Kurds hinder the evil plans of the traitors and report them to
border guards.

Meanwhile, Giko has set fire to the cotton and tries to hide, but
the peasants have put the fire out. Gayane unhesitatingly points him
out as the guilty one. Then the scoundrel threatens a terrible crime.
He seizes their small daughter, runs to a bridge spanning a violent
river, and threatens to throw the girl into a whirlpool if they do not
let him go free. A Cossack officer succeeds in getting the daughter
from him in time, but in the process Giko wounds his wife. However,
the people deliver him to judgment. Eventually, Guyane's wounds
heal and the kolkhoz has a holiday where guests of different nationalities gather. There, "piles of cotton speak of the kolkhoz abundance."[95]

An entirely new edition of *Gayane* was presented at Leningrad in 1952. In this version, the scene opens on a dark night. Amid torrents of rain an unknown figure appears. While examining a map, he looks about, listens, and frees himself from a parachute strap and flying suit. Then he heads toward a distant village in the mountains where lights twinkle.

In the next scene it is spring in the kolkhoz, and all are working happily except Giko, who is not Gayane's husband this time. Gayane, a brigadier, comes into the garden and Giko tries to embrace her. A young shepherd named Armen comes in and Gayane runs to meet him. He has found a brilliant piece of ore high in the mountains at his shepherd's station. Giko looks on in jealousy as Armen shows her his prize.

During the kolkhoz rest-hour there is dancing, and Giko again tries to embrace Gayane. Armen stops him and Giko tries to start a fight, but Gayane steps in between the two men. Suddenly, a group of visiting geologists comes, headed by the chief of the expedition, Kazakov. Behind him comes the Unknown, who has been hired to carry the baggage of the geologists. Gayane asks Armen to show the geologists his ore, and they are interested; they prepare to go on a reconnaissance trip. Armen shows them the map and the Unknown follows attentively. Suddenly Giko approaches the Unknown, a sign passes between them, and an agreement is made.

The geologists return with news that there is a large vein of ore in the mountains. Kazakov decides to go with the other geologists to survey it again and asks Gayane to take care of the sack of ore they have. She puts it behind a rug hanging in her hut. Night falls. The Unknown comes into Gayane's house and pretends to be ill, falling from exhaustion. She runs for water and while she is gone, the Unknown jumps up and hunts for the ore. When Gayane comes back, she understands that the enemy is before her, and he demands to know where she has hidden the ore. They skirmish, and the rug falls, revealing the niche where she hid it. The Unknown binds her hands and steals it, then sets fire to the house. As fire fills the room, Giko enters through a window. Gayane tells him about the Unknown and he is terrified at what he has done.

In the meantime, at their station in the mountains, a shepherd has found the stray parachute. The shepherds then realize the enemy has penetrated the Soviet land. Alarm and indignation fill their hearts. In the valley they see the fire raging and all hurry there. In the brightness of the flames they see flash momentarily the figure of the Unknown. A crowd of kolkhozniks surrounds the house, and the Unknown gets lost in them. He meets Giko and offers him a pack of money, but Giko throws the money in his face and tries to restrain him, being wounded in the process. Gayane runs to his rescue and the enemy aims at Gayane, but Armen runs up, grabs the enemy revolver and the frontier guards surround the enemy.

In the next scene it is fall and the kolkhozniks gather their plentiful harvest, bringing in huge baskets with fruit, wine-grapes, and other foods. Invited guests from the brother republics arrive— Russians, Ukrainians, Georgians, and others. The best brigade of the kolkhoz gets the Red Banner. Kazakov begs the leader to let Armen go away to study, and the leader agrees. Then all engage in their national dances. Tables are spread, and "with upraised glasses all praise free labor and the indestructible friendship of Soviet people and the beautiful Fatherland."[96]

Khachaturian, the composer of *Gayane*, is Armenian, although he never set foot in Armenia until he was thirty-six years old. In spite of the melodramatic plots linked with it, the music of *Gayane* has sold itself to worldwide audiences. Besides its numerous revivals in the U.S.S.R., the ballet has also been given in satellite cities, such as East Berlin, Leipzig, Bratislava, Košice, Olomouc, Sofia, and many others.[97]

Another Armenian ballet named *Marmar* tells the story of a shepherd Arame and his beloved Marmar. Their happiness is thwarted by a Prince Bakur who sees Marmar during a hunting trip and wants her for his concubine. To make Arame forget his loved one, he takes him into his retinue and tries to involve him in the loose life of his palace. The youth is steadfast, however, and Bakur has a new plan. He sends Arame into the kingdom of a three-headed monster in order to secure some life-giving water. Bakur meanwhile tries to win over Marmar, but, being unsuccessful, threatens her with death. However, the forces of nature come to her aid and turn her into a carved rock image which is submerged in an underground kingdom. However, Arame struggles successfully and secures the life-giving water, returns home and brings Marmar back to life with his trophy. Further attempts by Bakur and his party to take the girl induce the usual uprising of the people against the ruler.[98]

In the Armenian *dekada* of 1956 the ballet *Sevan* was presented. The activity of this ballet also takes place in one of the mountain kolkhozy of Soviet Armenia on the shore of Lake Sevan, another prime spot in the hydroelectric development of the area.[99] The characters of the ballet are simple Soviet people—collective farmers, fishers, builders of a hydroelectric station, and Komsomols. The production, according to description, sings of the creative labor of Soviet youth striving for the welfare of the beloved Homeland.

The story tells of the love of a young kolkhoznitsa, Ruzan, for a young engineer, Ruben, who is building a hydrostation on the lake. Another youth loves the girl—Azat, a brigadier of the fishing brigade who is energetic, temperamental, and passionate. However, the success of his brigade has turned his head and he tries to single himself out everywhere and oppose himself to the collective, thus manifesting traits alien to the ethical norms of Soviet society. Azat pursues Ruzan with his love, but the girl spurns him, so he seeks to shame her. Smarting of jealousy, he decides to get revenge against Ruben, whom he considers the cause of his misfortune. A storm arises on the lake and Ruben hurries to the locks of the dam in order to prevent disaster, but Azat puts a barrier in his path. They skirmish and Azat knocks Ruben out, then hides. Water breaks through the dam and floods

202

the kolkhoz plots. However, by heroic force the kolkhozniks succeed in diverting water from the gardens to save the harvest. Learning of Azat's crime, the kolkhozniks expel him from their midst. The ballet is concluded by a kolkhoz holiday on the occasion of the rich harvest and the wedding of Ruzan and Ruben.[100]

These are only some of the many ballets produced in the Soviet Union's drive to develop the national art of its minority groups. Mixed feelings are evoked by reading about them. Few honest critics could deny the obvious crudity and didacticism of many of their attempts. However, lacking some support of these national groups, for whatever motive it was given, the whole world would never have been treated to the wild artistry of Rudolf Nureyev. Neither would Frunze have known the dark-eyed loveliness of Biubiusara Beishenal-ieva, nor would Ulan-Ude have witnessed the elegant grace of Larissa Sakhianova. The world, Frunze, and Ulan-Ude would all be poorer if these artists had never had the chance to develop their powerful talents.

CHAPTER SEVEN

The Driving Forces

La danse, monsieur, n'est pas seulement un
plaisir, un amusement, non c'est une grand in-
terêt social.

—L. HALEVY [1]

THE continuous appearance of new
ballets in the U.S.S.R. which are based
upon social and political themes raises
interesting questions. The briefest introduction into the sophisticated world
of ballet leaves the impression that if the dancers were left to themselves, they would not be inclined toward portraying collective farms,
hydroelectric projects, or some other approved theme which appears
in Soviet ballet. How, then, does the Soviet state assure a continued
production of such works?

The answer lies in the fact that the entire apparatus is state controlled; the production of every material accessory to the art, from
the gigantic theatres to the ribbon on the ballerina's toe shoe is subject
to government approval. With this type of power the state can easily
decree the production of any type of ballet as simply as it can decree
an increase in the production of cotton.

The actual government agency for the control of ballet, as well as
for every other art in the U.S.S.R., is the Ministry of Culture. The
present ministry was formed in a reorganization of the governmental
apparatus which took place after the death of Stalin. Emerging in
1954, it superseded the old Committee on Affairs of the Arts, and is
classified as a Union-Republic Ministry. The head of this important
branch of government is Yekaterina Furtseva, a woman who joined
the Party in 1930 at the age of twenty and rose to power working in

the Moscow Party Organization. In 1952, at the Nineteenth Party Congress, she became a candidate member of the Central Committee of the Party, and in 1956 became a full member of the Party Central Committee, as well as Secretary of the Central Committee, and a candidate member of its Presidium. In 1957 she stood up against the faction called the Anti-Party Group, the enemies of Nikita Khrushchev who tried to dispose him. Shortly afterward, she was promoted to full membership in the Communist Party Presidium,[2] the only woman ever to occupy so high a post in the Party. In May, 1960, although given charge of the Ministry of Culture, she was dropped from the Secretariat. The course of her political career proceeded downward, resulting in her deposition from the Presidium at the Twenty-Second Party Congress in October, 1961. In 1963, Leonid F. Ilyichev, the head of the Agitation and Propaganda Department of the Central Committee of the Party, openly complained about "certain cultural leaders who have been influenced by alien ideas," and who had not controlled the stage sufficiently. Furtseva knew whom he meant, and promptly said that she welcomed Ilyichev's criticism.[3]

In 1968, Furtseva retains her job as Minister of Culture. This position entails great responsibility and brings inherent power of its own, for it deals with all the diverse aspects of Soviet cultural life. Under its aegis are all the theatres, institutions dealing with music or pictorial art, radio, television, museums and circuses, in addition to the coordination of the work of all publishing houses and many libraries. The Ministry "renders assistance" to trade union organizations and other cultural-enlightenment institutions. It also gives guidance to those professional organizations involving various arts, such as the Union of Soviet Composers.[4]

The branch of the ministry which directly affects ballet is the Department of Theatres and Musical Institutions. The major theatres, such as the Bolshoi and Leningrad Kirov, are directly controlled by this department of the central Ministry, though theatres in the Union-Republics are subject to the corresponding lower-level ministry in their own capitals. Theatres submit a quarterly plan of work which the appropriate ministry must approve. This allows the Ministry of Culture to make certain that no offensive productions creep into the repertoire. Bonuses are given if the theatres perform according to their plan. This method of operation has been criticized because productions were given before they had been sufficiently rehearsed, to meet the deadline of the quarterly plan. The Russians are accustomed to approach the production of a ballet in a leisurely manner, rehearsing it until the production is perfected. Therefore, they find the necessity of meeting such deadlines a bit alarming at times.

As an example of its method of control, in 1958 the Ministry of Culture of the U.S.S.R. issued a decree called "On Measures for the Further Development of Soviet Ballet Art." Musical theatres were ordered henceforth to include in their yearly plans not less than one ballet on contemporary or historical themes dealing with the life of the Soviet people. The ministry proposed to lead periodic concourses of balletmasters and producers, so that by working with the Union of Soviet Writers and the Union of Soviet Composers they might obtain librettos and scores for ballets on contemporary themes. It was suggested that the Department of Musical Institutions should systematically inform the theatres of the most interesting ballets that were taking place in the widespread parts of the Soviet Union, as well as in the Peoples' Democracies and other foreign states. The Ministry of Culture urged that more attention be given to the production of ballet films; specifically mentioned were *Sleeping Beauty* by the Kirov Ballet and *Red Poppy* by the Bolshoi.[5]

The Ministry also urged that the magazines *Teatr* and *Sovetskaia Muzyka* and the newspaper *Sovetskaia Kul'tura* give better reports on what was occurring in Soviet ballet. Those connected with ballet have periodically complained that they have no special journal dedicated to the dance, a just complaint for a nation having so much to report in this field. However, in the U.S.S.R., where every printing establishment is state-owned, there is no possibility of such a magazine appearing unless the government allocates the paper, the printing plant, and the personnel.

In the past the pictures which accompanied articles about ballet in the musical and theatrical journals were very small, and often with such poor focus that the dancers could not be identified. This, however, has improved in recent years. An English journalist writing about Soviet ballet wanted pictures of Semenova dancing at the Bolshoi. Semenova had wanted to use her own photographer and had asked the journalist to secure permission from Narkomindel. Permission was denied, and the journalist had to use pictures of the ballerina which had been taken during Semenova's visit to Paris in 1935.[6]

The Bolshoi Theatre has a five-story factory for production of such items as ballet slippers, costumes, wigs, leotards, and other ballet accouterments. Since it employs a sizable labor force of about 2,500 people—more than the number of spectators which the theatre can accommodate—state subsidies are necessary to sustain it.[7] Therein lies both its strength and its weakness.

The state would be powerless to demand that a theatre mount a certain type of ballet unless the personnel were capable of producing these works. Such ballets are not always made or performed willingly. One emigré dancer, when asked how the ballerinas portraying the role of a particular revolutionary heroine liked the part, immediately answered, "We hated it." However, the dancers and régisseurs learn what is expected of them in this respect during the years of their training and act accordingly if they want to continue to dance in the U.S.S.R. A dedicated dancer would rather dance than eat; in the U.S.S.R., in order to be able to do both, the dancer at times has to compromise a little bit.

IDEOLOGICAL FORMATION IN THE CHOREOGRAPHIC INSTITUTE

The Soviet Union points with pride to its choreographic institutes, which serve as centers for teaching the technique of ballet, as well as for inculcating a Communist mentality and forming a spirit of collective responsibility in the performers and régisseurs.

The boast is made that entrance to these schools is possible to a certain number of students each year from any segment of society, if they pass the rigid tests.[8] In Leningrad, sixty percent of the pupils are said to come from the working class and the rest from the intelligentsia.[9] A panel of doctors and experienced teachers determine whether the applicant's physical makeup and inherent talent will fit him for the career. Soviet sources like to contrast the present policy to that of the past, when the school did not admit students from the entire tsarist domain. In tsarist times there were definite stipulations about the background of pupils. For example, on August 21, 1888, a special statute was enacted which regularized certain aspects of the life of the imperial choreographic schools. The institutions were to receive as students nine- to eleven-year-old children of the Christian faith, Russian subjects, who had a suitable physical makeup. In addition, the young candidate had to know how to read and write Russian, had to"know the necessity of prayer," and at least have a beginning knowledge of numbers.[10]

There are now state choreographic schools in every capital of the union republics of the Soviet Union, but the two leading schools of ballet in the U.S.S.R. are the Moscow Choreographic Institute, which works in conjunction with the Bolshoi Theatre, and the Leningrad Vaganova Choreographic Institute, which works with the Leningrad Kirov Theatre. In the upheaval caused by war and revolution, both experienced a period when their doors were closed to students. Leningrad's period of inactivity was comparatively short compared to the situation in Moscow. There, the school closed in May, 1918, and remained closed for several years. In postwar years, some schools continued to operate for a time under private auspices, but gradually *Narkompros* took control of them. Ballet students, like all students, were given special rations during the difficult years, and if the school was under the jurisdiction of *Narkompros,* the rations were larger.[11]

208

However, some private schools continued to exist throughout the period of NEP. In 1929, an article in *Rabochii i Teatr* urged that the remaining private schools should be liquidated because of their "infamous exploitation of our youth."[12]

From the very early years of Soviet power, students in these ballet schools were required to take courses on the socialist movement, on Russia's political situation and its social development. Few arts demand as much dedication from its practitioners as ballet. In a dancer's life, long hours of daily, laborious practice drain his physical energy, and a real artist of the ballet is consumed by one aim: to perfect the art he loves. Understandably, many of the youths forced to take these courses shared the opinion of Igor Schwezoff, who studied in Leningrad:

> Nobody liked to have to do this; we were too enthusiastic about dance and the theatre to care anything for social or political matters; but it had to be taken with good grace—the pill to which our dancing was the sugar coating.[13]

Attention to ideological training was also apparent in the Bolshoi School of Moscow, once it opened. There "political-literacy" was introduced into the history course early in its existence.[14]

The choreographic institutes could scarcely remain apart from the controversy about the usefulness of ballet which took place in the 1920's. In 1929, a stormy meeting of the artistic council of the Leningrad Choreographic Institute took place. There, in order to answer the strident voices which had complained that ballet was not capable of taking its part in portraying Soviet life and inspiring Soviet man, the school introduced new subjects into the curriculum, including more character, acrobatic and grotesque-eccentric dancing. In a new five-year plan formulated in 1929 for the school, it was proposed to replace classical training in the first year with Swedish gymnastics, joined to elements of classical exercises. In all the remaining classes, less attention was to be given to ballet classics, and obligatory physical training was to be introduced.[15] This period was short lived, however, and the school soon adopted the strictly classical method of Agrippina Vaganova.

The decade of the 1930's brought significant changes in the choreographic schools, as well as changes in their official titles. In 1931, the Moscow school was officially called a *teknikum,* and in 1937, an *uchilishche,*[16] with Leningrad following suit. The number of choreographic students of the schools was greatly augmented in these years. In 1927, there had been 186 pupils in Leningrad, but by 1933, the number had grown to 466. There had been a seven-year course of training, which was no longer considered adequate, and a nine-year course was created. A revision of the general program of education was made, and "it was still more permeated with social-political content,"[17] with serious attention being given to history of the arts, including not only ballet history, but that of music, literature, graphic arts, and theatre in general. Similar changes took place in Moscow. Of special interest there was the introduction of a class of Choreodrama, taught by Igor Moiseyev, in which the students studied ways to express contemporary themes in dance. According to one of the school's administrators, this was one of the first attempts to apply the system of acting devised by Konstantin Stanislavsky to Soviet choreographic education.[18] The special method of Stanislavsky is now obligatory in all Soviet theatrical education, where it is employed to aid the portrayal of realism.[19] The Moscow institution also opened an *aspirantura,* an extended course for the training of Soviet choreography specialists. In 1937, the first class graduated from this department.[20] In later years, it prepared teachers to send to new schools in the union-republics.

Some idea of the actual time devoted to political education can be deduced from the hours which such training occupied in the advanced course in Moscow in the mid-1930's. In the first year of training, the course included three hours each week of history of the U.S.S.R., one hour of economic geography, one hour of military science, and four hours of history of the arts, including history of literature, the theatre, ballet, and art in general. In his second year, the student was exposed to two hours of political economy, one of economic geography, and four hours of history of the arts. In the final year, one hour a week was devoted to Leninism, one to the history of the Communist Party, and three to history of arts.[21] It must be remembered that in all of the history of arts, texts and lectures would be written and delivered from the very special Marxist-Leninist viewpoint, heavily impregnated with quotes from Lenin and Stalin, contrasting the art of the decadent bourgeois West with the healthy merits of socialist realism.

In Leningrad a pedagogical department was introduced in 1934, and "in the program of the pedagogical division, social-political subjects occupied a greater place.[22] According to the official account, this new emphasis being given to social-political subjects was soon evident in the work of the teachers and students, with a greater interest being shown toward Soviet themes. With special pride, they pointed to a contemporary concert number dealing with a frontier guard by E. P. Snetkova-Vecheslova.

The next step for Leningrad was the creation of a balletmasters' department in 1937, and as the Soviet accounts explain, such a job in their system needs special training:

> In a great measure it demands contemporary understanding of the tasks of Soviet Theatre, and the knowledge to evaluate its creativity critically, which of course, is not possible without a mastery of the theory of Marxism-Leninism.[23]

With this in mind, the program for the balletmaster was formulated, and the authors assure us that the teachers at the school and its pupils "conscientiously strove in these years to realize, in their modest sector, the will of the Soviet land and the ukases of the Party."[24]

Periodically, conferences were called to deal with questions of the ideological and cultural education of the future Soviet ballet actors. In 1938 in Moscow the first conference of this type took place. It was attended by teachers from Leningrad, Minsk, Sverdlovsk, and Kiev. At the conference, an attempt was made to formulate a united program. Their discussion brought out the fact that in former times only technique had been studied, but now their task was not simply to prepare dancers, but to train ballet actors able to portray the new heroes who were appearing in Soviet ballet performances. The young cadres had to learn how to reveal by means of their art the rich new inner world of the Soviet people. For this purpose, the conference discussed the further application of the method of Stanislavsky in ballet. In addition, according to the report of the meeting, "One of the cardinal points in the work of the conference was the discussion of the question of ideological-political education of the students." Recent efforts in this line by the Moscow choreographic school were held up as models for the rest of the participants at the meeting. In the Bolshoi school, the administration had arranged meetings of the pupils with Soviet aviators and with participants in the 1939 skir- mishes in Mongolia between Japanese and Russian soldiers in the area of Lake Khassan. Concerts were given by the students for Spanish students and for "the valorous warriors of the Red Army." The students had taken part in discussions concerning the international situation and the heroic struggle of the Spanish people. As the Mus- covite teachers affirmed, "all of this had undoubtedly a positive influence on the development of patriotic feelings on the part of the youthful students."[25] Work on a contemporary theme which emerged under the new emphasis was one by V. Bourmeister called *Granatometchiki*, "Grenade Throwers," in 1938. This ballet used music by the Spanish composer Albéniz. It "was penetrated with courageous heroism" and was "a worthy response of the young genera- tion of Soviet artists to the heroic struggle of the Spanish people against Fascism."[26]

In 1939, it was decided that Leningrad needed to deepen its political-education work. A systematic series of lectures and study courses was organized dealing with dialectical materialism, with methodological questions about art history, and with "A Short Course of the History of the Party." "Scientific" workers of the State University and Art-History Institutes were invited to deliver these lectures and guide the study groups.[27]

During wartime, the Bolshoi School was evacuated to Vasilursk on the Volga. There, they gave concerts for wounded soldiers in hospitals, and by such contacts "showed the children the grandeur of those freeing the country from Fascist oppressors." Their political education as well as choreographic education was carefully nurtured during the evacuation period, and the students heard such lectures as "Twenty-Five Years of the Great October Revolution," and "The Course of the Great Fatherland War." The displacement of war seemed to make little difference in the quality of its graduates, for Maya Plisetskaya and Raisa Struchkova both were graduated during these years.[28] The Leningrad Choreographic Institute was evacuated at first to the village of Polazne and then to Molotov, where the Kirov company was stationed. Classes continued in Leningrad for some who stayed during the siege.[29]

After the war, the choreographic institutes were involved in an intensification of ideological training which took place starting with Zhdanov's decree of August, 1946, as described by the Muscovite administrators:

> The care of the party concerning questions of special education [meaning political indoctrination] appeared in a series of investigations of schools by the raion committee of the Party at the end of the 1947–1948, when the *uchilishche* was given concrete directions for correcting its educational process.[30]

Guided by these decisions, the Communist Party members on the school's staff led an energetic struggle for strengthening the ideological-political training, qualitatively raising its level and bringing it into accordance with the mandates of Zhdanov which repeatedly appeared in *Pravda*.

In April, 1950, in conjunction with a review given by the pupils of the many ballet academies, there took place a second conference on choreographic formation. The basic idea of this conference, summoned by ukase of the Committee on Art Affairs, was to plan and urge a united system of training. Three questions were discussed especially: the raising of the level of ideological-political education of the future artists; the means to deepen the links of Soviet choreography with folk creativity; and the quality of "special education." At this meeting, speakers included L. M. Lavrovsky, artistic director of the Bolshoi; N. I. Tarasov, head of the department of classical dance at the Bolshoi; and N. P. Ivanovsky, artistic director of the Leningrad Institute. This time the conference reported the usual lack of work on Soviet themes, as well as a serious deficiency in the teaching of ballet history. In addition, insufficient attention was given in the courses to the struggle of realistic and antirealistic tendencies. As a result of the meeting, the older principles concerning the training of the dance actor were affirmed: they concluded that "only the actor, educated in the spirit of Soviet ideology, might fruitfully work on the creation of a form of art near and understood by the people." The conference speakers urged that the student should learn more character dance and should study methods of revealing the ideological content of music. The general aims of the school were reaffirmed: "The Soviet ballet school attempts to arm the young ballet generation by means of new, clear, mighty, and expressive choreographic speech, to answer to the tasks of socialist realism in ballet."[31]

In the same year, 1950, the Ministry of Higher Education of the U.S.S.R. ratified a set of "Regulations of the Choreographic Uchilishche in the State Order of Lenin Academic Bolshoi Theatre of the Union SSR." This document assured Bolshoi graduates a general education fully equal to that of the middle schools—thus "arming the future artists of the ballet with authentic scientific knowledge and a Marxist-Leninist outlook."[32] With the new program, "the creative method of socialist realism became a leading source in the education and formation of Soviet choreographic cadres." The program aimed to inculcate the students with the principles of Communist morals, and to develop within them the Communist attitude toward work.

Within the Bolshoi School there was organized a methodological department, a group formed for the purpose of discussion and testing new ways of teaching and producing new plans of study. In 1952 and 1953 they studied such problems as the application of the system of Konstantin Stanislavsky to choreographic art, as well as the problem of the introduction of elements of folklore into classic dance. In 1952, it was also reported that the methodological department was preparing a paper on "The Reactionary Essence of Contemporary Ballet of the Capitalistic States."[33]

At the April, 1950, meeting the participants had discussed the possibility of widening the school's concert repertoire by creating dances on contemporary Soviet themes, using more of the works of Soviet composers. Thus, in the fall of 1950, there was introduced at the Bolshoi School a new subject: Studies on Contemporary Themes, taught by V. Varkovitsky. In the course of the school year in each class there were contemporary studies, using themes dealing with such subjects as the revolutionary past of the Fatherland, the heroic contemporary life, the work of the Komsomols, the life on the country kolkozy and of Soviet school children, the friendship of peoples of the U.S.S.R. and the countries of the Peoples' Democracies, and the struggle for peace. These dances were created by the teachers and the pupils themselves, and it was obligatory for a pupil in the course of the teaching year to present one such independent composition. In the school recital, the children danced such works as *March of the Suvorovites,* undoubtedly honoring the eighteenth-century Russian General Alexander Suvorov. *Chapaevtsy,* showing little warriors imitating the glamorous deeds of the heroic Civil War partisan fighter

Chapaev,[34] the hero of a novel by Dmitri Furmanov, was probably not as exciting as the famous film also based upon the novel, but for shaping young minds, it was ingenious pedagogy.

In 1958, a Moscow institution, the Lunacharsky State Institute of Theatrical Art, established a department for the preparation of régisseur-balletmasters and has produced many talented graduates. The school, which is named GITIS, is empowered to bestow the highest academic titles and degrees which are quivalent to those granted by major educational institutes in the U.S.S.R. It has faculties for training theatrical, and ballet historians, and critics, and for research in Marxist-Leninist esthetics and other topics dealing with art and the theatre. The institution is also responsible for helping to draw up curriculum programs, study manuals, and outlines for new theatrical schools.[35] As an example of its work, a program drawn up in 1954 for the training of régisseurs assures the student that:

> Soviet theatre is an active bearer of the policy of the Communist Party and Soviet government. The activity of the régisseur in the theatre must be penetrated by the spirit of Communist ideology and Party spirit, of boundless devotion to socialist native land. The creative method of the Soviet régisseur is the method of socialist realism. The régisseur must know how to reveal the richness of Soviet reality and the superiority of the Soviet system, its culture and its art over the system, culture, and art of the bourgeois countries.[36]

From this research institution, several works on the history of ballet have emerged. Olga Martynova, a former ballerina of the Bolshoi Theatre, wrote and defended a dissertation on "The Creative Work of Yekaterina Geltser," and by unanimous vote of the sixteen members of the academic council she was granted the degree of Candidate of Arts. The magazine *Soviet Woman* pointed out that "before the revolution it could not have occurred to people that a ballerina could merit an academic degree"[37]—a statement that no one would challenge.

The schools at Moscow and Leningrad have been the focal points from which ballet training has been extended from Novosibirsk to Minsk, from Komi to Kazakhstan. A few individuals entered the choreographic institutes in the early 1920's from the outlying regions, such as Vaktang Chabukiani from Georgia, who studied in Leningrad, and Liubov Voinova-Shikanian of Armenia, who finished at the Bolshoi school in 1925. However, the real impetus to the development of national ballet began with the heated drive of the 1930's to give the national arts more recognition. In 1934, the Leningrad *teknikum* undertook measures in conjunction with the People's Commissariat of Education in the various Union-Republics to help prepare ballet cadres for the outlying regions.[38] Talent scouts searched out the local children who were promising candidates; when a substantial number from a given region would study at a major school, they were kept together as a national unit and received instruction in their own language from native teachers.[39] In 1961, out of 380 pupils registered at Leningrad, 260 were day students. The education of the national groups was done with great care, for the schools believed that the U.S.S.R. must educate its foster children to become politically conscious citizens who upon returning to their homeland would be the bearers of Soviet choreographic culture.[40]

The first groups of graduates from the national units fulfilled this goal and returning home passed on the balletic torch to students from the deserts and the mountain valleys. Eventually it was possible for their compatriots to see *Swan Lake* along with the ballets dealing with local lore and characters.

In 1946, a policy was inaugurated to bring groups of students from the satellite countries to Moscow and Leningrad for choreographic training. In 1955, in the post-Geneva atmosphere of goodwill, Anastasia Stephens, the daughter of Edmund Stephens, a *Time-Life* correspondent in Moscow, was allowed to study at the Moscow Choreographic Institute.[41] According to the report of a Hungarian student at Leningrad, they were free not to attend the political seminars and classes which Soviet students had to attend.

Komsomol units became an early part of the life of the choreographic schools, playing "no small role in the development of the community life of the Institute."[42] In one year, out of twenty-one students finishing at Leningrad, nineteen were members of the Komsomol unit, and six of them were destined to be future soloists. At the Komsomol meetings they would discuss the new roles they were preparing, and what they had read in preparation for their roles. They also expressed and discussed their opinions about the characters they were to portray. Such discussions were an effective tool in enabling the students to penetrate the "inner world" of their characters, and to interpret their heroes and heroines in the light of their ideology.

Komsomol units also exist in theatres, and at times they sponsor specific community projects, such as visiting a certain factory, army camp, or hospital. A part of the new Communist morality is the practice of openly criticizing the conduct of an errant member. Raisa Struchkova and her husband, Alexander Lapauri, were members of the theatrical Komsomol unit at the Bolshoi up to the age of thirty, and both have agreed that the organization helped them greatly in their work. Struchkova recounts that during her second year at the Bolshoi, while playing the role of Maria in *The Fountain of Bakhchisarai,* she missed a cue and ruined the program. At the next Komsomol meeting, her comrades held a *kritika,* and she was told that she was getting "too big for her boots." Struchkova declared she had never forgotten the lesson, and "it did me a power of good."[43] Pressure is often put upon some individuals to join the Komsomol. Rudolf Nureyev mentions that such pressure was exerted upon him, but he resisted, although both his parents were members of the Party.[44]

REWARDS FOR UNDERGOING TRAINING

The program of training which is required for the students of the choreographic schools is rigid and exacting. However, those who are able to take it know that they are receiving some of the best training

218

in the world for their art. Further, all expenses for the nine-year course of training are completely underwritten by the government—right down to the dance slippers. In their last four years of training, students can receive a stipend.[45] The choreographic schools also have the use of special vacation camps in the summer, and one American visitor to the Leningrad school remarked that the meal she had been served there was the best food she had during her stay in the Soviet Union.[46]

After graduation, the dancers are assured a steady career. Many of the graduates are taken into the Bolshoi or Kirov companies. Others may join the Maly, the Stanislavsky Musical Theatre, a theatre in the Union-Republics, or one of the many folk dance companies. After twenty years of service, a dancer can retire with a pension of thirty to fifty percent of his salary, but many prefer to teach. Galina Ulanova retired at a pension of 4,000 [old] rubles a month—1,000 rubles more than the pension of Nikolai Bulganin, who retired shortly before she did.[47] Ulanova's previous salary had been 6,000 rubles a month; this was the basic amount paid for her "norm" of five or six performances each month. If she danced more, her salary was increased. At the same time, a member of the *corps de ballet* made about 1,000 rubles, while Rudolf Nureyev reported that he made 2,000.

Sol Hurok once remarked, "Consciously or unconsciously, the Russian adores the artist, denies the artist nothing."[48] His statement, eminently true during tsarist days, still describes life in the present Soviet state, despite its claims of being a classless society. In tsarist times, there existed the custom whereby an artist could have a benefit performance after a stated period of service. Mathilde Kschessinska requested such a benefit performance after ten years on the stage and received it,[49] though less favored individuals had to serve twenty years before obtaining such a privilege. At these performances, the artists to be honored were allowed to keep a portion of the ticket sales, and they were showered with costly jewels, laces, and other gifts from admirers including the royal family. As a result of the accretion of such gifts, plus her handsome salary, Kschessinska was believed to be one of the richest women in Russia in her day. The days are gone when a ballerina is showered with jewels, but there are other compensations.

In 1939, to commemorate the sixtieth birthday of Stalin, a decree of the Council of People's Commissars established the Stalin prize to reward distinguished work in the many fields of art and science, thus formalizing the adulation which never had disappeared from Russian life.[50] A top Stalin prize carried a monetary reward of 100,000 rubles, while others amounted to 50,000 and 25,000 rubles. Among the first group of recipients of Stalin prizes were Natalia Dudinskaya, Olga Lepeshinskaya, Asaf Messerer, Marina Semenova, Galina Ulanova, Tamara Khanum, and Vakhtang Chabukiani.[51]

After the de-Stalinization campaign was inaugurated by Nikita Khrushchev in 1956, the Stalin prize became the Lenin prize, with a marked decrease in the number awarded. Efforts are made to display the prizes as rewards from "the people." Nominations are requested in the press, and appropriate sectors of the populace promptly respond. For examples, in 1962, a letter appeared in *Pravda* from the Collective of the Moscow Machine-Tool Factory "Red Proletariat" nominating the Moiseyev Folk Dance Ensemble for a prize,[52] which the ensemble later received. In the end, the recipients are chosen by a special committee which operates with the blessing of the Ministry of Culture.

There seems to be a growing practice for the Union-Republics to bestow laurels on their own native sons. In February, 1965, the Council of Ministers of the R.S.F.S.R. announced that in 1966, twelve prizes of 2,500 rubles each would be awarded for the best works of art produced in the Russian Republic in 1965.[53] Régisseurs, directors, balletmasters, choreographers, artists, and performers of dramatic and children's theatres are eligible. The Georgian Republic adopted a similar practice earlier, with prizes named to honor the Georgian poet Shotha Rusthveli. Besides these lucrative Soviet "Oscars," the government also bestows titles quite comparable in esteem to the British "Dame" or "Sir" carried by such artists as Margot Fonteyn and Frederick Ashton of the Royal Ballet. In the Soviet press, these titles are never omitted. The highest award is that of "People's Artist of the U.S.S.R.," which about a dozen ballet stars have received. The title "People's Artist of the R.S.F.S.R." or of another Union-Republic is more common. There are also lower-ranking "Honored Artists." The government also grants "Orders," such as the "Order of Lenin" or the "Order of the Red Banner of Labor." Dancers are at times also awarded Merit Badges and Labor Excellence Medals.

In Soviet society, the dancer is considered to be a real artist, a member of the intelligentsia, and not just a performing entertainer. In March, 1966, when the writers Andrei Siniavsky and Yuri Daniel were under arrest for having their works published abroad, a group of twenty-five Soviet intellectuals drew up a petition to warn the Party officials that any reversion to the days of Stalinism and the "cult of the personality" would not be accepted by the people or by Western Communist Parties. Noted writers and scientists, such as Viktor Nekrasov and Pyotr Kapitsa, signed the document, as did the ballerina Maya Plisetskaya.[54]

Many dancers, both non-Party and Party members, have taken part in the community life and its government. Among these are the venerable Agrippina Vaganova, who in 1939 was chosen as a deputy in the Kuibyshev Raion Soviet of Workers Deputies in Leningrad.[55] Galina Ulanova was also a deputy of the Leningrad Soviet of Workers Deputies when living there before the war.[56] After the war, when she took up residence in Moscow, she became a member of the Moscow City Soviet.[57] Olga Lepeshinskaya has served several terms in the same body, and Raisa Struchkova was elected to it as a representative of the Sverdlov District, the area in which the Bolshoi is located. Struchkova would receive constituents every first Monday of the month in a special room in the Bolshoi set aside for the purpose.[58] In 1966, ballerina Nina Timofeyeva took her place as deputy to the Supreme

Soviet from the Sverdlov district.[59] Several of the Central Asian dancers have held similar positions, including Tamara Khanum and Biubiusara Beishenalieva.[60]

Besides the official recognition and material rewards, theatrical artists have always been afforded many privileges not listed in the statute books in the U.S.S.R. In the early years, when Mathilde Kschessinska tried to induce her brother to migrate West, he replied that he would prefer to stay in Petrograd, for there artists had exceptional privileges and suffered few deprivations.[61] In 1933, while famine wracked vast areas of the U.S.S.R., a musician at the Vakhtangov Theatre reported that at their sumer camp, they received rations given only to responsible Party and government workers, and that he never before had as much good food as he enjoyed during that summer.[62] Their position has entitled high ranking artists to obtain preferential housing at times when ten ordinary people might have to occupy one room. Top-notch artists would also be able to buy fine clothes, cars, and many other luxury items unavailable to the ordinary citizens. This contrast in living standards may have been a factor in inducing artists to submit to the production of works which they knew were not artistic. It was the price paid for living a privileged life at a time when much of the population was existing in grinding poverty, with accompanying hunger and bad housing.

There are other intangible advantages. Tamara Karsavina's brother was once summoned before the Cheka, the secret police, for questioning. Karsavina reported:

These nocturnal examinations were particularly ominous, and my brother had incurred their [the Cheka's] special wrath. The Commissar was stern; he put before my brother one of the incriminating points: "You are in correspondence with abroad. Who are your correspondents?" "My sister." "What is her name?" "Same as mine: Karsavina." "You are the brother of Karsavina!" The Commisar veered around in his revolving chair. "Giselle is her best part, don't you think?" "I can't agree with you," said my brother, "I consider the *Firebird* one of her finest achievement." "Oh, do you?" The conversation wandered on to the principles and aims of the art; the prosecution was forgotten. "Won't you write to your sister?" asked the Commissar at parting. "Tell her to come back. Tell her she will be received with honours." My brother's sentence was to be exiled with all his family, the Government paying all the expenses.[63]

POLITICAL EDUCATION OF THEATRICAL WORKERS

Several agencies exist for the purpose of continuing the ideological education of theatrical workers after they have left the choreographic schools. One of these groups is the Russian Theatrical Society. This organization began in 1883 in St. Petersburg to help achieve a better social and legal status for actors in Russia. In the present day, the society still offers material assistance to theatrical people, although much of this type of service is now handled by trade unions. The RTO has two houses in which retired veterans of the stage can live, as well as six houses of rest. One very important work it performs is the manufacture of stage make-up, scenery, devices for sound effects, and various tools of the theatre.[64]

Perhaps its most significant work is in the educative role it plays. At the House of Actors in cities such as Moscow, Leningrad, Kazan, and Krasnodar, lectures and seminars for artistic workers are organized on topics that are being emphasized by the Party at the time. To aid its work, the RTO has a bibliographical department with vast reference files and a library of over 130,000 books dealing with theatrical questions. From this they send out "consultative materials" to the People's Democracies.[65] In conjunction with the Union of Writers R.S.F.S.R. and the Ministry of Culture, it puts out the magazine *Teatral'naia Zhizn'*, "Theatrical Life."

As examples of their work, in 1952, a group in the State Scientific Research Institute of Theatre and Music had made a special study of the inheritance of Konstantin Stanislavsky. This group, in cooperation with RTO, organized a series of lectures for workers of Moscow theatres. These included "Marxism and the Question of

Linguistics for Soviet Theatrical Art" and "The Leninist Theory of Expression and the System of K. S. Stanislavsky." Both of these were given by *kandidats* of philosophy in the research institute. There are corresponding theatrical societies in the Union-Republics, and these same lectures were given in different cities of the R.S.F.S.R.[66]

From the point of view of ballet, an interesting meeting took place in 1964 involving the All-Russian Theatrical Society, the House of Actors, and a special discussion club of the Bolshoi Theatre, which met to examine a book by Rostislav Zakharov called *The Art of the Balletmaster*. Zakharov's work was the subject of rather scathing *kritika,* and the general conclusion was that he gave himself too much credit in it, and that the work should not have been published without more consultation from other ballet workers. Igor Moiseyev pointed out in the discussion that the work did not reveal anything new about Soviet ballet, nor anything noteworthy about the problems of contemporary themes in ballet.[67]

In various cities, *Rabis,* the artistic trade union, has a headquarters which serves as a gathering place for similar artistic discussions. In Moscow, a filial branch of the University of Marxism-Leninism has existed in the Central House of Workers of Art since 1945. In 1952, it was reported that during the evening sessions of the previous year, eighty leading artists of the theatre finished the course, declaring afterwards that they could then more easily understand the ideological aspects of their job. Their courses had included lectures on the popular topics "The Leninist Theory of Expression and the System of Stanislavsky" and "The Moral Makeup of Soviet Man," as well as lectures on foreign policy, the history of the Communist Party, on the building of communism in the U.S.S.R. and the building of socialism in the People's Democracies.[68] However, in the following year a complaint was voiced that the attendance at these lectures was lower than it should be, and the Central Committee of *Rabis* declared its aim to be that every creative worker of art would complete the course at the University of Marxism-Leninism.[69]

The Driving Forces

In 1956, a series of discussions began with the topic, "Opera Theatre in the Struggle for a Soviet Repertoire." On another evening, ballet artists, composers, and authors of librettos took part in a discussion dedicated to "Paths of Creation of Soviet Ballet." A third meeting then discussed "On the Paths of Development of Soviet Operetta."[70]

As far as ballet or the musical theatre in general is concerned, one of the basic methods of influence over its production lies in the Union of Soviet Composers. The Union has various subsections including departments for children's music, choral music, symphonic and chamber music, and opera. In the words of Tikhon Khrennikov, the president of the Union, "It is a kind of tradition with us that all members of the Union show their work to their fellow members."[71] This means that a composer submits a piano score version of a proposed new ballet to the Union, and at one of its meetings it is played and dissected, and the composer is questioned about his inmost creative thoughts in composing various parts of it. Ballets are given this hearing by the opera commission of the Union, but at times another branch will take part. For example, in approving the score of two ballets destined for children, *Little Humpbacked Horse* and *Puss-in-Boots*, both the opera commission and youth commission took part.[72] In the special hearing for a ballet representing an outlying Republic, the folk music commission also took part.[73] At this point, a ballet could be either accepted or rejected, or sent back for major revisions, depending upon what the Union deemed expedient.

Close interaction exists among artistic agencies, with each one at times blaming the others for insufficient attention to some phase of their artistic life, especially during periods when Party heat is high. For example, *Sovetskaia Muzyka* complained in 1937 that there had not been enough *samokritika* in the Union of Soviet Composers, whereupon Aram Khachaturian complained that the Committee on Art Affairs did not give sufficient direction to the Union of Composers, and therefore the Union did not know its creative policies sufficiently.[74] It is not unheard of for a ballerina to appear before the Union of Soviet Composers, criticizing them for contributing little to ballet music in recent years and appealing to them to produce more; this was done by the ballerina Olga Lepeshinskaya in 1944.[75]

Since no special dance magazine is published in the U.S.S.R., the magazine of the Union of Soviet Composers, *Sovetskaia Muzyka*, provides one of the main sources for studying Soviet ballet. If a composer fails to attend meetings of the Union—which a few composers of great world stature manage to avoid—he can learn the current themes which the Party wants to stress from articles appearing in the journal.

Khrennikov affirmed that the Union appealed to its members to write about contemporary subjects, saying, "It is our task to help in the development of communism and to support the Communist Party in its endeavors. We believe that our main job as composers is to extol the ideals to which our people aspire."[76] However, Khrennikov hastened to add that this did not mean that the Union dictated to composers what they should do, since he himself was thinking of writing a ballet on the subject of a serf ballerina at the mansion of Count Sheremetev, which was not a contemporary theme.

Standing ultimately over all the agencies which strive to form the mentality of the ballet artist is the Communist Party itself. There is no secret made of this fact:

> The Communist Party directs agricultural, military, cultural, and other phases of the activity of the Soviet government. The direction consists above all in the fact that the Party, from a knowledge of the laws of social development, defines a clear political line. With the help of the mechanism of the Soviet government, by means of drawing the wide workers' mass into active state construction, it achieves a realization of the projected plan.[77]

As far as ballet is concerned, this means that in every major theatre there is a Party chief who fulfills various roles. His task of seeing that the theatre follows the correct Party line in art is aided by various other Party members among the dancers, musicians, and stage and maintenance crew. It would be incorrect to assume that most of the performing artists are Party members; however, its ranks include a sufficient number of them to carry out its mandates. Besides the active and vociferous Olga Lepeshinskaya and Viktorina Kriger, there are other well-known people of the dance world who are Party members, including the dancers Asaf Messerer and Raisa Struchkova; Professor Rostislav Zakharov, a teacher of choreography at GITIS; Lev Golovanov, a dancer with the Moiseyev Ensemble; and Sophia Golovkina, former dancer and present director of the Moscow Choreographic Institute.[78] It can usually be assumed that administrators of both theatres and choreographic institutes are Party members.

In the Bolshoi Theatre there is a paper published as an organ of the Party, the Komsomol and *Rabis,* called *Soviet Artist.* This serves as another organ of diffusing knowledge of such topics as "The Heritage of Konstantin Stanislavsky and Ballet," and articles by Olga Lepeshinskaya criticizing the lack of *sovremennost'* in ballet.[79]

With these many channels of communication open, whenever any important Party event is to take place, the enthusiasm of the artistic world is rallied to aid the cause. As one example among dozens of them, in 1952, it was reported that Party gatherings took place at the Bolshoi Theatre and nine other Moscow theatres for discussing the tasks facing the Party organization of the theatres in connection with the decisions of the Nineteenth Party Congress. It was reported that:

> Communists attending the gatherings with one soul spoke of the great significance of the decisions of the session, the historic speech of Stalin and his genial work *Economic Problems,* of the responsible tasks standing presently before workers of the theatres.[80]

Theatres throughout the U.S.S.R. also had evenings dedicated to the study of material related to the Nineteenth Party Congress.[81] A conclusion was reached at the Bolshoi meeting: an insufficient number of ideological-artistic productions on contemporary themes were being given. This particular meeting also spoke of the need for strengthening artistic discipline and for implanting feelings of responsibility in theatrical workers. It especially denounced régisseurs who forgot their responsibility for the ideological-artistic activity of the theatre as a whole. The meeting decided that there needed to be more attention given to *kritika* and *samokritika* in the theatres, with the Party organization exercising the *kritika*. Lately, it seemed that a theory had been bantered about in the Bolshoi Theatre that artists should not be criticized, for this would wound their psyches. The meeting disdainfully announced: "This theory is finished."[82]

Surprisingly enough, the Party organization of the theatres has not always been above censure itself. In 1938, for example, the Party director of the Kirov Theatre in Leningrad was soundly criticized for neglecting various phases of his job, such as directing the Komsomol organizations of the theatre. The Party organization was accused of not waging a sufficient struggle for the production of Soviet themes in their operas and ballets, and for failing to ferret out "saboteurs" who had "wrecked the repertoire plan."[83] Such criticism was typical of this great purge period in Soviet history when "wreckers" and "saboteurs" were thought to be lurking in every corner, if one were to believe the official line.

In the more relaxed period of the post-Stalin Thaw, the Party bureau of the Kirov came under public fire again. This time, *Pravda* noted that the ballet *Native Fields,* understandably, had been a magnificent flop, and had brought forth adverse criticism in the press. However, instead of taking the criticism to heart, the theatrical Party bureau had defended the ballet, with the theatre's newssheet publishing an editorial flatly rejecting criticism of the production. *Pravda* then complained that the Party bureau's action had prevented the theatre from learning the proper lessons from the failure of the production.[84]

The Party bureau of the theatre has been reported to be the mediator in quarrels between performers and administrators. In 1955, complaints arose against Konstantin Sergeyev, the head of the ballet troupe of the Kirov Theatre, and his wife, Natalia Dudinskaya. Veteran dancers said that conditions for creative work did not exist in the group, and that young dancers were not being given enough of a chance to perform. They cited the example of Nina Timofeyeva, who had managed to get a leading part in *Swan Lake* only because the chief balletmaster, Sergeyev, was absent at the time.[85] It seemed that he and his wife liked to keep the major roles for themselves. The following season, when Sergeyev was back, the Party organization of the theatre had to intervene so that Timofeyeva could continue to dance her role at times. An artistic collegium headed by Fyodor Lopukhov was formed to try to remedy the situation. Then Boris Fenster became chief balletmaster and conditions improved, with ten new productions being mounted in a few years. The talents of the young choreographers Yuri Grigorovich and Igor E. Belsky, and older ones such as Leonid Yacobson and Vakhtang Chabukiani were all utilized. Then in 1960 Fenster died and Sergeyev again assumed the leading role.

The year 1962 brought general unrest among artists in the U.S.S.R., and in April of that year, a group of dancers at the same Kirov Theatre, including Irina Kolpakova, Alla Osipenko, Alla Shelest, Ninel Kurgapkina, Olga Moiseyeva, Ninel Petrova, and Alla Sisova, complained openly in the press again that there was no artistic creativity in their organization because young talent was being stifled. They once more pointed out Sergeyev as the chief cause of the trouble, along with Natalia Dudinskaya, the chief teacher of the dancers.[86] A follow-up article pointed out that in January, at a meeting of the *Rabis* unit of the theatre, different aspects of the troupe's life had been examined and suggestions made for improving it. Soon after that, many questions regarding the work of the younger members were discussed in the Komsomol meeting. However, the board of directors of the theatre paid little attention to the proposals and did not try to eliminate the source of trouble. At this point, the Party bureau of the theatre again defended the complaining artists, saying that Sergeyev did not listen sufficiently to criticism, was not always objective in evaluating the work of the different dancers, that there was an absence of collegiality in their work, and that the complaints voiced in *Rabis* and the Komsomol were just. With the Party bureau's intervention there was formed a *kollegia* to discuss various aspects of theatrical life, and a system was worked out for the introduction of soloists into new parts.[87]

Thus the Party chief's role has broadened through the years. He has become not only the agent for seeing that the theatre fulfills its social and political duty of education and entertaining the masses in a manner befitting Soviet citizens, but his duties sometimes involve championing the causes of oppressed ballerinas—just as the Imperial Grand Dukes sometimes did in days of old.

The major government choreographic schools, though open to the whole population, can take only a minute percentage of the children who apply for training. For the remaining children who might want to learn ballet, there are other channels. Very few of these children can study in private classes. In the U.S.S.R., a private teacher can never operate on a large scale. First of all, there are no buildings available for private studios, and the teachers are not allowed to be employers. The only way this can be done is as it was done by a retired Bolshoi dancer named Kefevan Deviatkova. When she was old enough to be pensioned, she started teaching dancing in her own flat, using the backs of chairs as the supporting barre.[88]

The more regular channel of instruction is through the large state-sponsored apparatus called by the collective word, *samodeiatel'- nost'*, which might be translated "do it yourself" activities, but really refers to what Americans would call amateur theatre. This is the name given to cultural activity which takes place in thousands of factories, houses, and palaces of culture in cities and on collective farms, or in Pioneer Palaces and Komsomol organizations. These organizations had their predecessors in tsarist times in *Narodnye Doma* which first grew up in the 1890's. At that time, according to the Soviet version, the tsars built them to distract the people from political unrest or they were sponsored by such groups as temperance societies. Much of the theatrical work done in them was strictly amateur, but in certain establishments like the People's Palace in Petrograd, both opera and ballet soloists from the Maryinsky would sometimes perform, among them, Nijinsky.[89]

In 1918 there was organized in the Theatrical Department of *Narkompros* a division of worker-peasants' theatre, occupied with the task of developing this *samodeiatel'nost'* network. The Soviet Union emphasizes the fact that in promoting this, it is "eliminating the contradictions between physical and mental work,"[90] by giving the laborer the chance to appear on the stage to sing and dance. Through the years, the network of clubs has grown to the point where there are 115,000 of them, having some 1,500,000 participants.[91] These establishments serve as lecture centers and reading rooms, and are also used for the teaching of amateur arts.

In many of the Pioneer Palaces, a child can pick two hobby groups in which he wishes to participate; he can choose among ballet, chess, gymnastics, dramatics, drawing, or various other hobbies. Lessons can continue through high school days if he wishes. If his talent develops in an outstanding manner, his parents or teacher might appeal to have him received into one of the major choreographic institutes. From one Palace of Culture in Leningrad, over fifty children transferred to the main choreographic institutions, and thirty-five soloists and dancers of the *corps de ballet* in professional companies studied there during the eighty-five years of its life.[92] In the Moscow House of Young Pioneers in 1942 there was formed a Children's Song and Dance Ensemble which by 1954 included six hundred children. The children who worked with it remained there for several years, and the promising ones were sent to choreographic schools.[93]

These institutions serve many purposes. The Pioneer Palaces serve as a means of preventing delinquency in a nation where housing problems have been so bad for decades that there is literally no room at home to carry on any kind of hobby or recreational activity. Nikita Khrushchev voiced this along with another motive when he said: "When work in cultural-enlightenment institutions and ideological work in general is neglected, then sectarians and clergy step up their activities, and drunkenness and hooliganism appear.[94]

Many of these clubs are sponsored and financed by the All-Union Central Council of Trade-Unions. Appropriations for such clubs from 1929 to 1932 totaled 30,000,000 rubles. The Pioneer Palaces are financed by the Ministry of Education, with the Leningrad Pioneer Palace operating on a yearly budget of 600,000 rubles.[95]

For guiding the amateur art apparatus, there have existed since 1936 Houses of Folk Creativity in all major cities. These institutions render consultative aid to directors of amateur art institutions, aiding them in the selection of repertoire and visiting rehearsals of productions. The Houses of Folk Creativity also supervise the folk dance contests which are held yearly. In the R.S.F.S.R. there is the N. K. Krupskaya House of Folk Creativity which guides all subsidiary institutions. This organization works in close connection with the Union of Writers, the Union of Soviet Composers, and the all-Russian Theatrical Society.[96]

Along with classical ballet, other dances recommended for use in these amateur clubs frequently emphasize work themes. One of them, included in a manual of three dances for such use, is called *Brother-Parasites*. Its actions, described as follows, occupy one page, with the accompanying dance movements and music occupying the next twenty-four pages. In it, the stage is set as a meadow and two youths enter from different sides of the stage. They look sleepy and are dressed carelessly. They stand around and lazily greet each other. Then an energetic brigadier appears, notices the loafing pair, and begins to work.

The parasites shrug their shoulders, not knowing what to do. The brigadier leader then points to what they should start mowing, but the slackers gesture that they are sick and that mowing is too much work for them. But the brigadier is steadfast and demands that they get to work in short order, so the two youths begin to mow. Then the brigadier leaves, and the tempo of activity slackens; the youths are not used to such work. They stand about again, and draw from their pockets wooden spoons, indicating that they are already prepared to eat. Suddenly the brigadier leader appears. Angry at the conduct of the loafers, he snatches the spoons away and points out that they have to work to eat. The youths are embarrassed, and the brigadier measures out a plot which they must mow; only after that is done will they be allowed to eat. So the youths begin to work under the observation of the brigadier, the plot is mowed, and the brigadier is pleased.[97]

When the productions in such theatres have reached a high artistic and ideological level, the theatre can be granted the honorary title of *Narodnyi Teatr,* the People's Theatre. This transformation is achieved by confirmation of the appropriate trade union, military or other supervising authority. In 1964, there were 760 People's Theatres. Certain ones have the capacity and personnel to stage creditable ballets, including the Hammer and Sickle Factory Club in Moscow, the Kirov House of Culture in Leningrad, the Theatre of the Novokuznetsk Metallurgical Combine, and the Theatre of the Rybokombinat in Astrakhan.[98]

Achievements in ballet made by these groups are highly advertised in the Soviet press, pointing out to all the world that in the workers' state, culture is available to all. Very often, the papers will show two pictures, side by side. In one, a woman will be shown at her regular job, garbed in the shapeless, manly clothes of a factory worker, and in the other she will be shown delicately posed in her ballerina's *tutu.* For example, *Soviet Woman* in 1963 told about a certain Tatiana Shangina. Tatiana really operates a sewing machine at Atelier No. 4 in Leningrad, but she had been studying ballet for four years at the People's Theatre at the Gorky Palace of Culture in Leningrad. She became good enough to dance an *adagio* from *Swan Lake* at the Kremlin Theatre in Moscow, while keeping up with her sewing.[99]

Another picture showed a group of ballerinas in Yaroslavl in 1952 performing the *Dance of the Little Swans* from *Swan Lake*. One of these delicate maidens, Liudmilla Maslova, was the graduate of a construction technical school and during the day worked tirelessly at an apartment house construction site. Her friend, Tamara Kolobova, worked in a shoe factory. A third member, Nina Dondina, was a most gifted researcher at a scientific institute, while a fourth member, Faina Kuznetsova, was a renowned spinner who headed a Stakhanovite school for top-notch workers. They spent their evenings taking ballet lessons from Lev Dolmatsky at the club of the Yaroslavl Tire Factory.[100]

In 1965, in the newspaper of the teaching profession, *Uchitel'skaia Gazeta,* a picture appeared of Vera Fedorovna Pavlova, a school teacher. She studied dancing during her time of pedagogical studies and became so good that she was sent on a side tour to Germany.[101] In *Sovetskaia Muzyka* in 1964, two pictures of a certain Valentina Yaklokova were printed: one showing her performing the role of Niki in the ballet *La Bayadère* in her local People's Theatre in Novokuznetsk, and the other with Valentina dressed as a miner, the career which occupies her days.[102] In *Soviet Literature,* an article told of the Karaganda Ballet Theatre in Kazakhstan, whose ballet group was good enough to perform in 1963 at the Kremlin Palace of Congresses, as well as in the workers' clubs of the Likhachev Automobile Works in Moscow. This amateur ballet, which started life in a miner's club, included such diverse professional people as a coal-combine operator, a surgeon, an electrician, a schoolmistress, a stonemason, an engineer, and many others.[103] In all, there are over 10,000,000 adults who study dance in these amateur theatrical groups in Russia, which naturally makes them a most appreciative audience of the art.[104]

The types of ballets staged in these workers' clubs correspond somewhat to that which the main theatres produce. In the Gorky Palace of Culture in Leningrad there was presented, in 1953, the ballet *The Stone Flower,* using a score by A. Fridlender. Nina Karpovich, a student of a technical school, played Katerina, the heroine. Danila, the hero, was played both by Kirill Glushkov, an electric welder of the Kirov plant, and by Georgi Pinaev, a geology student of Leningrad University. The dance of the rock crystal was performed by Katia Fedorovna, a lathe operator at the Kirov plant. All of the participants had studied for ballet several years at the Gorky Palace of Culture, taught by experienced masters. More than 150 adults studied dance at the palace.[105]

In 1963, the choreographic studio in the First Five-Year Plan Palace of Culture in Leningrad gave a dance called *Cosmos—To Peace.* Another production was called *Buchenwald Tocsin,* and a third was named *Militant Youth.*[106] In 1965, a group at the Tikhvinsky Raion House of Culture of the Leningrad oblast gave an original choreographic composition also called *Cosmos.*[107]

One problem which has engaged the time of many workers of the ballet world is that of peace and disarmament. At a second All-Union Conference of Partisans of Peace held in 1950 at the Moscow House of Actors, speeches dedicated to peace were given by the ballet dancer Suzanna Zviagina and the ballet mistress Nadezhda Nadezhdina.[108] In 1962, when the movement had spread and an All-World Congress for General Disarmament and Peace was held in Moscow, a trade union dance group performed concert numbers warning of the danger of repeating Buchenwald, Auschwitz, and Hiroshima.[109] However, the most spectacular effort in this direction seemed to be the ballet entitled *To the Memory of Hiroshima,* given by the balletmaster Alexander Livshitz. He said that he conceived the idea for it while on tour in Japan with the Kirov Ballet Company, and had the opportunity to talk with some of the Japanese people. The ballet was then given at the Leningrad Kirov Palace of Culture.

The ballet begins with soft Japanese folk music, depicting a peaceful night where a mother sings a lullaby to her son, and lovers whisper their feelings to each other. Then the sun rises, the peaceful people leave for their work, and the lovers part. Suddenly, an atomic explosion destroys all the peace. The gigantic explosion brings suffering and death on all sides and horror to the survivors. In the background, a tragic requiem is played, but eventually the sad melody is replaced by a theme of resolution, of wrath, revolt, and struggle against this terrible evil. Then, according to the description, "people stand with raised fists, as if to say, 'Let there be no more Hiroshima!' "[110] *Pravda* described the ballet as a narration of "the sufferings of mothers losing their children, of the anger of the simple people of Japan, becoming sacrifices to the monstrous crime of atomic maniacs." *Pravda* also reported that the ballet was being prepared for presentation to the delegates of the forthcoming All-World Congress for General Disarmament and Peace.[111] The artists who danced in it were common people, including a cashier, a student, a chauffeur, an electrician, a telephone operator, and a garment factory worker.

On one occasion, *Pravda* poked a bit of fun at the excessive zeal of someone in the *samodeiatel'nost'* movement. Full appreciation of the article demands complete quoting:

Superphosphate Dance

Contemporary themes are still rarely reflected in choreographic art. There are no conquerers of the virgin land or builders of Bratsk among ballet heroes. We all understand that it is a difficult task to create such a ballet. Every attempt can only be welcomed.

Suddenly, we read *Golden Wheat* [a ballet in two acts and three scenes], and each new scene perplexes us more and more.

"First scene. A corner of a shop at a chemical combine. Whimsically curved pipes of machines in the background. Automatic control panel, stage left.

"Four girls in overalls run onstage. They go to the instruments, turn them on by pressing buttons, and mark down readings. Young men enter to relieve the girls; they join hands and dance, simulating the rhythm of machines."

They dance, let us remark, to the catchy tune of "Rondo March."

"A poster is lowered against the backdrop with the inscription: 'Plan fulfilled 106%.' The shift has finished its working day."

But, as we learn, the shock workers' exultation is premature. In the next episode, called "Achievement" performed to a "march": "Two workers appear upstage in the beams of spotlights. They triumphantly point to the higher indices of their shops. A second poster descends. Two more workers demonstrate very high achievement of their shop."

Then we have the "Dance of Labor." Ballerinas in overalls, "as if on a conveyor belt, move across the stage."

In passing, "the young people by dancing with vigorous movements express the joy of work," and "the dynamism grows."

The reader's perplexity also grows.

In the following scenes one sees Young Pioneers carrying bags. "The smallest Young Pioneer calls to all the other ones and explains why they are here: 'We need fertilizers!' " " 'Have some,' the workers say, dancing, 'you will have fertilizers, my boy.' " Then many boys appear on the stage, costumed in sacks bearing the inscriptions: "Superphosphate." They load themselves onto trucks with a gay dance.

In the second act there is an impressive little scene, "Fertilizers Arrive," performed to "Rondo Toccato."

Then "a machine drives on stage, represented by a group of boys. The machine advances, plowing, and fertilizing the soil and spreading superphosphate." Dances depict the rapid growth of an abundant harvest. We hear melodies called "Gallop" and "Agronomist and Worker Raise Scarlet Banner." The Young Pioneers blow bugles, beat drums, and "give a Young Pioneer salute to the audience."

"What are you trying to pull?" the reader is entitled to ask.

Unfortunately, the present writer did not invent all this. The "ballet in two acts and three scenes" was published in 100,000 copies in the magazine *Klub i Khudozhestvennaia Samodeiatel'nost'* "Club and Amateur Art," No. 2 of this year. The author of the ballet is K. Koshurnikov.

We repeat once more, we need choreographic and musical works on contemportary themes very urgently.

But what has been printed in *Klub i Khudozhestvennaia Samodeiatel'nost'* is neither art nor contemporary. One cannot "react" to the great and serious phenomena of our life with such tomfoolery.[112]

237

At this point, it might be apropos to point out to the non-Russian reader that the word *Pravda* means "truth."

While the existence of the large amateur art network gives the common people a chance to see and participate in ballet, the reverse side of the picture is also significant. Through these clubs, members of the ballet world are brought into contact with the people, both through giving concerts and assisting in the teaching of amateur classes.

The idea of artists going out to the byways to bring art to the people was not a Communist invention. Some artists of prerevolutionary Russia also went out of their way to perform for the lower classes of society. The developing social consciousness which prompted the building of the Narodnye Doma led Michel Fokine and sympathetic co-workers to entertain workers' audiences. However, Fokine had decided that in the form in which it then existed, ballet would not be suitable for the workers' audiences, so he gave performances for them with his balalaika instead.[113] At the same time, he resolved that ballet should be changed so that it would be better understood by the people.

When the Bolshevik Party came to power, artists began entertaining workers audiences constantly. Lenin believed very strongly that "art belongs to the people." In a conversation with Clara Zetkin, he emphasized that "it must have its deepest roots in the broad mass of workers. It must be understood and loved by them."[114] Because of this conviction, as well as the fact that art was deemed to be an effective educative force, the regime has encouraged artists both to perform for workers and to aid them in their amateur theatrical productions by their teaching and encouragement. This service is called by the name *obshchestvennaia nagruzka,* which means, literally, their "social load."

The new contact with the field and factory brought interesting returns. After performing for a factory in some outlying district,

238

The Driving Forces

Yekaterina Geltser and Vasily Tikhomirov's visit brought the following laudatory note in the factory paper:

The great Russian poet, Pushkin, when speaking about the "little feet of Terpsichore," could not imagine that "the flashing little feet of the academic ballet would one day become the subject of discussion, together with industrial plans, at a lunch-hour meeting of workers in the tool shop of the agricultural machinery works." Thus wrote the workers' paper of Rostov-on-Don *Bolshevitskaia Smena,* on April 3, 1930. In the course of the discussion, which was held in the dining hall after the show, the workers said: "The ballet used to be considered a 'superior' art, inaccessible to the masses. Today we saw something different when witnessing dances like *The Apple* and *The Internationale Sailor's Dance.* These dances stimulate tempo in production and help us in carrying out our industrial plans. The rhythm of the dance of *The Apple* fitted in well with our over fulfillment of our industrial plan by 19 percent. As your sailors danced, our hearts were profoundly stirred. It is the very 'apple' we have been striving for all these years. It is our very own. Draw us into the very center of your art, and by our criticism as workers we shall help you to produce many similar things and to merge your enthusiasm with the masses."[115]

Another well-known dancer who did a great deal of traveling in fulfillment of her *nagruzka* was Viktorina Kriger. In the 1930's she danced at Dnieprstroi, the Rostov agricultural machinery works, at Grozny oil fields, the Donbass coal mines, the textile mills of Ivanovo-Voznesensk, and other places. She graphically described how, on the tour, blaring loudspeakers would announce the performance outside the theatre and some neophyte spectator would wonderingly approach the cashier's box to inquire, "What do they sing in the ballet?"— whereupon the cashier would haughtily ignore the question and the spectator would proceed into the theatre, still wondering what they were going to sing in the ballet.[116]

It had been a practice, when the government was strongly pushing some industrial or agricultural project to recruit entertainers to go to the faraway spot and cheer the workers, upon whom superhuman demands were being levied. In the Ferghana Valley in Central Asia in the late 1930's, 160,000 collective farmers were building a canal 175 miles long. When the work was not proceeding at a pace to satisfy the government, 360 members of the Uzbek Opera and Ballet Theatre of Tashkent, as well as a group from the Uzbek Song and Dance Ensemble were brought to the work sites, giving fifty performances in twenty-five days. With this encouragement, it was reported that the daily "dig" rose from 2,500 cubic meters of earth to 4,071 cubic meters per day.[117]

One English observer in the 1930's noted that at the Freser Tool plant in Moscow, employing 3,000 workers, there was an operatic group of forty members and a ballet group meeting two times a week guided by a teacher from the Bolshoi.[118] The Bolshoi reportedly has a special link with the Burdenko Hospital, where they give performances for the patients and staff,[119] and are special patrons as well of the Gorky Vegetable State Farm near Moscow.[120] In 1961, a group of Bolshoi artists went to the site of the building of the Tsimiliansky hydroelectric generating station. This particular project was organized upon suggestion of the Department of Propaganda and Agitation of the All-Union Komsomol and the Komsomol organization of the Bolshoi Theatre.[121]

The examples are endless. In 1959, the Theatre of Opera and Ballet in Saratov was the patron of one of the local workers' brigades competing for the title of Brigade of Communist Labor. The theatre was also putting on performances for specialists of agriculture in surrounding raions and for young workers in the local chemical industry.[122] Artists participating in this type of activity are given wide publicity in the U.S.S.R. A special movie called *Bolshoi Concert* was made in 1951 showing Bolshoi artists arriving on a collective farm to give a concert for the kolkhozniks, to talk with the people, and to help train gifted youth on the farm. A review of the film recalls the complaints voiced in 1936 against *Bright Stream,* for it pointed out

240

that in the scene showing the arrival of the Bolshoi performers on the farm, overdressed actors appeared welcoming them instead of real farmers.[123]

FOLK DANCE

The network of amateur clubs serves as the channel for the state's encouragement of folk dance in the U.S.S.R., in keeping with the attention given to folk art in general. As a result of the emphasis given to national cultures in the mid-1930's, folk dance groups sprouted in hundreds of towns and cities, with even the NKVD having its own Song and Dance Ensemble. It became a practice to have nationwide contests of amateur art where these folk dance groups could display their skill. As a preliminary step, every year contests are held in amateur clubs throughout the U.S.S.R., and after a series of eliminating rounds, the best performers take part in the huge amateur art festival in Moscow. In 1956, 3,000,000 people were reported to have taken part in the preliminary contests in the U.S.S.R. Trade Union Festival of Amateur Art. There, it was possible to see performers from the length and width of the nation. Along with displays of classical ballet, there were dozens of numbers such as that given by a Kazakh folk dance group called Festival in Honor of a Miner-Hero of Labor.[124] Some of these amateur groups, while remaining amateurs, have amazing skill and were sent abroad to perform. In 1965, the Central Council of Trades Unions in East Germany and Poland invited a large group of Russian amateurs to visit their countries to perform for the workers.[125]

Other groups have grown into professional companies and have been designated as the official folk dance group of their Republic. All of these groups have learned the types of numbers which must be included in their repertoire. American Supreme Court Justice William O. Douglas, who made an extensive trip in Central Asia, reported that the Tatar Ensemble in Tashkent opened their program by praising Lenin. The Uzbek Ensemble had a finale in which the

241

dancers were dressed in the various costumes of different Soviet Republics and each group performed a dance appropriate to the Republic represented. Finally, four dancers dressed in red to represent the Russian Republic entered and executed the rapid twirling and stomping expected of them. In the end, the four Russians formed the hub of a huge wheel around which the other dancers formed spokes. While the giant wheel revolved, Miss Russia was hoisted high in the center, representing the role of Great Russia in uniting the various racial and religious groups in the nation and also pointing to the predominant role of Great Russia in the U.S.S.R.[126]

Another noteworthy feature is that new "folk" dances are continually being created predominantly on work themes. Uzbek folk dance has a new dance called the *Pakhta,* a dance of cotton growers, and *Pilia,* the dance of silkworm breeders. Their *Tanovar* is an older dance done by women, originated in past ages. It was supposed to depict the hard life of Uzbek women, but now it has changed its form and is intended to express in youthful, life-affirming dance the present happy life of the Uzbek woman who is no longer the slave of old feudal customs.[127] Russian sources repeatedly affirm that:

> There was often a melancholy tinge to the old Uzbek folk dances, particularly those of women. The new dances, while retaining the age-old traditions and characteristic traits of the Uzbek dance, are imbued with buoyant optimism, reflecting the tremendous changes that the October Revolution, carrying liberation from feudal and colonial oppression, has brought about in the life of the Uzbek people.[128]

At the Kirghiz *dekada* in 1958, a *Dance of Cotton Pickers* was given in which it was asserted "the spectators felt the joy, the poetry of labor on free earth."[129] The Moiseyev Company has developed a dance called *Bulba,* based upon on old Belorussian song which depicts the planting of potatoes, their growth, and the happiness of the people over a plentiful harvest.[130]

The recurrence of these manufactured "folk" dances raises interesting questions. While it is unquestionably true that the Soviets have greatly encouraged the creation and preservation of folk dance, there seems to be some substance to assertions made by émigré citizens regarding the authenticity of Soviet "folk" art in general. A member of a Ukrainian bandura orchestra affirmed:

> Samodeiatel'noe art is not developed on the basis of the spiritual necessity of the people, is not created by the people, but is made in party laboratories by poets and composers. This "folk creativity" later is transplanted locally for performance, as are all other party directives.[131]

This author claims that the amateur circles were a means of forcing out of the life of the workers the authentic folk songs and dances of their former inheritance, and that "all this strives to substitute a creativity, saturated with Bolshevik ideology, in order to educate the people to patriotism toward the socialist government." Another musician who formerly lived in the Soviet Union contended "the folk music garb which Soviet composers are obliged to wear to dress up their thoughts and feelings cannot be looked upon as genuine contact with the people."[132]

To confirm or deny such assertions on any large scale in the field of dance would literally involve research into the highways and byways of the Soviet Union. Here, the question is only raised, not answered.

CHAPTER EIGHT

Terpsichorean Diplomacy

I shall lay forever the ghost of Russian barbarism that haunts Europe, and I plan to do my exorcism with the proof of a culture so mighty in Russian hearts that it overshadows nobleborn and peasant alike with ardor and reverence in the presence of Art!

—SERGE DIAGILEV[1]

WHEN Stalin's government began its drive in the 1930's to give national folk art greater recognition, internal cohesion within the U.S.S.R. was one of the chief motives. Little did Stalin then realize that the rows of twirling dancers would some day become successful diplomats, and that one of the most widely-traveled groups from the U.S.S.R. would be the Moiseyev State Academic Folk Dance Ensemble, which was formed during the drive to recognize national arts.

The title "academic" was bestowed on this group in 1965 as a high honor.[2] Actually, it started life in 1936, after an important All-Union Festival of Folk Dance held in Moscow. At that time, Igor Moiseyev, who had achieved recognition as a choreographer for the Bolshoi, saw the vast possibilities of forming a permanent state folk dance group which would perform all the dances of the peoples of the U.S.S.R. The state was ripe for such a suggestion, and Moiseyev was given the necessary aid to form his very polished group. Their repertoire now includes dances from all over the U.S.S.R. and its satellites, and from many western countries. In the immediate postwar years, the group made extensive tours in the countries of Eastern Europe. At that time, the company staged a new number called *Dance of the Slavic People.* This was intended "to demonstrate to workers of the freed states the spiritual might and beauty of Soviet art, and it was dedicated to the indissoluble friendship of the Slavic people, who shoulder to shoulder had joined the battle for freedom."[3] It was said that another suite, called *Peace and Friendship,* "vividly conveys the people's love of life, their optimism and fortitude in the days of struggle for a happy future, their striving for peaceful coexistence and creative labor."[4] Among many others, the company has an amusing dance, not intended for United States viewers, called *Viva Cuba.* In it, dancers clad in Castro-like khakis and beards wield submachine guns and imitate a revolutionary demonstration. In the company's visits to Cuba, Raoul Castro presented the company with the banner of the Cuban revolution, and while he was in Russia later, he came to see *Viva* performed.[5]

In all, the Moiseyev group has traveled in over thirty-seven countries, and including television performances had reached a world audience of 100 million people by 1962.[6]

In 1955, the American musical production *Porgy and Bess* was performed in Moscow. Negotiations for a visit of the Moiseyev dancers to the United States were hindered by the American law demanding fingerprinting of foreign visitors. The Soviet government strongly objected to the practice and made good propaganda use of America's stand on the matter. *Izvestiia* declared, "In the Soviet Union, guests do not have to be fingerprinted upon entering the country, nor do they have to take upon themselves obligations, shameful for free people, as they do in the United States."[7] Urged by Secretary Dulles and Attorney General Herbert Brownell, the American Congress waived the law in September, 1957.[8] There were other difficulties involved in the negotiations; the Soviets were chagrined because the U.S.S.R. was not allowed to send the performers in its own jet planes, and the dancers had to travel in more costly commercial aircraft.[9] However, they finally appeared on the stage of the Metropolitan Opera House in April and May of 1958.

Wherever they have gone, the Moiseyev dancers have studied the local dance traditions. Therefore, in America, after a fabulous display of Georgian, Ukrainian, Uzbek, and a dozen other varieties of folk dance, the chorus begins a Virginia Reel. Someone in the audience begins to clap time, and all are spontaneously drawn into joyful participation. The 1966 program ended as the musicians played "Hail, Hail, the Gang's All Here." Carried away by the music and excitement the audience easily forgets the existence of the Cold War.

In a Moiseyev program in the United States, there is little that touches openly upon social or political questions. On closer examination, some of the points of emphasis bear noting. During the 1965 program, in a number called *Trepak*, a ridiculous, dishevelled drunkard comically enters the stage, chased by his broom-brandishing, shrewish wife. Anyone acquainted with the mores of socialist realism immediately wonders how he appeared on a Soviet program: is this the new Soviet man? The program settles all doubts. On the contrary, this is a dance taken from a cycle of choreographic pictures entitled *Scenes from the Past*. The past is depicted in a foolish, laughable manner, described in the program as "Chekhovian" scenes which no longer appear in Soviet life.[10] Contrasted to the old life, there are presented "Soviet Scenes," which show heroic incidents, such as *Partisans* or *Day on Board a Ship*, or *Street of a Kolkhoz Village*, which displays the bright gaiety of life on the collective farm. All these scenes are described by the program as differing radically from peasant life before the Russian revolution.

Since they are constantly told that capitalistic art is on the downgrade, Soviet citizens who have come to the West for the first time are often surprised. According to the *New York Times*, after Igor Moiseyev returned to the Soviet Union from his American tour, he gave a three-and-a-half-hour talk to 600 theatrical workers in the House of Actors in Moscow. The talk, sponsored by the Union of Soviet Friendship Societies, was entitled "The Cultural Life of America." Moiseyev said that he wished to concentrate on the positive aspects of American culture and leave the negative elements "to those responsible for such things."[11] He praised American music and general cultural life. It was later reported that Moiseyev was called to see Nikolai A. Mikhailov, the Minister of Culture, where he was warned to weigh his words and to give a more "balanced" report in the future about his visits abroad. A talk by Moiseyev which was scheduled to be given at the House of Journalists was canceled.[12]

Moiseyev is well aware of his great responsibility and made it clear on one occasion that he realizes the group has a broader mission than simply to dance. He said:

> I think that in our days artistic prestige is inseparable from political prestige. In any case, our art, which would appear to be quite remote from political passions, could not exercise such a strong aesthetic and emotional influence if it were not so politically well-defined and purposeful, if it were not Soviet art in the fullest sense of the term.
>
> The audiences of our performances abroad judge us not only by our choreography and artistic skill. Above all they judge us as representatives of our country, our people, the art of the Soviet Union as a whole. And we like to tell of our people, so fond of life and straightforward, so proud and sincere; we enjoy telling at the top of our voices what kind of people our fellow countrymen are. We take pride in our political mission.[13]

At times, however, politics has been painful for the company. During their first performance in Argentina, anticommunist demonstrators threw teargas bombs onto the stage and orchestra pit. The dancers managed to keep dancing, accompanied by an orchestra that was temporarily blinded. In the final count, the incident probably was of more propaganda value to the company than to the demonstrators.

BERYOZKA ENSEMBLE

Another professional group, called the State Choreographic Beryozka Ensemble, also grew out of the amateur dance movement. In 1948, at a Collective Farmers' Art Festival of the Russian Federation, the audience very enthusiastically received the dances of a group of collective farm girls from the Kalinin region.[14] This suggested to the leader, Nadezhda Nadezhdina, that a women's dance group might be permanently successful. Three girls who were employees of a needle trades factory in Moscow, a few Bolshoi graduates, and some farm girls made up the original group. The ensemble has met world success, for there are some very lovely numbers in their repertoire. Asked in Norway what kind of dances they performed, the reply had a familiar ring: "Old dances describing the hard lot of Russian women before the Revolution, and modern dances expressive of their bright and happy present."[15] Their dances are done in old-fashioned, long, full-skirted costumes, and wherever they go they are pictured as representatives of the charm of the new Soviet woman. Upon seeing their performance, one Soviet composer remarked:

> Nadezhdina seeks to bring out in every dance the . . . beauty and charm of Russian women's dances, and the spirit of life, profound lyricism and purity characteristic of them. . . . The vivid, optimistic art of the ensemble has won it the appreciation of the Soviet concert audiences.[16]

RED ARMY SONG AND DANCE ENSEMBLE

Another well-traveled group is the Red-Banner A. V. Aleksandrov Ensemble of Song and Dance of the Soviet Army. The group was started in 1928 to aid the "political, military, and cultural education of the personnel of the Red Army and Navy."[17] In the beginning it had twelve members, but has since grown to 300 singers and dancers. In 1937, the ensemble performed in Czechoslovakia and at the world's fair in Paris, where it scored great success.[18] An article in *Pravda* about the usefulness of its many tours abroad declared that many people living in foreign countries are often exposed only to evil-intentioned propaganda, and that concerts of this ensemble convey the truth about the Soviet homeland, about its peace-loving people with their strength and confidence in the future. In the same article, an English citizen was reported to have said, "If this is the Red Army, then they are

Aurora and Prince Desiré in Tschaikovsky's ballet *Sleeping Beauty,* danced by Maximova and Khokhlov.

Bessmertnova as Odette and Fadeyechev as the prince in Tschaikovsky's
ballet *Swan Lake* at the Bolshoi Theatre.

always welcome in our town, in our hotel. They are gentlemen and good guests."[19]

CLASSICAL BALLET OUTSIDE RUSSIA

A Soviet source once indignantly quoted a story attributed to the Moral Rearmament group. According to the tale, when Stalin was first asked to send the Bolshoi Ballet on an American tour, he replied that he would like to do it, but he was having trouble on the Manchurian border and needed them there.[20] Whether true or false, Soviet ballet artists have indeed conquered worldwide audiences and achieved a tremendous amount of good will for their homeland.

Along with their revolutionary productions, the system of vast state support of Soviet art enables the U.S.S.R. to continue to produce long, full-evening ballets of the standard classics, which demand mass scenes of people. American companies, even if they wanted to imitate them, could seldom afford to stage these gigantic works. The high salaries of performers, union stage hands, musicians, makeup artists, and other expenses are encountered by theatrical managers in the American capitalistic free enterprise system. These costs afford no real problem in the Soviet structure.

Many of the newer Soviet ballets which alternate with the old classics in their own repertoire are obviously nonexportable.[21] When given in the United States and Western Europe, some of their noteworthy examples of "socialist realism" evoked comments ranging from ridicule to polite silence. From bitter experience, the Soviet companies have thus learned to keep such productions at home, or at least within the boundaries of satellite nations. where the press is controllable. This leaves their companies no great choice of tour repertoire; they have to present the old classics. Since they do these exquisitely and devotedly, world audiences are justifiably captivated by them, and a visit from such a foreign troupe affords many countries of the world, including America, a welcome chance to see a full-length *Swan Lake* or *Sleeping Beauty*.

249

EARLIER CULTURAL EXCHANGES

Cultural exchanges of ballet dancers are not a new practice for either Western Europeans or Russians. In 1802, Ivan Valberkh was sent to Paris at the expense of the imperial theatres in order to perfect his dance technique.[22] Foreign audiences have been charmed by ballerinas at least since 1844, when the St. Petersburg dancer Tatiana Smirnova went abroad. She gained great success in Brussels and Paris. In the former city, Smirnova gave some of her earnings from a benefit performance for the use of the poor, which endeared her to the Belgiums even more.[23]

The next year, the dancer Elena Andreanova traveled abroad and she, too, was warmly received in Paris, Hamburg, and Milan, as well as in London in 1852.[24] In 1850, Nadezhda Bogdanova began studies in Paris and danced successfully there and in Germany, Poland, Hungary, and Italy.[25] Then came the turn of the Muscovite ballerina, Zinaida Richard, who entertained Paris and London in 1857 and 1858. Zinaida Richard was perhaps the first, but assuredly not the last Russian dancer to lose her heart in Paris, and as a result to abandon her career in Russia; she married a French dancer, Louis Mérante.[26]

During these years an influx of foreign artists also came to Russia to display their art or to teach. A Soviet author explains that this period of decay in Western ballet brought to Russia a stream of Western European choreographers: Marie Taglioni, Fanny Elssler, Carlotta Grisi, Lucille Grahn, Amalia Ferraris, Carolina Rosati, Jules Perrot, Artur Saint-Léon, Jean and Marius Petipa, Virginia Zucci, Carlotta Brianza, Pierrina Legnani, Enrico Cechetti, and Christian Johanson.[27]

After the turn of the century, there were numerous tours by Russians, such as one in 1908 organized by Adolf Bolm. The group, which included Anna Pavlova, danced in Berlin, Prague, and in Sweden. In Sweden, the king bestowed on the group the title "Artibus Litteras."[28] The following year, Diagilev organized his famous group.

Opportunities for such artistic exchange have more often than not been at the mercy of the political situation. In 1894, France and Russia entered an alliance which England joined in 1907, to form the Triple Entente. The formation of the entente was part of the scheme of "balance of power" politics to meet the alliance of Germany and Austria-Hungary on the opposite side. When Serge Diagilev began to organize his first tour, he presented his plea for funds to the Russian government on the basis of the great propaganda value for Russian art which his troupe would have in Western Europe. Diagilev was granted a promise of the subsidy, but never received it because of intramural political troubles with Kschessinska.[29]

During the Paris tour of the Ballet Russe in 1912, when Nijinsky danced the part of the young faun in Debussy's impressionistic ballet *L'Après-Midi d'un Faune,* there was fear that Franco-Russian relations might be harmed. The ballet originally contained a final gesture by the faun which shocked a part of the audience by its suggestion of obscenity. M. Gaston Calmette, the editor of the Parisian newspaper *Le Figaro,* wrote an editorial about the performance, castigating its "vile movements of erotic bestiality."[30]

Officials of the Russian embassy explained to Diagilev that Calmette and *Le Figaro* really were attacking Raymond Poincaré and the Russian ambassador Alexander Izvolsky, who at that time were trying to strengthen the Franco-Russian entente, so that Calmette's thrusts against the ballet were really a means of attacking the *rapprochement* itself. Another Parisian newspaper, *Le Matin,* then entered the fray with an article by the great sculptor Auguste Rodin, who lauded the ballet for embodying the ancient Greek ideals of harmony and beauty. Calmette's stinging reply to Rodin in *Le Figaro,* began a pro-Rodin campaign which eventually enlisted the support of such men as Emile Loubet, Raymond Poincaré, Léon Bourgeois, Georges Clemenceau, Aristide Briand, Jacques Barthou, Gabriel Hanotaux, Anatole France, Frederick Mistral, Jules Lamaître, Claude Monet, Albert Besnard, Maurice Barres, and several others.[31] In the end, the Parisian police intervened, and Nijinsky had to modify the gesture in future performances.[32] The incident neither strengthened nor weakened the entente, but it did give Diagilev publicity, in which he gloried.

After the Bolshevik rise to power, exchanges took place for a time in a comparatively free manner. From 1920 to 1922, Viktorina Kriger toured Europe and North America. In the Soviet view, Kriger had "to dispel the myth that the Bolsheviks wanted to dynamite the old Russian culture, and that art dragged out a miserable existence in the new revolutionary Russia."[33] In Russia, a top ballerina usually has to dance about four performances a month, since the theatres offer a mixed repertoire of operas and ballets. Therefore, when Russian dancers have to appear every night while on tour in the West, they find it physically exhausting, and many have returned home with the impression that American dancers are exploited like all the other slaves of capitalism. Kriger wrote that she was appalled to find that in New York actors had to perform five or six times a day. She said that for twenty weeks in New York she had to dance daily, performing the ballet *Fairy Doll* sixty-five times.[34] By the end of the fifteenth week, she had intense pain in her right knee, and at the end of the twentieth week could not dance, but had to recuperate in bed for six weeks without bending her leg. New York's impression of Kriger was quite favorable, for one newspaper hailed her as "second only to Pavlova,"[35] while another remarked that she "proved by her alluring dancing that press agents can tell the truth."[36] In 1935, Kriger was artistic director of a group of Soviet performers who attended an international festival of folk dance in London.[37]

The "modern" dancers also did their share of traveling in the 1920's. When Isadora Duncan left Russia, one of her pupils, Irma Duncan, bravely carried on with the school amid great hardships. In late 1926, she took her little troupe of dancers on a tour through Siberia. While on the Pacific coast of Russia, she asked permission, and unexpectedly received it, to take her touring company to Harbin, China. Young and adventurous, Irma Duncan then proceeded to visit other Chinese cities. These were times of great stress in Sino-Soviet relations, when a break between the U.S.S.R. and Chiang Kai-shek seemed imminent. At a New Year's party in the Soviet embassy in Shanghai in 1927, the Soviet ambassador personally asked that the group go to Hankow to perform for the Chinese nationalists. Miss Duncan explained the reason for their urging her to go: "The Soviet Embassy saw in our dancers a providential means of extending a friendly gesture to Chiang Kai-shek. In other words, they tried to use us as propaganda to help smooth the ruffled feathers of the Chinese-Russian entente."[38] Before leaving China, she was honored by a banquet attended by Madame Sun Yat-sen, Chiang Kai-shek, Foreign Minister Eugen Chen, and Mikhail Borodin, the well-known Russian advisor in China. At this point, the rift was too great for terpsichorean diplomacy to mend, and the formal break in diplomatic relations between Russia and nationalist China came in December, 1927. In Moscow, Eugen Chen's daughter Sylvia soon became Irma Duncan's first Chinese pupil. Later Sylvia Chen was reported to be studying at the studio of Vera Maya and was said to be the most engaging performer at a recital of Maya's pupils in the year 1928.[39]

In 1929, Valeska Gert, a "modern" dancer from Germany, performed in the U.S.S.R. through the arrangements of VOKS,[40] the Soviet All-Union Society for Cultural Links Abroad. In the Soviet description, Gert drew many elements from the great contemporary European city, such as unruliness of movement, eroticism approaching the level of sensuality, and a somewhat indecent bravado.[41]

The little trickle of exchanges continued, with Asaf Messerer and his sister Sulamith performing successfully in Riga, Latvia, in 1929,[42] with Asaf returning in 1933. The United States gave diplomatic recognition to Soviet Russia in 1933, and from January 12 to 20, 1934, two veteran Soviet dancers performed in America: Vakhtang Chabukiani and Tatiana Vecheslova. They danced in New York, Boston, Chicago, Detroit, Los Angeles, and San Francisco. Chabukiani and Vecheslova recall that in San Francisco the Society of Maxim Gorky presented them with a wreath decked with red ribbons on which was written in gold letters: "The Proletarians of San Francisco send their greetings to the Soviet artists as beautiful representatives of Soviet art."[43] One American author asked Vecheslova and Chabukiani "how it was the technique of the ballet they brought with them had not been victimized by propaganda." The pair dutifully answered:

> How could it be? We are trained in a ballet school that gives us not only our training in dance, but also an academic education. The only obvious manifestation of revolutionary theory is that we are taught dialectical materialism. . . . In dancing we did experiment. . . . Several productions were put on, emphasizing the new theories of the dance as developed in Germany and elsewhere, but we found that the public refused to come and see them.[44]

A second Franco-Russian entente facilitated exchanges between the two countries in the 1930's. In 1932, France and the Soviet Union signed a nonaggression treaty. In 1933, Asaf Messerer performed in Paris, amazing many by his technique, but meeting the standard Western critique of Soviet ballet: "l'absense . . . de tout élément de nouveauté creatrice."[45] In the face of Hitler's growing power, a five-year treaty of military assistance was signed between France and the Soviet Union in May, 1935. The French government, desiring at this point to please the Soviet government, invited them to send a Soviet dancer to Paris to perform. The Russians sent Marina Semenova, the wife of Lev Karakhan, who was himself prominent in the Soviet diplomatic service before he fell a victim of the Stalinist purges. Semenova was well received by the general audience, although Parisian critics, perhaps used to the other-worldly portrayal of Giselle by Olga Spessivtzeva, complained that Semonova's interpretation emphasized Giselle's peasant condition, while failing to express the psychological dimensions of the role,[46] and that she endowed the part with "insupportable realism."[47]

In the years when Soviet dance was being firmly channeled into classical paths, the visits of some American dancers to the Soviet

Union served to underscore some paradoxical contrasts between the paths of evolution of the art of dance in the two countries. In the depressed years of the 1930's in the United States, noteworthy groups of modern dancers with such intriguing names as the Harlem Proletariats and The Rebel Dancers were formed to dramatize by dance such themes as class struggle, Negro rights, antiwar issues, and fascism. Some of these groups came together in New York for conventions in 1934 and 1935. There, it was possible to see such works as *Comintern,* performed by a group called the Red Dancers; *Pioneer March,* performed by the Junior Red Dancers; *Uprising,* by the New Dance Group; and an *Antiwar Cycle* done by the Theatre Union Dance Group, and many others.[48] Anna Sokolow, the guiding hand of the latter group, was one of the first American modern dancers to perform in Russia after Isadora Duncan. She danced in Moscow in 1934.[49] The following year at least two people involved with the American modern dance movement performed in Russia: Pauline Koner and Dhimah. Pauline Koner felt that she had found the nucleus of a Soviet modern dance movement in the Physical Culture Institute at Leningrad, where she had taught.[50] An article in the Soviet press explained that one might dispute the worth of Koner's dance, but one could not fail to recognize her freshness, vividness, and expressiveness.[51] The second voyager, Dhimah, was an Egyptian who had studied under Germany's Mary Wigman, but who had been dancing in New York in the years preceding her Russian trip.[52] All the American emissaries discovered that, as far as revolutionary dance technique was concerned, there was more to be seen in New York than in Russia.

Exchanges took place with satellite countries soon after the guns of World War II were silent. Also in 1945, Ulanova danced in Vienna,[53] and in 1951 Asaf Messerer and Vasily Tikhomirov appeared in a concert group in the same city.[54] The year 1951 brought Russian ballet to Italy for the first time in recent years. Regrettably, from the start Soviet artists have had to experience inconveniences resulting from the fact that they represent a government which many people fear and distrust. Ulanova was invited at this time to perform at a Florentine music festival. However, an election was pending, and her performance date was postponed. She had to wait nearly two weeks in Florence without performing—until the election was over. It was reported that at one point her appearance was actually cancelled, but Mayor Fabiani of Florence, a Communist, secured a reversal of the cancellation.[55] She was then invited to perform at La Scala Opera House in Milan and did so. Performances in other Italian cities were scheduled, but she was then given notice to leave Italy within twenty-four hours. Characteristically, Ulanova reported that the people and workers had been especially kind to her by repairing the badly pitted La Scala stage floor and by bringing flowers to the Soviet performers when they were told to go home, thus clearly showing their displeasure with the government's orders for their departure.[56] At home, Ulanova also emphasized the theme of the hard life of artists in the West, the insecurity of their lives, and the exploitation of their youthful energy which exhausted them before they were really ripe artists. She deplored the talent which was wasted and underdeveloped because of the high cost of artistic education.[57]

In later years, happier exchanges took place between Italy and the U.S.S.R. In 1955, Soviet performers brought the ballet *Romeo and Juliet* to the land of the Capulets and Montagues, where it was enthusiastically received.[58]

After Stalin's death in April, 1953, the doors to the West gradually opened wider. In November, 1953, a delegation of Soviet artists and scientists came to England. The group included Georgi Farmaniants from the Bolshoi, Alla Shelest and Konstantin Shatilov from the Kirov Theatre, the Uzbek dancer Galia Izmailova, and a trio from the Piatnitsky Song and Dance Group.[59] The next year, Raisa Struchkova and Alexander Lapauri of the Bolshoi Theatre came to Britain for concerts inaugurating British-Soviet Friendship month. Some of their performances were reminiscent of the old postrevolutionary "meetings," for the spectators were urged to buy certain newspapers, to belong to certain societies, and the dancers performed against a background of British and Soviet flags, sharing the stage with various officials and members of the diplomatic corps, including Jacob Malik, the Soviet ambassador.[60] An Uzbek dancer named Gulnora Mavaeva performed a dance called *Spring,* which described an Uzbek sowing seed, washing clothes, sewing, and carrying on a courtship. The delegation included several more performers, including the violinist David Oistrakh, Aram Khachaturian, and a few circus artists and jugglers.[61] Besides appearing in London, they performed in industrial towns such as Cardiff, Manchester, Liverpool, Bristol, Newcastle, and Stockton. In the same year, a delegation of six Soviet artists, including Sophia Golovkina and Leonid Zhukov, gave several performances in Canada.[62]

One of the most unfortunate occurrences in the history of ballet exchanges also took place in 1954. An agreement had been negotiated between the two governments whereby the Comédie Française would perform in Russia and the Bolshoi Ballet would dance in Paris. The French actors had completed their tour in Russia and the Russians had actually arrived in Paris to perform. At this point, due to the military situation in Indo-China and as the fall of Dien Bien Phu became imminent, the scheduled May 7 performance of the Bolshoi artists was postponed until May 10. At this time, the policy of the French government was under strong attack in the Assemblée Nationale, and on May 10, the Soviet dancers learned that their performance was postponed indefinitely by the French government. The French Premier had told them that it was impossible to assure their safety, and the dancers packed their bags for home. The Soviet press tried to make the most advantageous use of a bad situation, emphasizing the fact that the French people had really wanted the dancers to stay, but that the government had overridden their will. Their press reported that the dancers were taken to the airfield in a roundabout way to prevent their meeting French citizens who wanted to bid them *au revoir.* At the airport, the police tried to hold back several hundred people who gathered there anyway. Finally, they let some of the citizens through the lines to give flowers to the performers, whereupon the ingenious Frenchmen began to divide up their flowers so that more people could get through the police lines. Ulanova declared, "We know the people of France sincerely regretted the whole thing."[63]

The Soviet press reported that various French intellectuals, including Frédérick and Irene Joliot-Curie had published a letter in the paper *L'Humanité* protesting the government's policy, saying that the action "might prejudice for many years efforts toward free exchange of ideas and people."[64]

Meanwhile, according to Soviet sources, the group had received invitations to perform instead in England, Denmark, Holland, Greece, Egypt, Latin America, and the German Democratic Republic. They chose Berlin and danced at the Friedrichstadt Palace. On one occasion, French delegates to a trade union conference in Berlin came on stage and presented them with flowers. They gave one performance especially for West Berliners and also performed at a House of Culture for miners.[65] A review of the program which appeared in the Western press centered about a theme which became a standard criticism of the Soviet productions. Though their technical ability was considered stupendous, the realism displayed in their performance of *Bronze Horseman* did not appeal to the Western critic, who showed surprise at the outmoded decors and costumes and the absence of creative choreography.[66]

In July, 1955, the Geneva Summit Conference brought an era of comparatively good feelings into East-West relationships. At this meeting, Anthony Eden strongly urged more cultural contacts and the Soviet delegate, Nikolai Bulganin, was very amenable to the idea.[67] Immediately there began to appear in the Soviet press articles such as one by Olga Lepeshinskaya, entitled "We Should Meet,"[68] urging the further development of such contacts. At the Twentieth Party Congress in 1956, Nikita Khrushchev reaffirmed the Soviet aim of seeking to establish more firm and friendly relations with the West.[69]

This new attitude resulted in a visit of Igor Moiseyev's Folk Dance Ensemble to France, followed in July, 1956, by the ballet company of the Stanislavsky Nemirovich-Danchenko Musical Theatre of Moscow. They performed *Swan Lake* and some other standard fare, along with *Shore of Happiness* with its incredible military tank disintegrating on stage. The first glimpse by a Western audience of this particular brand of Soviet realism brought the usual reaction: universal surprise was registered that the Soviets were still clinging to trends which had not been in evidence in the West for many decades. The composer Henri Sauguet, who had written a ballet produced by the Ballet Russe, wrote an article entitled "So Diagilev Accomplished a Revolution in Vain!" The French reaction rubbed a very sensitive point; and Soviet critics in turn deplored the fact that the French critics, accustomed to the pseudo-innovations and modernistic ballets which grew in Diagilev's path, could not appreciate their realistic approach. Their press complained that French critics ignored what was to the Soviet world "the basic criterion of a work, its idea value," and that "content interested them little."[70]

In the spring of 1956, Ninette de Valois, the guiding force of the British Sadler's Wells Ballet, went to Moscow to negotiate exchange visits of the British company and the Bolshoi.[71] Again the visit by the Bolshoi dancers was almost curtailed by another incident. A Soviet sportswoman, an Olympics contestant named Nina Ponomareva, was in Britain in August, 1956. As she was leaving a shop on Oxford Street, the athlete was accused of having failed to pay for merchandise from the shop.[72] The Soviet press treated her arrest as a deliberate provocation, and there were serious doubts whether Britain would see the Bolshoi performers. Various members of the administration, orchestra, and dancers of the company, including Mikhail Chulaki, Galina Ulanova, A. Melik-Pachaiev, Raisa Struchkova, Yuri Faier, Asaf Messerer, Vladimir Ryndin, Alexander Radunsky, Georgi Farmaniants, Yadviga Sangovich and Yuri Kondratiev sent the following letter to the editor of *Izvestiia:*

Naturally, great anxiety reigns in the collective of our troupe. In fact, what guarantee is there that a provocation like that which was aimed at Nina Ponomareva in London will not be repeated against one of us? What guarantee is there that our collective can appear in London under normal conditions without fearing that someone from the collective will be subjected to outrages or other forms of persecution? In such circumstances the trip to London of the Bolshoi Theatre can not be carried out. We declare that we shall not allow any member of our collective to be subject to the danger of any sort of provocation. That is why we pose the question of whether the collective of the ballet troupe of our theatre may go to London under the given conditions.[73]

Meanwhile, Nina Ponomareva was sheltered in the Soviet embassy, the scenery of the Bolshoi company lay in British docks, uncleared, and some of the British people interpreted the Soviet letter as blackmail to force the British government to drop the case of the athlete.[74] However, the exchange finally took place, and the Soviet company was enthusiastically received in Britain. At home, after the visit, one of the dancers, Yekaterina Sheveleva, reported:

> The bourgeois press tries to avoid mentioning the successes of the Soviet Union in the international arena in science, technology, art, literature, and sports. English newspapers could not avoid writing of the exceptional triumph of the Bolshoi artists in London. But the press passed over in silence the concluding performance of the Soviet artists at Covent Garden, with its more than half-hour ovation and cries from the boxes and galleries saying, "Long live friendship" and "Greetings to the country which has created such art!"
>
> Once, when Soviet artists were returning after a performance at Covent Garden, simple Londoners—industrial, office and professional workers—linked hands, forming a living chain in order to guard the artists from troublesome distributors of slanderous leaflets.[75]

This time, British dancers did not have a chance to enjoy an equal triumph, for international events again prevented their visit to the Soviet Union. The Hungarian Revolution of November, 1956, and the concomitant involvement of Britain and France in the Suez crisis prompted a cancellation of the visit. Mikhail Chulaki of the Bolshoi

Theatre received the following telegram from Sir David Webster, General Administrator of the Royal Opera House, Covent Garden:

> In view of public opinion in this country, which strongly condemns the renewed suppression by Soviet forces of Hungarian liberty and independence, the Royal Opera House, Covent Garden, has consulted Her Majesty's Government and the Soviet Relations Committee of the British Council. It has been unanimously agreed that in present circumstances the projected visit of the Sadler's Wells Ballet to Moscow cannot take place.[76]

Chulaki answered Webster with a counterthrust:

> We understand that the reason for your refusal to come to the Soviet Union is not the events in Hungary referred to in your cable, but the correct position of the Soviet government, which has the unanimous support of all Soviet people, on the Anglo-French and Israeli aggressive agitation against the freedom and independence of the Egyptian people.
>
> As regards the events in Hungary, we recommend that you refer to the published documents of the Hungarian Revolutionary Workers' and Peasants' Government and also to material about the brutalities of the White Terror in Hungary published in various places, including the American press.[77]

Although the British visit did not take place this time, by 1958 an exchange was finally made between the ballet of the French Opéra and the Bolshoi Ballet Company. The visit of a major Western company to Russia was bound to bring into sharp focus the differences in esthetic doctrines between Russia and the West. More information is necessary for a proper understanding of the criticisms the U.S.S.R. leveled against Western ballet.

To many Americans, aware of the postrevolutionary period of free love in Russia, it comes as a surprise to find Soviet art usually free from anything that would disturb the sensibilities of a Victorian governess. Official sources depict the West as the citadel of decayed morals and depravity, and its artists are prime perpetrators of this vileness. The Soviet youth newspaper, *Komsomolskaia Pravda*, has declared:

> Searching out ways to the minds of youth, bourgeois propaganda places more and more hope on its art, music, and dances in trying to reach the minds of young people. . . . It stresses art that awakens animal instincts and that preaches egoism, cruelty, and a thirst for unhealthy pleasures. . . . Apologists for the bourgeois way of life place their hope on licentious and hysterical jazz rubbish, on dances with pornographic overtones, on concoctions by artists that relieve man of the necessity of thinking.[78]

More pointedly, the *Bol'shaia Entsiklopediia* decried many West European and American ballets:

> [They express] a hideous picture of the decay of reactionary bourgeois culture. Just as in the other forms of bourgeois art, the present ballet of capitalistic countries serves the reactionary aims of imperialism. In it are preached submissiveness to fate (*Dante Sonata*—London); . . . death as a "higher rest" (*Le Jeune Homme et la Mort*—Paris); insanity (*Night Shadow*—U.S.A.); murder and violence. . . .[79]

Actually, in the years when Soviet ballet was passing through its wild, experimental period, pioneers of the American modern dance movement were developing a new idiom of movement to represent themes hitherto unexpressed in dance. The teachings of Sigmund Freud, which had led twentieth-century man to probe his own consciousness, found expression in literature, in music, and on canvas. However, if only the strict, established vocabulary of classical ballet could be employed, problems were posed in the dance expression of such a phenomenon as Freudian frustration. Thus the "moderns" began to experiment with new movements. Just as the expressionist painters used distortion and exaggeration of bodily parts to show more intense emotion, in the same manner, modern dancers used bodily contractions and tense gestures to explore in dance the profundities of man's inner world.[80]

In opposition to this trend, the official Soviet doctrine preaches that because of its excessive, morbid probing of the unconscious spheres of the human psyche, the bourgeois art of the West has progressively decayed.[81] During the intense postwar drive to purify Soviet artistic life of decadent Western tendencies, *Bolshevik*, the official ideological organ of the Communist Party of the Soviet Union, printed an article that was merely an elaboration of Zhdanov's creed. It denounced "the ideological teachers of West European decadence, the epigones of subjective idealism—Nietzsche, Bergson, and Freud," who preached the destruction of all laws of social development, of morality and reason, and exalted the subconscious, bestial instincts of man, along with his zoological individualism, mysticism, and eroticism.[82] The article said that this phenomenon was accompanied in literature by an inevitable decay of form, citing the works of Proust, Joyce, Dos Passos, Céline, Sartre, and the "religious eroticism of Akhmatova" as examples of such decay.

The Soviet condemnation of Freudian themes in art thus stems from a deep-seated antagonism toward the works of the renowned psychologist. Their view states:

> Freudianism is a typical product of bourgeois ideological reaction in the epoch of imperialism, used by the bourgeois ideologues as a weapon for stupefying the masses in the interests of imperialism in the struggle against Marxism.
>
> *   *   *
>
> With the aid of psychoanalysis, the reactionary followers of Freud try to persuade the worker that all the difficulties of his life stem from within himself and not from bourgeois society or from the essential consequences of the productive relations of an exploiters' society. [The latter statement is the view of Karl Marx][83]

Such condemnations in the U.S.S.R. are not meant to be personal critiques. Any artist knows that such an article in *Bolshevik* or *Voprosy Filosofii* is a guideline which all creative endeavor must follow. This is exactly the pattern in this case, as in countless others. On April 24, 1948, B. V. Asafiev, speaking at the First All-Union

Congress of Soviet Composers, criticized the gloomy pessimism and mysticism of bourgeois society as depicted in the works of Hartmann, Spengler, Bergson, Nietzsche, and Swedenborg, and he deplored the fact that the West must search for peace of mind in "the twilight of the Freudian theory of the subconscious." After castigating the paintings of Cézanne, Matisse, Picasso, and Cocteau, he criticized the music of Arnold Schönberg, Alban Berg, Anton von Webern, Ernst Křenek, Paul Hindemith, Olivier Messaiën, Gian-Carlo Menotti, and Benjamin Britten, concluding that "all these composers are penetrated by a spirit of extreme subjectivism, mysticism, obscurantism, and loathsome imbecility."[84]

In subsequent years, it was the turn of Western ballet to be the subject of a parallel critique. In an article called "Corruption of the Art of Ballet in the West," the author pointed out general faults of Western art, declaring that it attempted to draw the advanced members of society away from political and social questions, and thus to occupy their attention with an art low in ideology, but replete with gangsters, variety show girls, adultery, and various other unsavory features of bourgeois society. She declared: "On the stages of capitalist states more and more there appear ballets directly propagandizing a reactionary, cosmopolitan ideology, the cult of death, of criminality, and of depravity, fitted to educate the mercenaries so needed by plundering, American imperialism."[85]

Western ballet theatre was judged to be guilty of the general faults of all Western art, for it, too, based its librettos upon the works of authors under *Bolshevik's* interdict: Proust, Freud, and Sartre.[86] The corruption of Western ballet was due not only to its employment of themes by these authors, but also because it used sets by the surrealist artists Salvador Dali and Leslie Hurry. In imitation of a recent article in *Izvestiia,* she also complained that one of the causes of Western ballet's corruption was its employment of "the cacophony of Stravinsky." As examples, the article pointed to *Undertow, Pillar of Fire, Dante Sonata, Checkmate, Le Jeune Homme et la Mort,* and

Labyrinthe. All of these were guilty of toying with Freudian frustration themes, of expressing a type of morbid self-probing not permitted in Soviet art, or of other deviations from their esthetic rules.

Thus, Western companies with a repertoire of ballets reflecting the ideas of the interdicted Western thinkers were bound to face a wall of cultivated misunderstanding when their work should be reviewed in the U.S.S.R.

The Ballet of the French Opéra was the first to experience this brand of Soviet criticism. Many of the French ballets were well received by both critics and ordinary citizens. However, Soviet comments about certain works in their repertoire were consistent with their general ideological views. The French company performed the ballet *Les Mirages* with music by Henri Sauguet, the composer who had made a searing remark about Diagilev's vain revolution, after the Stanislavsky Ballet had danced in Paris. The choreography of the ballet was by Serge Lifar, an ex-Russian whose reported connivance with Hitler's Parisian occupation forces during World War II had been mentioned in the Soviet press.[87] *Les Mirages* has been called one of Lifar's most poetic ballets. It attempts to portray "human existence in the midst of deceptions, up to the hour of final solitude, when man remains isolated with his shadow before indifferent nature."[88] Soviet statements indicated that critics detected in the ballet traces of the influence of the existentialist philosopher Jean-Paul Sartre. Viktorina Kriger remarked that a healthy organism would not accept deviations from the norm; neither could Soviet society accept such a ballet as *Les Mirages,* for its citizenry had no contact with the problem of "the eternal loneliness of man."[89] Mikhail Gabovich likewise complained of the ballet because it mirrored the philosophy of the "cult of the solitary human being."[90]

The Fundamentals of Marxism-Leninism, which both Kriger and Gabovich have undoubtedly studied, declares that Soviet Communist doctrine cannot accept Sartrean ideas that the individual is alone in an alien world, that he lives an "unreal" existence in relation to other men, that society robs man of his individuality, and that struggle is futile because the world is absurd and history is meaningless. In contrast, communism preaches that man's labor as a member of society redeems and raises him above the animal world and gives meaning and purpose to life.[91] Therefore, there can be no eternal loneliness of man in Soviet society.

In the summer of 1958, Soviet dancers from the Bolshoi Ballet and the Moiseyev Folk Dance Ensemble scored a wide success with audiences at the Brussels World's Fair.[92] There were less heartening moments in 1958 in the field of cultural exchanges. The Bolshoi Company had been invited to perform in Athens in the spring of 1958, but Greek Minister of Labor Kapodistrias made the announcement that the troupe would not be allowed to perform because of election campaigns which were in process at the time.[93]

However, such setbacks were well-balanced by new triumphs. A most significant step occurred when an agreement was signed January 27, 1958, by American Ambassador William S. B. Lacy and Soviet representative Georgi N. Zaroubin.[94] This ultimately led to the performance of the Bolshoi Ballet Company in the United States in 1959 and to the exchange trip of the American Ballet Theatre in Russia in 1960. The Russians were heartily received by American audiences, which could overlook such a work as *We Stalingraders* in the light of the overpowering brilliance of *Giselle*, danced by Ulanova. Americans, like Frenchmen and Englishmen, were surprised at the seeming absence of newer artistic trends in their works, but general judgment still placed the performers themselves at the top of the world's hierarchy of dance. Their tour became a source of keen pride to Nikita Khrushchev, who gloated over the supremacy of Soviet ballet during his visit to the United States in 1959. Angered at the refusal of American authorities to let him see Disneyland, Khrushchev had emitted his famous phrase, "We will bury you," only a few days before he spoke at a dinner in a Los Angeles film studio. While reminiscing there about his poor background, Khrushchev became garrulous as he described his culturally-starved youth:

> I remember I was in the Kuban region. . . . I lived in the house of a
> very interesting bourgeois intellectual family. The mistress of the house
> was a graduate of a noble ladies education establishment in St. Peters-
> burg. I suppose I still had coal on my hands. . . . They started asking me
> questions. "Well, all right," they said, "But what do you understand in
> the ballet?—you a miner?" And I must admit that at that time I not
> only had never seen a ballet; I had never seen a ballerina. So I did not
> know what it was—what sort of a dish it was and what you ate it with.
> And I said, "Wait, it will all come."
>
> If she were to have asked me then what it was that would come, I
> would not have given her any reply—I did not know what would come.
> But I did know that the new and the good happy life would come.
> Now, I have a question for you. Which country has the best ballet?
> Yours? You do not even have a permanent opera and ballet theatre.
> Your theatres thrive on what is given them by rich people. In our coun-
> try it is the state that gives it money. And the best ballet is in the Soviet
> Union. It is our pride. And you paid a worthy tribute to our ballet
> when it came here to the United States. . . . I am not going to lavish
> praise on it, but see yourselves which art is on the upsurge and which
> is on the downgrade.[95]

The next day Khrushchev gave his famous burlesque performance,
mocking the cancan he had seen performed by Shirley MacLaine
during his visit to the Hollywood studio. According to a Soviet source,
Khrushchev remarked, "You want to know what I think of the cancan?
From my point of view it is immoral. Good actors are made to do
things for the entertainment of satiated and depraved people."[96]
The Soviet source then proceeded to explain that the staging of the
dance was probably no accident, but a provocation by someone who
wanted to destroy the cordial understanding born in Hollywood
between Khrushchev and American actors. Khrushchev used the
incident to make another point: "This is what you call freedom.
Freedom for the girls to show their backsides. To us it's pornography.
The culture of a people who want pornography."[97]

After the U–2 episode of May, 1960, there was a good deal of doubt whether the reciprocal visit of the American Ballet Theatre would occur.[98] Finally, the path was cleared, and the American group was inspected while performing in Holland. The censors were two Soviet citizens: Alexei Tchichinadze, a dancer, and M. Gorokhov, the First Secretary of the Soviet Embassy in Holland.[99] The American company had planned to perform several ballets which the Soviet authorities vetoed. One work, *Billy the Kid,* was canceled. Billy, in their view, had no sufficient moral or social purpose for killing his victims.[100] Lucia Chase, the director of the company, brought up the subject of Stenka Razin, but to no avail.

In 1950, the same company had performed *Fall River Legend* in Berlin. On December 12, 1950, the Soviet-controlled newspapers in Berlin used the ballet as a juicy propaganda piece, calling it "dancing murder."[101] *Fall River Legend* was indeed a story of murder. It was based upon a famous case in America, the axe-murders attributed to Lizzie Borden of Fall River, Massachusetts, in the late nineteenth century. *Fall River Legend* was no ordinary melodrama. One critic remarked that he felt it revealed the morasses of abnormal psychology with more brilliance and depth than the works of all American playwrights during the last twenty-five years.[102] Though stunningly performed, the ballet was exactly the kind of work which the Soviet press had labeled typical American decadence, and the censor in Holland had to exclude Lizzie Borden from the U.S.S.R. along with Billy the Kid.

Of the ballets which were subsequently allowed in the U.S.S.R., some met with criticisms entirely in keeping with normal Soviet criteria. One such work was *Lilac Garden,* a drama of couples in love who are parted by a marriage of convenience. A Soviet reviewer referred to it as "a so-called psychological ballet,"[103] decrying the fact that in it, "a feeling of tragic doom predominates," not in keeping with Soviet optimism. On the other hand, their critics almost universally praised *The Duel* by William Dollar, an artistic depiction in ballet of Torquato Tasso's *Jerusalem Delivered.* In the danced version, haughty crusaders are depicted, one of whom kills the girl he loves while she, too, is clad in armor. The Soviet critic called it "an open and consistent condemnation of war, of bloodshed, of feuds and their tragic consequences."[104] Other criticisms and evaluations of the company's repertoire were in keeping with their standard principles. Soviet authors seldom missed an opportunity to point out that the company had no permanent location in America, and was doomed to a nomadic life.[105]

In 1961, the West became acquainted with the Leningrad State Kirov Ballet. After the company's performance in Paris on June 16, 1961, the most dramatic incident in the history of Soviet cultural exchanges occurred. The brilliant Tatar dancer Rudolf Nureyev had never found it easy to conform, and there were indications that his superiors feared his independent spirit.

When the American Ballet Theatre danced in Russia in 1960, Nureyev, who had learned English, was sent to dance in Berlin with a group of circus performers.[106] While the Kirov Ballet danced in Paris, Nureyev had toured the city and seemed too independent to please Soviet authorities. At the airport he was informed that he was not to go on to London with the troupe, but was to return home to the Soviet Union. Fearing that his future chances for dancing might be curtailed, Nureyev requested political asylum of the French government. Having decided to stay in the West, he accepted a contract with the Marquis de Cuevas Ballet Company. Soviet authorities resorted to strong pressures to force his return to the U.S.S.R. His mother was brought from Bashkiria to Moscow to make daily phone calls and plead with her son to return; and at one performance French Communists threw broken glass on the stage to show their displeasure with the man who had deserted communism.[107] When the Paris Opéra attempted to engage him to dance in *Giselle*, the Soviet ambassador to France threatened to suspend cultural exchanges between the two countries, and the Opéra rescinded the contract with Nureyev.[108] In Athens, Sviatoslav Richter, the Soviet pianist, canceled his engagement to play at a festival where Nureyev was also scheduled to dance.[109] In spite of pressure on the British government, Nureyev signed a contract with the Royal Ballet and has won fame as the captivating partner of Margot Fonteyn. The rest of the Kirov company, with Nureyev's picture deleted from the programs, proceeded to complete their tour. In spite of the fact that they were introduced to London audiences with the unpopular, moralistic *Stone Flower*, which in the view of a British critic harked back to Victorian melodrama,[110] the West was universally impressed with this fine company. The company, in turn, was apparently impressed with Western dentistry; they made headlines by using the services of British state-subsidized dentists.[111]

This time, the British company, now called the Royal Ballet, had the opportunity of repaying the visit. Their tour passed without incident, bringing forth a minimum of adverse comments against such ballets as *Rinaldo and Armida,* and *La Peri,* which were labeled as "exotic, sentimental poesy."[112]

Exchanges of subsequent years continued to bring forth comments that emphasized the marked differences in the evaluative criteria on both sides of the Iron Curtain. For example, in 1962 the Bolshoi Ballet company again returned to America and made another triumphal tour. This time, the repertoire included the garish, expensive *Spartacus,* complete with gladiatorial contests, slave girl dancing, and all the gaudy trappings expected of a Roman extravaganza. It was, literally, socialist realism to end all socialist realism—in America. The New York critics flagellated the production. *New York Times* writer Allen Hughes labeled it "one of the most preposterous theatrical exercises" he had ever seen.[113] Understandably, on September 18, 1962, the headlines carried the news that the Bolshoi company, in a shift of programs, had canceled three planned showings of *Spartacus.*[114]

In 1962, George Balanchine's elegant New York City Ballet danced in Russia. Balanchine's visit even more sharply emphasized the differences in the art practiced by the two countries. Through long years of collaboration with Igor Stravinsky, Balanchine has evolved his own austere style of intricate choreographic patterns which uniquely mirror the complicated rhythms and harmonies of Stravinsky's music. His company has also successfully performed the works of Anton von Webern, Arnold Schönberg, and Benjamin Britten—all of whom were castigated by Asafiev in 1948. Balanchine has no essential need for "content" in his works; for him, the dance suffices. The company operates with a minimum of scenery, and for costumes the dancers often wear leotards or unadorned, short adaptations of Greek tunics. Western audiences and critics, long exposed to abstract art, to 12-tone music, and to an art in general which emphasizes form instead of content, have developed a taste for this type of presentation. Because of the state-imposed doctrine of socialist realism, Soviet audiences have had an entirely different type of esthetic education through the decades.

During the Soviet tour, Balanchine's group performed such works as *Fanfare* by Benjamin Britten, *Agon* and *Apollo* by Stravinsky, *Episodes* by Anton von Webern, as well as a good portion of the work of such "standard" composers as Tchaikovsky.[115] Balanchine's visit came at a time of general ferment in the artistic world of the U.S.S.R. and his style was bound to stir some excitement. Many Soviet viewers were astounded and fascinated with the works, but Soviet critics know how they are supposed to respond in print to "formalism" in art. There were the standard comments about the evident lack of content. Aram Khachaturian, while complaining of Balanchine's adherence to the principle of "plotlessness,"[116] also remarked that if Balanchine had done the choreography for his *Spartacus,* it would not have been such a flop. Balanchine begged to differ with him; he declared that *Spartacus,* like much of Russia's contemporary ballet, excessively emphasized plot and decoration to the expense of dance and music, and was therefore hopeless from the beginning.[117]

One critic, excessively sensitized toward works which did not conform to the officially imposed rosy-visioned Soviet *weltanschauung,* did not approve of *La Valse,* whose "choreographic impressionism," depicted frantically whirling couples suggesting "desperate searching for happiness, brief and transient meetings, evanescent, illusory dreams, the sudden crashing of human hopes."[118] Another critic complained that *Western Symphony* was "vulgar," adding, "our people consider any psychological overstrain or nervous tensity incompatible with the radiant and elevated art of ballet."[119] Rostislav Zakharov, a well-known Soviet choreographer, said that Balanchine's adherence to formal quests was unacceptable to Soviet ballet, which was based upon content, plot, kinship with the people, and realism.[120] Another author affirmed that the lack of a guiding idea impoverished the creative possibilities of the talented group.[121]

Balanchine himself gave a press interview which was subsequently printed in *Sovetskii Artist.* Knowing perfectly well the Soviet view, Balanchine calmly affirmed his own creed: "The ballet as such is a rich art form that should not be an illustration of even the most meaningful literary primary source. The ballet will speak for itself and about itself. Ballet is flowers, beauty, poetry . . ."[122] Further, he remarked that he was always sorry to see a skilled ballerina using her talent to depict only some literary theme, and added, "Yes, if you like, I am an adherent of art for art's sake." There were bound to be comments against such a blatant contradiction of Soviet principles. Alexander Lapauri was quick to answer in the press that the Soviet Union wanted a ballet art which posed and solved great social questions, and which spoke not only of beauty but also of man's great thoughts and feelings.[123] Perhaps a truer gauge of the impact made by Balanchine can be judged from the fact that, in late 1962, Galina Ulanova called for the creation of a new experimental ballet theatre in the U.S.S.R. that would exchange experiences with foreigners. She said, "I dream about a theatre of seeking, experiments, trials—a theatre where the contemporary performance would be born."[124] The timing of Ulanova's letter was surprising, for it came during the period of the heated efforts of Nikita Khrushchev to degrade abstract art. Ulanova also cautiously acknowledged the campaign, said she approved of the official condemnation of abstract paintings, and made it clear she was not advocating any radical departures from Khrushchev's policies.

The spring of 1963 brought several manifestations that some Soviet officials feared the magnetism of some of the theories of Western artistic invaders of the U.S.S.R. It was reported that the head of the Leningrad regional party committee was nervous about Western influences that seemed to be permeating the Kirov Company,[125] and in his own picturesque way, Khrushchev conveyed the same fear during a long tirade on March 8, 1963. While he was probably primarily speaking about social and folk dance, such comments could be expected to apply in general to the entire field of dance:

> A feeling of objection is also evoked by some so-called modern dances, brought into our country from the West. I have had a chance to travel a lot around the country. I have seen Russian, Ukrainian, Kazakh, Uzbek, Armenian, Georgian, and other dances. These are beautiful dances. To watch them is pleasant. But the so-called modern, fashionable dances are simply something obscene, the devil knows what! They say that one can see such indecent things only in the religious sect of Shakers. I cannot attest to this, because I have never attended their meeting. (Laughter in the hall.)[126]

Another chance for Soviet critics to evaluate the American dance world came in October, 1963, when the Robert Joffrey Ballet Company performed in the U.S.S.R. The young company was replete with technically competent dancers working under exciting artistic direction. Their performances evoked the normal responses. A veteran critic, Natalia Roslavleva, especially noted the ballet *Feast of Ashes*. This was quite understandable on several counts. First of all, it dealt with Spain—a favorite subject of Soviet propaganda art—when it could be shown in an unhealthy light. Further, *Feast of Ashes* is a strikingly unforgettable, highly dramatic ballet, loaded with enough "content" to make a Soviet choreographer envious. It depicts the trials of a beautiful young Spanish girl, frustrated in love both by a domineering mother and by the Church. The latter is represented in the ballet by processing monks, brandishing a large cross, who prevent the girl from being united with the man she loves. Frustrated in her efforts to achieve happiness, she commits suicide. In Russia, the title was *House of Suffering,* and to the Soviet critic, it was "the most interesting of the whole repertoire."[127]

Another ballet performed by the company brought adverse printed criticism, also completely logical from their point of view. In America, the ballet was called *Time Out of Mind,* but the Soviet title was *At the Dawn of Humanity.* It has no plot. In the earlier version the dancers, clad in white leotards, moved in startling contrast against a bright red backdrop on which a solitary large black spot was painted. Their swiftly moving, highly complex choreographic patterns created a general impression of Man in his mad, ceaseless drive toward Girl. In the beginning of the ballet, the man, according to a graphic and correct Soviet description, appeared to represent prehistoric people with dangling, apelike arms hanging down while they walked in a squatty manner.[128] It was a startling work and probably many Soviet viewers found it breathtaking, but its bald probing of man's lower instincts would clearly bar its full acceptance in the U.S.S.R. The general comment was one of disapproval. Their critics said that it could only aim to degrade man by denuding his animal nature and by showing his utter helplessness in overcoming his own restless, primitive instincts. Soviet spectators were said to have interpreted the work either as a comment on contemporary American life or as the awakening of love against the background of primitive instincts. Typically, a reviewer said of the whole tour, "Evidently the company has a wide-ranging creative program. But what its credo is we do not know, or its goals."[129]

The precarious financial existence under which American companies have had to function has continually provided anticapitalist grist for the Soviet propaganda mills. In 1965, Natalia Dudinskaya reported in *Sovetskaia Kul'tura* that Joffrey's company had fallen apart because his patron, who formerly subsidized the troupe, presently refused to give them the means to exist and "because of his [sic] caprice all the troupe was left without work."[130]

In 1966, the American Ballet Theatre again toured the Soviet Union, performing such works as *Fall River Legend* and *Billy the Kid*—not allowed by the Soviet censor in 1960. The Ballet Theatre tour followed a spring tour by the Bolshoi Ballet in America where the Soviets performed their own version of Stravinsky's *Rite of Spring*. Both were indications that the harsh days of Stalinism had disappeared, but neither should be construed in any way as signs of complete artistic freedom in the U.S.S.R. The rule laid down by Leonid F. Ilyichev in 1962 still stands: "We have full freedom to struggle for communism. We do not and cannot have freedom to struggle against communism."[131]

CULTURAL CONTACTS WITH ASIA AND AFRICA

The U.S.S.R. has sent its best artists to other countries of Asia and Africa to display Soviet prowess in dance. In China, western classical ballet had made little headway before the communist government was established in 1949. When large groups of Russian technicians and cultural workers came to China at the invitation of the new regime, balletmasters of the highest quality began the Peking School of Dancing in 1954. For five years, teachers from the Moscow Bolshoi and Leningrad Kirov companies trained cadres of Chinese dancers. The Russian teacher mentioned most gratefully in the Chinese press was Pyotr A. Gusev, who had been associated with George Balanchine in the Leningrad Young Ballet Group in the 1920's.

One of the first works to be staged under Russian tutelage was a "dance drama" called *Dove of Peace*.[132] by 1958, the Chinese pupils were sufficiently well-trained to stage *Swan Lake*. In 1959, the Experimental Ballet Troupe of the Peking School of Dancing was instituted and many Soviet and western classics were produced. Chinese folk dances and folk tales were incorporated in the ballet, resulting in such works as *Maid of the Sea* and *Magic Lotus Lantern.*

When the political situation between the U.S.S.R. and Red China began to deteriorate in 1958, the Russian teachers were recalled. By this time, the Chinese students were able to continue the art, although after the Russians left ballet and dance in general became militant political tools, and the main efforts of the Chinese companies were channeled to the production of works such as *Red Detachment of Women.*[133] In the struggle between Liu Shao-chi and Mao Tse-tung, Mao's forces castigated many government officials who wished to follow a line of greater reconciliation with the U.S.S.R.; one of the charges against Liu Shao-chi was that he had praised bourgeois ballets such as *Swan Lake* while opposing China's own ballet and symphonic music.[134] *Swan Lake,* probably because of its true Russian origin, was denounced most stridently, being called "a symbol of the political and artistic stagnation that exists in the Soviet Union."[135]

As far as ballet technique is concerned, the Chinese were well-taught by the Russians and trained observers have noted the performers' arched backs, split leaps, and high leg extensions which have become identified with "the Bolshoi style" of dance.[136]

In 1954, a delegation of Bolshoi artists went to India, including Maya Plisetskaya. There were mixed accounts in the Indian press about their reception, ranging from glowing praise to an acid review declaring that India should in return send a troupe of snake charmers to Russia.[137] However, there are never any such mixed reports in the Soviet press when Indian artists appear there; the comments are always uniformly ecstatic. When Indian performers, including Gopinath and Tara Chowdhry, danced in Russia in 1956, a typical review read: "It was a warm welcome that Muscovites gave their dear guests, the masters of Indian art who paid a return visit to the capital of the Soviet Union, following the concerts of Soviet artists in India."[138]

Terpsichorean Diplomacy

There has followed a continued stream of articles in the Soviet press in recent years about Indian dance, music, and art of all forms. The former Minister of Culture, Nikolai Mikhailov, has pointed out that "the music, songs, and dances of India are of a unique beauty. Like all her art, they breathe a spirit of true nobility, a feeling of high humanism, and are deeply poetic."[139]

Soviet audiences and critics, whose tastes for various forms of national dances have been studiously cultivated by Soviet ruling circles, are usually warmly responsive to the many dancers who come to the U.S.S.R. from Asia and Africa, and the glowing reception the artists receive undoubtedly aids in cementing friendship with these people.

Ruins of the famed temples at Angkor in Cambodia give evidence that dance was a well-developed and esteemed art among the Khmers, one of the ancestral races of the present Cambodians. It became a custom for the ruler's children to train as performers in the royal dancing group, and today the lovely young daughter of Prince Norodom Sihanouk is the star of the Royal Cambodian Ballet. In 1964, the Royal Cambodian Ballet danced in Moscow and in the concluding number of the performance, the Cambodians staged a *Dance of Friendship and Greeting*. In it, tiny flags of the U.S.S.R. and Cambodia, blossoming like magic flowers, emerged from the hands of the dancers, whereupon the Soviet audience burst into a loud ovation. As the Russian reporter described it, "This warm applause expressed not only admiration for the astounding mastery of the Cambodian actors but also the cordiality and spiritual warmth that mark relations between the peoples of the Soviet Union and Cambodia."[140] Several days later, in the middle of the first page of *Pravda* a large, prominent notice appeared:

To His Excellency
Mr. Nikita Khrushchev

My daughter, Bopkha Devi, reports to me from Moscow that your excellency rendered honor to our Royal Ballet by being present at the première in the Soviet capital and singularly inspired our artists by your high evaluation of the performance of classical Khmer dances.

Allow me to express to you my very deep gratitude and to assure the Soviet government, ruling circles, and all our Soviet friends of our sincere gratitude for the organization of the extensive cultural arrangements in Kiev, Leningrad, and Moscow.

I am sure that this unforgettable visit of our Royal Ballet in the U.S.S.R. has aided the strengthening of the deep friendship uniting both our states.

Norodom Sihanouk
Head of State of Cambodia[141]

In 1957, stars of the Bolshoi Theatre toured Japan. This was a noteworthy occurrence, for, as the Soviet press explained, in pre-World War II days, Japanese militarists had organized "control over thoughts" and "witch hunts," hermetically sealing Japan from any knowledge of the true life of the Soviet people. Then, when the American occupation forces came into the country, they erected a bamboo curtain to fence Japan from the U.S.S.R. Under American influence, in restaurants, casinos, and cabarets there began to appear "naked women, coiling in silly poses," all the more regrettable because the Japanese women formerly had been unusually modest and shy. Along with this unhealthy element, the Americans also brought their gambling automats, which impoverished poor Japanese. When the Soviet dance troupe arrived, they were warmly greeted, although three American pilots tore down the Soviet flag from the hotel in which the artists were staying. The dancers made friends with Japanese performers, among them one of the leading artists of the Tokyo Kabuki Theatre, Ichikawa Ennosuke, who told them that when he was young he had visited Europe and had introduced elements of the ballet he had seen into the Kabuki dances. Since he had been taken to task for it by traditionalists of his art, he was glad to have the Soviets there to show how correct he had been in introducing it. The Russians pointed out that the Japanese were trying to develop ballet, but it was not state supported, and therefore the dancers had

278

to serve in shops, restaurants, and dressmaking establishments to earn
their living while also trying to dance. The Soviet troupe asked to
give a performance for plain working people, which they did in the
Kokusai Stadium.[142] Japanese dancers have been invited to study at
the Bolshoi school. In 1960, in Tokyo there was opened the Tchaikovsky Ballet School with Sulamith Messerer and Alexei Varlamov
as principal instructors.[143]

There have been many Asiatic students who have been the guests
of the Soviet government for choreographic education in the U.S.S.R.
A student from Indonesia, Farida Utoino, charmed all in the Soviet
capital by her Javanese dances, portraying a girl at work in the rice
fields, dressing for a festival, or carrying a water jug from a spring.
In the commencement recital of the Bolshoi graduating class she was
given a small part in a ballet suite called *Africa*. She was reported as
saying to her husband, a fellow Indonesian student in Moscow: "I
long to return to Djakarta and stage a ballet, our own Indonesian
ballet! But its heroes will not be legendary figures of antiquity; they
will be you and me, our friends and our people. These times we live
in are as heroic as those of the Ramayana, aren't they?"[144]

In the countries of Asia and Africa which they visited, some Soviet
performers were inclined to exploit the issue of race when an occasion
presented itself. In one report of a trip to Australia made by Bolshoi
members, the remark was made:

> Speaking of rights, . . . at one reception a member of our company,
> Esfandiar Kashani, [an Armenian] noticed a young, dark-skinned
> couple standing diffidently apart. He went over and shook hands with
> them and engaged them in conversation. Suddenly he noticed that
> tears had welled up in the eyes of the young woman. They were, he
> learned, native Australians, "aborigines" and unaccustomed to being
> treated as equals by whites.[145]

This policy of being "all things to all men" has been pursued
with equal persistence in Africa. In 1965, the Armenian State Folk
Dance Ensemble was sent to tour Algiers, Morocco, Tunis, Israel, and

Iran. In Tunis, they gave a concert to aid sufferers from a recent flood, an act which Soviet press reported was warmly received.[146] Besides the humanitarian role, the U.S.S.R. persistently grasps at opportunities to build a world image of itself as the patron of artistic development in countries which have not had the material means to nourish their own arts.

In Cairo, a delegation consisting of Uzbek dancer Galia Izmailova, ballerina Irina Tikhomirnova, and several others performed in 1956.[147] In 1958, Minister of Culture Mikhailov went to the United Arab Republic where he paved the way for greater cultural exchanges of students, actors, musicians, and other artists and sportsmen. Olga Lepeshinskaya, Irina Tikhomirnova, and Vladimir Preobrazhensky also toured the country in this year.[148] The Egyptian Minister of National Guidance, Fathy Radwan, was in Moscow in November, 1958, and there he received an assurance of stipends for training of Egyptian specialists in theatrical arts, cinema, dance, and music in the U.S.S.R. At the same time, the U.S.S.R. agreed to send balletmasters to Egypt to render aid in establishing a ballet school for the national development of the art.[149]

In 1958, Soviet balletmaster Sergei Pavlov came to Egypt, along with specialists in dance from Moscow, Leningrad, and Novosibirsk, in order "to lift the cultural level of the Egyptian people," a remark which an Egyptian rightfully proud of his own ancient culture might not have appreciated. In Egypt, according to the Soviet press, their task was not simple because the Moslem custom forbade girls to appear in the traditional garb of the ballerina to study the dance. However, the Soviet teachers persevered in the face of difficulties, and in 1961 they had trained enough dancers to produce the ballet *Nutcracker* in conjunction with more polished artists from Novosibirsk. In 1966, there were to emerge the first fully-trained graduates of the Egyptian ballet school established by Soviet teachers.[150]

A glance at the Soviet press in recent years brings the impression

280

that one of the topics of the hour in the U.S.S.R. is African art. There have been numerous visits of folk dancers from Africa. The National Ensemble from Ghana, called Obadzen, visited there in 1961.[151] In 1964, the National Ballet of the Republic of Guinea appeared in the capital.[152] In 1965, the National Ballet of Senegal displayed through dance the celebration of their harvest holidays, their work of gathering peanuts, the rest of fishermen and boatmen, and the songs and dances of their youth.[153] All of these groups were met by warm appreciation and were much publicized in the Soviet press.

YOUTH FESTIVALS

One of the means used by the U.S.S.R. for displaying its excellent dancers has been the World Youth Festivals. The first one of these events took place in 1947 in Prague, Czechoslovakia, and they were held every two years thereafter. A standard part of the program of the festivals has been a vast display of folk dance. At the Sixth Festival, large ensembles from the ballets *The Stone Flower* and *Gayane* performed simultaneously on four rostra in Dynamo Stadium in Moscow.[154] The Soviet Union sends its best performers to entertain the visitors, and contests have been held for both folk and classical ballet at the gatherings. At the Seventh Youth Festival in 1959 in Vienna, the winners included Alla Sisova, Yekaterina Maximova, Vladimir Vasiliev, Elena Riabinkina, G. Seliutsky, Irina Kolpakova, Yuri Soloviev, and Rudolf Nureyev.[155]

The festivals reveal that the dancers of satellite countries have learned some of the Soviet methods of incorporating "content" into their works. In 1949, the Ensemble of the Hungarian People's Army, according to the description, "saturated their folk dance with sharp social content." Some of the characters were ancient rich men, looking haughtily down on poor peasants. "But gradually, to the general pleasure of the public, everything changed, and the rich men were driven away in shame." The Chinese collective gave a *Dance with*

Drums, which the reporter avowed could only have been given by a strong and revolutionary people. The dance was followed by stormy applause and from the audience arose cries of greeting to Mao Tse-tung and Joseph Stalin.[156]

In the folk dance contest during the same year, the jury decided to give the prizes to the Soviet delegation. One judge, an unnamed American ballerina, brought forth the objection that the dancers had displayed such mastery that they could not be counted as folk dancers, and should not be judged along with amateurs. Further discussion pointed out to the American that in the U.S.S.R., the border between *samodeiatel' nyi* and professional dance was very thin, and if their workers showed such mastery, it only "bore witness to the differences in conditions of the life of the people of the U.S.S.R. and, 'let us say, America.' " In the end, the American judge had to take away her objection. The fact was restated by the reporter that "where capitalism remains, folk culture does not grow."[157]

At the final session of the festival, the ballet *The Flames of Paris* was performed. It evoked the rhythmic, stormy applause which is given as a special sign of pleasure by Soviet audiences. To the organized accompaniment of the applause a thousand people in all languages cried, "Long live Stalin! Long live Komsomol!" This applause lasted ten minutes, whereupon Yuri Faier struck up the "Hymn to Democratic Youth."[158]

At one of the concerts in the 1951 Berlin festival, Maya Plisetskaya reported that a Negro delegate from the United States came up to some Soviet participants with tears in his eyes. He said, "If only my mother could see this." In one account of the story, he said his mother had never known anything in her life but contempt and humiliation as a laundress, charwoman, or nanny.[159] In another account, she died of grief after the lynching of her oldest son.[160] Now, her other son was bemoaning the fact that she could not know about the U.S.S.R. where "the highest human culture, the culture of socialism, exists, and how deeply it esteems the worth of man."[161]

282

During the same 1951 festival, a youth from Ceylon staged a
dance reminiscent of Isadora Duncan's Muscovite performance. At
the beginning of the number, his arms contorted and writhed to
reveal they were enchained. As the dance progressed, he struggled
to free himself from the chains by stretching his muscles to the limit,
and when he finally broke them, he received a grand ovation.[162]
This was the era of the Korean War, and the North Korean dancer
An Son Khi enacted the role of a mother trying to save her child as
bombs exploded on the stage. Her efforts were in vain, and the child
died. Then the enemy appeared, her eyes became fiery, and the
fragile woman became a fearless defender of the motherland.[163] Later,
at the 1953 festival, the same An Son Khi did a dance called *Morning*,
symbolizing the awakening of freed Korea to a new life.[164]

In June, 1964, the practice was begun of having an international
ballet competition at Varna, Bulgaria, chiefly attended by the U.S.S.R.
and the satellite countries. Performers eighteen to thirty years old
were eligible, and Galina Ulanova was one member of the jury.[165]
Soviet performers took most of the top prizes, but creditable representatives from some of the satellite countries also carried awards
home.

Thus, the art which a zealous ideology once tried to suppress has
in later times become the shining light of the Soviets. On Western
tours, at the World's Fair, at Youth Festivals, at Varna, Soviet dance
heads the list of attractions whereby the U.S.S.R. attempts to show
its cultural superiority, its solicitude for the classics, and its attention
to the development of folk culture both at home and abroad. Its brilliance is at times dimmed by the demands of socialist realism or short
circuited into stultifying propaganda themes, but the light is still
sufficiently glorious to dispel the ghost of Russian barbarism to people
throughout the world. Knowing this, the U.S.S.R. has continued to
urge these contacts. In the Party Program enunciated in 1961 as a plan
for the completion of the Communist edifice, the document affirmed
that:

The Party considers it necessary to expand the Soviet Union's cultural relations with the countries of the socialist system and with all other countries for the purposes of pooling scientific and cultural achievements and of bringing about mutual understanding and friendship among the peoples.[166]

Knowing that the exchanges are very good propaganda for the U.S.S.R., the question would naturally arise about whether the West would have more to gain by continuing them or stopping them. The words of the American who negotiated the original exchange agreement in 1958 are therefore worth considering. Ambassador Lacy declared:

Every Russian who comes to the United States under this program has an opportunity to see our country as it really is and not as it is presented by Communist propaganda. Every American visiting the Soviet Union shows what Americans are really like. For instance, the Russians have high standards of music. So do we. And we wish them to understand that we are not the money-mad imperialists they make us out to be in their government's propaganda.[167]

Lacy's statement has merit, for Soviet performers who have come to America have gone home with the awareness that they have much to learn, as well as to give, from contacts with the West. Also, when a Soviet artist builds a passionate circle of admirers around the globe, it increases his stature at home. Plisetskaya could more readily sign a petition displeasing to many important Party and governmental officials with the knowledge that should harm come to her an enraged howl would be elicited from her vociferous and demonstrative fans throughout the world. In the terrible days of the 1930's no Soviet ballerina had such a wide world following; Ulanova or any of her co-workers could have joined the huddled masses interred in slave camps and her name would have meant no more to the West than the thousands of other Russians who populated the camps.

CHAPTER NINE

Fifty Years of Ballet in Retrospect

I'm fed to the teeth with agit-prop,
I'd like to scribble for you love ballads

* * *

But I mastered myself, and crushed under foot
The throat of my very own songs.

VLADIMIR MAYAKOVSKY [1]

A BRIEF glance into the history of ballet under the tsars brought forth evidence that the art had indeed been censored. When *Sumbeka* displeased the tsar, orders came forth that no ballet should be presented which either insulted personalities or disparaged government or religion. Numerous ballets during tsarist times were based upon political themes, the most outstanding ones being those of Ivan Valberkh during the Napoleonic Wars. However, the quaintness and the contemporaneity of Valberkh's ballets were matched by such works as *Roxana, the Belle of Montenegro* during Russo-Turkish War of 1878.

There was direct interference by the tsar in the ballet world, which he considered his private amusement. The Ministry of Court not only controlled the purse strings which supported the art, but the tsar himself interceded upon occasion to please a favorite. When the revolution of 1917 came to Russia, many of the dancers, facing famine and sickness in their homeland, migrated permanently abroad and eventually spread their marvelous art throughout the world.

In 1917, a mysterious Madame S. remarked to Ambassador Paléologue:

It is not political and social ideas which interest and excite our masses in a revolution; they don't understand them at all. It is the dramatic spectacles which send them crazy—processions with red flags. . . . looting and fires, particularly the fires, which make such a wonderful effect at night. . . . We're a theatrical race . . . too imaginative, too much the artist and musician. It will do us a bad turn someday.[2]

After the revolution, the state was wise enough to enlist the services of the theatrical workers who stayed in Russia. Their art could spread sympathy for the revolution to simple workers and peasants who could be much more easily stirred by an emotional theatrical experience than by the abstruse logic of the dialectic.

Thus in the years of civil war following the revolution, ballet, too, was duly enlisted in the campaign to form the revolutionary mentality and raise the cultural level of the Russian common man. To serve as an attraction for the workers' attendance at political speeches, a ballerina would be asked to perform, thus bringing a bit of glamour, a moment of escape and relaxation in a cold, hungry, stark, and dismal world.

It was not the easiest feat to rivet the attention of the Russian peasant and proletarian to a long production of *Swan Lake,* which he had never been trained to appreciate. The theatre had to approach the new audience at its own level before leading them on to greater heights of esthetic experience. *Proletkult* attempted to entertain the worker by putting on acrobatic performances or juggling acts more in keeping with the past experience of the new spectator. In similar striving to reach the proletarian, ballet absorbed some of these feats and changed its style as it incorporated new elements of acrobatics, including the startling, difficult lifts and running dives which have so amazed Western audiences.

Ballet could easily have perished as an art form in the years following the revolution in Russia. In the terrible days of 1919, some citizens could see better uses for fuel than in heating the big Bolshoi Theatre. Lenin, as well as Lunacharsky, knew that it was a piece of "pure *pomeshchik* culture." Nikolai Bukharin, the powerful editor of *Pravda,* pained Lunacharsky by articles which appeared in that organ of the press as early as 1919, insinuating that ballet should

286

forget its fairy-tale past and start portraying revolutionary subjects. As for the powerful Leon Trotsky, his remark to Fyodor Chaliapin that he could not give food to ballerinas when the army was starving was consonant with his general view that everything should be subordinate to the revolution, and there was no time to build even a proletarian culture.

Lunacharsky's own devotion to ballet was never guided by pure theories of art for art's sake. He gladly agreed to Isadora Duncan's migration to Russia because he had dreams and visions of great proletarian festivals of dance in the style of the ancient Greeks. Yet he distinguished between the type of work which he expected from the propagandistic theatres under the aegis of *Glavpolitprosvet* and the work of the Academic Theatres, which were to concentrate on artistry. He knew that the proletariat would soon tire of only didactic works, and he supported the preservation of the old classical heritage in many ways, cleverly twisting the arguments of the opposition so that it seemed that anyone who questioned his position in the matter was not a true and faithful Party member. Fearing that Russia would lose so many of its artists of the dance that it would be impossible to carry on the imperial heritage, Lunacharsky went to great lengths to show the artists who remained, such as Yekaterina Geltser, how much the state valued their work.

The unstable period after the revolution was a time of fascinating experimentation in all arts, and ballet also felt this invigorating release of the creative spirit. Times were difficult and money was scarce for new costumes, new scenery, and all the other expenses of new productions. However, Russia did not lack new ballets in these hard times; although they did not have enough food in 1920 and 1921, the Russians did have *Firebird* and *Petrushka*. Faced with the cost of making the whole nation literate, Lunacharsky and Lenin felt they could justify the expense involved in preserving Russia's monuments of the past (in stone and in dance) better than they could excuse the expense of mounting some of the startling new theatrical works which innovators wished to produce. Thus many of the older classics were preserved, while many of the new ballets of the 1920's which tried to portray revolutionary themes were utter failures. In the case of Stravinsky's *Pulchinella,* usually conceded to be a fine production in the U.S.S.R., there simply was not enough foreign currency to pay royalties outside the country to produce it. Perhaps this factor explains in greater measure the zeal with which the regime began to urge the production of ballets by native Soviet composers who had not migrated abroad, such as Boris Asafiev, Reingold Gliere, Alexander Krein, or Dmitri Shostakovich.

While the Western-oriented ASM held power in the musical world of the U.S.S.R. during the 1920's, it was possible to hear many works of such composers as Stravinsky. However, ASM was superseded by RAPM in the later years of the decade. The fanatical policy of this organization encouraged the writing of mass songs, the employment of folk music, and the elimination of anything from the musical world of the U.S.S.R. which could not be understood by the simple worker or peasant. Naturally, such policies were reflected in dance, especially in regard to the incorporation of elements of folk dance into classical ballet. This factor became a *sine qua non* of a successful new Soviet ballet in the eyes of trained critics.

While the Soviet Union has never ceased to preserve the revered classics, it has made changes in them appropriate in a workers' state. *Giselle's* Hilarion, a man of the people, is not as villainous as his Western counterparts because "the people" should not be portrayed in a sinister manner on a Soviet stage. Along with the old classics, numerous new ballets produced during the years of Soviet power have dealt with blatantly propagandistic themes, ranging from the subtle to the absurd.

In his study of Soviet methods of propaganda, Frederick Barghoorn has pointed out several of their special aims. One has been to picture the United States as a decadent civilization which wishes to corrupt all the workers of the world—in contrast to the U.S.S.R., the champion of folk cultures and patron of all fine art throughout the world.[3] In countless ways these aims are reflected in Soviet ballet. Critical articles can be found in their press pointing to examples of decadence in American and all Western ballet, with its employment of Freudian and Sartrean themes, its plotless and formalistic ballets. *Undertow, Time Out of Mind,* and many other examples have been used to show the bankruptcy of Western art with its morbid concern for themes of despair, of murder, of unwholesome sexual desires. In contrast to such Western "madness," in their ballets, the U.S.S.R. has presented a national image of itself as a bright, happy land where workers are diligently engaged in building new hydroelectric projects, draining swamps, overfulfilling production quotas, outlawing obsolete and superstitious local customs and replacing them with an enlightened, humane policy of social improvement. Many ballets, especially of the Central-Asian Union Republics, show woman in her sad role under the former theocratic and autocratic system of local government. With the coming of Soviet power, everything was changed for her: the throwing off of the yashmak and the embracing of Soviet power freed her from slavery to brutish marriage practices and consequent seclusion in her husband's home. Under the Communist regime, the new heroine could now marry the man she loved and pursue the career she chose, whether that of cotton picker or ballerina. All these themes have been shown in ballets.

As far as possible, the U.S.S.R. has certainly attempted to embody Marxist principles and ideas in its ballets. Time after time, ballets have been presented which exalted or urged revolution. This list is seemingly endless: *Stenka Razin, Carmagnole, Laurencia, The Flames of Paris, Red Poppy, Serf Ballerina, Smerch, Red Whirlwind, Lilea, Prince-Lake, The Rising Dawn, In the Name of Love, Heart of the Hills, Last Ball, Tavria, Spartacus,* and many others. The number is sufficiently great to preclude any possibility that the use of this theme is merely accidental.

To Marx, religion was an opiate of the people, and the U.S.S.R.

theatrical world has stressed this concept. Certain ballet productions have purposely made religion appear both stupid and vile, including *Night on Bald Mountain*, *Tale of a Fox*, *Light and Shade*, and *Laima*.

The Leninist principle of anti-imperialism has been reflected in the famous *Red Poppy* as well as in *Ferendzhi* and *Path of Thunder*. These same ballets reveal the manner in which the Soviet propaganda apparatus approaches the racial question. The evil of the Western position is portrayed in all of these ballets dealing with imperialistic subjects, as well as in *Rigonda*, *Golden Age*, and *The Little Stork*. In the latter two, the Soviet citizen is pictured as the friend and helper of the minority races of the earth in their struggles against oppression.

Ballet has been equally busy occupying itself with the various vicissitudes of Soviet foreign policy. Quarrels with Japan in 1939 brought forth *Svetlana*, while sympathy for the revolution in Spain in the 1930's brought *Laurencia*. Antagonism to American aid in the Marshall Plan urged the production of *Under Italian Skies*. Dances have been used consistently to portray antiwar themes, such as *In Memory of Hiroshima*, or to show the brutality of the enemies of the U.S.S.R., as in *To the Heart of Marika*, or *Dawn*.

A score of ballets preach lessons of sheer Russian patriotism, such as *Bronze Horseman*, *Shore of Hope*, *Tatiana*, and *Svetlana*. In countless ballets portraying some heroic character from the Union Republics, the heroine will be saved from some difficult situation by Russian friends, and in the end of such ballets, there is a standard "Dance of Friendship of Nations," showing all the national groups of the U.S.S.R. displaying their folk dances to each other, thus enhancing their national camaraderie.

In the festivals of national art which have taken place in Moscow, the government has taken great care to show the Union Republics that it values their art and its possible contributions to Soviet society. As a result of Soviet policies, ballet collectives now exist where, in truth, not even folk dance had existed previously. From their description, it seems that some of the ballets staged in these outlying Republics have sunk to the "agitka" level more profoundly than they ever did in Muscovite or Leningrad theatres. But the mere existence of the art in these far outposts of civilization is a remarkable accomplishment, and the Soviet Union takes great pains to let the world know of their efforts in this respect. On a local level, ballets have commonly served to instill attitudes which the regime wishes the people to have. In the Baltic states, the ballets *Audrone, Laima,* and *Amulet of Freedom* show the perfidy of the German knights. In Tadzhikstan they could learn of the cruel Basmachi from *Two Roses,* and in Armenia, of the treacherous Dashnaktsutiun from *Sona.*

The question of whether such ballets might have been produced spontaneously, without state or party insistence, scarcely seems worth examining. Russian artistic ability in music, dance, painting, and literature captured the admiration of the entire world long before the revolution; few could dispute the fact that the people have inherent good taste and artistic potential. It is somewhat amazing that artists of the nation which produced *Swan Lake* or *Firebird* would voluntarily produce *Native Fields* or *Tatiana* without official urging. The example has been cited where the Ministry of Culture ordered in 1958 that each opera and ballet theatre should produce one contemporary ballet a year. If a theatre should have other plans, the Party chief is on hand, in the theatre, to see that such directives are enforced.

The policy of the Communist Party and Soviet government of compelling the ballet world to produce these utilitarian works explains in great part the impression which Soviet companies have made upon the West in cultural exchange programs. Almost universally, the Western comment has been one of marvel at the technique of the dancers, but at the same time of amazement at the lack of originality and creativity in their choreography. Because dance training is state financed every step of the way, scientific methods of pedagogy can be evolved at state expense, and the Soviet performer has his technical potentialities developed to the very limit of his powers during his

291

student training period and theatrical career. However, the system also assures that the future performer, and especially the choreographer, will be well armed with knowledge of his nation's official ideology and current position on questions of foreign policy. Part of the very training program involves learning ways of expressing such themes in dance. These lessons in ideology, while obligatory, do not consume so much time that the young dancer's technique suffers from it. In regard to choreography, however, the story has been different. The production of any ballet, good or bad, consumes the full time of the choreographer. If a talented balletmaster must spend weeks or months producing a poor work such as *Black Gold,* it means he is kept from the truly artistic work he might do if given free reign.

Further, ballets which must "preach" or tell a story often necessarily involve more mime than dance; therefore, the chances for evolving the type of dance in which Western choreographers have excelled have simply not been available in the U.S.S.R. Choreographers such as Goleizovsky, who apparently found it hard to conform their ideas to the regime's demands, have found on occasion that the stage doors of the great theatres were closed to them, and if they wished to pursue a dance career, it had to be in some smaller, distant outpost of the U.S.S.R. After the initial period of free creativity in the U.S.S.R., experimental groups promoted by men such as Nikolai Foregger and the imitators of Isadora Duncan withered away. The Moscow Dramatic Ballet is a case in point. With the tremendous lack of housing facilities in Moscow, the group was asked to transfer to Leningrad. Perhaps the chief reason for its demise was the government's desire to eliminate such experimental groups, to reduce the number of ballet companies in Moscow to one—the Bolshoi, with the company of the Stanislavsky Nemirovich-Danchenko Musical Theatre being added later.

Because Soviet ballet, along with all art, has been assigned a mission in the U.S.S.R., tsarist censorship practices pale in comparison with the policy of the Soviet government. There was no equal in tsarist times to the classification of ballets in the *Repertoire Index* published in 1929.[4] Also, as Communists would say, more than a quantitative difference exists between the two policies, for a qualitative change took place in censorship and repertoire control practices when Soviet power became completely entrenched. Never did tsarist officials attempt to impose a positive, all-encompassing esthetical doctrine upon any art in the manner the Soviet regime has promoted socialist realism. This imposition of socialist realism since 1932 has affected every facet of the production of ballets. No musical score could be adopted for use which violated its canons demanding bright, cheerful melodies. Composers were urged to incorporate folk tunes at the same time that they were forbidden the use of atonal music with strange harmonies and rhythms, or of any music which expressed introspection, despair, or moods alien to a society busily and happily building a bright new life. Just as the production of the "mass song" was supposed to occupy the composer's talent, so it was made clear to choreographers that their ballets should include mass scenes showing the mighty wave of "the people" triumphing over feudal oppressors, imperialists, or whoever happened to be the villain of the hour.

In Soviet ballets, realism on the stage has been carried to great lengths as far as scenery, stage effects, and costumes are concerned. Diagilev's ballet revolved around the avant-garde painters of Russia for inspiration, producing unforgettable results. "Socialist realism," imposed in the construction of scenery, brought forth the nineteenth-century flats which amazed Western audiences during early Soviet cultural exchanges, since they expected to see some evidence that *Mir Iskusstva* had once exercised its talents in Russia. In reading of the fabulous floods, fires, storms, and realistic underwater scenes which predominate in Soviet ballets, the question arises about the motivation for such displays. Would the Soviet spectator be drawn to a boldly propagandistic work on its own dramatic or choreographic merits if it lacked such startling tricks produced by the stage crew? The same question arises in regard to the fabulous virtuoso feats performed by the dancers themselves. Few Americans would be interested in seeing *The Flames of Paris* on the basis of its plot, music, or scenery. However, if a potential audience had been given some hint of the recklessly daredevil leaps and heroic style of Yuri Vladimirov, playing the role of Jérome, the spectator might be drawn to a performance just to see such skill and virtuosity while trying to forget its banal setting.

Ballet, like all the arts in the U.S.S.R., has been subject to direct Party action in times when stringent general pressure has been applied. The first noteworthy period of this type began in 1936 with the publication of the decree, "Confusion Instead of Music," in *Pravda*. Only a short time later, the unfortunate composer Shostakovich endured a second Party condemnation in the decree entitled "Ballet Fraud." The publication of these decrees came soon after the beginning of the Stakhanovite movement, with its excessive urging of increased production quotas. In the years after the decrees, political purges left scarcely any family in the U.S.S.R. free or unafraid. The Party's action against Shostakovich was a warning to the artistic world that certain production standards were expected from them.

In the case of *Bright Stream,* there seems to be some correlation between the fact that the government was currently renewing its policy toward national minorities. *Bright Stream* did not do justice to the folklore, the costumes, the songs, or the dances of the Kuban Cossacks which it was supposed to represent. Formerly, neither had the Soviet government in general done justice to the aspirations of these people. Cossacks had not been allowed to enlist as units in the Red Army, and the Kuban had been less colorful during the 1920's for lack of the dashing, showy uniforms of the men of the region. In 1936, with the threat of war very evident, the government was following a new policy geared toward gaining the allegiance of these people. The Party's decree on *Bright Stream* advertised the new attitude.

During 1946, the next period of increased pressure upon art, there was no direct decree published against any ballet, but the ballet world was affected by Zhdanov's criticism of Muradeli's *Great Friendship,* and his words made it clear that he wanted ballet to portray heroes of the war and of contemporary life. Works such as *Tatiana,* and *Shore of Happiness* resulted from his criticism. His condemnation of the authors Akhmatova and Zoschenko was reflected in the removal from the repertoire of the Bolshoi the ballet *Crimson Sails,* with its reliance on the fulfillment of dreams to bring human happiness. Such a ballet was inappropriate for a nation which had to struggle with all its might to recover from the losses inflicted on their homeland by war.

In the artistic crackdown of spring, 1962, Nikita Khrushchev and Leonid Ilyichev vented most of their wrath upon writers and painters. However, there were enough remarks made about jazz and the type of dance which accompanies it to make it clear to the Soviet professional dancers that they should not be completely carried away by works which Western companies were showing during the cultural exchange tours.

Besides bringing some much-needed fresh air into the world of Russian ballet, the cultural exchange program has proven eminently successful from the U.S.S.R.'s point of view. Appreciative audiences throughout the globe have justifiably marveled at the artistry of the Soviet performers. Concomitantly, the U.S.S.R. has shown great appreciation when performers of traditional dances of other nations have performed in their land. For Africans, the discovery that some white men are interested in recognizing, applauding, and even supporting their culture is a happy change from long decades of indifference and denigration of African cultural achievements. To Asians, justly proud of their own ancient, graceful dances, the U.S.S.R. has been no less cordial. Knowing well that such a man as Norodom Sihanouk could not be touched in a more sensitive point than his fatherly pride toward a beautiful dancing daughter, the press of the U.S.S.R. extended warm appreciation of the Royal Ballet of Cambodia. In contrast, during Soviet exchanges with Japan, attempts were made to point out the manner in which American occupation had corrupted the delicate, modest Japanese women. They also took any available opportunity to emphasize the difficulties lying in the path of the development of ballet, as well as all art, in a society which lacked state subsidies for such purposes.

The comparison between the economically secure life of the Soviet dancer and the precarious existence of the dancer in the West has always been an effective propaganda point for the U.S.S.R. The West has been typified as the citadel of decadence, where true art has no chance of growing because corrupt capitalists want only to satiate the people with their own low tastes. Consequently, the U.S.S.R. has preached that the Western artist really knows no freedom because he must cater to these low tastes of the rich patrons. *Lost Illusions* showed the sad state of one nineteenth-century artist in France whose creative potential was stifled in a capitalistic society. *Into the Port Came* Russia showed a talented Italian girl who could not free herself from the grip of the dance hall until her Soviet friends arrived to help her. The Belorussian ballet, *Dream*, shows a similar picture of a Soviet girl exiled in the West where an artist has no chance to use or develop talent; only after returning to the Soviet homeland does she find artistic fulfillment. And in his picturesque comments about the cancan which he saw in Hollywood, Nikita Khrushchev was only echoing Lenin's teaching of 1905 about the freedom of the Western artist to produce pornography. In the U.S.S.R., on the contrary, the artist has freedom to build a communist society.

After they have returned home from tours abroad, numerous Soviet dancers have written articles revealing to their fellow Soviet countrymen the difficult life of the unappreciated artist of the West. For Igor Moiseyev, who had a different tale to tell about Western art, there were warnings that such reports in the future must be "more balanced."

In spite of periods of repression in the arts, the government of

Plisetskaya in the title role of Stravinsky's ballet *The Firebird* at the Bolshoi Theatre, with Fadeyechev as Ivan.

Cartoon satirizing the political work of Olga
Lepeshinskaya.

Russia has always shown great deference to artists as a whole, and few sectors of Soviet society have known such privileges or enjoyed such esteem as their ballet artists. The high carbohydrate diet of the normal Soviet woman is evident in her high tendency to obesity; the slim ballerina, who has had a high protein diet since childhood, stands in great contrast to her fellow countrywomen. Titles, material gains, and a multitude of intangible rewards have repaid the hard work which is the lot of a dancer in any society. In a country where luxuries are available to only a small privileged group, strong motivation for achievement in dance has existed for those with the talent to pursue such a career. In the West, in spite of a lifetime of training, a great ballerina seldom achieves the fabulous wealth which some less talented movie actresses have gained. But in the Soviet Union, the *prima ballerina* of a large theatre has few rivals in fame or fortune, although the buying power of her salary probably does not enable her to have many of the luxuries which an upper middle class American family has come to expect.

Many Soviet ballet stars have been active as political workers, such as Olga Lepeshinskaya, whose voice has been recorded at numerous conferences of art workers, actively promoting the current policy of the Party or prodding her fellow artistic workers on to greater achievements. On the opposite side, there are scores of artists who regard the interference of the Party and State in their art as a colossal nuisance, and who would like nothing more than to be allowed simply to be artists. However, the Soviet performer is not left alone. Once a Soviet ballet artist joins a theatrical collective, his in-service ideological training continues through the theatrical Komsomol or Party unit if he is a member. His mentality is further formed by lectures sponsored by the All-Russian Theatrical Society, by *Rabis,* or simply by the talks and discussions which take place in every theatre.

In like manner, composers of ballets must spend a great deal of time attending such meetings and lectures, especially in periods when the government is applying particular pressure. For truly creative

297

artists, attendance at such functions would often be an unwelcome and frustrating infringement on their time.

Thus, Soviet ballet is guided to reflect all the temperature changes which occur in the artistic climate of the U.S.S.R. In a state where all the artistic unions are controlled by the Party and government, where the production of every material necessity for the art is done ultimately only with government approval, where the regime controls every theatre, every loom for knitting leotards, and every press for printing musical scores, there can be no artistic liberalism without the government allowing it. Today, many things are now permissible in Soviet ballet which were forbidden the ballet of the 1930's under Stalin. The works of Stravinsky periodically appear in new ballets which do not in any way match the "formalistic" style that Balanchine uses in choreographing his works, but the mere fact that Stravinsky's music is played shows a reversal from Stalinist policies. As hostility between Red China and the Soviet Union increases, there is less likelihood of the appearance of works akin to the flagrantly anti-American *Under Italian Skies.* In fact, if old patterns continue, there are probably ballets being planned at the present time to show the evil of life in Red China. It seems probable that there will continue to be "positive heroes" in Soviet ballets, and there will still be speeches urging the ballet world to draw closer to the life of the people. It is unlikely that the words *"soderzhanie," "narodnost' "* and *"sovremennost' "* will soon disappear from the vocabularies of Soviet ballet critics and authors of librettos.

However, in surveying the early history of the art, a fervent ballet-omane can be grateful that ballet continued to exist at all in Russia after the revolution. The fact that it survived days of famine, typhus, trade-union threats, and countless other disturbances of its former hothouse existence, is to the everlasting credit of Anatoly Lunacharsky, with his admirable ability for convincing a somewhat dubious Lenin of the correctness of his stand. Russian ballet still lives, stronger by far than in imperial days. The technique has been preserved. However, until the day arrives when that same creative fire will be allowed *full* freedom in Russia, when a supreme young artist like Bessmert-nova can be assured that she will never have to stoop, like the supreme young artist Ulanova, to slapping a Fascist on a ballet stage—or an American, or a Chinaman—the twentieth-century balletomane can only recall the translation of the classic lines of his great nineteenth-century counterpart, Alexander Pushkin:

> Shall I yet see you winging
> Your way in soulful flight and *free*
> My fair Russian Terpsichore?

CLASSIFICATION OF BALLETS GIVEN IN

Repertoire Index of 1929[1]

THE RATINGS GIVEN WERE:

A   The best works ideologically; universally recommended for presentation.
B   Ideologically acceptable and permitted without hindrance.
C   Not completely supportable ideologically but not forbidden. Rehearsal for examination purposes required.
D   Ideologically acceptable but usually primitive in content, form, and language. Timed to a special political campaign or historical date.
E   Forbidden.

Title of Ballet	Composer	Rating
Le Corsaire	Adam	C
Giselle	Adam	C
Egyptian Nights	Arenskii	C
The Poor Bride	Armsheimer	C
Fairy Doll	Bayer	E
Smerch	Beer	E
Chopiniana (Les Sylphides)	Chopin	A
Coppélia	Delibes	B
Bolsheviks	Deshevov	B

1. Alphabetized by English spelling of composer's name.

Title of Ballet	Composer	Rating
Les Millions d'Arlequin	Drigo	B
The Magic Flute	Drigo	B
Cinderella	Fittinghof-Schell	C
Raymonda	Glazunov	B
The Seasons	Glazunov	B
The Trials of Damis	Glazunov	B
Chrysis	Gliere	C
Red Poppy	Gliere	A
Jota Aragonesa	Glinka	B
Walpurgis Night	Gounod	B
The Ice Maiden	Grieg	C
The Vestal Virgin	Ivanov	E
Svetlana	Klenovsky	C
Danta	Konius	C
Serf Ballerina	Korchmarev	C
Magic Mirror	Koroshchenko	C
The Swan	Lecocq	C
Le Carillon	Massenet	C
Camargo	Minkus	C
Don Quixote	Minkus	C
Fiametta	Minkus	C
La Bayadère	Minkus	C
La Fille des Neiges	Minkus	C
Le Papillon	Minkus	C
Les Bandits	Minkus	C
The Little Goldfish	Minkus	C
The Magic Pills	Minkus	C
Roxana	Minkus	C
Zoraya	Minkus	C
Number 0, or the Wreck of the Council of Five	Nikulin	E
Chout	Prokofiev	A
Le Pas d'Acier	Prokofiev	A
Esmeralda	Pugni	C
Katerina	Pugni	C
La Fille du Pharaon	Pugni	C
Tsar Kandavl (Le Roi Candaule)	Pugni	C

Repertoire Index, 1929

Title of Ballet	Composer	Rating
The Little Humpbacked Horse	Pugni	C
The Pearl of Seville	Pugni	C
Vain Precautions	Pugni	C
Daphnis et Chloé	Ravel	B
Capriccio Espagnole	Rimsky-Korsakov	A
Le Coq d'Or	Rimsky-Korsakov	A
Mlada	Rimsky-Korsakov	C
La Vigne	Rubinstein	C
Teolinda	Schubert	B
Carnaval	Schumann	A
La Sylphide[2]	Schumann	A
Firebird	Stravinsky	A
Les Noces	Stravinsky	A
L'Histoire du Soldat	Stravinsky	A
Petrushka	Stravinsky	A
Pulchinella	Stravinsky	A
Tale of a Fox (Renard)	Stravinsky	A
Nutcracker	Tchaikovsky	B
Sleeping Beauty	Tchaikovsky	B
Swan Lake	Tchaikovsky	B
The Masque of Red Death	Tcherepnine	C
Gypsies	Thomas	B
Joseph the Beautiful	Vasilenko	B

2. Schumann was listed here instead of Jean M. Schneitzhoeffer.

LIST OF BALLETS

Title of Ballet	Composer	Balletmaster	Date and Place of First Performance[1] (cited herein)
Adventures of Aldar-Qos	K.A. Korchmarev	N. Kholfin	October 31, 1942; Ashkhabad
Amulet of Freedom	A. Skulte	E. Changa	May 9, 1950; Riga
Anar	V. Vlasov, V. Fere	N. Kholfin, V. Kozlov	November 7, 1940; Frunze
Ashik Kerib	B. Asafiev	B. Fenster	December 3, 1940; Maly
Audrone	Yu. Indra	V. Grivitskas	May 18, 1957; Vilnius
Ballerina (Guilnara)	G. Mushel	P. Iorkin, M. Turgunbaeva	July 14, 1949; Tashkent
Beautiful Angara	L. Knipper, B. Yampilov	I. Moiseyev, M. Zaslavsky	February 4, 1959; Ulan-Ude
Bela	V. Deshevov	B. Fenster	June 25, 1961; Len. Ch. Inst.
Bela	B. Moshkov	T. Ramonova	March 3, 1955; Perm
The Betrothed	Yu. Pakalnis	B. Kelbauskas	December 4, 1963; Kaunas
Black Gold	V. Gomoliaka	A. Berdovsky, N. Yefremov	October 7, 1957; Donetsk
Bolt	D. Shostakovich	F. Lopukhov	April 8, 1931; Len. GATOB
Bright Stream	D. Shostakovich	F. Lopukhov	April 4, 1935; Maly
Bronze Horseman	R. Gliere	R. Zakharov	March 14, 1949; Kirov
By the Blue Sea	E. Rusinov	S. Pavlov, Z. Vasilieva	June 26, 1955; Odessa

By the Friendship Road (formerly Dzhungar Gate)	L. Stepanov, N. Tlendeyev	Yu. Kovalev, R. Zakharov, D. Abirov	1958 Kazakh Dekada; Moscow
Capriccio Espagnole	Rimsky-Korsakov	L. Zhukov	May 9, 1923; Bolshoi
Carmagnole	V. Femilidi	M. Moiseyev	October 17, 1930; Odessa
Carnaval	S. Vasilenko	K. Goleizovsky	November 20, 1928; Moscow Experimental Theatre
Cholpon (Morning Star)	M. Raukhverger	L. Kramarevsky	December 30, 1944; Frunze
Chout	S. Prokofiev	M. Dyskovsky	January 27, 1928; Kiev
Christmas Eve	B. Asafiev	V. Varkovitsky	June 15, 1938; Kirov
Crane Song	L. Stepanov, Z. Ismagilov	N. Anisimova	March 20, 1944; Ufa
Crimson Sails	V. Yurovsky	A. Radunsky, N. Popko, L. Pospekhin	December 12, 1942; Kuibyshev
Dawn	V. Zagorsky	V. Varkovitsky	January 27, 1960; Kishinev
Demon	S. Tsintsadze	V. Chabukiani	April 30, 1961; Tbilisi
Dilbar	A. Lensky	G. Valamat-zade	November 7, 1954; Dushanbe
Distant Planet	B. Maizel	K. Sergeyev	April 12, 1963; Kirov
Dream	I. Akbarov	B. Zavialov, G. Izmailova	February 3, 1959; Tashkent
Dream	E. Glebov	N. Stukolkina, A. Andreyev	October 6, 1961; Minsk

Title of Ballet	Composer	Balletmaster	Date and Place of First Performance[1] (cited herein)
Egyptian Nights (Cleopatra)	A. Arensky et al.	I. Arbatov	1938; Sverdlovsk
Egyptian Nights (Cleopatra)	A. Arensky et al.	F. Lopukhov	1962; Kirov
Esmeralda	C. Pugni	V. Tikhomirov	February 7, 1926; Bolshoi
Esmeralda	C. Pugni, R. Gliere	A. Vaganova, S. Radlov (Régisseur)	April 23, 1935; Kirov
Fadetta	L. Delibes	L. Lavrovsky	March 21, 1934; Len. Ch. Inst.
Fair at Soroshinsk	V. Gomoliaka	N. Tregubov	1955; Donetsk
Ferendzhi	B. Yanovsky	P. Kretov, N. Foregger (Rég.)	October, 1930; Kharkov
Festival of Love (Lesson of Life)	Yu. Znatokov	N. Tregubov	November 7, 1960; Odessa
Firebird	I. Stravinsky	F. Lopukhov	October 2, 1921; GATOB
Firebird	I. Stravinsky	S. Vlasov, N. Simachev	June 30, 1964; Bolshoi
The Flames of Paris	B. Asafiev	V. Vainonen	November 6, 1932; GATOB
Footballist	V. Oransky	L. Lashchilin, I. Moiseyev	March 30, 1930; Bolshoi
For Peace	D. Toradze	V. Chabukiani	June 17, 1953; Tbilisi
Fountain of Bakhchisarai	B. Asafiev	R. Zakharov	September 28, 1934; Kirov
Gayane	A. Khachaturian	N. Anisimova	December 9, 1942; Kolotov

306

Ballet	Composer	Choreographer	Premiere
Gavroche	B. Bitov, E. Kornblit	V. Varkovitsky	February 28, 1958; Maly
Giuliandom	E. Brusilovsky	T. Khanum, I. Arbatov	March 3, 1940; Tashkent
Giulnazira	N. Sabitov	S. Drechin	January 14, 1963; Ufa
Giulshen	S. Gadzhibekov	G. Almas-zade, S. Dadashev (Rég.)	December 30, 1950; Baku
The Golden Age	D. Shostakovich	V. Vainonen, L. Yacobson, V. Chesnakov	October 26, 1930; GATOB
Gorda	D. Toradze	V. Chabukiani	December 30, 1949; Tbilisi
The Greatness of Creation	Beethoven	F. Lopukhov	March 7, 1923; GATOB
Gypsies	S. Vasilenko	N. Kholfin	October 3, 1937; Leningrad tour of V. Kriger's Ballet
Happiness	A. Khachaturian	I. Arbatov	October 24, 1939; Erevan
Heart of the Hills	A. Balanchivadze	V. Chabukiani	June 28, 1938; Kirov
Heroic Poem (Geologists)	N. Karetnikov	N. Kasatkina, V. Vasilëv	January 26, 1964; Bolshoi
L'Histoire du Soldat (Tale of a Soldier and the Devil)	I. Stravinsky	E. Sube	July 5, 1963; Estonia
L'Histoire du Soldat	I. Stravinsky	?	1964; Bolshoi
Iag-Mort	Ya. Perepelitsa	G. Vakhovsky	August 21, 1961; Syktyvkar

307

Title of Ballet	Composer	Balletmaster	Date and Place of First Performance[1] (cited herein)
The Ice Maiden	E. Grieg, B. Asafiev	F. Lopukhov	April 27, 1927; GATOB
In Memory of Hiroshima	Yanusa Ivanov	A. Livshits	1962; Kirov Palace of Culture, Leningrad
In the Name of Love	Zh. Batuev, B. Maizel	M. Zaslavsky	February 4, 1959; Ulan-Ude
Into the Port Came Russia	V. Soloviev-Sedoi	R. Zakharov	February 14, 1964; Kirov Theatre
Joan of Arc	N. Peiko	V. Bourmeister	December 29, 1957; Stanislavsky, Moscow
Joseph the Beautiful	S. Vasilenko	K. Goleizovsky	March 3, 1925; Experimental Theatre, Moscow
Kalevipoeg	E. Kapp	Kh. Tokhvelman	March 27, 1948; Estonia
Katerina	A. Rubinstein, A. Adam, E. Dubovsky, P. Feldt	L. Lavrovsky	May 25, 1935; Len. Ch. Inst.
Kalkaman i Mamyr	V. Velikanov	L. Zhukov	June 24, 1938; Alma-Ata
Khustka Dovbusha (Shawl of Dovbush)	A. Kos-Anatolsky	N. Tregubov	March 23, 1951; L'vov
Komedianty	R. Gliere	A. Cherkrygin	April 5, 1931; Bolshoi Fil.

308

Laima	A. Liepins	E. Tangieva-Birzniek	June 27, 1947; Riga
Last Ball	Yu. Biriukov	K. Muller	October 17, 1961; L'vov
Laurencia	A. Krein	V. Chabukiani	March 22, 1939; Kirov Theatre
Leili and Mejnun	S. Balasanian	G. Valamat-zade	November 7, 1947; Dushanbe
Levsha	B. Aleksandrov	Ya. Romanovsky	December 29, 1954; Sverdlovsk
Lieutenant Kizhe	S. Prokofiev	A. Lapauri, O. Tarasova	February 10, 1963; Bolshoi
Life	A. Balanchivadze	L. Lavrovsky	1948; Bolshoi
Light and Shade	G. Vagner	N. Stukolkina	February 13, 1963; Minsk
Lilea	K. Dankevich	G. Berezova	August 26, 1940; Kiev
Little Humpbacked Horse	R. Shchedrin	A. Radunsky	March 4, 1960; Bolshoi
Little Stork	D. Klebanov	A. Radunsky	June 6. 1937; Moscow Ch. Inst.
Lola	S. Vasilenko	V. Bourmeister	June 25, 1943; Stanislavsky
Lost Illusions	B. Asafiev	R. Zakharov	December 31, 1935; Kirov Theatre
Maiden's Tower	A. Badalbeili	S. Kevorkov, V. Vronsky	April 18, 1940; Baku
Maltakva	Sh. Taktakishvili	D. Dzhavrishvili, V. Litvinenko	April 4, 1938; Tbilisi
Marmar	E. Oganesian	Z. Muradian, I. Arbatov	March 9, 1957; Erevan
Marusia Boguslavka	A. Svechnikov	S. Sergeyev	November 23, 1951; Kiev
Masquerade	L. Laputin	O. Dadishkiliani	March 23, 1956; Novosibirsk
Mistress into Maid	B. Asafiev	R. Zakharov	March 14, 1946; Bolshoi Fil.
Mother	A. Scriabin	L. Yacobson	1960(?), Leningrad
Mountain Tale	A. Kliucharev	Kh. Safiullin, E. Voitovich	April 12, 1951; Ufa

Title of Ballet	Composer	Balletmaster	Date and Place of First Performance[1] (cited herein)
Native Fields	N. Chervinsky	A. Andreyev	June 4, 1953; Kirov Theatre
Night on Bald Mountain	M. Mussorgsky, Rimsky-Korsakov	F. Lopukhov	March 16, 1924; GATOB
The Nightingale	M. Kroshner	M. Moiseyev	May 5, 1939; Odessa
Nutcracker	Tchaikovsky	F. Lopukhov	October 27, 1929; GATOB
On the Eve	I. Shvarts	K. Boiarsky	November 16, 1960; Maly
On the Sea Shore	J. Juzeliunas	V. Grivitskas, A. Messerer	May 10, 1953; Vilhius
Orpheus	I. Stravinsky	K. Boiarsky	March 26, 1962; Maly
Othello	A. Machavariani	V. Chabukiani	November 27, 1957; Tbilisi
Paganini	S. Rachmaninov	L. Lavrovsky	April 7, 1960; Bolshoi
Pan Kaniowski	M. Verikovsky	V. Litvinenko	April 19, 1931; Kharkov
Partisan Days	B. Asafiev	V. Vainonen	May 10, 1937; Kirov
Path of Thunder	K. Karaev	K. Sergeyev	January 4, 1958; Kirov Theatre
Petrushka	I. Stravinsky	L. Leontiev, based on Fokine	November 20, 1920; GATOB
Petty Bourgeois from Tuscany	V. Nakhabin	N. Bolotov, P. Virsky	April 2, 1936; Dnepropetrovsk
Prince-Lake	V. Zolotarev	K. Muller	January 15, 1948; Minsk
Praise to the Cosmonaut	Yu. Biriukov	S. Drechin	1962; L'vov
Pulchinella	I. Stravinsky, G. Pergolese	F. Lopukhov	May 15, 1926; GATOB

Prisoner of the Caucasus	B. Asafiev	L. Lavrovsky	April 14, 1938; Maly
Red Poppy	R. Gliere	L. Lashchilin, V. Tikhomirov	June 14, 1927; Bolshoi
Red Whirlwind (Bolsheviks)	V. Deshevov	F. Lopukhov	October 29, 1924; GATOB
Rigonda	R. Grinblat	E. Tangieva-Birzniek	September 12, 1959; Riga
Rising Dawn (Betrothed)	Yu. Pakalnis	B. Kelbauskas	December 4, 1943; Kaunas
Rite of Spring	I. Stravinsky	N. Kasatkina, V. Vasilёv	1965; Bolshoi
Romeo and Juliet	S. Prokofiev	L. Lavrovsky	January 11, 1940; Kirov Theatre
Rostislava	H. Zhukovsky	V. Vronsky	December 4, 1955; Kiev
Sampo	G. Sinisalo	I. Smirnov	March 27, 1959; Petrozavodsk
Serf Ballerina	K. Korchmarev	F. Lopukhov	December 11, 1927; GATOB
Sevan	G. Égiazarian	I. Arbatov	February 11, 1956; Erevan
Seven Beauties	K. Karaev	P. Gusev, G. Almas-zade	November 7, 1952; Baku
Seventh Symphony (Leningrad Symphony)	D. Shostakovich	I. Belsky	April 14, 1961; Kirov Theatre
Shore of Happiness	A. Spadevekkia	V. Bourmeister	November 6, 1948; Stanislavsky
Shore of Hope	A. Petrov	I. Belsky	June 16, 1959; Kirov Theatre
Shurale	F. Yarullin	L. Zhukov, G. Tagirov	March 12, 1945; Kazan
Sinatle (Light)	G. Kiladze	V. Chabukiani	March 16, 1947; Tbilisi

Title of Ballet	Composer	Balletmaster	Date and Place of First Performance[1] (cited herein)
The Sisters	L. Kogan	V. Boichenko	February 3, 1959; Kishinev
Smerch	B. Beer	K. Goleizovsky	November 6, 1927; Bolshoi Fil.
Sona	E. Aramian	I. Arbatov, A. Garibian, Z. Muradian	December 29, 1957; Erevan
Song of the Forest	M. Skorulsky	S. Sergeyev	February 25, 1946; Kiev
Spartacus	A. Khachaturian	L. Yacobson	December 27, 1956; Kirov Theatre
Spartacus	A. Khachaturian	I. Moiseyev	March 11, 1958; Bolshoi
The Stationmaster	A. Petrov	Yu. Vorontosov, M. Mikhailov	May 9, 1955; Len. Ch. Inst.
Stenka Razin	A. Glazunov	A. Gorsky	November 6, 1918; Bolshoi
Stone Guest	B. Asafiev, M. Glinka	L. Yacobson	June 26, 1946; Len. Ch. Inst.
Substitute Bride	G. Vagner	K. Muller	December 21, 1958; Minsk
Stronger than Death	I. Shvarts	L. Yacobson	1960(?), Leningrad
Svetlana	D. Klebanov	N. Popko, A. Radunsky, L. Pospekhin	December 20, 1939; Bolshoi Fil.
Tale of the Dead Tsarevna and the Family of Bogatyrs	V. Deshevov	A. Andreyev, B. Fenster	June 16, 1949; Maly
Tale of a Fox, Rooster and Ram (Renard)	I. Stravinsky	F. Lopukhov	January 2, 1927; GATOB
Tale of a Priest and His Worker Balda	M. Chulaki	V. Varkovitsky	January 9, 1940; Maly

Title	Composer	Choreographer	Premiere
Tale of a Stone Flower	A. Fridlender	K. Muller	August 5, 1944; Sverdlovsk
Tale of a Stone Flower	S. Prokofiev	L. Lavrovsky	February 12, 1954; Bolshoi
Taras Bulba	V. Soloviev-Sedoi	F. Lopukhov	December 12, 1940; Kirov Theatre
Tatiana (Daughter of the People)	A. Krein	V. Bourmeister	June 12, 1947; Kirov Theatre
Tavria	B. Nakhabin	I. Kovtunov	September 19, 1959; Kharkov
Three Fat Men	V. Oransky	I. Moiseyev	March 1, 1935; Bolshoi
Tiina	L. Auster	B. Fenster	December 30, 1955; Estonia
Timur and His Command	A. Nesterov	G. Yazvinsky	November 17, 1956; Gorky
To the Heart of Marika	B. Moshkov	G. Yazvinsky	November 25, 1959; Sverdlovsk
Tsar Kandavl (Le Roi Candaule)	C. Pugni	L. Leontiev	March 1, 1924; GATOB
Two Roses	A. Lensky	K. Goleizovsky	1941; Dushanbe
Under Italian Skies	V. Yurovsky	R. Zakharov, S. Sergeyev	September 25, 1952; Kiev
Vanina Vanini	N. Karetnikov	N. Kasatkina, V. Vasilév	May 25, 1962; Bolshoi
We Stalingraders	Potapov	V. Varkovitsky	Bolshoi
Youth	M. Chulaki	B. Fenster	December 9, 1949; Maly

1. "Maly" refers to the Leningrad Maly Opera Theatre; "Stanislavsky," to the Stanislavsky and Nemirovich-Danchenko Musical Theatre, Moscow; and "GATOB," to the State Academic Theatre of Opera and Ballet, Leningrad. Its name was later changed to the Leningrad Kirov Theatre of Opera and Ballet. "Kirov" refers to the latter; used also by the Leningrad Choreographic Institute.

313

SELECTED BIBLIOGRAPHY

BOOKS, THEATRICAL PROGRAMS, PAMPHLETS

Abramskii, I.P., I.F. Belza, K.K. Sakva, and M.I. Chulaki. *Bol'shoi Teatr SSSR Opera. Balet.* Moscow: Gosudarstvennoe Muzykal'noe Izdatel'stvo, 1958.

Akademiia Khudozhestv SSSR. *Ocherki Marksistsko-Leninskoi Estetiki.* Moscow: Izdatel'stvo Akademii Khudozhestv SSSR, 1960.

Akademiia Nauk SSSR. Institut Istorii Iskusstv. *Istoriia Russkoi Sovetskoi Muzyka.* 4 vols. Moscow: Gosudarstvennoe Muzykal'noe Izdatel'stvo, 1956–1963.

———. *Teatr i Muzyka. Dokumenty i Materialy.* Moscow: Izdatel'stvo Akademii Nauk SSSR, 1963.

Ananov, I.N. *Ministerstva v SSSR.* Moscow: Gosudarstvennoe Izdatel'stvo Iuridicheskoi Literatury, 1960.

Andreeva, Maria Sergeevna. *Kommunisticheskaia Partiia-Organizator Kul'turno-Prosvetitel'noi Raboty v SSSR 1917–1933.* Moscow: Vysshaia Shkola, 1963.

Anisimov, A., ed. *Aistenok. Gosudarstvennyi Ordena Lenina Akademicheskii Bol'shoi Teatr SSSR.* Moscow: Iskusstvo, 1951.

———. ed. *Bakhchisaraiskii Fontan. Gosudarstvennyi Ordena Lenina Akademicheskii Bol'shoi Teatr SSSR.* Moscow: Iskusstvo, 1951.

Arapov, Pimen'. *Lietopis' Russkago Teatra.* St. Petersburg: Tipografii N. Tiblens, 1861.

Aristophanes. *Five Comedies of Aristophanes,* translated by Benjamin Bickley Rogers. Garden City: Doubleday, 1955.

314

Selected Bibliography

Asaf'ev, B.V. [Igor' Glebov]. *Izbrannye Trudy.* 5 vols. Moscow: Izdatel'stvo Akademii Nauk SSSR, 1952–1957.

———. *Kniga o Stravinskom.* Leningrad: "Triton," 1929.

Aubrey, Henry G. *Co-existence: Economic Challenge and Response.* Washington, D.C.: National Planning Association, 1961.

Babitsky, Paul, and John Rimberg. *The Soviet Film Industry.* New York: Praeger, 1955.

Bakhrushin, Iu. A. *Istoriia Russkogo Baleta.* Moscow: Izdatel'stvo Sovetskaia Rossia, 1965.

Ballet Annual, XII, 1958. London: A. & C. Black, 1957.

Les Ballets du Grand Théâtre de Moscou. Paris: Editions Cercle d'art, 1958.

Barghoorn, Frederick C. *The Soviet Cultural Offensive. The Role of Cultural Diplomacy in Soviet Foreign Policy.* Princeton: University Press, 1960.

———. *Soviet Foreign Propaganda.* Princeton: University Press, 1964.

Beaumont, Cyril W. *Ballet Design. Past and Present.* London: Studio Publications, 1946.

———. *Ballets. Past and Present. Being a Third Supplement to the Complete Book of Ballets.* London: Putnam, 1955.

———. *Complete Book of Ballets.* London: Putnam, 1956.

———. *A History of Ballet in Russia, 1613–1881.* London: Beaumont, 1942.

———. *A Short History of Ballet.* London: Beaumont, 1947.

———. *Supplement to a Complete Book of Ballets.* London: Beaumont, 1942.

Bellew, Hélène. *Ballet in Moscow Today.* London: Thames and Hudson, 1956.

Benois. Alexandre. *Memoirs,* translated by Moura Budberg. London: Chatto and Windus, 1960.

———. *Reminiscences of the Russian Ballet.* Translated by Mary Britnieva. London: Putnam, 1941.

Benton, William. *This is the Challenge. The Benton Reports of 1956–1958 on the Nature of the Soviet Threat.* New York: Associated College Presses, 1958.

Bereday, George Z.J., William W. Brickman, and Gerald H. Read. *The Changing Soviet School.* The Comparative Education Society Field Study of the U.S.S.R. Cambridge: Riverside Press, 1960.

Bernandt, G. *Slovar' Oper. Vpervye Postaylennykh ili Isdannykh v Dorevoliutsionnoi Rossii v SSSR.* Moscow: Sovetskii Kompozitor, 1962.

Bertenson, Sergei. *Vokrug Iskusstva.* Hollywood, 1957.

Bezpalov, V.F. *Teatry v Dni Revoliutsii 1917.* Leningrad: Academia, 1927.

Blass, Ernst. *Das Wesen der Neuen Tanzkunst.* Weimar: Erich Lichtenstein, 1921.

Blok, Aleksandr. *Dnevnik Al. Bloka,* edited by P.N. Medvedev. 2 vols. Leningrad: Izdatel'stvo Pisatelei v Leningrade, 1928.

Bocharnikova, E., and O. Martynova. *Moskovskoe Khoreograficheskoe Uchilishche. Kratkii Istoricheskii Ocherk.* Moscow: Iskusstvo, 1954.

Bochenski, J.M. *Soviet Russian Dialectical Materialism [Diamat].* Dordrecht, Holland: D. Reidel, 1963.

Bogdanov-Berezovskii, Valerian. *Galina Sergeevna Ulanova.* 2nd ed. Moscow: Iskusstvo, 1961.

————. ed. *Muzykal'naia Zhizn' Leningrada. Sbornik Statei.* Leningrad: Sovetskii Kompozitor, 1961.

————. *Stat'i o Balete.* Leningrad: Sovetskii Kompozitor, 1962.

————. *Teatr Opery i Baleta imeni S.M. Kirova.* Leningrad: Iskusstvo, 1959.

Bogoiavlenskii, S.K. *Moskovskii Teatr pri Tsarkh Aleksee i Petre. Materialy Sobrannye Izdanie Imperatorskago Obshchestva Istorii i Drevnostei Rossiiskikh pri Moskovskom Universitete.* Moscow: 1914.

Bol'shaia Sovetskaia Entsiklopediia. 1930 Edition.

Bol'shaia Sovetskaia Entsiklopediia. 1950 Edition.

Bonnot, Yves. *Ballets de Moscou. Par la Troupe du Théâtre Lyrique National Stanislavski et Nemirovitch-Dantchenko.* Paris: Editions Cercle d'Art, 1956.

Borisoglebskii, M.V. *Materialy po Istorii Russkogo Baleta. Proshloe Baletnogo Otdeleniia Peterburgskogo Teatral'nogo Uchilishcha, nyne Leningradskogo Gosudarstvennogo Khoreograficheskogo Uchilishcha.* Leningrad: Leningradskoe Gosudarstvennoe Khoreograficheskoe Uchilishche, 1938–1939.

Borland, Harriet. *Soviet Literary Theory and Practice During the First Five-Year Plan, 1928–1932.* New York: King's Crown Press, 1950.

Bourman, Anatole, in collaboration with D. Lyman. *The Tragedy of Nijinsky.* New York: McGraw-Hill, 1936.

Brants, Georgs. *Latviešu Balets.* Riga: Izdevniecība Tāle, 1937.

Brodskii, N.L., V.L. L'vov-Rogachevskii, and N.P. Siderov. *Literaturnye Manifesty.* Moscow: Federatsii, 1929.

Selected Bibliography

Brown, Benjamin W. *Theatre at the Left*. Providence, R.I.: The Booke Shop, 1938.

Brown, Edward J. *The Proletarian Episode in Russian Literature, 1928–1932*. New York: Columbia University Press, 1953.

Bryce, Mayo. *Fine Arts Education in the Soviet Union*. U.S. Department of Health, Education, and Welfare. Washington, D.C., U.S. Government Printing Office, 1963.

Bukharin, N. *Culture in Two Worlds*. New York: International Publishers, 1934.

————. *Historical Materialism. A System of Sociology*. Authorized translation of 3d Russian edition. New York: Russell and Russell, 1965.

Carter, Huntley. *The New Spirit of the Russian Theatres, 1917–1928*. New York: Brentano's, 1929.

Chaliapin, Feodor. *Man and Mask. Forty Years in the Life of a Singer*, translated by Phyllis Mégroz. New York: Knopf, 1932.

Chaliapine, Feodore Ivanovich. *Pages from My Life. An Autobiography*, translated by H.M. Buck. New York: Harper's, 1927.

Chen, Jack. *Soviet Arts and Artists*. London: The Pilot Press, 1945.

Chernyshevsky, N.G. *Selected Philosophical Essays*. Moscow: Foreign Languages Publishing House, 1953.

Chistiakova, V. *V Mire Tantsa*. Leningrad: Iskusstvo, 1964.

Chudnovskii, M. *Viktorina Kriger*. Moscow: Iskusstvo, 1964.

Chujoy, Anatole, ed. *The Dance Encyclopedia*. New York: A.S. Barnes, 1949.

Communist Party of the Soviet Union. Programme. 22d Congress of the C.P.S.U. Moscow: Foreign Languages Publishing House, 1961.

Compan, Charles. *Tantsoval'nyi Slovar', Soderzhashchii v Sebe Istoriiu, Pravila i Osnovaniia Tantsoval'nago Iskusstva, s Kriticheskimi Rasmyshleniiami i Liubopytnymi Anekdotami, Otnosiashchimsia k Drevnim i novym Tantsam,* translated from the French. Moscow: V Universitetskoi Tipografii u V. Okorokona, 1790.

Dana, H.W.L. *Handbook on Soviet Drama*. New York: The American Russian Institute, 1938.

Dandré, Victor. *Anna Pavlova*. London: Cassell, 1932.

Daniels, Robert V., ed. *A Documentary History of Communism*. 2 vols. New York: Vintage Books, 1960.

Danilevich, Lev. Vasil'evich. *Kniga O Sovetskoi Muzyke*. Moscow: Gosudarstvennoe Muzykal'noe Izdatel'stvo, 1962.

Desti, Mary. *The Untold Story. The Life of Isadora Duncan, 1921–1927.* New York: Horace Liveright, 1929.

Drizen, N.V. *Dramaticheskaia Tsenzura Dvukh Epokh 1825–1881.* Petrograd: Kinoizdatel'stvo Prometei, 1917.

———. *Materialy K Istorii Russkago Teatra.* Moscow: Postavshch. Dvora Ego Velichestva, 1905.

Druskin, M. *Ocherki po Istorii Tantsoval'noi Muzyki.* Leningrad: Leningradskaia Filarmoniia, 1936.

Druskin, M.S., L. Lavrosvskii, P. Fel'dt, et al. *Fadetta. Balet v 3 Deistviakh Muzyka Leo Deliba. Sbornik Statei k Postanovke Balete v Gosudarstvennom Akademicheskom Malom Opernom Teatre.* Leningrad, 1936.

Duncan, Irma. *Duncan Dancer. An Autobiography of Irma Duncan.* Middletown, Conn.: Wesleyan University Press, 1966.

Duncan, Isadora. *My Life.* New York: Garden City Publishing, 1927.

Dymshits, A.L. *Teatr i Zhizn'.* Moscow: Iskusstvo, 1958.

Dynnik, Tatiana. *Krepostnoi Teatr.* Moscow: Academia, 1933.

Eastman, Max. *Artists in Uniform. A Study of Literature and Bureaucratism.* New York: Knopf, 1934.

El'iash, Nikolai. *Russkaia Terpsikhora.* Moscow: Izdatel'stvo Sovetskaia Rossia, 1965.

Elizarova, N.A. *Teatry Sheremetevyk.* Moscow: Izdanie Ostankinskogo Dvortsa-Muzeia, 1944.

Ely, Colonel Louis B., ed. *The Red Army Today.* Harrisburg, Pa.: The Military Service Publishing Co., 1953.

Evreinov, Nikolai Nikolaevich. *Histoire du Théâtre Russe.* Preface et adaptation française de G. Welter. Paris: Editions du Chêne, 1947.

Ezhegodnik Imperatorskikh Teatrov Sezon 1890–1891 gg. St. Petersburg: Tipografiia Imperatorskikh Teatrov, 1892.

———. *Sezon 1893–1894 gg.* St. Petersburg: Tipografiia Imperatorskikh Teatrov, 1895.

Famintsyn, Aleksandr. *Skomorokhi na Rusi.* St. Petersburg: Tipografiia E. Arngol'da, 1889.

Feuer, Lewis S. ed. *Marx and Engels. Basic Writings on Politics and Philosophy.* Garden City: Doubleday, 1959.

Fisin, S., ed. *Svetlyi Ruchei. Komediinyi Balet v 3 Deistviakh i 4 Kartinakh. Sbornik Statei i Materialov k Postanovke Baleta v Gosudarstvennom Akademicheskom Malom Opernom Teatre.* Leningrad: 1935.

Selected Bibliography

Fokine, Vitale, trans., and Anatole Chujoy, ed. *Fokine. Memoirs of a Ballet Master*. Boston: Little, Brown, 1961.

Frangopulo, Marietta. *Leonid Sergeevich Leont'ev. Tridtsat'piat' Let Stsenicheskoi Deiatel'nosti*. Leningrad: VTO, 1939.

———. and L. Entelis. *75 Baletnikh Libretto*. Leningrad: Sovetskii Kompozitor, 1960.

Freeman, Joseph, Joshuah Kunitz, and Louis Lozowick. *Voices of October: Art and Literature in Soviet Russia*. New York: Vanguard, 1930.

Friche, V.M. "Freidizm i Iskusstvo," in *Problemy Iskusstvovedeniia. Sbornik Statei po Voprosam Sotsiologii Iskusstva i Literatury*. 2nd ed. Moscow: Gosudarstvennoe Izdatel'stvo Khudozhestvennoi Literatury, 1931, pp. 48–68.

Fülöp-Miller, René, and Joseph Gregor. *The Russian Theater: Its Character and History, with Especial Reference to the Revolutionary Period*, translated by Paul England. Philadelphia: Lippincott, 1929.

Fundamentals of Marxism-Leninism. Manual, translated by Clemens Dutt. Moscow: Foreign Languages Publishing House, 1963.

Gorchakov, Nikolai A. *The Theater in Soviet Russia*, translated by Edgar Lehrman. New York: Columbia University, 1958.

Gosudarstvennaia Akademiia Iskusstvoznaniia. *Istoriia Sovetskogo Teatra. Tom I. Petrogradskie Teatry na Poroge Oktiabria i v Epokhu Voennogo Kommunizma 1917–1921*. Leningrad: Leningradskoe Otdelenie Gosudarstvennogo Izdatel'stva Khudozhestvennoi Literatury, 1933.

Grant, Douglas, ed. *The Humanities in Soviet Higher Education*. Toronto: University of Toronto Press, 1960.

Grosheva, Elena. *Bol'shoi Teatr SSSR. v Proshlom i Nastoiashchem*. Moscow: Sovetskii Kompozitor, 1962.

Gruilow, Leo, ed. *Current Soviet Policies II. The Documentary Record of the 20th Communist Party Congress and Its Aftermath*. New York: Frederick A. Praeger, 1957.

Gsovsky, Vladimir. *Soviet Civil Law. Private Rights and Their Background under the Soviet Regime*. 2 vols. Ann Arbor: University of Michigan Law School, 1948.

Haskell, Arnold L. *Balletomania. The Story of an Obsession*. New York: Simon and Schuster, 1934.

———. *Diaghileff. His Artistic and Private Life*. In collaboration with Walter Nouvel. New York: Simon and Schuster, 1935.

————. *The Russian Genius in Ballet.* New York: Pergamon Press, 1963.

Hindus, Maurice. *The Cossacks, The Story of a Warrior People.* New York: Doubleday, 1945.

Hurok, S. *S. Hurok Presents. A Memoir of the Dance World.* New York: Hermitage House, 1953.

Hyden, Walford. *Pavlova.* Boston: Little, Brown, 1931.

Iakobson, L.V., and I.V. Golubovskii, eds. *Khoreograficheskie Miniatury.* Leningrad, 1960.

Il'chev, Leonid Fedorovich. *Iskusstvo Prinadlezhit Narodu.* Moscow: Gospolitizdat, 1963.

Jasny, Naum. *The Socialized Agriculture of the U.S.S.R. Plans and Performances.* Palo Alto: Stanford University Press, 1949.

Jelagin, Juri. *Taming of the Arts,* translated by Nicholas Wreden. New York: Dutton, 1951.

Johnson, Priscilla. *Khrushchev and the Arts: the Politics of Soviet Culture. Documents Selected and Edited by Priscilla Johnson and Leopold Labedz.* Cambridge, Mass.: MIT Press, 1965.

Juviler, Nina. "Soviet Art. A Report for the Use of Specialists in the Field of Art Planning to Visit the Soviet Union." New York: Institute of International Education, 1964.

Kahn, Albert E. *Days with Ulanova.* New York: Simon and Schuster, 1962.

Kalinin, M. *O Molodezhi.* 2nd ed. Moscow: Izdatel'stvo TsK VLKSM, Molodaia Gvardiia, 1939.

————. *O Voprosakh Sotsialisticheskoi Kul'tury. Sbornik Statei i Rechei 1925–1938 gg.* Moscow: Gosudarstvennoe Izdaltel'stvo Politicheskoi Literatury, 1938.

Karlinskaia-Skudina, G.S. *Balet.* Moscow: Gosudarstvennoe Muzykal'noe Izdatel'stvo, 1960.

Karsavina, Tamara. *Theatre Street. The Reminiscences of Tamara Karsavina.* Revised Edition. New York: Dutton, 1961.

Katonova, S. *Balety R.M. Gliera.* Moscow: Sovetskii Kompozitor, 1960.

————. *Balety S. Prokof'eva.* Moscow Sovetskii Kompozitor, 1962.

————. *Muzyka v Balete.* Leningrad: Muzgiz, 1961.

Kharlamov and O. Vadeyev, eds. *Face to Face. The Story of N.S. Khrushchev's Visit to the U.S.A., September 15–27, 1959.* Printed U.S.S.R.

Khudozhniki Sovetskogo Teatra (1916–1935). Makety, Eskizy, Dekoratsii i Kostiumov, Kukly. Katalog Vystavki Teatral'nogo-Dekoratsionnogo Iskusstvo. Leningrad: VTO, 1936.

Selected Bibliography

Kirtoka, A.M. Manuilov. *Moldavskii Gosudarstvennyi Teatr Opery i Baleta.* Kishinev: Gosudarstvennoe Izdatel'stvo "Kartiia Moldoveniaske," 1960.

Kiselev, M.S. "Balet," in *Ocherki Sovetskogo Muzykal'nogo Tvorchestva.* Tom I, edited by B.V. Asaf'ev. Moscow: Muzgiz, 1947.

Kleiber, Boris A. *Russisk Ballett.* Nasjonalforlaget, 1946.

Klingender, F.D. *Marxism and Modern Art. An Approach to Socialist Realism.* London: Laurence and Wishart, 1943.

Koegler, Horst. *Bolschoi-Ballet. Das Ballett des Grossen Akademischen Theaters der UdSSR in Moskau.* Berlin: Rembrandt Verlag, 1959.

Komitet po Delam Uskusstv pri SNK SSSR. *Dve Rozy. Balet v 4 Aktakh.* Moscow: Iskusstvo, 1941.

―――. *Gosudarstvennyi Teatr Opery i Baleta imeni A.A. Spendiarova.* Moscow: Iskusstvo, 1939.

Kommunisticheskaia Partiia Sovetskogo Soiuza v Rezoliutsiiakh i Resheniiak. S''ezdov, Konferentsii i Plenumov TsK. Chast'III 1930–1954. Moscow: Gosudarstvennoe Izdatel'stvo Politicheskoi Literatury, 1954.

Kostetskii, I.V. *Sovetskaia Teatral'naia Politika i Sistema Stanislavskogo.* Munich: Institut po Izycheniu SSSR, 1956.

Kovach, Nora, and Istvan Rabovsky. *Leap Through the Curtain,* told by George Mikes. New York: Dutton, 1956.

Kozlov, Iu. M. *Sovetskoe Administrativnoe Pravo.* Moscow: Izdatel'stvo Iuridicheskaia Literatura, 1964.

―――. *Upravlenie v Oblasti Administrativno-Politicheskoi Deiatel'nosti Sovetskogo Gosudarstva.* Moscow: Izdatel'stvo Moskovskogo Universiteta, 1961.

Krasovskaia, Vera. *Russkii Baletnyi Teatr ot Vozniknoveniia do Srediny* XIX *Veka.* Leningrad: Iskusstvo, 1958.

―――. *Russkii Baletnyi Teatr. Vtoroi Poloviny* XIX *Veka.* Moscow: Iskusstvo, 1963.

―――. *Vakhtang Chabukiani.* Moscow: Iskusstvo, 1956.

Krebs, Stanley Dale. *Soviet Composers and the Development of Soviet Music.* Unpublished Ph.D. dissertation, University of Washington, 1963.

Kremshevskaia, G. *Nataliia Dudinskaia.* Moscow: Iskusstvo, 1964.

Kriger, Viktorina. *Moi Zapiski. Teatral'nye Memuary.* Moscow: Academia, 1930.

321

————. *Vakhtang Chabukiani. Stranitsy iz Tvorcheskoi Zhizni.* Moscow: Izdatel'stvo "Znanie," 1960.

Krivosheeva, A. *Esteticheskie Vzgliady A.V. Lunacharskogo.* Moscow: Iskusstvo, 1939.

Krylov, S.M. *Puti Razvitiia Teatr. Stenograficheskii Otchet i Resheniia Partiinogo Soveshaniia po Voprosam Teatra pri Agitprope TsK VKP (b) v Mae 1927 g.* Moscow: Kinopechat', 1927.

Kulski, W.W. *The Soviet Regime. Communism in Practice.* Syracuse: Syracuse University Press, 1959.

Kytasty, Hryhory. *Some Aspects of Ukrainian Music under the Soviets.* Research Program on the U.S.S.R., 1954. New York: Columbia University Archives.

Lasarew, W.N. *Die Malerei und die Skulptur der Kiewer Rus. Vol. I of Geschichte der Russischen Kunst.* Dresden: Verlag der Kunst, 1957.

Lashin, A.G. *Kul'turno-Vospitatel'naia Deiatel'nost' Sovetskogo Gosudarstva.* Moscow: Gosudarstvennoe Izdatel'stvo Iuridicheskoi Literatury, 1955.

————. *Mestnye Organy Gosudarstvennoi Vlasti v SSSR.* Gospolitizdat, 1955.

Laurent, Jean, and Julie Sazonova. *Serge Lifar. Renovateur du Ballet Français.* Paris: Buchet/Chastel, Corrêa, 1960.

Lawson, Joan. *Ballet in the U.S.S.R.* London: Society for Cultural Relations between Peoples of the British Commonwealth and the U.S.S.R., 1943.

Lebedev, A.A. *A. V. Lunacharskii. Esteticheskie Vzgliady.* Moscow: Iskusstvo, 1962.

Lederman, Minna, ed. *Stravinsky in the Theatre.* New York: Pellegrini and Cudahy, 1949.

Legat, Nikolai Gustavovich. *Ballet Russe. Memoirs by Nicholas Legat,* translated by Sir Paul Dukes. London: Methuen, 1939.

Lehmann-Haupt, Hellmut. *Art Under a Dictatorship.* New York: Oxford University Press, 1954.

Lenin, V. I. *Lenin o Kul'ture i Iskusstvo,* edited by L. G. Tamashin. Moscow: Iskusstvo, 1956.

————. "Party Organization and Party Literature," Vol. x of *Selected Works.* London: Laurence and Wishart, 1962.

Lenine, V. I. *Sur la Litterature et l'Art. Textes Choisis Précedés d'une Etude par Jean Fréville.* Paris: Editions Sociales, 1957.

Selected Bibliography

Leningrad Gosudarstvennyi Akademicheskii Teatr Opery i Baleta imeni S. M. Kirova. *Utrachennye Illiuzii. Khoreograficheskii Roman*. Leningrad: 1936.

Leningradskii Gosudarstvennyi Institut Teatra, Muzyki i Kinematografii. *Muzyka Sovetskogo Baleta. Sbornik Statei*. Moscow: Gosudarstvennoe Muzykal'noe Izdatel'stvo, 1962.

Levine, Irving R. *Main Street U.S.S.R.* Garden City: Doubleday, 1959.

Levinson, Andrei. *Staryi i Novyi Balet*. Petrograd: Izdatel'stvo Svobodnoe *Iskusstvo*, 1917.

Levit, S. *Sovetskaia Muzyka v Bor'be za Mir*. Moscow: Izdatel'stvo SSSR, 1957.

Lieven, Prince Peter. [Liven, Petr Aleksandrovich]. *The Birth of Ballet Russe*, translated by L. Zarine. Boston: Houghton Mifflin, 1936.

Lifar, Serge. *History of Russian Ballet from Its Origins to the Present Day*, translated by Arnold L. Haskell. London: Hutchinson, 1954.

————. *Serge Diaghilev, His Life, His Work, His Legend*. New York: Putnam's, 1940.

Lifshitz, M. *The Philosophy of Art of Karl Marx*. New York: Critics Group, 1938.

Litinskii, G. I. *Muzykal'naia Kul'tura Avtonomnykh Respublik RSFSR*. Moscow: Muzgiz, 1957.

Liukom, E. M. *Moia Rabota v Balete*. Leningrad: VTO, 1940.

Livanova, Tamara. *Ocherki i Materialy po Istorii Russkoi Muzykal'noi Kul'tury*. Vol. I. Moscow: Iskusstvo, 1938.

London, Kurt. *The Seven Soviet Arts*. London: Faber and Faber, 1937.

Lopukhov, Fedor. *Shest'desiat Let v Balete. Vospominaniia i Zapiski Baletmeistera*, edited by Iurii Slonimskii. Moscow: Iskusstvo, 1966.

Lunacharskii, Anatolii. *Sobranie Sochinenii*. 4 vols. Moscow: Khudozhestvennaia Literatura, 1964.

————. *O Teatre i Dramaturgii. Izbrannye Stat'i*. 2 vols. Moscow: Iskusstvo, 1958.

————. *Stat'i o Teatre i Dramaturgii*. Moscow: Iskusstvo, 1938.

————. *Teatr i Revoliutsiia*. Moscow: Gosizdat, 1924.

————. *V Mire Muzyki. Stati i Rechi*, edited by G. B. Bernandt and I. A. Sats. Moscow: Sovetskii Kompozitor, 1958.

————. *Voprosy Literatury i Dramaturgii*. Leningrad: Rossiiskii Institut Istorii Iskusstv, 1924.

L'vov, I. *Kirgizskii Teatr; Ocherk Istorii*. Moscow: Iskusstvo, 1953.

L'vov-Anokhin, Boris. *Alla Shelest*. Moscow: Iskusstvo, 1964.

MacDougall, Allan Ross. *Isadora: A Revolutionary in Art and Love*. New York: Thos. Nelson, 1960.

MacLeod, Joseph. *Actors Across the Volga. A Study of the 19th Century Russian Theatre and of Soviet Theatres in War*. London: George Allen and Unwin, 1946.

Manchester, Phyllis Winifred. *The Rose and the Star: Ballet in England and Russia Compared by P. W. Manchester and Iris Morley*. London: V. Gollancz, 1949.

Markov, P.A. *The Soviet Theatre*. New York: Putnam's, 1935.

Martynova, Ol'ga. *Ekaterina Gel'tser*. Moscow: Iskusstvo, 1965.

Marx, Karl. *Economic and Philosophic Manuscripts*. Moscow: Foreign Languages Press, 1961.

———. *The German Ideology*. New York: International Publishers, 1963.

———. *Selected Works,* edited by Ed. V. Adoratsky. 2 vols. Moscow: Cooperative Publishing Society of Foreign Workers in the U.S.S.R., 1935.

——— and Friedrich Engels. *Literature and Art. Selections from Their Writings*. New York: International Publishers, 1949.

Masefield, John, and Edward Seago. *Tribute to Ballet in Poems by John Masefield*. London: Collins, 1938.

Mathewson, Rufus W. *The Positive Hero in Russian Literature*. New York: Columbia University Press, 1958.

Mehnert, Klaus. *Stalin versus Marx. The Stalinist Historical Doctrine*. London: G. Allen and Unwin, 1952.

Meisel, James H. and Edward S. Kozera. *Materials for the Study of the Soviet System. State and Party Constitutions, Laws, Decrees, Decisions, and Official Statements of Leaders in Translation*. 2d ed. Ann Arbor: George Wahr, 1953.

Moiseyev Dance Company [Program of U.S. Tour, 1965]. New York: S. Hurok Company, 1965.

Molotov, V., "What is Stakhanovism?" Speech delivered at the First All-Union Conference of Stakhanovites. New York: International Publishers, 1936.

Monas, Sidney. *The Third Section. Police and Society in Russia under Nicholas I*. Cambridge: Harvard University Press, 1961.

Moore, Lillian, ed. *Russian Ballet Master—The Memoirs of Marius Petipa,* translated by Helen Whittaker. London: Adam and Charles Black, 1958.

Morley, Iris. *Soviet Ballet*. London: Collins, 1945.

Selected Bibliography

Morozov, P.O. *Istoriia Russkago Teatr do Poloviny* XVIII *Stoletiia*. St. Petersburg: V. Demakov, 1889.

Moseley, Philip E. *The Kremlin and World Politics. Studies in Soviet Policy
and Action*. New York: Vintage Books, 1960.

———, ed. *The Soviet Union, 1922–1962*. New York: Praeger, 1953.

Moskovskii Bol'shoi Teatr 1825–1925. Moscow: Izdanie Upravleniia Gosu-
darstvennykh Akademicheskikh Teatrov, n.d.

Nekrasov, N.A. *Izbrannye Poemy*. 2 vols. Moscow: Gosizdat Khudozhestvennoi Literatury, 1962.

Nijinsky, Romola. *Nijinsky*. New York: Simon and Schuster, 1934.

Nisnevich, Soma Gerasimovna. *Belaruskaia Narodnaia Pesnia i Muzychnai
Dramaturgi Natsyianalnykh Oper i Baletau*. Minsk: Redaktsyia Muzychnai Literatury, 1962.

N'iu-Iuork, Siti Balet. Gastroli v SSSR. Moscow: Ministerstvo Kul'tury
SSSR, 1962.

Nureyev, Rudolf. *Nureyev. An Autobiography*. New York: Dutton, 1963.

*O Literature i Iskusstve. Sbornik Dokumentov, Izdanie Vtoroe, Dopolnen-
noe*. Moscow: Izdatel'stvo "Sovetskaia Rossia," 1960.

Olearius, Adam. *The Voyages and Travels of the Ambassadors from the
Duke of Holstein, to the Great Duke of Muscovy, and the King of Persia,
Begun in the Year MDCXXXIII and finish'd in MDCXXXIX. Con-
taining a compleat History of Muscovy, Tartary, Persia and other
Adjacent Countries*. In Seven Books. Rendered in English by John
Davies of Kidwell. London: Printed for Thomas Dring, 1662.

Olkhovsky, Andrey. *Music under the Soviets. The Agony of an Art*. Praeger,
1955.

Orlov, Georgii. *Muzykal'naia Literatura. Bibliograficheskii Ukazatel'
Knizhnoi i Zhurnal'noi Literatury o Muzyke na Russkom Iazyke*. Leningrad: Leningradskaia Filarmoniia, 1935.

Outline History of the U.S.S.R. Moscow: Foreign Languages Publishing
House, 1960.

Pantiukhova, L. *Leningradskoe Gosudarstvennoe Khoreograficheskoe
Uchilishche*. Moscow: Iskusstvo, 1948.

Pevsner, Alexei. *A biographical sketch of my brothers naum gabo and
antoine pevsner*, translated by Richard Scammell and W.R. Burke.
Amsterdam: Augustin and Choonman, 1964.

Pipes, Richard. *The Formation of the Soviet Union. Communism and
Nationalism. 1917–1923*. Cambridge: Harvard University Press, 1954.

Plato. *The Laws of Plato,* translated by A.E. Taylor. London: J.M. Dent, 1934.

Pleshcheev, Aleksandr. *Nash Balet (1673–1899). Balet v Rossii do Nachala XIX Stoletiia i Balet v S. Peterburge do 1899 Goda. Vtoroe Dopolnennoe Izdanie s Predisloviem K.A. Skal'kovskago.* St. Petersburg: Izdanie F.A. Pereiaslavtseva i A.A. Pleshcheeva, 1899.

Programma Kursa. "Rezhissura i Masterstvo Aktera." Moscow: Iskusstvo, 1954.

Programme of the Communist Party of the Soviet Union. 22nd Congress. Moscow: Foreign Languages Publishing House, 1961.

Prokofief, S. *Autobiography: Articles, Reminiscences.* Moscow: Foreign Languages Publishing House, n.d.

Protiv Formalizma, Naturalizma v Iskusstve. Sbornik Statei. Moscow: OGIZ, 1937.

Punina, Z., Iu. Kharlamov, N. Foregger, Kollektiva Geptakhor, T. Glebov i Z. Verbova s Predisloviem A.A. Gvozdeva. *Ritm i Kul'tura Tantsa. Sbornik Statei.* Leningrad: Academia, 1926.

Pushkin, Alexander. *The Works of Alexander Pushkin,* edited by Avrahm Yarmolinsky. New York: Random House, 1936.

Racster, Ol'ga. *The Master of the Russian Ballet. The Memoirs of Cav. Enrico Cecchetti.* London: Hutchinson, 1922.

Rauch, Georg von. *A History of Soviet Russia,* translated by Peter and Annette Jacobsohn. New York: Praeger, 1963.

Ravich, N.A., ed. *Glavnyi Komitet po Kontroliu za Repertuorom, Repertuarnyi Ukazatel'. Spisok Razreshennykh i Zapreshchennykh k Ispolneniiu na Stsene Proizvedenii.* Moscow: Teakinopechat', 1929.

Reiss, Francoise. *Nijinsky* translated by Helen and Stephen Haskell. New York: Pitman, 1957.

Reitenfel's, Iakob. [Reutenfels, Jakob]. *Skazaniia Svetleishemu Gertsogu Toskanomu Koz'me Tret'emu o Moskovii.* Vol. III, translated from Latin to Russian by Aleksei Stankevich. Moscow: Obshchestvo Rasprostraneniia Poleznykh Knig, 1905.

Rimberg, John David. *The Motion Picture in the Soviet Union. A Sociological Analysis.* Ph.D. dissertation, Department of Political Science, Columbia University, 1959.

Romanovsky-Krassinsky, H.S.H. The Princess [Kschessinska, Mathilde]. *Dancing in Petersburg. A Memoir of Imperial Russia, Exile, and the Ballet,* translated by Arnold Haskell. Garden City: Doubleday, 1961.

Selected Bibliography

Rossiiskii Featr, ili Polnoe Sobranie Vsekh Rossiiskikh Sochinenii, Chast' XVIII. St. Petersburg: Pri Imperatorskoi Akademii Nauk, 1788.

Sayler, Oliver M. *The Russian Theatre.* New York: Brentano's, 1922.

———. *The Russian Theatre under the Revolution.* Boston: Little, Brown, 1920.

Schaikevitch, André. *Olga Spessivtzeva. Magicienne Envoutée.* Paris: Librairie les Lettres, 1954.

Schwartz, Harry. *Russia's Soviet Economy.* Englewood Cliffs: Prentice-Hall. 1954 and 1960 editions.

Schwezoff, Igor. *Russian Somersault.* New York: Harper, 1936.

Seduro, Vladimir, "Belorussian Opera and Ballet." Unpublished manuscript, Columbia University Archives.

———. *The Byelorussian Theater and Drama,* edited by Edgar H. Lehrman, Foreword by Ernest J. Simmons. New York: Research Program on the U.S.S.R., 1955.

Seroff, Victor Ilyich. *Dmitri Shostakovich. The Life and Background of a Soviet Composer.* New York: Knopf, 1943.

Shaverdian, A. *Bol'shoi Teatr Soiuza SSR.* Moscow: Gosudarstvennoe Muzykal'noe Izdatel'stvo, 1952.

Shchipunov, P., ed. *Leningradskoe Gosudarstvennoe Khoreograficheskoe Uchilishche.* Leningrad: Iskusstvo, 1940.

Shirokii, Iurii. *Tamara Khanum.* Moscow: Iskusstvo, 1941.

Shteinpress, Boris B., ed. *Iz Muzykal'nogo Proshlogo: Sbnornik Statei.* Moscow: Muzgiz, 1960.

Shtelin, Iakob [Jacob Staehlin von Storcksburg]. *Muzyka i Balet v Rossii XVIII Veka,* translated from German by B.I. Zagurskii. Leningrad: Muzykal'noe Izdatel'stvo "Triton," 1935.

Sil'vo, L.G. *Opyt Alfabitnago Ukazatelia Baletam, Pantomimam, Divertissementam 1672–1900.* St. Petersburg: N.I. Evstifeeva, 1900.

Simmons, Ernest J., ed. *Through the Glass of Soviet Literature. Views of Russian Society.* New York: Columbia University Press, 1953.

Skalkovskii, Konstantin. *V Teatral'nom Mire. Nabliudeniia, Vospominaniia, i Razsuzhdeniia.* St. Petersburg: A.S. Suvorin, 1899.

———. [Baletoman]. *Balet. Ego Istoriia i Mesto v Riadu Iziashykh Iskusstv.* St. Petersburg: A.S. Suvorin, 1882.

Slonim, Marc. *The Russian Theatre. From the Empire to the Soviets.* Cleveland: World Publishing Company, 1951.

Slonimskii, Iurii [Yuri Slonimsky]. *The Bolshoi Ballet*. 2d ed. Moscow: Foreign Languages Publishing House, 1960.

———. *Egipetski Nochi. Muzyka Arenskogo. Shopeniana, Muzyka Shopena. Karnaval. Muzyka Shumana*. Leningrad: Leningradskii Akademicheskii Teatr Opery i Baleta, 1935.

———. *Mastera Baleta*. Leningrad: Iskusstvo, 1937.

———. *Sovetskii Balet. Materialy k Istorii Sovetskogo Baletnogo Teatra*. Moscow: Iskusstvo, 1950.

———, ed. *Soviet Ballet*. New York: Philosophical Society, 1947.

———, ed. *"Zhar Ptitsa" i "Petrushka" I.F. Stravinskogo*. Leningrad: Gosudarstvennoe Muzykal'noe Izdatel'stvo, 1963.

———. Y. Bocharnikova, M. Gabovich, G. Ulanova, *The Bolshoi Ballet Story*. New York: Heller and Heller, 1959.

———. *Music Since 1900*. 3d ed. New York: Coleman-Ross Company, 1949.

Spisok Chinov Ministerstva Imperatorskago Dvora 1914 Goda. St. Petersburg: R. Golike i A. Vil'borg.

Spravochnik Partiinogo Rabotnika. Moscow: *Izdatel'stvo Politicheskoi Literatury*, 1959.

Stalin, Joseph. *Marxism and the National Question. Selected Writings and Speeches*. New York: International Publishers, 1942.

———. *Problems of Leninism*. Moscow: Foreign Languages Publishing House, 1940.

———. *Sochineniia*. 13 vols. Moscow: OGIZ, 1947.

———. "Speech at the First All-Union Conference of Stakhanovites, Nov. 17, 1935," translated by A. Fineberg. Moscow: Cooperative Publishing Society of Foreign Workers in the U.S.S.R., 1935.

Stals, Georgs. *Latviešu Balets*. Riga: J. Kadila Apgads, 1943.

Stanishevs'kyi, Iu. *Ukrains'kyi Radians'kyi Balet*. Kiev: Mystetsvo, 1963.

Stanislavsky, Constantin. *My Life in Art*, translated by J.J. Robbins. Boston: Little, Brown, 1938.

Stefanovych. M. *Kyivs'kyi Derzhavnyi Ordena Lenina Akademichnyi Teatr Operi ta Baletu URSR imeni T.G. Shevchenka. Istorichnyi Narys*. Kiev: Ministerstva kul'tury URSR, 1960.

Stevens, Edmund. *This Is Russia Uncensored*. Introduction by Walter Bedell Smith. New York: Didier, 1950.

Stravinsky, Igor, and Robert Craft. *Dialogues and a Diary*. New York: Doubleday, 1963.

Stravinsky and the Dance. A Survey of Ballet Productions 1910–1962. Foreword by Genevieve Oswald. The Dance Collection of New York Public Library, 1962.

Studenikin, S.S., V.A. Vlasov, and I.I. Evtikhiev. *Sovetskoe Administrativnoe Pravo*. Moscow: Gosudarstvennoe Izdatel'stvo Iuridicheskoi Literatury, 1950.

Surits, E. *Vsë o Balete. Slovar' Spravochnik*. Moscow: Izdatel'stvo Muzyka, 1966.

Svetlov, V. [Ivchenko, Valerian Iakovlevich]. *Sovremennyi Balet*. St. Petersburg, 1911.

———. *Terpsikhora. Stat'i, Ocherki, Zametki*. St. Petersburg, 1906.

Swayze, Harold. *Political Control of Literature in the U.S.S.R., 1946–1959*. Cambridge: Harvard University Press, 1962.

Tarasenko, G. Ia. *Leningradskii Gosudarstvennyi Ordena Lenina Malyi Opernyi Teatr*. Leningrad, 1940.

Teatral'naia Entsiklopediia. 5 vols. Moscow: Izdatel'stvo Sovetskaia Entsiklopediia, 1961–1967.

Teatral'naia Moskva. Mosreklamspravizdat, 1929.

Teatral'naia Moskva. Teatr, Muzyka, Kino Putevoditel 1927–8. Izdatel'stvo MKKh.

Teatral'naia Moskva. Spravochnik. Izdatel'stvo Gazety, "Sovetskoe Iskusstvo," 1947.

Teliakovskii. V.A. *Imperatorskie Teatry i 1905 God*. Leningrad: Academia, 1926.

———. *Vospominaniia 1898–1917*. Peterburg: Vremia, 1924.

Terry, Walter. *Ballet*. New York: Dell Laurel Edition, 1959.

Tertz, Abram [Andrei Siniavskii]. *On Socialist Realism*. Introduction by Czeslaw Milosz, translated by George Dennis. New York: Pantheon, 1960.

Tigranov, G. *Armianskii Muzykal'nyi Teatr. Ocherki i Materialy*. Tom II. Erevan: Aipetrat, 1960.

Timasheff, Nicholas. *The Great Retreat. The Growth and Decline of Communism in Russia*. New York: Dutton, 1946.

Tolstoy, Leo. *What is Art and Essays on Art*. Translated by Aylmer Maude. London: Oxford University Press, 1959.

Tri Siuzhetnykh Tantsa. Repertuar Khudozhestvennoi Samodeiatel'nosti No. 22. Moscow: Izdatel'stvo Iskusstvo, 1962.

Triska, Jan F., ed. *Soviet Communism: Programs and Rules. Official Texts of 1919, 1952, (1956), 1961*. San Francisco: Chandler, 1962.

Trotsky, Leon. *Literature and Revolution.* New York: Russell and Russell, 1957.

Tsulukidze, A. *Gruzinskaia Muzykal'naia Kul'tura. Sbornik Statei.* Moscow: Gosudarstvennoe Muzykal'noe Izdatel'stvo, 1957.

U.S.S.R. Constitution. *Fundamental Law of the Union of Soviet Socialist Republics. As Amended by the Seventh Session of the Fifth Supreme Soviet of the U.S.S.R.* Moscow: Foreign Languages Publishing House, 1962.

U.S. Department of State, Bureau of Intelligence and Research, Division of Biographic Information. *Directory of Soviet Officials. Biographic Directory No. 272. Vol. 1. Personnel in the Communist Party, Government and Mass Organization of the U.S.S.R. and R.S.F.S.R.* August, 1960.

U.S. House of Representatives. 86th Congress, Second Session, December, 1960. Committee on Un-American Activities. *Facts on Communism. Volume II. The Soviet Union, from Lenin to Khrushchev.* Washington, D.C.: U.S. Government Printing Office, 1961.

Ustinov, T.M., Baranchikova, M., and Kh. Mikkel'. *Baletmeister i Kollektiv.* Moscow: Iskusstvo, 1963.

Vaganova, Agrippina Iakovlevna. *Stat'i, Vospominaniia, Materialy.* Leningrad: Iskusstvo, 1958.

Vaillat, Leandre. *Ballets de l'Opéra de Paris.* Paris: Compagnie Française des Arts Graphiques, 1943.

Val'berkh, Ivan. *Iz Arkhiva Baletmeistera. Dnevnik, Perepiska, Stsenarii,* edited by Iurii Slonimskii. Moscow: Iskusstvo, 1948.

Vazem, E.O. *Zapiski Baleriny.* Moscow: Iskusstvo, 1937.

Vecheslova, Tat'iana. *Ia-Balerina.* Moscow: Iskusstvo, 1964.

Vladimirov, N. *Cultural Facilities in the U.S.S.R.* Moscow: Progress Publishers, n.d.

Volkov, Nikolai E. *Dvor Russkikh Imperatorov v Ego Proshlom i Nastoiashchem.* St. Petersburg: R. Golike, 1900.

Volynskii, A.L. [Flekser']. *Kniga Likovanii. Azbuka Klassicheskogo Tantsa.* Leningrad: Izdanie Khoreograficheskogo Tekhnikuma, 1925.

Voprosy Kul'tury pri Diktature Proletariate. Sbornik. Moscow: Gosudarstvennoe Izdatel'stvo, 1925.

Vserossiiskii Tsentral'nyi Ispolnitel'nyi Komitet, III Sessiia XX Sozyva. Stenograficheskii Otchet. Moscow: Izdanie VTsIK, 1926.

Vserossiiskii Tsentral'nyi Sovet Professional'nykh Soiuzov. Moscow: 1920.

Selected Bibliography

Vsesoiunznaia Kommunisticheskaia Partiia (Bol'shevikov). *VKP(b) v Reso-liutsiiakh i Resheniiakh. S'ezdov, Konferentsii i Plenumov TsK.* 2 vols. Moscow: OGIZ, Gospolitizdat, 1941.

Vsevolodskii-Gerngross, V. *Istoriia Teatral'nago Obrazovanniia v Rossii.* Tom I. St. Petersburg: Izdanie Direktsii Imperatorskikh Teatrov, 1913.

———. *Teatr pri Aleksee Mikhailoviche.* Moscow: Ob'edinenie, 1914.

———. *Teatr v Rossii pri Imperatritse Anne Ionnovne i imperatore Ioanne Antonoviche.* St. Petersburg: Tipografiia Imperatorskikh SPB Teatrov, 1914.

Weaver, John. *An Essay towards an History of Dancing.* London: J. Tonson, 1712.

Werth, Alexander. *Musical Uproar in Moscow.* London: Turnstile Press, 1949.

Yarmolinsky, Avram. *Literature under Communism: the Literary Policy of the Communist Party of the Soviet Union from the End of World War II to the Death of Stalin.* Bloomington, Ind.: Indiana University Press, 1960.

Zabelin, I. *Domashnyi Byt' Russkikh Tsarits v* xvi *i* xvii *st. Vol.* ii. Moscow: Tipografiia Gracheva, 1872.

Zakharov, R. *Besedy o Tantse.* Moscow: Izdatel'stvo VTs SPS Profizdat, 1963.

———. *Iskusstvo Baletmeistera.* Moscow: Iskusstvo, 1954.

Zavalishin, Vyacheslav. *Early Soviet Writers.* New York: Praeger, 1958.

Zeglovsky, Valentin. *Ballet Crusade,* translated from Russian. Melbourne: Reed and Harris, 1944.

Zetkin, Klara. *Reminiscences of Lenin.* London: Modern Books, 1929.

Zhdanov, Andrei. *Essays on Literature, Philosophy, and Music.* New York: International Publishers, 1950.

———, Maxim Gorky, N. Bukharin, K. Radek, and A. Stetsky. *Problems of Soviet Literature. Reports and Speeches of the First Soviet Writers Congress.* New York: International Publishers, n.d.

Zhurnaly Komissii po Razsmotreniiu Finansovykh Smet Ustanovlenii Ministerstvo Imperatorskago Dvora na 1914 God. St. Petersburg: Tipografiia Glavnago Upravleniia Udelov, 1914.

ARTICLES

Abbé, James E. "Russia's Revolution of the Dance," *Dancing Times,* December, 1930, 281–284.

Alexeyev, M. "Academic Degree for Ballerina," *Soviet Woman,* June, 1956, 43.

"The All-Russian Theatrical Society," *Soviet Literature,* No. 4 (1952), 182–183.

Al'tman, Iogann. "Vozrozhdennoi Narod, Vozrozhdennoe Iskusstvo," *Teatr,* No. 11 (1940), 21–35.

Andreeva, E. "Gazeta Bol-shogo Teatr," *Sovetskaia Muzyka,* No. 2 (1953), 104–105.

"Angliiskie Vpechateleniia i Vstrechi," *Teatr,* No 4 (1955), 158–159.

Arsen'ev, I.A. "Slovo Zhivoe o Nezhivykh," *Istoricheskii Viestnik,* xxvii (1887), 69–81.

Asaf'ev, B. "Za Novuiu Muzykal'nuiu Estetiku, za Sotsialisticheskii Realism, Na S"ezd Sovetskikh Kompozitorov," *Sovetskaia Muzyka,* No. 2 (1948), 12–22.

Ashrafi, M. "Strana Tsvetushchei Muzykal'noi Kul'tury," *Sovetskaia Muzyka,* No. 10–11 (1938), 71–74.

Babochkina, Nina. "Bolshoi in the U.S.," *USSR,* September, 1962, 50–51.

Barnes, Clive. "The Ballet of the Kirov Opera," *Dance and Dancers,* February, 1965, 26–31.

Battey, Jean. "A Special, Privileged World. How the Kirov Ballet School, 'The Hothouse of Russian Ballet,' Nurtures Its Future Dance Artists," *Dance Magazine,* xxxv (October, 1961), 34–37.

Behrman, Renate. "The Latvian Ballet," *Dancing Times,* October, 1937, 11–13.

Belorusets, I. "Svet i Teni," *Sovetskaia Muzyka,* No. 6 (1963), 65–67.

Belosel'skii, A. "Molodye Kadry Baleta," *Teatr,* No. 12 (1952), 87–88.

Benton, William. "Should We Continue the Cultural Exchanges with the USSR?" *Saturday Review,* xlv (October 27, 1962), 17–20, 39–40.

Berezantseva, Tatyana, "Leili and Mejnun," *Soviet Woman,* No. 7 (1960), 22.

Berko, M. "Balet 'Sona'," *Sovetskaia Muzyka,* No. 6 (1958), 147–50.

Bloch, Gilbert. "Problèmes Actuels du Ballet Sovietique," *La Danse,* August, 1958, 15–17.

Boelza, Igor. "Music in Wartime. Plenum of the Union of Soviet Composers in Moscow," *International Literature,* No. 6 (1944), 72–73.

Bogdanov-Berezovskii, V. "Geroicheskii Balet," *Sovetskaia Muzyka,* No. 3 (1958), 77–82.

Bondarenko, P. P., and M. Kh. Rabinovich, "Nauchno Soveshchanie po

Voprosam Ideologicheskoi Bor'by s Sovremennym Freidizmom," *Voprosy Filosofii,* No. 2 (1959), 164–170.

Boromé, Joseph A. "The Bolshoi Theater and Opera," *Russian Review,* XXIV (January, 1965), 52–74.

Brodersen, Iurii. "Legalisatsiia Prisposoblenchestva," *Rabochii i Teatr,* No. 60–61 (1930), 2–3.

———. "Otvet Tov. L. Iakobsonu. Tribuna Tvorcheskoi Diskussii. Na Povestke—Baletnyi Teatr," *Rabochii i Teatr.* No. 26 (1931), 8–9.

———. "Sovetskaia Tantsoval'naia Komediia," *Sovetskii Teatr,* No. 8 (1935), 10–11.

———. "Valeska Gert Tantsuet," *Rabochii i Teatr,* No. 11 (1929), 7.

———. "V Ak. Baleta Neblagopoluchno," *Rabochii i Teatr,"* No. 20 (1928), 6.

Bromfield, Louis. "Fall River Legend," *Theatre Arts,* CCL (June–July, 1948), 30.

Buchler, Walter. "Ballet in Soviet Russia," *Dancing Times,* June, 1937, 284–287.

Byrdin, F.A. "Vospominaniia Artista ob Imperatore Nikolae Pavloviche," *Istoricheskii Viestnik,* XXIII (1886), 144–153.

Cazden, Norman. "What's Happening in Soviet Music?" *Masses and Mainstream,* April, 1948, 11–25.

Chabukiani, V. "Dramaticheskii Obraz v Baleta," *Rabochii i Teatr,* No. 11 (1937), 25.

"Chairman Mao's Line for Literature and Art Is the Line for Literature and Art Throughout the World," *Peking Review* (January 1, 1967), 25.

Cheliapov, N. "K Itogam Diskussii na Mauzykal'nom Fronte," *Sovetskaia Muzyka,* No. 3 (1936), 3–9.

Chen-I-Wan, "American Dancers in Moscow," *New Theatre,* August, 1935, 21.

Chernova, N. "Miniatury Goleizovskogo," *Teatr,* No. 4 (1962), 140–141.

Chesnokov, E. "Podgotovka Baletnykh Kadrov," *Rabochii i Teatr,* No. 26 (1934), 2.

Chirkov, A. "V Partiinoi Organizatsii Teatra," *Iskusstvo i Zhizn',* July, 1938, 11.

Christout, Marie-Françoise, "Presstime," *Dance Magazine,* XXXVII, March, 1963, 82.

Chudnovsky, Mikhail. "New York City Ballet As I See It," *Dance Magazine,* XXVII, January, 1963, 36–39.

Chujoy, Anatole. "Russian Balletomania," *Dance Index,* VII, January-February, 1948.

Chulkov, G. "Dramaticheskii Balet," *Sovremennyi Teatr,* October 23, 1928, 680.

Clarke, Mary. "Lieutenant Kije," *Dancing Times,* September, 1963, 684.

Cohen, Selma Jeanne. "Avant-Garde Choreography," *Dance Magazine,* XXXVI (June, 1962), 22–24, 57.

Coleman, Emily. "Russia's Best," *Newsweek,* LIII, Part II, April 13, 1959, 111–117.

Coleman, Francis. "Canadian Dateline," *Dance Magazine,* XXVIII, June, 1954, 78.

Cripps, Sir Stafford. "The Cultural Importance of Ballet," *Dancing Times,* August, 1942, 537–538.

Dal Negro, L. "Return from Moscow," *New Theatre,* December, 1934, 27.

"Dance," *Time Magazine,* LXXXV, April 16, 1965, 48–52.

Danilov, S.S. "Revoliutsiia, 1905–7 Godov i Russkii Teatr," *Teatr,* No. 7 (1955), 116–126.

Dashicheva, Alexandra. "Lieutenant Kizhe," *Soviet Literature,* No. 9 (1963), 172–175.

———. "Vtoroe Rozdenie 'Krasnyi Mak' v Bol'shom Teatre," *Teatr,* No. 2 (1950), 25–34.

"Dekada Uzbezskogo Iskusstvo," *Sovetskaia Muzyka,* No. 2 (1959), 203.

Deriabin, Peter, and Frank Gibney. "Kremlin Intrigue and Debauchery," *Life,* XLVI (March 30, 1959), 80–92.

Dhimah. "I Dance for Moscow," *New Theatre,* October, 1935, 24–25.

"Diskussii 'Iskusstvo Baletmeistera,'" *Sovetskaia Muzyka,* No. 6 (1955), 156.

"Dlia Delegatov Kongressa," *Teatr,* No. 10 (1962), 170.

Dolgopolov, M. "The Oldest Ballet School," *Dancing Times,* April, 1944, 308–309.

"Dom Rabotnikov Iskusstv v Novom Sezone," *Teatr,* No. 9 (1952), 151.

Douglas, William O. "Soviet Colonialism—Product of Terror," *Look,* XIX, December 13, 1955, 35–43.

Driesen, N. de. "Les Origines du Ballet en Russie. Le Ballet des Serfs," *Archives Internationales de la Danse,* April 15, 1935, 38–40.

Dubrovin, N. "Russkaia Zhizn v Nachale XIX Veka," *Russkaia Starina,* XCVII, January, 1899, 3–38.

Eaving, V. [Iving]. "The Ballet in the U.S.S.R.," *Soviet Travel,* No. 5 (1932), 33–35.

Selected Bibliography

Edwards, Sushil. "Ulanova Talks. Interview to Sushil Edwards," *Dance and Dancers,* December, 1957, 18.

Efros, Adam. "Aisedora Denkan," *Teatral'noe Obozrenie,* No. 1 (1921), 8–9.

Eisenberg, Emmanuel. "Diagnosis of the Dance," *New Theatre,* July-August, 1934, 24–25.

Ellis, David. "Notes on the Bolshoi School and Its Influence in the East," *Dancing Times,* February, 1958, 220.

Elyash, Nikolai. "American Ballet," *USSR,* June, 1964, 56–57.

"Entuziast Kazakhskoi Khoreografii," *Teatr,* No. 9 (1959), 159

"Epikur," *Stolitsa i Usad'ba,* April 15, 1917, 23.

"Esche o Baleta 'Alye Parusa'," *Sovetskaia Muzyka,* No. 11 (1950), 110.

Fadeev, A. "O Literaturnoi Kritike," *Bol'shevik,* No. 13 (1947), 20–35.

Farkhadova, R. "Pervaia Azerbaidzhanskaia Balerina," *Sovetskaia Muzyka,* No. 1 (1964), 59–63.

Fevral'skii, A. "¡Pasaremos!" *Sovetskaia Muzyka,* No. 1 (1939), 97–98.

Fizer, John. "The Problem of the Unconscious in the Creative Process as Treated by Soviet Aesthetics," *The Journal of Aesthetics and Art Criticism,* XXI, Summer, 1963, 399–406.

"For Leninist Adherence to the Principle in Questions of Literature and the Arts," *Kommunist,* No. 10 (1957), 13–22. *Current Digest of the Soviet Press,* IX:33, September 25, 1957, 3–6.

Franks, A.H. "Leningrad State Kirov Ballet," *Dancing Times,* July, 1961, 599–601.

———. "The New Russian Film," *Dancing Times,* August, 1954, 670.

Freidkina, L. "Lenin i Teatr," *Teatr,* No. 8 (1937), 25–42.

Gabovich, M. "Sovremannaia Tema v Baleta," *Teatral'nyi Al'manakh. Sbornik Statei i Materialov, Vserossiiskoe Teatral'noe Obshchestvo,* 1947.

Gabovitch, M. "Brillante Maîtrise du Ballet Français," *Etudes Soviétiques,* July, 1958, 15–21.

Gaudrimas, Iu. "Novyi Litovskii Balet," *Sovetskaia Muzyka,* No. 12 (1957), 76–79.

"Gazetnoe obozrenie," *Teatr,* No. 2 (1958), 150–153.

"Gazetnoe obozrenie," *Teatr,* No. 3 (1958), pp. 125–128.

"Geroi Respublikanskoi Ispanii," *Sovetskaia Muzyka,* No. 5 (1939), pp. 100–104.

Ginsburg, S.L. "Muzykal'nyi Teatr Gruzinskogo Naroda," *Iskusstvo i Zhihn',* No. 9 (1938), 21.

335

Goian, Georg. "Natsional'nyi Balet," *Teatral'nyi Al'manakh,* 1946, 63–85.

Golubov-Potapov, V. "Sovremennost' i Fantasiia," *Teatr,* No. 10 (1940), 128–143.

Gordon, Celia. "Palaces for Children and Workers," *Soviet Woman,* No. 5 (1961), 24–25.

Gosberg, A. " 'Serdtse gor',—Balet A. Balachivadze,' " *Sovetskaia Muzyka,* No. 8 (1938), 58–65.

Graham, Rockwell. "Harbingers of the New Russia," *American Dancer,* February, 1934, 6, 19.

Grant, Frances R. "The Russian Ballet," *Art and Archaeology,* XIII, February, 1922, 69–77.

Gray, Camilla. "Soviet Ballet, An English Dancer's Impression," *Dancing Times,* December, 1955, 152–153, 165.

Grigorovich, Iurii. "Fedor Lopukhov," *Teatr,* No. 7 (1965), pp. 81–85.

Grinberg, M. " 'Komedianty' v Bol'shom Teatre," *Proletarskii Muzykant,* No. 5 (1931), 38–39.

Grosheva, E. "Novyi Pushkinskii Balet 'Mednyi Vsadnik' R. Gliera," *Sovetskaia Muzyka,* No. 9 (1949), 26–34.

Gubaidullin, N. "Novyi Bashkirskii Balet," *Sovetskaia Muzyka,* No. 9 (1963), 60–61.

"Hail the Victories of Mao Tse-tung's Line on Literature and Art," *Peking Review,* June 30, 1967, 34.

Harutovsky, B. "The Classical Tradition and Innovation in Music," *Soviet Literature,* No. 6 (1948), 126–132.

Haskell, Arnold. "Bolshoi Theatre Ballet. Background to the Season," *Ballet Annual,* XII (1958), 14–24.

———. "L'Affaire Nureyev," *Dancing Times,* March, 1963, 336.

Hering, Doris. "First Impressions of the Bolshoi Ballet," *Dance Magazine,* XXXIII, June, 1959, 38, 40, 78–81.

Horie, Muraichi, "Japanese-Soviet Friendship," *Culture and Life,* No. 3 (1957), 43–45.

Hughes, Langston, "Tamara Khanum," *Theatre Arts Monthly,* XVIII, November, 1934, 832–834.

I., A. "Khoreograficheskie Kompozitsii Kas'iana Goleizovskogo," *Sovetskaia Muzyka,* No. 8 (1960), 204–205.

Iakobson, L. "Na Povestke—Baletnyi Teatr," *Rabochii i Teatr,* No. 26 (1931), 6–7.

Iankovskii, M. "Bolt," *Rabochii i Teatr,* No. 11 (1931), 11.

Selected Bibliography

"Ideologicheskaia Platforma Vserossiiskii Assotsiatsii Proletarskikh Muzyk-antov," *Muzykal'naia Nov'*, No. 12 (1924), 24–25.

Ignat'eva, M. "Po-delevomu o Prazdnichnom. Spektakli Litovskogo Teatra Opery i Baleta na Vsesoiuznom Festivale," *Teatr*, No. 3 (1958), 71–76.

Il'ichev, L. F. "Creative Work for the People in the Name of Communism," *Soviet Literature*, No. 2 (1963), Supplement.

"In Brief," *Soviet Literature*, No. 4 (1963), 177.

"Iskusstvo, na Vysotu Sotsialisticheskoi Epokhi. K VII S"ezdy leninskoi Partii," *Rabochii i Teatr*, No. 3 (1934), 1.

Iutkevich, S. "Golub' Mira Priletaet v Pekin," *Teatr*. No. 4 (1951), 99–106.

Ivanova, Svetlana. "Iag Mort," *Teatr*, No. 7 (1962), 129–131.

Iving, V. "O Russkoi Shkole Klasicheskogo Tantsa," *Teatral'nyi Al'-manakh*, 1947, 256–283.

———. "Spektakl' V. Maiia," *Sovremennyi Teatr*, June 3, 1928, 447.

Johnson, Priscilla. "The Regime and the Intellectuals. A Window on Party Politics. Winter, 1962–Summer, 1963." Special Supplement. *Problems of Communism*, XII.

Juviler, Nina. "Art and Artists in the U.S.S.R.," *Problems of Communism*, XI, No. 3, June, 1962, 41–55.

Kann, E. "Muzykal'nyi Teatr im. Stanislavskogo i Nemirovicha Danchenko v Dni Voiny," *Teatral'nyi Almanakh*, 1944, 122–133.

Karelova, I. "Novyi Uzbekskii Balet," *Sovetskaia Muzyka*, No. 10 (1952), 58–63.

Katonova, S. "Romantika Liubvi i Podviga, 'Bereg Nadezhdy'," *Sovetskaia Muzyka*, No. 9 (1959), 16–22.

Kh., G. "Kompozitory Revoliutsionnoi Ispanii," *Sovetskaia Muzyka*, No. 7 (1938), p. 105–106.

Khatchaturian, Aram. "O Tvorcheskoi Smelosti i Vdoknovenii," *Sovetskaia Muzyka*, No. 11 (1953), 7–13.

Khrennikov, Tikhon. "Serdechnyi Privet ot Stravinskogo," *Ogonek*, August 6, 1961, 12.

"Kronika Teatral'noi Zhizni," *Teatr*, No. 11 (1950), 115–116.

Khrushchev, N.S. "Za Tesnuiu Sviaz' Literatury i Iskusstva s Zhizniu Naroda," *Kommunist*, No. 2 (1957), 11–29.

"Khrushchev on Modern Art . . ." *Encounter*, xx, April, 1963, 102–103.

"Kievskaia Gazeta o Balete Shostakovicha," *Proletarskii Muzykant*, No. 1 (1931), 46.

Kirillova, Irina. "Ballet at the Moscow Festival," *Dancing Times,* December, 1957, 116–119.

Klas, Anna. "Balet E. Kappa 'Kalevipoeg,' " *Sovetskaia Muzyka,* No. 6 (1949), 44–47.

Kondakov, N.P. "O Freskakh Liesnits Kievo Sofiiskago Sobora," *Zapiski Imperatorskago Russkago Arkheologicheskago Obshchestva.* III. Novaia Seriia (St. Petersburg, 1888), 287–306.

Kondratov, Yuri. "The 'Secret' of the Soviet Ballet," *Culture and Life,* No. 2 (1961), 41–42.

Koner, Paulie. "Russia Dances," *New Theatre,* October, 1936, 22–23.

Krasovskaia, Vera. "Razlozhenie Baletnogo Iskusstva na Zapade," *Teatr,* No. 10 (1950), 100–105.

Kriger, Viktorina. "Klassika—Osnova Baletnoi Ucheby," *Sovremennyi Teatr,* September 2, 1928, 556.

Kunitz, Joshua. "The Shostakovich Affair," *New Masses,* June 9, 1936, 115–118.

L.L. "Balet K. Korchmareva, 'Krepostnaia Balerina,' " *Muzyka i Revoliutsiia,* No. 12 (1927), 10–12.

"Laureaty Konkursov Venskogo Festivalia Molodezhi," *Sovetskaia Muzyka,* No. 9 (1959), 201.

Lawson, Joan. "Another New Soviet Ballet 'Laurencia,' " *Dancing Times,* October, 1940, 11–13.

———. "The Heart of the Hills. A New Departure in Soviet Ballet," *Dancing Times,* July, 1939, 389–392.

———. [J.L.]. "More Russian Visitors," *Dancing Times,* December, 1954, 149.

———. "Pages from the History of Russian Ballet." *Dancing Times,* December, 1940, 116–118; January, 1941, 201–203; February, 1941, 261–263; March, 1941, 334–336; April, 1941, 385–387; May, 1941, 541–543.

———. "A Short History of Soviet Ballet, 1917–1943," *Dance Index,* II (June-July, 1943).

———. "The Soviet Dancers," *Dancing Times,* January, 1955, 219.

Leontovskaia, T., and I. Il'in. "Pod Nebom Italii," *Sovetskaia Muzyka,* No. 12 (1952), 73–76.

Lepeshinskaya, Olga, "Japanese Impressions," *Soviet Woman,* No. 3 (1958), 39–41.

Levine, Irving R., "Khrushchev's Prettiest Propaganda," *This Week Magazine,* April 19, 1959. Supplement to *New York Herald Tribune.*

Selected Bibliography

Livshits, A. "Pervyi Belorusskii Balet 'Solovei,' " *Sovetskaia Muzyka,* No. 11 (1939), 75–80.

Lobacheva, E. "Latyshskii Balet. 'Rigonda,' " *Sovetskaia Muzyka,* No. 11 (1959), 111–114.

Lopukhov, Fedor. "Deklaratsiia F. Lopukhova," *Zhizn' Iskusstva,* December 8, 1929, 6.

Lukacs, George. "Problems of Marxist Culture," *Masses and Mainstream,* June, 1948, 6–18.

Lunacharskii, A. "Khronika. Iubilei E.V. Gel'tser," *Kul'tura Teatra,* No. 1 (April 5, 1921), 56–58.

———. "Novye Puti Opery i Baleta," *Proletarskii Muzykant,* No. 5 (1930), 4–10.

———. "O Teatral'noi Politike," *Zhizn' Iskusstva,* February 22, 1927, 6.

———. "O Zadachakh Teatra v Sviazi s Reformoi Narkomprosa," *Kul'tura Teatra,* No. 4, April 5, 1921, 1–5.

Lutskaya, E. "American Ballet," *Culture and Life,* No. 13 (1960), 38–39.

———. [Lutskaia, E.] "Biubiusara Beishenalieva," *Teatr,* No. 2 (1959), 72–76.

L'vov, Nikolai. "Tanets i Sovremennost'," *Zhizn' Iskusstva,* February 8, 1927, 6.

Lvov-Anokhin, Boris. "Balanchine's Ballet in Moscow," *Soviet Literature,* No. 3 (1963), 163–167.

McLanathan, Richard B. "Art in the Soviet Union," *Atlantic Monthly,* ccv, No. 6, June, 1960, 74–76.

Maizel', B. "O Podvige Cheloveka," *Sovetskaia Muzyka,* No. 2 (1963), 148–149.

Makanowitzky, Barbara. "Music to Serve the State," *Russian Review,* xxiv, July, 1965, 266–277.

Maksimova, E. "Buriatskie Spektakli v Moskve," *Sovetskaia Muzyka,* No. 2 (1960), 110–114.

Malkov, N. "Novaia Muzyka i Kul'tura Ispolnitel'stva v Perekhodnuiu Epokhu," *Novaia Muzyka,* No. 1 (1927), 33–49.

Manchester, P.W. "The Soviet Ballet," *Center,* I. No. 6, 19–21.

Martin, John. "Isadora Duncan and Basic Dance," *Dance Index,* I, January, 1942, 4–12.

———. "John Martin Visits Russia," *Dance Magazine,* xxx, September, 1956, 14–21, 58–64.

339

Martinov, I. "Avstriiskie Vpechatleniia," *Sovetskaia Muzyka,* No. 1 (1951), 77–83.

Mei, Emil. "Baletnaia Molodezh' na Rasputi'i," *Sovremennyi Teatr,* September 2, 1928, 557.

Michener, Wendy. "Jeanne d'Arc in Moscow," *Dance and Dancers,* September, 1958, 22–23.

Mihajlov, Mihajlo. "Moscow Summer, 1964," *New Leader,* XLVIII, March 29, 1965, 4–38.

Mikhailov, G. "Ritmika v Ispanskoi Narodnoi Muzyke," *Sovetskaia Muzyka,* No. 7 (1938), 97–102.

Militsyna, Nina. "Soviet Ballet Today," *Dancing Times,* May, 1949, 435–437.

Mlodik, A. "Tamara Khanum," *Teatr,* No. 10 (1939), 133–136.

Mogilevskaya, G., and B. Pokrovsky. "The House We Live In," *Soviet Woman,* No. 7 (1960) 14–17.

Moiseyev, Igor. "Searching, Planning, Dreaming," *Soviet Literature,* No. 7 (1962), 150–156.

"Molodye Sily Baleta—Vecher 'Molodogo Baleta,' " *Zhizn' Iskusstva,* May 27, 1928, 6–7.

Montagu-Nathan, M. "The Strange Case of Professor Assafiev," *Music and Letters,* XXXVIII, October, 1957, 335–340.

"Moskva," *Teatr,* No. 8 (1952), 157–158.

Moskva, Vasilii. "Zametki o Balete: Moskovskie Prem'ery 'Karman'ola,' " *Sovetskii Teatr,* July-August, 1932, 36–37.

Munro, Thomas. "Marxist Theory of Art History. Socio-Economic Determinism and the Dialectical Process," *Journal of Esthetics and Art Criticism,* XVIII, No. 4, July, 1960, 430–445.

"Muzyka v Antireligioznoi Propagande," *Proletarskii Muzykant,* No. 2 (1930), 37.

Myers, Margaret. "The Dance in Moscow," *New Theatre,* October, 1934, 25.

N., "Krasnyi Mak v Mosk. Narvskom Dome Kul'tury," *Zhizn' Iskusstva,* January 13, 1929, 12.

"Na Pomoshch' Ispanskomu Narodu!" *Sovetskaia Muzyka,* No. 11 (1936), 80.

Nabokov, Ivan, and Elizabeth Carmichael. "Balanchine," *Horizon,* III, No. 3, January, 1961, 44–56.

Nabokov, Nicolas. "The Music Purge," *Politics,* V, No. 2 (1948), 102–106.

Selected Bibliography

Nadezhdina, N. "The Beryozka Dancers Abroad," *Soviet Literature*, No. 1 (1954), 148–152.

Narodny, Ivan. "Red Russia Reforms Its Ballet," *Dance Magazine*, XI (March, 1929), 33, 55.

Nasilov, N. "Balet," *Zhizn' Iskusstva*, November 9, 1926, 8.

——. "Zakrytie Baletnogo Sezona," *Zhizn' Iskusstva*, June 22, 1926, 15.

"Needleworker and Ballerina," *Soviet Woman*, No. 12 (1963), 31.

"Novyi Kurs Gosbaletnogo Uchilishcha," *Zhizn' Iskusstva*, September 8, 1929, 13.

"Novyi Moskovskii Sezon," *Teatr*, No. 11 (1962), 148.

"O Teatral'noi Politike," *Zhizn' Iskusstva*, February 22, 1927, 6.

"Ob Obrazovanii Vsesoiuznovo Komiteta po Delam Iskusstv pri SNK Soiuza SSSR," *Rabochii i Teatr*, No. 2 (1937), 2–3.

"Ob Opera 'Velikaia Druzhba' V. Muradeli," Postanovlenie TsK VKP(b). *Bol'shevik*, No. 3 (1948), 10–14.

"Oblastnye Teatry Obmenivaiutsia Opytom," *Teatr*, No. 9 (1952), 148.

Olesha, Yuri. "About Formalism," *International Literature*, No. 6 (1936), 86–92.

Ol'khovich, E., and V. Zemlemerov, "V Narodnykh Teatrakh Leningrada," *Sovetskaia Muzyka*, No. 11 (1963), 103–104.

"Ot Kompozitorov i Muzykovedov Goroda Moskvy Velikomu Vozhdiu Sovetskogo Naroda Tovarishchu Stalinu," *Sovetskaia Muzyka*, No. 1 (1948), 27–28.

Palatsky, Eugene. "In Russia with American Ballet Theatre," *Dance Magazine*, XXXIV (December, 1960), 28–31, 66.

"Paulina Koner," *Rabochii i Teatr*, No. 3 (1935), 20–21.

Peiko, N. " 'Marmar.' Novyi Armianskii Balet," *Sovetskaia Muzyka*, No. 6 (1957), 69–73.

"Perspektivy GOTOB," *Zhizn' Iskusstva*, September 29, 1929, 13.

"Pervyi S"ezd Rabis," *Teatr*, No. 5 (1954), 191.

"Pesnia Bratstva," *Teatral'naia Zhizn'*, No. 4 (1965), 5.

Peters, Kurt. "Russian Dancers in Berlin," *Dancing Times*, July, 1954, 607.

Petrushanskaya, R. "In Memory of Hiroshima," *Soviet Woman*, No. 8 (1963), 34–35.

Pierre, André. "Les Ballets Soviétiques et l'Amour de la Danse en URSS," *Formes et Coulers*, No. 4 (1948), unpaged.

"Pis'mo Pablo Kazal'sa," *Sovetskaia Muzyka*, No. 1 (1939), 106.

"Pis'mo Iaponski Baleriny," *Teatr*, No. 4 (1956), 187.

Plavskin, Zakhar. "Lope de Vega in the U.S.S.R.," *Soviet Literature*, No. 11 (1962), 127–132.

Pleasant, Richard. "Message to Congress," *Dance Magazine*, XXXIII, August, 1959, 44–49, 68–69.

"Plenum TsK Soiuza Rabotnikov Iskusstv," *Teatr*, No. 2 (1952), 146.

Plisetskaia, Maiia. "Neugasimoe Flamia. Zametki Uchastniki III Vsemirnogo Festivalia Molodezhi," *Teatr*, No. 11 (1951), 98–104.

"Pod Znakom Kritiki i Samokritiki," *Teatr*, No. 1 (1953), pp. 142–144.

"Podgotovka Artistov Baletnogo Teatra," *Teatr*, No. 12 (1952), 150.

Poggioli, Renato. "About Soviet Culture: or the Twilight of Poetry and Art," *Yale Review*, XLIX, December, 1959, 198–214.

"Politicheskoe Prosveshchenie Akterov," *Teatr*, No. 7 (1952), p. 149.

"Programma Kul'turno Prosvetitel'noi Raboty Partii," *Vlast' Sovetov*, No. 8–9 (1919), 18.

Prokofiev, S. "Tvorcheskie Plany," *Sovetskaia Muzyka*, No. 1 (1953), 19.

"Protiv Formalizma i Fal'shi. Tvorcheskaia Diskussia v Leningradskom Sovetskikh Kompozitorov," *Sovetskaia Muzyka*, No. 5 (1936), 28–73.

"Protiv Formalizma i Fal'shi. Tvorcheskaia Diskussiia v Moskovskom Soiuze Sovetskikh Kompozitorov," *Sovetskaia Muzyka*, No. 3 (1936), 16–60.

R. "Arest Russkogo Baleta," *Zhizn' Iskusstva*, July 27, 1926, 20.

Rabinovich, D. "Moldavskie Opery i Balety," *Sovetskaia Muzyka*, No. 8 (1960), 110–118.

"Rabis i Sotsperestroika Iskusstva. Boevoi Prikaz po Armii Iskusstv," *Zhizn' Iskusstva*, December 8, 1929, 15.

"Rabis po Sluzhbu Piatiletke!" *Rabochii i Teatr*, No. 50 (1930), 1.

Raffé, W.G. "Ballet Training in the U.S.S.R.," *Dancing Times*, February, 1936, 641–647.

———. "Modern Ballet in the Soviet Union," *Dancing Times*, August, 1937, 543–545.

Ravich, N.A. "Bol'shoi Teatr na Perelome," *Rabochii i Teatr*, No. 22 (1930), 12–13.

"The Red Poppy," *Soviet Woman*, No. 3 (1950), 50–52.

Reiser, Max. "Russian Aesthetics Today and Their Historical Background," *The Journal of Aesthetics and Art Criticism*, XXII, Fall, 1963, 47–53.

Reiss, Françoise. "Chronique: l'Esthetique du Ballet Sovietique," *Revue d'Esthetique*, XI (1958), 190–199.

Rittikh, M. "Balet o Molodosti i Druzhbe," *Sovetskaia Muzyka*, No. 5 (1960), 107–109.

———. "Komy Nuzhen Takoi Spektakl'?" *Sovetskaia Muzyka,* No. 5 (1950), 33–34.

———. "Poslednyi Bal," *Sovetskaia Muzyka*, No. 10 (1962), 78–86.

"Romeo i Dzhul'etta v Italii," *Sovetskaia Muzyka*, No. 10 (1955), 151–152.

Roslavleva, N. "Amerikanskii Teatr Baleta," *Muzykal'naia Zhizn'*, October, 1960. Dance Collection, New York Public Library.

Roslavleva, Natalia. "Heroic Geologists," *Dancing Times*, July, 1964, 528–529.

———. "The Leningrad State Kirov Ballet," *Dancing Times*, June, 1961, 543–547.

———. "A Lively Controversy on New York City Ballet Soviet Season," *Dancing Times*, January, 1963, 229.

———. "The Most American. Russian Opinions about the Joffrey Ballet," *Dancing Times*, March, 1964, 311.

———. "Stanislavski and the Dance," *Dance Perspectives*, XXIII (September, 1965).

Rostislavov, A. "Khudozhestvennaia Letopis'," *Apollon*, No. 2–3 (1917), 65–69.

Ruge, Gerd. "Report from Moscow, Composer's Dilemma," *Survey*, No. 37, July-September, 1961, 43–52.

Rumnev, Aleksandr. "Realizm v Tantse," *Zhizn' Iskusstva*, September 29, 1929, 6.

Russell, Sam. "Backstage with a Bol'shoi Ballerina," *Soviet Woman*, July, 1958, 13, 45.

"The Russian Ballet Is French and the French Ballet Is Russian," *Réalites*, March, 1957, 43–49.

Sadko. "Krasnyi Mak v Bol'shom Teatra," *Zhizn' Iskusstva*, June 28, 1927, 4.

Scheuer, L. Frank. "Messerer in Paris," *Dancing Times*, May, 1933, 134–135.

———. "Semenova in 'Giselle.' Our Paris Letter," *Dancing Times*, February, 1936, 637–640.

Schiller, F. "Marx and Engels on Balzac. Unpublished Correspondence of Friedrich Engels," *International Literature*, No. 3 (1933), 113–124.

Sedin, L. "Moral Charlatanry. Book Review of *Ideology and Co-Existence*," New York, 1959, in *New Times*, No. 27 (1960), 28–30.

Sh., G. "Pesnia o Grenade," *Sovetskaia Muzyka*, No. 7 (1938), 103–105.

Shantyr', T. " 'Gornaia Byl'," *Sovetskaia Muzyka*, No. 3 (1960), 100–102.

343

————. Rozhdenie Moldavskogo Baleta. Balet L. Kogana 'Sestry' " *Sovetskaia Muzyka,* No. 6 (1959), 115–118.

"Shchelkunchik," *Rabochii i Teatr,* No. 45 (1929), 7.

Sheiko, I. "They Met in Moscow," *Soviet Woman,* No. 12 (1962), 14–15.

"Shock Waves in Moscow," *Time,* LXXX, October 12, 1962, 57.

Shumskaia, N. "Gruzinskii Teatr na Dekade," *Sovetskaia Muzyka,* No. 6 (1958), 134–141.

"Shuty i Skomorokhi v Drevnostii i Noveishee Vremia," *Istoricheskii Viestnik,* XXXI (1888), 208–220; 453–474; 688–690.

Skeaping, Mary. "Ballet in China. Peking Ballet School," *Dancing Times* (April, 1961), 412–415.

Slonimsky, Nicholas. "Development of Soviet Music." *Research Bulletin on the Soviet Union.* American Institute for Cultural Relations with the Soviet Union, II, April 30, 1937.

————. "Soviet Music and Musician," *Slavonic Review,* XXII, December, 1944, 1–18.

————. "Soviet Music Unchained," *Panorama,* June, 1934, 5.

Slonimsky, Yuri. "Talent and the Ballet," Translated by Martin Kamin. *Atlantic Monthly,* CCV, June, 1960, 101–104.

————. "Torzhestvo Russkogo Baleta," *Iskusstvo i Zhizn',* No. 5 (1938), 11–14.

Slusser, Robert M. "Soviet Music Since the Death of Stalin," *The Annals of the American Academy of Political and Social Science,* CCCIII, January, 1956, 116–125.

Sollertinskii, I. "Baletmeister Fedor Lopukhov," *Zhizn' Iskusstva,* April 26, 1927, 4.

————. "Kakoi zhe Balet Nam v Sushchosti Nuzhen?" *Zhizn' Iskusstva,* October 2, 1929, 5.

————. "Problem Baletnogo Stsenariia," *Zhizn' Isskusstva,* October 21, 1928, 12–13.

————. " 'Svetlyi Ruchei' v Gos. Malom Opernom Teatr," *Rabochii i Teatr,* No. 12 (1935), 14–15.

Sollertinskii, I. "Za Novyi Khoreograficheskii Teatr," *Zhizn' Iskusstva,* June 17, 1928, 5.

Solodovnikov, A. "The Composer and the Theater—a Few Words on Bolshoi Theater Plans," *Sovetskaya Muzyka,* No. 4 (1949); *Current Digest of the Soviet Press,* 1:28, August 9, 1949, 16–19.

"Soviet Dancers in London," *Dancing Times,* December, 1953, 137.

344

"Stone Carvers of the Urals," *Soviet Literature,* No. 8 (1953), 146.

Surits, E. "Iskusstvo Baleta i Ego Burzhuaznye Istolkovateli," *Teatr,* No. 7 (1961), 183–187.

———. "Prava li Frantsuzskaia Kritika," *Teatr,* No. 11 (1956), 75–81.

Sviridova, I. "Obrazy Nashikh Sovremennikov v Balete. Novyi Azerbaidzhanskii Balet 'Giul'shen'," *Sovetskaia Muszyka,* No. 6 (1951), 49–54.

Swift, Mary Grace. "Ballet in Communist China," *Dance Magazine,* November, 1967, 61–65.

T., I. " 'Prekrasnyi Iosif,' i 'Karnaval' v Gatobe," *Zhizn' Iskusstva,* February 3, 1929, 8–9.

"Talanty Kirgizii," *Sovetskii Soiuz,* No. 10 (1958), 8–17.

Tal'nikov, D. "Kompozitor i Dve Baleriny," *Teatr,* No. 5 (1940), 51–62.

———. "Puti Sovetskogo Baleta," *Krasnaia Nov',* No. 5 (1936), 213–225.

"Teatr Narodnogo Tvorchestva," *Teatr i Dramaturgiia,* May, 1936, 249–255.

Tigranov, G. "Balet 'Sevan' G. Egiazariana," *Sovetskaia Muzyka,* No. 7 (1956), 17–22.

Tikhomirnova, Irina. "My Favourite Roles," *Soviet Woman,* No. 4 (1951), 28.

"Timur i Ego Komanda," *Sovetskaia Muzyka,* No. 5 (1957), 112–116.

Tiumeneva, G. "Meshchanin iz Toskany," *Sovetskaia Muzyka,* No. 12 (1936), 15–23.

"Tol'ka Fakty," *Teatr,* No. 4 (1959), 132.

Trotsky, Leon. "The Betrayal of Russian Culture," *Saturday Review of Literature,* xv, February 27, 1937, 3–4, 12.

Tsekhnovitser, Orest. "Novaia Muzyka i Proletariat," *Novaia Muzyka,* 1 (5) (1927–1928), 5–6, 15.

"Tsentral'nyi Dom Rabotnikov Iskusstv," *Teatr,* No. 2 (1956), 171.

Tsepyuk, Nina. "Uzbekistan," *Dance and Dancers,* November, 1953, 13.

Tserbakova, T. "Minskaia Prem'era," *Sovetskaia Muzyka,* No. 4 (1962), 53–56.

Turkel'taub, I. "Na Baletnom Perekrestke," *Zhizn' Iskusstva,* October 6, 1929, 4.

Ulanova, Galina. "Bright Image of Chinese Heroine," *Soviet Woman,* No. 2 (1950), 53.

———. "Shkola Baleriny," *Novyi Mir,* No. 3 (1954), 210–222.

Urzhumsky, Nikolai. "The Woman of the Celestial Mountains," *Soviet Woman,* No. 1 (1956), 24–27.

"Uslovia Konkursa na Libretto Sovetskogo Baleta," *Zhizn' Iskusstva,* January 13, 1929, 2.

"U.S.S.R. Minister of Culture N. Mikhailov on Cultural Relations with the United Arab Republic," *New Times,* No. 17 (1958), 13.

Uznadze, Nelli. "Prima Ballerina," *Soviet Woman,* No. 6 (1959), 22.

"V Baletnom Uchilishche," *Zhizn' Iskusstva,* July 7, 1929, 16.

"V Kaire, Beirute i Damaske," *Teatr,* No. 2 (1956), 178–179.

"V Ministerstve Kul'tury SSSR," *Sovetskaia Muzyka,* No. 3 (1958), 159.

"V Ministerstve Kul'tury SSSR. O Merkah po Dalneishemu Razvitiu Sovetskogo Baletnogo Iskusstva," *Teatr,* No. 2 (1958), 155–156.

"V Muzykal'noi i Teatral'noi Sektsiakh VOKS," *Sovetskaia Muzyka,* No. 10 (1951), 107–108.

"V Neskol'ko Strok," *Sovetskaia Muzyka,* No. 5 (1951), 133.

"V Soiuze Kompozitorov," *Sovetskaia Muzyka,* No. 4 (1956), 203–204. No. 7 (1956), 156; No. 10 (1951), 156.

"V Universitetakh Marksizma-Leninizma," *Teatr,* No. 9 (1952), 145.

Vanslov, V. "Dalekaiia Planeta," *Sovetskaia Muzyka,* No. 11 (1963), 63–66.

"Vdoknovliaiushchii Primer, Zametki o Vsemirnom Festivale Demokraticheskoi Molodezhi 1949 Goda," *Teatr,* No. 11 (1949), 19–29.

"Veliki Dokument Epokh. O Nedostatkakh Partiinoi Raboty i Merakh Likvidatsii Trotskikh i Inykh Dvurushnikov,"*Sovetskaia Muzyka,* No. 4 (1937), 5–10.

Vecheslova, Tatiana. "Vmeste s Chabukiani," *Teatr,* No. 10 (1963), 75–80.

"'Vesna Sviashchennaia' Stravinskogo v Ispolnenii Orkestra GABT i Dirizhera Fritsa Stidri," *Muzyka i Revoliutsiia,* No. 4 (1926), 32.

Viaz'min, N. "Kustari ot Baleta. Chastnye Baletnye Shkoly Dolzhny Byt' Likvidirovany!" *Rabochii i Teatr,* No. 43 (1929), 3.

Vol'berg, M. "Leili and Medzhnun," *Sovetskaia Muzyka,* No. 6 (1949), 40–43.

Volkov, N. "Baletnyi God," *Teatral'naia Dekada,* October 1, 1934, 9.

Voyce, Arthur. "Soviet Art and Architecture: Recent Developments," *Annals of American Academy of Political and Social Sciences,* CCCIII, January, 1956, 104–115.

Vsevolodskii, V. "Pravda o Balete," *Zhizn' Iskusstva,* April 14, 1929, 5.

"Vyvesti Balet na Novuiu Dorogu," *Rabochii i Teatr,* No. 50 (1929), 5.

"When Evening Comes," *Soviet Woman,* No. 2 (1952), 20–21.

Williams, Albert Rhys. "The People Are Dancing," *Soviet Russia Today,* May, 1937, 12–13, 42.

Selected Bibliography

Winckley, Rosemary. "Russian Journey," *Dance and Dancers,* June, 1965, 24–28.
"The World and the Theatre," *Theatre Arts,* CCXLII (July, 1940), 464.
Wylie, Grace. "Dance Convention," *New Theatre,* July-August, 1934, 29.
Yakhontova, M. "Balzac and Modern Times," *Soviet Literature,* No. 5 (1949), 161–168.
"Za 10 Dnei," *Rabochii i Teatr,* No. 1 (1932), 23.
"Zarubezhnyi Konsul'tatsii VTO," *Teatr,* No. 1 (1956), 183.
Zeleransky, N. "A People's Actress," *Soviet Woman,* No. 1 (1947), 42–45.
Zhitomirskii, D. "Spartak," *Sovetskaia Muzyka,* No. 4 (1956), 7–13.
Zoete, Beryl de. "Maggio Musicale, 1951," *Ballet,* September, 1951, 19–24.
Zvyagina, Suzanna. "The Other End of the World," *New Times,* No. 51 (1959), 29–31.

NEWSPAPERS

Baltimore Sun
Camoedia
The Christian Science Monitor
Dance News
Izvestiia
Komsomol'skaia Pravda
Krasnaia Gazeta
Leningradskaia Pravda
London Observer
London Times
New York American
New York Herald
New York Herald Tribune
  and *This Week Magazine*
New York Journal of Commerce
  and *Commercial Review*
New York Post
New York Times
News (Trud)
Pravda
Sovetskaia Kul'tura
Uchitel'skaia Gazeta
Washington Post

NOTES

INTRODUCTION

1. *An Essay towards an history of dancing* (London, 1712), p. 2.

2. *Five Comedies of Aristophanes*, trans. Benjamin Bickley Rogers (Garden City, 1955), p. 97.

3. To mention only a few works: Ernest J. Simmons, ed., *Through the Glass of Soviet Literature* (New York, 1953); Harold Swayze, *Political Control of Literature in the U.S.S.R., 1946–1959* (Cambridge, 1962); Avram Yarmolinsky, *Literature under Communism: the Literary Policy of the Communist Party of the Soviet Union from the End of World War II to the Death of Stalin* (Bloomington, 1960).

4. Andrey Olkhovsky, *Music under the Soviets. The Agony of an Art* (New York, 1955); Philip Mosely, "Freedom of Artistic Expression and Scientific Inquiry in Russia," in *The Kremlin and World Politics. Studies in Soviet Policy and Action* (New York, 1960), pp. 91–128; Robert Slusser, "Soviet Music since the Death of Stalin," *Annals of the American Academy of Political Science*, CCCIII (January, 1956), 116–125.

5. Nikolai A. Gorchakov, *The Theater in Soviet Russia*, trans. Edgar Lehrman (New York, 1958); Marc Slonim, *The Russian Theatre. From the Empire to the Soviets* (Cleveland, 1951).

6. Paul Babitsky and John Rimberg, *The Soviet Film Industry* (New York, 1955).

7. A. Voyce, "Soviet Art and Architecture," *Annals of the American Academy of Political Science*, CCCIII (January, 1956), 104–115; B. K. McLanathan, "Art in the Soviet Union," *Atlantic Monthly*, CCV (June, 1960), 74–6; Nina Juviler, "Art and Artists in the U.S.S.R. Forbidden Fruit," *Problems of Communism*, XI (May–June, 1962), 41–55.

8. (New York, 1966).

9. Renato Poggioli, "About Soviet Culture: Or the Twilight of Poetry and Art," *Yale Review*, XLIX (December, 1959), 211.

348

Notes

10. Richard Pleasant, "Message to Congress," *Dance Magazine*, XXXIII (August, 1959), 69.

11. *The Russian Theater* (New York, 1922), pp. 7–8.

12. Albert Rhys Williams, *The Soviets* (New York, 1937), p. 410.

13. E.g. "John Martin Visits Russia," *Dance Magazine*, XXX (September, 1956), 20.

14. Iris Morley, *Soviet Ballet* (London, 1945), p. 13.

CHAPTER ONE

1. A. V. Lunacharskii, "Lenin i Iskusstvo," in *Lenin o Kul'ture i Iskusstve*, ed. L. G. Tamashin (Moscow, 1956), p. 5.

2. Anatole Chujoy, "Russian Balletomania," *Dance Index*, VII (January–February, 1948); V. A. Teliakovskii, *Vospominaniia 1898–1917* (Leningrad, 1924), p. 67.

3. The historiographical trend was reversed by a decree of the Council of People's Commissars of the U.S.S.R. and of the Central Committee of the All-Union Communist Party (Bolsheviks), "On the Teaching of Civic History in Schools of the U.S.S.R." May 16, 1934, in Robert V. Daniels, ed., *A Documentary History of Communism*, 2 vols. (New York, 1960), II, 39. The significance of the decree is explained by Klaus Mehnert, *Stalin versus Marx. The Stalinist Historical Doctrine* (London, 1952), pp. 11–34.

4. Joseph Stalin, *Marxism and the National Question. Selected Writings and Speeches* (New York, 1942), p. 207.

5. See, for example, W. W. Kulski, *The Soviet Regime. Communism in Practice* (Syracuse, 1959), pp. 74–75.

6. "Ulanova Talks. Interview to Sushil Edwards," *Dance and Dancers* (December, 1957), 18.

7. V. Svetlov, *Terpsikhora. Stat'i, Ocherki, Zametki* (St. Petersburg, 1906), p. 155. Svetlov was the husband of ballerina Vera Trefilova.

8. A. Vaganova, "Sovetskii Balet i Klassicheskii Tanets," in *Stat'i, Vospominaniia, Materialy* (Leningrad, 1958), pp. 68–69.

9. G. S. Karlinskaia-Skudina, *Balet* (Moscow, 1960), p. 7.

10. Rostislav Zakharov, *Besedy o Tantse* (Moscow, 1963), p. 6.

11. E. Surits, "Iskusstvo Baleta i Ego Burzhuaznye Istolkovateli," *Teatr*, No. 7 (1961), 185.

12. N. P. Kondakov, "O Freskakh Liesnits Kievo Sofiiskago Sobora," *Zapiski Imperatorskago Russkago Arkheologicheskago Obshchestva*. III Novaia Seriia (St. Petersburg, 1888), 287–306; "Shuty i Skomorokhi v Drevnostii i Noveishee Vremia," *Istoricheskii Viestnik*, XXXI (1888), 208–220; 453–474; 688–709.

13. Aleksandr Famintsyn, *Skomorokhi na Rusi* (St. Petersburg, 1889).

14. V. Vsevolodskii-Gerngross, *Teatr pri Aleksee Mikhailovich* (Moscow, 1914), p. 54.

15. Adam Olearius, *The Voyages and Travels of the Ambassadors from the Duke of Holstein, to the Great Duke of Muscovy, and the King of Persia*, trans. John Davies (London, 1662), p. 9.

16. I. Zabelin, *Domashnyi Byt' Russkikh Tsarits v* XVI *i* XVII *st.* (Moscow, 1872), II, 475–476.

17. N. V. Drizen, *Materialy k Istorii Russkago Teatra* (Moscow, 1905), p. 213.

18. Pimen' Arapov, *Lietopis' Russkago Teatr* (St. Petersburg, 1861), p. 12. Arapov gives the date as Nov. 2, 1673. Authorities differ about it, e.g. A. Plescheev, *Nash balet'* (St. Petersburg, 1899), p. 29, gives the date as 1672.

19. P. O. Morozov, *Istoriia Russkago Teatr do Poloviny* XVIII *Stoletiia* (St. Petersburg, 1889), p. 190. The German verses are reproduced here with the spelling and capitalization of Morozov.

20. *Zabelin*, p. 479. Iakob Reitenfel's [Jacob Reutenfels] *Shazaniia Svetleishemu Gertsogu Toskanomu Koz'me Tret'emu o Moskovii* Padua, 1680, trans. from Latin to Russian by Aleksei Stankevich (Moscow, 1906), III, 88–89. Again authorities differ on dates. Zabelin gives February 17, 1672.

21. Konstantin A. Skal'kovskii [Baletoman], *Balet. Ego Istoriia i Mesto v Riadu Iziashykh Iskusstv* (St. Petersburg, 1882), p. 150.

22. Arapov, p. 17.

23. Svetlov, p. 108.

24. Vera M. Krasovskaia, *Russkii Baletnyi Teatr ot Vozniknoveniia do Serediny* XIX *Veka* (Leningrad, 1958), p. 33.

25. Arapov, p. 28.

26. *Dnevnik Kammer-iunkera Berkhgol'tsa, Vedennyi Im v Rossii v Tsarstvovanie Petra Velikago s 1721–1725 God,* trans. I. Ammon., 4 vols. (Moscow, 1857), I, 228.

27. A. O. Kornilovich, *Sochineniia i Pis'ma* (Moscow, 1957), p. 186.

28. Vsevolodskii-Gerngross, *Teatr v Rossii pri Imperatritse Anne Ionnovne i Imperatore Ionne Antonoviche* (St. Petersburg, 1914), pp. 64–65.

29. M. V. Borisoglebskii, *Materialy po Istorii Russkogo Baleta. Proshloe Baletnogo Otdeleniia Peterburgskogo Teatral'nogo Uchilishcha, nyne Leningradskogo Gosudarstvennogo Khoreograficheskogo Uchilishcha* (Leningrad, 1939), I, 21.

30. A. I. Leshkov, "Balet v Moskve," in *Moskovskii Bol'shoi Teatr 1825–1925* (Moscow, 1925), p. 163.

31. V. Mikhnevich, *Russkaia Zhenshchina* XVIII *Stoletiia. Istoricheskie Etiudy* (Kiev, 1895), p. 70. Kornilovich, pp. 186-187.

32. "Pribezhishche Dobrodeteli. Stikhotvorstvo i Raspolozhenie Dramy G. Sumarokova, Muzyka G. Raupakha, Tantsy i Osnovanie Dramy Gil'ferdinga. Teatral'nye Ukrasheniya G. Perezinotti," in *Rossiiskii Featr, ili Polnoe Sobranie Vsekh Rossiiskikh Sochinenii,* chast' XVIII (St. Petersburg, 1788), pp. 99–134. The volume classifies the work as a ballet, although it contains elements of drama and singing.

33. Iakob Shtelin [Jacob Staehlin von Storcksburg], *Muzyka i Balet v Rossii* XVIII *Veka,* trans. from German by B. I. Zagurskii (Leningrad, 1935), p. 160.

34. Krasovskaia, p. 28.

35. Shtelin, pp. 164–168.

Notes

36. Krasovskaia, p. 52.

37. Ibid., p. 32.

38. Borisoglebskii, I, 30; trans. by Joan Lawson, entitled, "Pages from the History of Russian Ballet," *Dancing Times,* No. 364 (January, 1941), 203.

39. Chujoy, p. 49; Skal'kovskii, p. 342; Teliakovskii, pp. 15, 44, 56, 66; also *Spisok Chinov Ministerstva Imperatorskago Dvora 1914 Goda* (St. Petersburg, 1914).

40. Chujoy, p. 49.

41. Ibid. and Skal'kovskii, p. 345.

42. Prince Peter Lieven, *The Birth of Ballet Russe,* trans. by L. Zarine (Boston, 1936), p. 66. Also *Zhurnaly Komissii po Razsmotreniiu Finansovykh Smet Ustanovlenii Minis-terstvo Imperatorskago Dvora na 1914 Goda* (St. Petersburg, 1914), pp. 88, 168.

43. V. Vsevolodskii-Gerngross, *Teatr v Rossii v Epoku Otechestvennoi Voiny* (St. Petersburg, 1912), p. 40.

44. Nikolai Egorovich Volkov, *Dvor Russikh Imperatorov v Ego Proshlom i Nastoia-shchem* (St. Petersburg, 1900), p. 95.

45. Krasovskaia, p. 60. Also Yuri Slonimsky, *The Bolshoi Ballet,* 2nd ed. (Moscow, 1960), p. 8.

46. V. Vsevolodskii-Gerngross, *Istoriia Teatral'nago Obrazovaniia v Rossii,* (St. Peters-burg, 1913), I, 326.

47. Leshkov, p. 167.

48. Ibid., p. 172.

49. Vsevolodskii-Gerngross, *Istoriia Tealtra'nago Obrazovaniia,* I, 265, 341–346; E. Bocharnikova and O. Martynova, *Moskovskoe Khoreograficheskoe Uchilishche* (Moscow, 1954), pp. 8–12.

50. Borisoglebskii, I, 60.

51. V. A. Kollar, "Ocherk Istorii Muzykal'nogo Teatra v Nizhnem Novgorode," in Boris S. Shteinpress, ed., *Iz Muzykal'nogo Proshlogo. Sbornik Statei* (Moscow, 1960), p. 295. The whole ballet repertoire of the serf theatre is given in Tatiana Dynnik, *Krepos-tnoi Teatr* (Moscow, 1933), pp. 256–305.

52. N. A. Elizarova, *Teatry Sheremetevykh* (Moscow, 1944), p. 307; N. de Driesen, "Les Origines du Ballet en Russie. Le Ballet des Serfs," *Archives Internationales de la Danse* (April 15, 1935), 38–40.

53. I. A. Arsen'ev, "Slovo Zhivoe o Nezhivykh," *Istoricheskii Viestnik,* XXVII (1887), 76–77.

54. N. Dubrovin, "Russkaiia Zhizn' v Nachale XIX Veka," *Russkaia Starina,* XCVII (January, 1899), 16.

55. Leshkov, p. 172.

56. Iurii Slonimskii, ed., in Ivan Val'berkh, *Iz Arkhiva Baletmeistera. Dnevnik, Perepiska, Stsenarii* (Moscow, 1948), p. 36.

57. Ibid., pp. 151–156.

58. Ibid., p. 37.

59. Val'berkh, pp. 157–165.

60. F. A. Byrdin, "Vospominaniia Artista ob Imperatore Nikolae Pavloviche," *Istoricheskii Viestnik*, XXIII (1886), 151.

61. N. V. Drizen, *Dramaticheskaia Tsenzura Dvukh Epokh 1825–1881* (Petrograd, 1917), pp. 13–15. In 1778 the Russian poet Mikhail M. Kheraskov had written his heroic poem "Rossiada" on the same subject. On the censorship apparatus see Sidney Monas, *The Third Section. Police and Society in Russia under Nicholas I* (Cambridge, 1961).

62. Ibid., pp. 8–9. Also Iurii Slonimskii, *Mastera Baleta* (Leningrad, 1937), pp. 121–122.

63. Vaganova, pp. 77–78.

64. V. Chistiakova, *V Mire Tantsa* (Leningrad, 1964), p. 15.

65. Drizen, *Dramaticheskaia Tsenzura*, p. 99.

66. H. S. H. The Princess Romanovsky-Krassinsky (Mathilde Kschessinska), *Dancing in Petersburg. A Memoir of Imperial Russia, Exile, and the Ballet*, trans. Arnold Haskell (Garden City, 1961), p. 72. V. A. Teliakovskii, *Vospominaniia, 1898–1917* (Petrograd, 1924), p. 254.

67. Ibid., pp. 57–58.

68. Ibid., p. 82.

69. Borisoglebskii, II, 63.

70. E. O. Vazem, *Zapiski Baleriny* (Moscow, 1937), p. 132.

71. Mikhnevich, pp. 280, 293.

72. Alexandre Benois, *Reminiscences of the Russian Ballet*, trans. Mary Britnieva (London, 1947), p. 50.

73. Anatole Bourman, in collaboration with D. Lyman, *The Tragedy of Nijinsky* (New York, 1936), p. 60.

74. Fedor Lopukhov, *Shest'desiat Let v Balete. Vospominaniia i Zapiski Baletmeistera* (Moscow, 1966), pp. 125–126.

75. Lopukhov, p. 123.

76. V. A. Teliakovskii, *Imperatorskie Teatry i 1905 God* (Leningrad, 1926), p. 30. S. S. Danilov, "Revoliutsiia 1905–1907 Godov i Russkii Teatr," *Teatr* No. 7 (1955), 116–126, gives a typical Soviet account of the proceedings.

77. Teliakovskii, p. 40.

78. Ibid., pp. 135–139.

79. Lopukhov, p. 124.

80. Tamara Karsavina, *Theatre Street. The Reminiscences of Tamara Karsavina* (New York, 1961), p. 162.

81. Lopukhov, pp. 124–125.

82. Feodor Chaliapin, *Man and Mask. Forty Years in the Life of a Singer*, trans. Phyllis Mégroz (New York, 1932), p. 199.

83. Floristan XXVI was meant to symbolize Louis XIV.

84. McLanathan, p. 75.

85. "Mir Iskusstva," in *Bol'shaiia Sovetskaia Entsiklopediia*, 2nd ed., 1950, XXVII, 565.

86. Lieven, p. 42.

87. Benois, p. 217.

88. Arnold L. Haskell, *Diaghileff. His Artistic and Private Life* (New York, 1935), p. 182.

89. Serge Lifar, *A History of Russian Ballet from Its Origins to the Present Day*, trans. Arnold Haskell (London, 1954), p. 226; Romanovsky-Krassinsky, p. 111.

90. Lifar, p. 237.

91. Maurice Paléologue, *An Ambassador's Memoirs*, trans. F. A. Holt, 3 vols. (New York, 1925), II, 242.

92. V. Bogdanov-Berezovskii, "Muzykal'naia Kul'tura Baleta," in *Stat'i o Balete* (Leningrad, 1962), p. 66.

93. V. Bogdanov-Berezovskii, *Teatr Opery i Baleta Imeni S. M. Kirova* (Leningrad, 1959), p. 20.

94. E.g. Walter Buchler, "Ballet in Soviet Russia," *Dancing Times* (June, 1937), 387.

CHAPTER TWO

1. "Come All Ye," in John Masefield and Edward Seago, *Tribute to Ballet in Poems by John Masefield* (London, 1938), p. 34.

2. "Eugene Onegin," in *The Works of Alexander Pushkin*, ed. Avraham Yarmolinsky (New York, 1936), p. 119.

3. Iurii Slonimskii, *Sovetskii Balet* (Moscow, 1950), p. 26.

4. "*Epikur*, No. 79 (April 15, 1917), 23.

5. E. M. Liukom, *Moia Rabota v Balete* (Leningrad, 1940), p. 19.

6. "Ekaterina Vasil'evna Gel'tser," *Pravda* (December 14, 1962).

7. Paléologue, I, 166.

8. Ibid., II, 185.

9. Ibid., III, 214.

10. Ibid., III, 230.

11. Romanovsky-Krassinsky, p. 167.

12. V. F. Bezpalov, *Teatry v Dni Revoliutsii 1917* (Leningrad, 1927), p. 41.

13. Paléologue, III, 290.

14. Sergei Bertenson, *Vokrug Iskusstva* (Hollywood, 1957), p. 212.

15. Bezpalov, p. 45; Bertenson, p. 215.

16. Bertenson, p. 210.

17. Ibid., p. 211.

18. A. Rostislavov, "Khudozhestvennaia Letopis'," *Apollon*, No. 2–3 (1917), 65, 69.

19. Bertenson, p. 215.

20. Vitale Fokine, trans., and Anatole Chujoy, ed., *Fokine. Memoirs of a Ballet Master* (Boston, 1961), p. 238.

21. Karsavina, p. 261.

22. Lopukhov, p. 192.

23. Bertensen, p. 212. These *politsmeistery* were often officers wounded in former campaigns.

353

24. Ibid., pp. 236–237. Meyerhold was directing operas in the Marinsky at the time.

25. Bertenson, pp. 238, 270.

26. Bezpalov, p. 103. The name "State Commission for Enlightenment" was changed in June, 1918, to "People's Commissariat for Enlightenment," subsequently shortened to *Narkompros.*

27. Ibid., p. 107. Also Nikolai Evreinov, *Histoire du Théâtre Russe* (Paris, 1947), p. 410.

28. Lopukhov, p. 189.

29. "Dekret ob Ob'edinenii Teatral'nogo Dela," *Izvestiia VTsIK* (September 9, 1919).

30. "Programma Rossiiskoi Kommunisticheskoi Partii (Bol'shevikov)," in *Vsesoiuznaia Kommunisticheskaia Partiia (Bol'shevikov) VKP(b) v Rezoliutsiakh i Resheniakh, S"ezdov, Konferentsii, i Plenumov Ts K.* Chast' I 1898–1925 (Moscow, 1941), p. 289.

31. Constantin Stanislavsky, *My Life in Art,* trans. J. J. Robbins (Boston, 1938), pp. 554–555.

32. Liukom, p. 19.

33. Chaliapin, p. 316. Trotsky held that the energy of the proletariat should be spent in conquering power, not in building a culture. In his view, there would be no "Proletarian Culture," strictly speaking, because the proletarians would soon abolish their own class characteristics. Leon Trotsky, *Literature and Revolution* (New York, 1957), p. 185.

34. André Schaikevitch, *Olga Spessivtzeva. Magicienne Envoutée* (Paris, 1954), pp. 48–49.

35. "Political Propaganda and Educational Activity in the Villages. A Resolution of the 8th Convention of the Russian Communist Labor Party," *Soviet Russia,* I (July 12, 1919), 13.

36. "Programma Kul'turno Prosvetitel'nyi Raboty Partii," *Vlast' Sovetov,* No. 8–9 (1919), 18.

37. *Pravda* (November 1, 1919).

38. V. Bogdanov-Berezovskii, *Teatr imeni Kirova,* p. 27.

39. Karsavina, p. 266.

40. Galina Ulanova, "Shkola Baleriny," *Novyi Mir,* No. 3 (1954), 210.

41. O. Martynova, *Ekaterina Gel'tser* (Moscow, 1956), p. 72.

42. Aleksandr Blok, *Dnevnik Al. Bloka,* ed. P. N. Medvedev, 2 vols. (Leningrad, 1928), II, 68. Pugachev was another very famous leader of a peasant revolt in the Volga River basin in 1773–1775.

43. "Teatr i Iskusstvo," *Izvestiia* (November 12, 1918).

44. *Krasnaia gazeta* (November 18, 1918). A ballet by the same name had been given by M. Fokine at a charity performance in 1915; Fokine and Chujoy, p. 305.

45. A. A. [sic] "Vesti ob Iskusstve," *Pravda* (February 11, 1919).

46: Lunacharskii, "Lenin i Iskusstvo," p. 527. A *pomeshchik* was a landowner in tsarist times.

47. Max Eastman, *Artists in Uniform: a Study of Literature and Bureaucratism* (New York, 1934), pp. 224–225; E. Malinovskaia, "Sovetuias' s Il'ichem," *Izvestiia* (March 31,

1963); Adolf Verbitsky, "Deciding the Bolshoi's Fate," *U.S.S.R. Soviet Life Today*, No. 4 (79) (April, 1963), 51; A. Krivosheeva, *Esteticheskie Vzgliady A. V. Lunacharskogo* (Moscow, 1939), p. 107; L. Freidkina, "Lenin i Teatr," *Teatr*, No. 8 (1937), 31.

48. "Balet," in *Bol'shaia Sovetskaia Entsiklopediia*, 2nd ed. (Moscow, 1950), IV, 126.

49. "Poshcheschina Obshchestvennomu Vkusu," in N. L. Brodskii, V. L. L'vov-Rogachevskii and N. P. Siderov, *Literaturnye Manifesty* (Moscow, 1929), p. 77; "LEF," ibid., pp. 228–237.

50. "Deklaratsiia Literaturnogo Tsentra Konstruktivistov," ibid., pp. 258–260.

51. Alexei Pevsner, *a biographical sketch of my brothers naum gabo and antoine pevsner*, trans. richard scammell and w. r. burke (Amsterdam, 1964).

52. "Konstruktivism," in *Bol'shaia Entsiklopediia*, 2nd ed., XXII, 437.

53. Ibid. Nikolai A. Gorchakov, *The Theater in Soviet Russia*, trans. Edgar Lehrman (New York, 1958), p. 176, insert #5 gives illustration.

54. Anatole Chujoy, ed. *The Dance Encyclopedia* (New York, 1949), pp. 46, 74.

55. Excerpt from "A Contribution to the Critique of Political Economy," in Lewis S. Feuer, ed., *Marx and Engels. Basic Writings on Politics and Philosophy* (Garden City, 1959), p. 43.

56. "Proletkul't," in Brodskii, pp. 139–141.

57. "Ot Redaktsii," *Proletarskaia Kul'tura*, No. 3 (1918), 38.

58. "O Proletarskoi Kul'ture," (October 8, 1920), in *Lenin o Kul'ture i Iskusstve*, pp. 301–302.

59. Rene Fülöp-Miller and Joseph Gregor, *The Russian Theater: Its Character and History, with Especial Reference to the Revolutionary Period*. trans. Paul England (Philadelphia, 1929), p. 71.

60. Edward J. Brown, *The Proletarian Episode in Russian Literature 1928–1932* (New York, 1953), pp. 13, 70, 256.

61. "VAPP. Platform Vsesoiuznoi Assotsiatsii Proletarskikh Pisatelei," (January, 1925), in Brodskii, p. 196.

62. Translation of decree in Olkhovsky, pp. 278–279.

63. Nicholas Slonimsky, "Soviet Music and Musicians," *Slavonic Review*, XXII (December, 1944), 1.

64. Akademiia Nauk SSSR, *Istoriia Russkoi Sovetskoi Muzyki*, 5 vols. (Moscow, 1956–1963), I, 36. In future references, this work will be designated *IRSM*.

65. Meyerhold wanted to stage this ballet of Prokofiev's in 1929 at the Bolshoi Theatre. However, in Slonimskii's opinion, the ballet "slanderously narrated the events of October and the Civil War" and was taken out while still in preparation. Slonimskii, *Sovetskii Balet*, p. 41; also *IRSM*, I, 215.

66. Orest Tsekhnovitser, "Novaia Muzyka i Proletariat," *Novaia Muzyka*, Vypusk 1, V (1927–1928), 5–6, 15.

67. *IRSM*, I, 35.

68. Olkhovsky, p. 148.

69. "Ideologicheskaia Platforma Vserossiiskii Assotsiatsii Proletarskikh Muzykantov," *Muzykal'naia Nov'*, No. 12 (1924), 24–25.

70. The philosophical battle dealt with an interpretation of "Dialectical Materialism." Bukharin's group denied that any qualitative differences existed between phases in the production of matter. The opposition, on the contrary, emphasized the "dialectic" aspect, saying that matter evolved by means of qualitative "leaps." Bukharin's mechanists led the struggle until 1925, but the Deborinites held sway between 1925 and 1930. A decree of the Central Committee of the Party on January 25, 1931, formally condemned the Deborinites. Trotsky was banished by Stalin in 1929; Bukharin was purged in 1938. See J. M. Bochenski, *Soviet Russian Dialectical Materialism. Diamat* (Dordrecht, Holland, 1963), pp. 32–36.

71. Olkhovsky, p. 279.

72. A. Gvozdev in A. Punina, Iu. Kharlamov et al., *Pitm i Kul'tura Tantsa* (Leningrad, 1926), p. 4.

73. N. Foregger in *Ritm i Kul'tura Tantsa*, p. 45. VTsSPS stood for All-Union Central Soviet of Trade Unions, whose leader was Mikhail P. Tomsky.

74. Fülöp-Miller and Gregor, p. 71.

75. N. Foregger, p. 47.

76. Ibid., p. 52.

77. Karl Marx, *Economic and Philosophic Manuscripts* (Moscow, 1961), p. 71.

78. Nikolai Bukharin, *Culture in Two Worlds* (New York, 1934), p. 31. Bukharin probably wrote more in detail about the evolution of society and the art of dance than any other early Soviet ideologue; e.g. Nikolai Bukharin, *Historical Materialism. A System of Sociology*, authorized trans. of 3rd Russian ed. (New York, 1965), pp. 192–196.

79. Huntley Carter, *The New Spirit of the Russian Theatres* (New York, 1929), p. 153.

80. Gosudarstvennaia Akademiia Iskusstvoznaniia, *Istoriia Sovetskogo Teatra* (Leningrad, 1933), I, 344.

81. Vera Krasovskaia, *Vakhtang Chabukiani* (Moscow, 1956), pp. 9–10.

82. *Moiseyev Dance Company*, Program of U.S. Tour, 1965 (New York, 1965), unpaged.

83. Isadora Duncan, *My Life* (New York, 1927), p. 357.

84. According to Juri Jelagin, *Taming of the Arts,* p. 238, "God Save the Tsar" was the sole musical composition forbidden in Russia in 1917.

85. Alan Ross MacDougall, *Isadora: A Revolutionary in Art and Love* (New York, 1960), p. 199. "Khronika. Vecher A. Dunkan," *Izvestiia* (November 5, 1921). Reviews not too complimentary are contained in Adam Efros, "Aisedora Denkan," *Teatral'noe Obozrenie*, No. 1 (1921), 8–9, and Igor Schwezoff, *Russian Somersault* (New York, 1936), p. 140.

86. A. Lunacharskii, "Nasha Gost'ia," in A. Lunacharskii, *O Teatre i Dramaturgii. Izbrannye Stat'i,* 2 vols. (Moscow, 1958), II, 274.

87. Some listed in MacDougall, p. 247; others in *Teatral'naia Moskva*, 1935, p. 68. "Pioneers" refers to the youth group in Russia younger than Komsomol.

Notes

88. Irma Duncan, *Duncan Dancer. An Autobiography of Irma Duncan* (Middletown, Conn., 1966), pp. 321–322, 333–334.

89. Mary Desti, *The Untold Story. The Life of Isadora Duncan* (New York, 1929), pp. 101–102.

90. A. Anisimov, "Purge Vaudeville of Foreign Influences," *Sovetskoye Iskusstvo* (March 19, 1949), trans. in *Current Digest of the Soviet Press*, I:16 (May 17, 1949), 74.

91. Kollektiv Geptakhor, "Geptakhor," in *Ritm i Kul'tura Tantsa,* pp. 55–65. Similar studios of T. Grebova and Z. Berbova are also described pp. 66–73 and 74–77; also A. Siderov, "The Dance Art in Russia," *New York Times* (August 7, 1932).

92. V. Iving, "Spektakli V. Maiia," *Sovremennyi Teatr* (June 3, 1928), 447; James E. Abbé, "Russia's Revolution of the Dance," *Dancing Times* (December, 1930), 284; *Teatral'naia Moskva, 1935,* p. 68.

93. Nikolai El'iash, *Russkaia Terpsikhora* (Moscow, 1965), p. 150.

94. Slonimskii, *Sovetskii balet,* p. 70; Lopukhov, pp. 206–207. "Balanchin," in *Teatral'naia Entsiklopediia* (Moscow, 1961), I, 383; Bogdanov-Berezovskii, *Teatr imeni S. M. Kirova,* p. 56.

95. "Molodye Sily Baleta—Vecher 'Molodogo Baleta'," *Zhizn' Iskusstva* (May 27, 1928), 6–7.

96. Iu. Brodersen, "V Ak. Baleta Neblagopoluchno," *Rabochii i Teatr,* No. 20 (1928), 6.

97. Oliver Sayler, *The Russian Theater* (New York, 1922), pp. 111–114.

98. G. Chulkov, "Dramaticheskii balet," *Sovremennyi Teatr* (October 23, 1928), 680.

99. Ibid. Also I. Turkel'taub, "Na Baletnom Perekrestke," *Zhizn' Iskusstva* (October 6, 1929), 4.

100. Introduction to Viktorina Kriger, *Moi Zapiski. Teatral'nye Memuary* (Moscow, 1930), p. 8.

101. Ibid.

102. Viktorina Kriger, "Klassika—Osnova Baletnoi Ucheby," *Sovremennyi Teatr* (September 2, 1928), 556.

103. M. Chudnovskii, *Viktorina Kriger* (Moscow, 1964), p. 43.

CHAPTER THREE

1. Ivan Sollertinskii, "Kakoi zhe Balet Nam v Sushchnosti Nuzhen?" *Zhizn' Iskusstva* (October 6, 1929), 5.

2. A. Lunacharskii, "K Voprosu o Repertuare," *Teatr i Revoliutsiia* (Moscow, 1924), p. 83.

3. "Teatr i Revoliutsiia," in ibid., pp. 36–38.

4. Ibid., p. 38, 40.

5. Shortened form of *Glavnyi Politiko-Prosvetitel'nyi Komitet,* the Chief Political-Enlightenment Committee.

6. "O Glavpolitprosvete i Agitatsionno-Propagandistkikh Zadachakh Partii," in

VKP(b) v Resoliutsiiakh i Resheniiakh, I, 379; also, Maria Sergeevna Andreeva, *Kommunisticheskaia Partiia-Organizator Kul'turno-Prosvetitel'noi Raboty v SSSR 1917–1933* (Moscow, 1963), pp. 29–31.

7. A. A. Gvozdev and A. Piotrovskii, "Petrogradskie Teatry i Prazdnestva v Epokhu Voennogo Kommunizma," in Gosudarstvennaia Akademiia Iskusstvoznaniia, *Istoriia Sovetskogo Teatra* Tom I. *Petrogradskie Teatry na Poroge Oktiabria i v Epokhu Voennogo Kommunizma 1917–1921* (Leningrad, 1933), p. 108.

8. A. Lunacharskii, "O Zadachakh Teatra v Sviazi s Reformoi Narkomprosa," *Kul'tura Teatra*, No. 4 (April 5, 1921), 1.

9. A. Lunacharskii, "La Lutte de Classe dans l'Art," *Iskoustvo* (January, 1929), in V. I. Lenine, *Sur la Littérature et l'Art. Textes Choises Précedés d'une Etude par Jean Fréville* (Paris, 1957), pp. 217–218.

10. Alexander Herzen (1812–1870) was a Russian author who strongly criticized the tsarist government.

11. Lunacharskii refers here to a fable called "The Cock and the Pearl-Grain," by the Russian Aesop, Ivan Krylov.

12. A. Lunacharskii, "Khronika. Iubilei E. V. Gel'tser," *Kul'tura Teatra*, No. 1 (April 5, 1921), 56–58.

13. "Pervyi S''ezd Rabis," *Teatr*, No. 5 (1954), 191.

14. *Vserossiiskii Tsentral'nyi Sovet Professional'nykh Soiuzov* (Moscow, 1920), p. 2. Pamphlet is bound in volume entitled *Capital and Labor*, New York Public Library.

15. *Izvestiia* (November 5, 1921), 2. Elena Konstantinova Malinovskaya had been a Party member since 1905. After the February Revolution, she had organized the artistic-enlightenment department of the Moscow Soviet, and after the October Revolution held dominant positions in the Moscow theatrical administration apparatus. Leonid V. Sobinov was a famous tenor who became head of the Bolshoi in 1921, but had to relinquish his job to Malinovskaya after a short time.

16. Ibid., (November 18, 1921), 2.

17. Igor Schwezoff, *Russian Somersault* (New York, 1936), p. 242.

18. Ibid., p. 243.

19. Ibid., p. 261.

20. Ibid., p. 265.

21. Iurii Slonimskii, ed., *"Zhar Ptitsa" i "Petrushka" I. F. Stravinskogo* (Leningrad, 1963), pp. 3–4.

22. *IRSM*, I, 45.

23. This ballet was called *Le Renard* in the West.

24. M. Stefanovych, *Kyivs'kyi Derzhavnyi Ordena Lenina Akademichnyi Teatr Operi ta Baletu URSR imeni T. G. Shevchenka. Istorichnyi Narys* (Kiev, 1960), p. 198. The ballet's Ukrainian name was *Blazen*.

25. "Po Voprosam Propagandy, Pechati i Agitatsii," in *VKP(b) v Resoliutsiiakh i Resheniiakh*, I, 512.

26. Slonimskii, *Sovetskii Balet*, p. 46.

Notes

27. Ibid., pp. 46–47.

28. "Balet," in *Bol'shaia Sovetskaia Entsiklopediia* (1950 ed.), IV, 126.

29. V. Bogdanov-Berezovskii, *Teatr imeni Kirova*, p. 54.

30. Slonimskii, *Sovetskii balet,* p. 54.

31. Lopukhov, p. 53.

32. Ibid., p. 225.

33. *Krasnaia Gazeta,* No. 246 (1924). "Smychka" was a term used by Bol'sheviks from 1921 to 1928 to refer to the close connection between town and village. The Russian peasant had been stubborn when forced to yield farm products to feed the city proletariat after the Bol'shevik seizure of power in 1917. In 1921, Lenin said a tax would replace the forced appropriations and the town and country should live in harmony; a *smychka* should exist. See Vladimir Zenzinov, "The Bol'sheviks and the Peasant," in *The Soviet Union 1922–1962,* ed. Philip Moseley (New York, 1953), pp. 33–43.

34. *IRSM,* I, 205.

35. Slonimskii, *Sovetskii Balet,* pp. 54, 60.

36. S. Voskresenskii, "Vyvod," *Rabochii i Teatr,* No. 8 (1924), quoted in Bogdanov-Berezovskii, *Teatr imeni Kirova,* p. 103.

37. Iurii Slonimskii, "Puti Baletmeistera Lopukhova," introduction to Lopukhov, p. 36. *The Ice Maiden* was revived in 1964 in Novosibirsk. Pictured in *Life,* LX (April 22, 1966).

38. I. Sollertinskii, "Baletmeister Fedor Lopukhov," *Zhizn' Iskusstva* (April 26, 1927), 4.

39. Lopukhov, p. 247.

40. Ibid., pp. 31, 247–248.

41. Bogdanov-Berezovskii, *Teatr imeni Kirova,* p. 104.

42. Slonimskii, *Sovetskii Balet,* p. 87. Libretto in L. L. [sic], "Balet K. Korchmareva, 'Krepostnaia Balerina,' " *Muzyka i Revoliutsiia,* No. 12 (1927), 11–12. The theme of the serf ballerina has been popular. In 1935, Leonid Lavrovskii staged a tragic ballet about a serf-dancer called *Katerina.* It was first given for a graduation performance of the Leningrad Choreographic Institute and was later incorporated into the Kirov repertoire. E. Surits *Vsë o Balete. Slovar' Spravochnik* (Moscow, 1966), p. 370.

43. "Shchelkunchik," *Rabochii i Teatr,* No. 45 (1929), 7.

44. "Deklaratsiia F. Lopukhova," *Zhizn' Iskusstva* (December 8, 1929), 6.

45. Slonimskii, *Sovetskii Balet,* p. 48.

46. Slonimskii in Lopukhov, p. 15.

47. Later the Bolshoi Filial Theatre.

48. M. Druskin, *Ocherki po Istorii Tantsoval'noi Muzyki* (Leningrad, 1936), p. 186.

49. *IRSM,* I, 207.

50. Ibid.

51. *Teatral'naiia Moskva, 1929* (Moscow, 1929), p. 25.

52. Slonimskii, *Sovetskii Balet,* p. 50.

53. I. T., "Prekrasnyi Iosif, i Karnaval v Gatobe," *Zhizn' Iskusstva* (February 3, 1929), 8–9.

54. V. Eaving, "The Ballet in the U.S.S.R.," *Soviet Travel*, No. 3 (1932), 33–35; see also *Teatral'naia Entsiklopediia*, II, 30–31.

55. Clive Barnes, "Bolshoi's 'Don Quixote' Stars a Radiant Couple at the Met," *New York Times* (April 24, 1966).

56. N. Nasilov, "Zakrytie Baletnogo Sezona," *Zhizn' Iskusstva* (June 22, 1926), 15.

57. N. Nasilov, "Balet," *Zhizn' Iskusstva* (November 9, 1926), 8.

58. "Dlia Chego My Sokhraniaem Bol'shoi Teatr?" in *V Mire Muzyki. Stat'i i Rechi*, ed. G. B. Bernandt and I. A. Sats (Moscow, 1958), p. 298.

59. Ibid., p. 303.

60. *Tsentral'nyi Ispolnitel'nyi Komitet*.

61. III Sessiia Vserossiiskogo Tsentral'nogo Ispolnitel'nogo Komiteta, XX Sozyva, *Stenograficheskii Otchet* (Moscow, 1926), p. 59. Volkov's remark is on p. 119.

62. Ibid., pp. 137–139. The author is indebted to Mr. Howard Holter for pointing out this quotation.

63. Ekaterina Gel'tser, "Slava Russkogo Baleta," *Izvestiia* (May 26, 1951).

64. Moscow, n.d.

65. Iosif Stalin, "Politicheskii Otchet Tsentral'nogo Komitet," 14th Session VKP(b), December 18, 1925, *Sochineniia*, 13 vols. (Moscow, 1947), VII, 293–294.

66. George Von Rauch, *A History of the Soviet Union*, trans. Peter and Annette Jacobsohn (New York, 1963), p. 202.

67. "The Red Poppy," *Soviet Woman*, No. 3 (1950), 50–52.

68. *IRSM*, I, 212.

69. Valentin Zeglovsky, *Ballet Crusade* (Melbourne, 1944), p. 53.

70. M. Frangopulo and L. Entelis, *75 Baletnikh Libretto* (Leningrad, 1960), p. 8.

71. Viktorina Kriger, "Krasnyi Mak," *Izvestiia* (February 3, 1950).

72. A. Dashicheva, "Vtoroe Rozhdenie 'Krasnyi Mak' v Bol'shom Teatre," *Teatr*, No. 2 (1950), 26.

73. Slonimskii, *Sovetskii Balet*, p. 77.

74. Sadko, "Krasnyi Mak v Bol'shom Teatre," *Zhizn' Iskusstva* (June 28, 1927), 4.

75. Aleksandr Rumnev, "Realism v Tantse," *Zhizn' Iskusstva* (September 29, 1929), 6.

76. N. [sic], "Krasnyi Mak v Mosk. Narvskom Dome Kul'tury," *Zhizn' Iskusstva* (January 13, 1939), 12.

77. M. Kalinin, "Rech' na VIII s"ezde VLKSM, May 13, 1928," in *O Molodezhi*, 2nd ed., (Moscow, 1939), p. 88.

78. *Teatral'naia Moskva* (1929), p. 25. A Soviet musical theatre has a mixed repertoire of both operas and ballets. Ballet dancers and opera singers belong to one theatrical company which is permanently based in one theatre. The capitals of Union Republics have their own opera and ballet theatres. With the triumph of communism in China in 1949, *Red Flower* was performed throughout the U.S.S.R. It was mounted by local companies in the following cities:

Notes

1949: Kiev, Perm, Riga, Saratov, Shakhty, Frunze, Ufa, Vilnius.

1959: Sverdlovsk, Gorkii, Alma-Ata, Minsk, Novosibirsk, Dushanbe, Tallin, Kuibyshev, and Bucharest, Rumania.

1951: Tbilisi, Ulan Ude, Ashkabad and Sofia, Bulgaria.

Teatral'naia Entsiklopediia, ed. P. A. Markov (Moscow, 1964), III, 257.

79. Slonimskii, *Sovetskii Balet,* p. 85.

80. Ibid., p. 79.

81. Ibid.

82. "Rabis i Sotsperestroika Iskusstva. Boevoi Prikaz po Armii Iskusstv," *Zhizn' Iskusstva* (December 8, 1929), 15.

83. "Rabis po Sluzhbu Piatiletke!" *Rabochii i Teatr,* No. 50 (1930), 1.

84. "Glavrepertkom" *Teatral'naia Entsiklopediia,* I, 1184. The full name is *Glavnyi Repertuarnyi Komitet.*

85. "O Teatral'noi Politike," *Zhizn' Iskusstva* (February 22, 1927), 6.

86. Ibid.

87. S. M. Krylov, ed., *Puti Razvitiia Teatra. Stenograficheskii Otchet i Resheniia Partiinogo Soveshaniia po Voprosam Teatra pri Agitprope TsK VKP(b) v Mae 1927 g.* (Moscow, 1927), p. 503.

88. Ibid., pp. 507, 486.

89. *Glaviskusstvo* is the shortened form of *Glavnoe Upravlenie po Delam Khudozhestvennoi Literatury i Iskusstva. Teatral'naia Entsiklopediia,* I, 1183–84.

90. N. A. Ravich, ed., Glavnyi Komitet po Kontroliu za Repertuarom, *Repertuarnyi Ukazatel'. Spisok Razreshennykh i Zapreshchennykh k Ispolneniiu na Stene Proizvedenii* (Moscow, 1929), p. 4. See Appendix, p. 301.

91. Ibid., p. 6.

92. Ibid., pp. 139–150. The ballet *Golden Wheat,* described below in Chapter VII, is a worthy example of Class D. Schumann was listed incorrectly as the composer of *Sylphide* instead of J. M. Schneitzhoeffer. *Fairy Doll* was given as the graduation performance of Asaf Messerer in 1926.

93. "Perspektivy GOTOB," *Zhizn' Iskusstva* (September 29, 1929), 13.

94. Nikolai L'vov, "Tanets i Sovremennost'," *Zhizn' Iskusstva* (February 8, 1927), 6.

95. I. Sollertinskii, "Za Novyi Khoreograficheskii Teatr," *Zhizn' Iskusstva* (June 17, 1928), 5.

96. Ibid., 6.

97. I. Sollertinskii, "Problem Baletnogo Stsenarii," *Zhizn' Iskusstva* (October 21, 1928), 12–13.

98. Emil Mei, "Baletnaia Molodezh' na Rasput'i," *Sovremennyi Teatr,* No. 36 (September 2, 1928), 557.

99. Aleksandr Rumnev, "Realism v Tantse," loc. cit., p. 6.

100. L. Iakobson, "Na Povestke—Baletnyi Teatr," *Rabochii i Teatr,* No. 26 (1931), 6–7.

101. Ibid., p. 7.

102. Iu. Brodersen, "Otvet Tov. L. Iakobsonu," *Rabochii i Teatr,* No. 26 (1931), 8.

103. V. Vsevolodskii, "Pravda o Balete," *Zhizn' Iskusstva* (April 14, 1929), 5.

104. A. V. Lunacharskii, "Novye Puti Opery i Baleta," Document read May 12, 1930 at Bolshoi Theatre. *Proletarskii Muzykant*, No. 5 (1930), 4–5.

105. *Zhizn' Iskusstva* (January 13, 1929), 2.

106. This part was played by a young ballerina named Galina Ulanova.

107. Slonimskii, *Sovetskii Balet*, pp. 88–89; Cyril Beaumont, *A Complete Book of Ballets* (London, 1956), pp. 1025–30.

108. M. Stefanovych, p. 199.

109. "Kievskaia Gazeta o Balete Shostakovicha," *Proletarskii Muzykant*, No. 1 (1931), 46. The Russian performance received no better review from Iu. Brodersen, "Legalisatsiia Prisposoblenchestva," *Rabochii i Teatr*, No. 60–61 (1930), 2–3.

110. Ravich, "Bol'shoi Teatr na Perelome," *Rabochii i Teatr*, No. 22 (1930), 12.

111. *IRSM*, I, 215.

112. Ravich, 13.

113. Lunacharskii, "Novye Puti Opery i Baleta," loc. cit., p. 7.

114. Lopukhov, p. 257. The Blue Blouse had grown out of the propagandistic device of "living newspapers," where characters would illustrate passages from newspapers being read to illiterate workers' audiences, or would garnish them with dancing, acrobatics, songs, or gymnastics. TRAM was a primitively propagandistic proletarian theatre whose formation was assisted by RAPP, and which continued under the active leadership of the Komsomol. See Gorchakov, pp. 145–146, 280.

115. D. Tal'nikov, "Puti Sovetskogo Baleta," *Krasnaia Nov'*, No. 5 (1936), 221.

116. Marshal Budënny was a popular cavalry officer in the Red Army in the civil war after the revolution.

117. M. Iankovskii, "Bolt" *Rabochii i Teatr*, No. 11 (1931), 11.

118. *IRSM*, I, 217.

119. Iankovskii, 11.

120. Lopukhov, pp. 258–259.

CHAPTER FOUR

1. *The Laws of Plato,* trans. A. E. Taylor (New York, 1934), p. 34.

2. Mihajlo Mihajlov, "Moscow Summer 1964," *New Leader,* XLVIII (March 29, 1965), 10.

3. N. Vladimirov, *Cultural Facilities in the U.S.S.R.* (Moscow, n.d.), p. 26.

4. M. Frangopulo and L. Entelis, p. 8.

5. The term is described in detail by Rufus W. Mathewson, *The Positive Hero in Russian Literature* (New York, 1958).

6. Olkhovsky, pp. 49–58.

7. Nina Juviler, "Soviet Art. A Report for the Use of Specialists in the Field of Art Planning to Visit the Soviet Union," (New York, 1964), p. 9.

8. Walford Hyden, *Pavlova* (Boston, 1931), p. 34.

Notes

9. Lifar, *History of Russian Ballet*, p. 61.

10. Camilla Gray, "Soviet Ballet. An English Dancer's Impression," *Dancing Times* (December, 1955), 152.

11. Howard Taubman, "Stagecraft in Soviet Theatre Found Impressive by Visitor," *New York Times* (July 1, 1958).

12. Vaganova, pp. 77–80.

13. Slonimskii, *Sovetskii Balet*, p. 116.

14. Vasilii Moskva, "Zametki o Balete: Moskovskie Prem'ery 'Karman'ola,'" *Sovetskii Teatr* (July-August, 1932), 36.

15. "Za 10 dnei," *Rabochii i Teatr*, No. 1 (1932), 23.

16. Frangopulo and Entelis, pp. 26–28.

17. Slonimskii, *Sovetskii Balet*, p. 117.

18. Ibid., p. 107.

19. A. H. F., "The New Russian Film," *Dancing Times* (August, 1954), 670.

20. Committee on Un-American Activities, House of Representatives. 86th Congress, 2nd Session, December, 1960. *Facts on Communism. Volume II: The Soviet Union, from Lenin to Khrushchev* (Washington, 1961), pp. 164–169.

21. J. Stalin, "The Policy of Eliminating the Kulaks as a Class," *Problems of Leninism* (Moscow, 1940), pp. 328–332.

22. Leonid Lavrovskii, "Baletmeister o Spektakle," in M. S. Druskin, L. Lavrovskii, P. Fel'dt, et al., *Fadetta. Balet v 3 Deistviakh Muzyka Leo Deliba. Sbornik Statei k Postanovke Baleta v Gosudarstvennom Akademicheskom Malom Opernom Teatre* (Leningrad, 1936), p. 18.

23. Slonimskii, *Sovetskii Balet*, p. 122.

24. A. Anisimov, ed., *Bakhchisaraiskii Fontan. Gosudarstvennyi Ordena Lenina Akademicheskii Bol'shoi Teatr SSSR* (Moscow, 1951), p. 23.

25. Stanley D. Krebs, *Soviet Composers and the Development of Soviet Music*, unpublished doctoral dissertation, University of Washington, 1963, p. 102.

26. Edmund Stevens, *This Is Russia Uncensored* (New York, 1950), pp. 104–105.

27. Benjamin W. Brown, *Theatre at the Left* (Providence, R.I., 1938), p. 44.

28. El'iash, p. 185.

29. Karl Marx, "Manifesto of the Communist Party," in *Selected Works*, ed. V. Adoratsky, 2 vols. (Moscow, 1935), I, 207.

30. V. I. Lenin, "Partiinaia Organizatsiia i Partiinaia Literatura," *Sochineniia*, 35 vols., 4th ed. (Moscow, 1947), x, 48.

31. F. Schiller, "Marx and Engels on Balzac. Unpublished Correspondence of Friedrich Engels," *International Literature*, No. 3 (1933), 114; M. Yakhontova, "Balzac and Modern Times," *Soviet Literature*, No. 5 (1949), 168.

32. Slonimskii, *Sovetskii Balet*, p. 147.

33. B. Asaf'ev, "Muzykal'naia Dramaturgiia Spektaklia," in Leningrad Gosudarstvennyi Akademicheskii Teatr Opery i Baleta Imeni S. M. Kirova *Utrachennye Illiuzii. Khoregraficheskii Roman* (Leningrad, 1936), p. 10.

34. Leon Trotsky, "The Betrayal of Russian Culture," *Saturday Review of Literature,* xv (February 27, 1937), 4.

35. "Ob Obrazovanii Vsesoiuznovo Komiteta Po Delam Iskusstv Pri SNK Soiuza SSSR," *Rabochii i teatr,* No. 2 (1937), 2–3; see also "Komitet Po Delam Iskusstv," *Teatral'naia Entsiklopediia,* III, 166.

36. Hryhony Kytasty, "Some Aspects of Ukrainian Music under the Soviets," (New York, 1954), p. 9; Juri Jelagin, *Taming of the Arts,* trans. Nicholas Wreden (New York, 1951), p. 105.

37. *Outline History of the U.S.S.R.* (Moscow, 1960), p. 423.

38. "Vyvesti Balet Na Novuiu Dorogu," *Rabochii i Teatr,* No. 50 (1929), 5.

39. Vladimir Gsovsky, *Soviet Civil Law. Private Rights and Their Background under the Soviet Regime,* 2 vols. (Ann Arbor, 1948), I, 118, and II, 759, 762; Nicholas Timasheff, *The Great Retreat. The Growth and Decline of Communism in Russia* (New York, 1946), pp. 193–196.

40. "Iskusstvo, Na Vysotu Sotsialisticheskoi Epokhi. K. VII S"ezdu Leninskoi Partii," *Rabochii i Teatr,* No. 3 (1934), 1.

41. G. Bernandt, *Slovar' Oper. Vpervye Postavlennykh Ili Izdannykh v Dorevoliutsionnoi Rossii v SSSR* (Moscow, 1962), p. 157–158.

42. *Pravda* (January 28, 1936).

43. Jelagin, p. 212.

44. *Communist Manifesto,* p. 225.

45. A. Lunacharskii, *Problemy Narodnogo Obrazovaniia. Sbornik Statei* (Moscow, 1923), pp. 99–101.

46. Robert V. Daniels, ed., *A Documentary History of Communism,* 2 vols. (New York, 1962), II, 40–41.

47. Vladimir Seduro, *The Byelorussian Theater and Drama,* ed. Edgar H. Lehrmann (New York, 1955), p. 81.

48. Kytasty, p. 6.

49. Maurice Hindus, *The Cossacks. The Story of a Warrior People* (New York, 1945), p. 107; Colonel Louis B. Ely, ed., *The Red Army Today* (Harrisburg, Pa., 1953), p. 86.

50. Hindus, p. 111.

51. Timasheff, p. 271. Some information here was given by a Kuban Cossack now living in New York; see also Viktor I. Seroff, *Dmitri Shostakovich, The Life and Background of a Soviet Composer* (New York, 1943), pp. 222–229.

52. N. Volkov, "Baletnyi God," *Teatral'naia Dekada* (October 1, 1934), 9.

53. W. G. Raffé, "Modern Ballet in the Soviet Union," *Dancing Times* (August, 1937), 545.

54. Cyril W. Beaumont, *Complete Book of Ballets* (London, 1956), pp. 1052–56.

55. S. Fisin, ed., *Svetlyi Ruchei. Komediinyi Balet v 3 Deistviakh i 4 Kartinakh. Sbornik Statei i Materialov k Postanovke Baleta v Gosudarstvennom Akademicheskom Malom Opernom Teatre* (Leningrad, 1935), p. 3.

Notes

56. Ibid., p. 6.

57. Joseph Stalin, "Speech at the First All-Union Conference of Stakhanovites," November 17, 1935, trans. A. Fineberg (Moscow, 1935).

58. V. M. Molotov, "What Is Stakhanovism?" Speech delivered at the First All-Union Conference of Stakhanovites (New York, 1936), p. 18. The goal of elimination of such differences has been mentioned in Marxist works since 1846 when Marx wrote *The German Ideology* (New York, 1963), p. 44.

59. Fisin, p. 10.

60. Iurii Slonimskii, ed., in Fedor Lopukhov, *Shest'desiat Let v Balete. Vospominaniia i Zapiski Baletmeistera* (Moscow, 1966), p. 56.

61. I. Sollertinskii, " 'Svetlyi Ruchei' v Gos. Malom Opernom Teatre," *Rabochii i Teatr,* No. 12 (1935), 14–15.

62. Iur. Brodersen, "Sovetskaia Tantsoval'naia Komediia," *Sovetskii Teatr,* No. 8 (1935), 10.

63. Ibid., p. 11.

64. In tsarist times, peasants in ballets were usually "paysans," an affected imitation of the real type.

The reference to the Kuban Cossacks in this announcement was not an isolated comment in *Pravda.* In subsequent weeks, several pictures appeared showing the Kuban Cossacks in their uniforms, with a letter from one of the Cossacks professing firm adherence to the Soviet authorities. See "Pis'mo Kubanskikh Kazakov Tov. Voroshilovu" (March 5, 1936); "Sovetskie Kazaki" (February 18 and March 20, 1936), pictures.

65. The poem quoted here, written by Nikolai A. Nekrasov (1821–1878), is entitled "Ballet." The full work is contained in N. A. Nekrasov, *Izbrannye Poemy,* 2 vols. (Moscow, 1962), I, 259–260.

66. The documents are collected in one volume: *Protiv Formalizma, Naturalizma v Iskusstve. Sbornik Statei* (Moscow, 1937). Philip E. Mosely explains their significance in "Freedom of Artistic Expression and Scientific Inquiry in Russia," in *The Kremlin and World Politics,* pp. 91–128.

67. Jelagin, p. 152. Such meetings took place all over the U.S.S.R.; e.g., Seduro, p. 136, reports them in Belorussia.

68. Igor V. Kostetskii, *Sovetskaia Teatral'naia Politika i Sistema Stanislavskogo,* (Munich, 1956), pp. 91–93.

69. Lopukhov, pp. 273–274.

70. Jelagin, p. 238.

71. Kurt London, *The Seven Soviet Arts* (London, 1937), p. 97.

72. N. Cheliapov, "K Itogam Diskussii Na Muzykal'nom Fronte," *Sovetskaia Muzyka,* No. 3 (1936), 4.

73. "Protiv Formalizma i Fal'shi. Tvorcheskaia Diskussia v Moskovskom Soiuze Sovetskikh Kompozitorov. Vystuplenie Tov. Belogo," ibid., 29.

74. Iur. Keldysh, ibid., 112–113.

75. "Vystuplenie Tov. Fere," ibid., 48.

76. "Rezoliutsiia Rasshirennogo Plenuma Pravleniia Leningradskogo Soiuza Sov. Kompozitorov," ibid., 14.

77. "Protiv Formalizma i Fal'shi. Tvorcheskaia Diskussia v Leningradskom Soiuze Sovetskikh Kompozitorov. Vystuplenie Tov. Chernetskoi," *Sovetskaia Muzyka*, No. 5 (1936), 60.

78. "Vystuplenie Tov. Chulaki," ibid., 63. Mikhail Chulaki later became director of the Bolshoi Theatre.

79. B. Asaf'ev, "Volnuiushchie Voprosy (Vmesto Vystupleniia Na Tvorcheskoi Diskussii), ibid., 26.

80. D. Tal'nikov, "Puti Sovetskogo Baleta," *Krasnaia Nov'*, No. 5 (1936), 213–225.

81. Yuri Olesha, "About Formalism," *International Literature*, No. 6 (1936), 87–88.

82. Jelagin, p. 100.

83. Slonimskii, *Sovetskii Balet,* p. 174.

84. Ibid., pp. 174–175.

85. "Dmitri L. Klebanov," *Teatral'naia Entsiklopediia*, III, 68.

86. Frangopulo and Entelis, p. 130.

87. A. Anisimov, ed., *Aistenok. Gosudarstvennyi Ordena Lenina Akademicheskii Bol'shoi Teatr SSSR* (Moscow, 1951), p. 21.

88. Ibid., p. 14, and Slonimskii, *Sovetskii Balet,* p. 155.

89. "Timur i Ego Komanda," *Sovetskaia Muzyka*, No. 5 (1957), 113.

90. Martynova, pp. 76–77.

91. Zakhar Plavskin, "Lope de Vega in the U.S.S.R.," *Soviet Literature*, No. 11 (1962), 128.

92. M. Grinberg, " 'Komedianty' v Bol'shom Teatre," *Proletarskii Muzykant*, No. 5 (1931), 39.

93. "Na Pomoshch' Ispanskomu Narodu!" *Sovetskaia Muzyka*, No. 11 (1936), 80.

94. E.g., "Pis'mo Pablo Kazal'sa," *Sovetskaia Muzyka*, No. 1 (1939), 106; A. Fevral'skii, "¡Pasaremos!" ibid., 97–98; "Geroi Respublikanskoi Ispanii," ibid., No. 5 (1939), 100–104; G. Kh., "Kompozitory Revoliutsionnoi Ispanii," ibid., No. 7 (1938), 105–106; G. Mikhailov, "Ritmika v Ispanskoi Narodnoi Muzyke," ibid., 97–102; G. Sh., "Pesnia o Grenade," ibid., 103–104.

95. V. Chabukiani, "Dramaticheskii Obraz v Balete," *Rabochii i Teatr*, No. 11 (1937), 25.

96. Slonimskii, *Sovetskii Balet,* pp. 360, 364.

97. Nelli Uznadze, "Prima Ballerina," *Soviet Woman*, No. 6 (1959), 22. The ballet is also described by Joan Lawson, "Another New Soviet Ballet, *Laurencia*," *Dancing Times* (October, 1940), 12.

98. Von Rauch, *A History of Soviet Russia,* pp. 281–282.

99. Slonimskii, *Sovetskii Balet,* pp. 201–202.

100. "Ol'ga V. Lepeshinskaia," *Teatral'naia Entsiklopediia*, III, 504.

Notes

101. Peter Deriabin and Frank Gibney, "Kremlin Intrigue and Debauchery," *Life*, XLVI (March 30, 1959), 90.

CHAPTER FIVE

1. "Za Tesnuiu Sviaz' Literatury i Iskusstva s Zhizn'iu Naroda," *Kommunist*, No. 12 (August, 1957), 24.

2. Iurii Slonimskii, *Sovetskii Balet*, pp. 238–243. In 1937 Ukrainian musicians were told to put anti-Polish songs in their repertoire. See Kytasty, p. 18.

3. Ibid., p. 260. Albert E. Kahn, *Days with Ulanova* (New York, 1962), p. 118.

4. Slonimskii, *Sovetskii Balet*, p. 262.

5. Ibid., p. 260.

6. Harold Swayze, *Political Control of Literature in the U.S.S.R. 1946–1959* (Cambridge, 1962), p. 28.

7. "O Podgotovke i Perepodgotovke Rukovodiashchikh Partiinykh i Sovetskikh Rabotnikov," in *Kommunisticheskaia Partiia Sovetskogo Soiuza v Rezoliutsiiakh i Resheniiakh S"ezdov, Konferentsii i Plenumov TsK. Chast'* III *1930–1954.* (Moscow, 1954), pp. 476–484. Subsequently designated *KPPS*.

8. "O Zhurnalakh 'Zvezda' i 'Leningrad' " in ibid., pp. 485–488.

9. Andrei A. Zhdanov, *Essays on Literature, Philosophy, and Music* (New York, 1950), p. 22.

10. Ibid., p. 25.

11. Olkhovsky, p. 284. The entire decree is given pp. 280–285.

12. "Ot Kompozitorov i Muzykovedov Goroda Moskvy Velikomu Vozhdiu Sovetskogo Naroda Tovarishchu Stalinu," *Sovetskaia Muzyka*, No. 1 (1948), p. 28.

13. Zhdanov, p. 90.

14. M. Gabovich, "Sovremennaia Tema V Balete," *Teatral'nyi Almanak* (Moscow, 1947), 123.

15. "Vystupleniia Na Soveshchanii," *Sovetskaia Muzyka*, No. 1 (1947), 33–34, 51.

16. L. A. Entelis, compiler, *100 Baletnykh Libretto* (Moscow-Leningrad, 1966), pp. 297–299.

17. Zhdanov, p. 13.

18. M. Rittikh, "Komy Nuzhen Takoi Spektakl' " *Sovetskaia Muzyka*, No. 5 (1950), 33–34.

19. "Eshche o Balete 'Alye Parusa!' " *Sovetskaia Muzyka*, No. 11 (1950), 110.

20. D. Tal'nikov, "Kompozitor i Dve Baleriny," *Teatr*, No. 5 (1940), 54.

21. V. Golubov-Potapov, "Sovremennost' i Fantasiia," *Teatr*, No. 10 (1940), 135.

22. Zhdanov, p. 27.

23. Slonimskii, *Sovetskii Balet*, p. 292.

24. Ibid., pp. 298–299, and Frangopulo and Entelis, pp. 232–234.

25. Nina Militsyna, "Soviet Ballet Today," *Dancing Times* (May, 1949) 435–437.

26. "Bolshoi Ballet in Peking," *Peking Review* (October 6, 1959), 36.

27. Natalia Roslavleva, "The Leningrad State Kirov Ballet," *Dancing Times* (June, 1961), 543.

28. L. V. Iakobson and I. V. Golubovskii, eds., "Khoreograficheskie Miniatury," (Leningrad, 1960), p. 30.

29. Ibid., p. 25.

30. Frangopulo and Entelis, pp. 283–286.

31. M. Rittikh, "Balet o Molodosti i Druzhbe," *Sovetskaia Muzyka*, No. 5 (1960), 107–109.

32. "Bolshoi Theater in New Season—Interview with Bolshoi Theater Director A. V. Solovnikov," *Komsomolskaya Pravda* (September 5, 1950), 4; *CDSP*, II:39 (November 11, 1950), 38.

33. T. Leontovskaia and I. Il'in, "Pod Nebom Italii," *Sovetskaia Muzyka*, No. 12 (1952), 73–76; see also A. Filippenko, "Pod Nebom Italii," *Pravda* (November 16, 1952).

34. Galina Ulanova, "Shkola Baleriny," *Novyi Mir*, No. 3 (1954), 222.

35. "V Port Voshla 'Rossia,'" *Sovetskaia Kul'tura* (September 9, 1965). Also M. Korolev, "Deistvie Proiskhodit v Nashi Dni," *Pravda* (September 6, 1962).

36. Galina Ulanova, "Bright Image of Chinese Heroine," *Soviet Woman*, No. 2 (1950), 53.

37. V. Krasovskaia, "Bereg Nadezhdy," *Pravda* (October 9, 1959). S. Katonova, "Romantika Liubvi i Podviga, 'Bereg Nadezhdy,'" *Sovetskaia Muzyka*, No. 9 (1959), 17–18.

38. Nikolai El'iash, *Russkaia Terpsikhora* (Moscow, 1965), p. 199. Slonimskii, *Sovetskii Balet*, pp. 252–253.

39. E. Surits, *Vsë o balete*, pp. 376–377, 392.

40. Rosemary Winckley, "Russian Journey," *Dance and Dancers* (June, 1965), 26. A. Medvedev and E. Svetlanov, "Balet po Stendaliu," *Izvestiia* (October 9, 1962).

41. Frangopulo and Entelis, pp. 58–60.

42. Karl Marx and Friedrich Engels, *Literature and Art. Selections from Their Writings* (New York, 1949), p. 145.

43. Walter Terry, "De Mille Out De Milled," *New York Herald Tribune* (September 16, 1962).

44. "Serious Errors of the Magazine *Sovetskaya Muzyka*," *Sovetskaya Kultura* (October 5, 1957). CDSP, IX:39 (November 6, 1957), 11.

45. D. Zhitomirskii, "Spartak," *Sovetskaia Muzyka*, No. 4 (1956), 7.

46. Alexandra Dashicheva, "Lieutenant Kizhe" *Soviet Literature* (No. 9, 1963), pp. 172–175. Also described by Clive Barnes, "The Ballet of the Kirov Opera," *Dance and Dancers* (February, 1965), 28, and Mary Clarke, "Lieutenant Kije," *Dancing Times* (September, 1963), 684.

47. Frangopulo and Entelis, pp. 270–272.

48. V. Chevychelov, "Rezervy Donbassa—Na Slyzhbu Rodine," *Pravda* (March 29, 1950).

49. Ruben Simonov, "Balet Na Sovremennuiu Temu," *Pravda* (December 14, 1953).

50. S. Prokofiev, "Tvorcheskie Plany," *Sovetskaia Muzyka*, No. 1 (1953), 19.

51. Frangopulo and Entelis, pp. 195–198, gives plot. Review by John Martin, "Ballet *Stone Flower," New York Times* (May 5, 1959).

52. "Stone Carvers of the Urals," *Soviet Literature*, No. 8 (1953), 146.

53. Natalia Roslavleva, "Heroic Geologists," *Dancing Times* (July, 1964), 529.

54. E. Grosheva, "Novyi Pushkinskii Balet 'Mednyi Vsadnik' R. Gliera," *Sovetskaia Muzyka*, No. 9 (1949), 26–34.

55. Ibid.

56. Nate White, "Soviet Ballet, Opera Point Up Contrasts With U.S. Artistry," *The Christian Science Monitor* (August 9, 1960).

57. V. Bogdanov-Berezovskii, *Stat'i o Balete* (Leningrad, 1962), pp. 107–108.

58. "Muzyka v Antireligioznoi Propagande," *Proletarskii Muzykant*, No. 2 (1930), 37. Lenin was once reported saying that except for the theatre, there was nothing with which they might replace religion. See Max Eastman, *Artists in Uniform*, p. 224.

59. Rothbart is the evil magician in *Swan Lake*, and Carabosse is the evil fairy in *Sleeping Beauty*, who in a recent Kirov version wears the costume of a nun in one scene.

60. V. Bogdanov-Berezovskii, "Geroicheskii Balet," *Sovetskaia Muzyka*, No. 3 (1958), 78.

61. Wendy Michener, "Jeanne d'Arc in Moscow," *Dance and Dancers* (September, 1958), 22–23; Frangopulo and Entelis, pp. 178–179.

62. Leonid Lavrovsky, "Rachmaninov and Paganini," *Culture and Life*, No. 9 (1960), 42.

63. Dmitri Shostakovich, "Some Vital Problems of Music Composition," Pravda (June 17, 1956), in *CDSP*, VIII:22 (July 11, 1956), 8–10.

64. "Za Leninskuiu Printsipial'nost' v Voprosakh Literatury i Iskusstva," *Kommunist*, No. 10 (July, 1957), 13–22.

65. "On the Correction of Mistakes in Appraisal of the Operas *The Great Friendship, Bogdan Khmelnitsky*, and *With All My Heart*. Decision of the C C of the CPSU," *Soviet Literature*, No. 6 (1958), Supplement.

66. N. Chernova, "Miniatiury Goleizovskogo," *Teatr*, No. 4 (1962), 140. A. I., "Khoreograficheskie Kompozitsii Kas'iana Goleizovskogo," *Sovetskaia Muzyka*, No. 8 (1960), 204–205.

67. "Khrushchev on Modern Art . . ." Stenographic account of his comments, *Encounter*, XX (April, 1963), 102. An excellent explanation of the events is contained in Priscilla Johnson, *Khrushchev and the Arts; the Politics of Soviet Culture. Documents Selected and Edited by Priscilla Johnson and Leopold Labedz* (Cambridge, Mass., 1965).

68. "Creative Work for the People in the Name of Communism," Speech of L. F. Ilyichov. *Soviet Literature*, No. 2 (1963), Supplement, 7.

69. L. F. Ilyichev, "Young Writers and Artists Should Serve Great Ideals," Meeting of December 26, 1962, *Sovestkaya Kultura* (January 10, 1963), 1–3; *CDSP* XV:2 (February 6, 1963), 10.

70. "Vysokaia Ideonost' i Khudozhestvennoe Masterstvo—Velikaia Sila Sovetskoi Literatury i Iskusstva," *Pravda* (March 10, 1963).

369

71. N. Malkov, "Novaia Muzyka i Kul'tura Ispolnitel'stva v Perekhodnuiu Epokhu," *Novaia Muzyka,* No. 1 (1927), 47.

72. "'Vesna Sviashchennaia' Stravinskogo v Ispolnenii Orkestra GABT i Dirizhera Fritsa Stidri," *Muzyka i Revoliutsiia,* No. 4 (1926), 32.

73. *IRSM,* I, 10.

74. B. Harutovsky, "The Classical Tradition and Innovation in Music," *Soviet Literature,* No. 6 (1948), 126.

75. I. V. Nest'ev, "Dollarovaia Kakofoniia," *Izvestiia* (January 7, 1951).

76. Slonimskii, *"Zhar-Ptitsa" i "Petrushka,"* p. 28.

77. Tikhon Khrennikov, "Serdechnyi Privet Ot Stravinskogo," *Ogonëk,* No. 32 (August 6, 1961), 12.

78. "Priem N. S. Khrushchevym I. F. Stravinskogo," *Pravda* (October 12, 1962).

79. A review is in A. Dashicheva, " 'Za' i 'Protiv.' Balet ili Simfoniia," *Sovetskaia Kul'tura* (August 3, 1965). Dazh-Bog is an ancient pagan Slavic god.

80. *Programme of the Communist Party of the Soviet Union,* 22nd Congress (Moscow, 1961), p. 48.

81. *Fundamentals of Marxism-Leninism. Manual,* trans. Clemens Dutt (Moscow, 1963), p. 413.

82. Entelis, pp. 121–127; V. Bogdanov-Berezovskii, "Tropoiu Groma," *Izvestiia* (January 24, 1958); S. Gadzhibekov, "Tropoiu Groma," *Pravda* (March 29, 1961).

83. "Kara Karaev," *Teatral'naia Entsiklopediia,* II, 1130.

84. " 'Colonialism' in a Russian Ballet," *New York Times* (October 25, 1959).

85. Krebs, p. 433.

86. E. Lobacheva, "Latyshskii Balet, 'Rigonda,' " *Sovetskaia Muzyka,* No. 11 (1959), 111; Frangopulo and Entelis, pp. 92–94.

87. V. Vanslov, "Dalekaiia Planeta," *Sovetskaia Muzyka,* No. 11 (1963), 63; T. Tserbakova, "Minskaia Prem'era," *Sovetskaia Muzyka,* No. 4 (1962), 53–56.

88. "Na Stolichnoi Stsene," *Izvestiia* (June 14, 1963).

89. "Novyi Moskovskii Sezon," *Teatr,* No. 11 (1962). 148.

90. B. Maizel', "O Podvige Cheloveka," *Sovetskaia Muzyka,* No. 2 (1963), 148.

91. Vanslov, p. 66.

CHAPTER SIX

1. "O Tvorcheskoi Smelosti i Vdoknovenii," *Sovetskaia Muzyka,* No. 11 (1953), p. 7.

2. *Constitution. Fundamental Law of the Union of Soviet Socialist Republics* (Moscow, 1962), p. 101.

3. See, for example, Frederick Barghoorn, *Soviet Foreign Propaganda* (Princeton, 1964), pp. 226, 241; Henry G. Aubrey, *Coexistence: Economic Challenge and Response* (Washington, 1961), p. 17.

4. *Fundamentals of Marxism-Leninism,* p. 394.

5. Kytasty, p. 31

Notes

6. Jelagin, p. 232.

7. "Gazetnoe Obozrenie," *Teatr*, No. 3 (1958), 127.

8. "Deiateli Gruzinskogo Iskusstva i Literatury V Moskve," *Izvestiia* (March 18, 1948).

9. "Zakliuchitel'nyi Kontsert Dekady Uzbekskoi Literatury i Iskusstva," *Pravda* (November 28, 1951).

10. Irina Tikhomirnova, "My Favourite Roles," *Soviet Woman*, No. 4 (1951), 28.

11. M. Stefanovych, p. 11.

12. Iu. Stanishevs'kyi, *Ukrains'kyi Radians'kyi Balet* (Kiev, 1963), pp. 23–27.

13. Ibid., pp. 33–34.

14. G. Tiumeneva, "Meshchanin iz Toskany," *Sovetskaia Muzyka*, No. 12 (1936), 22.

15. "New Soviet Ballet," *Izvestiia* (March 28, 1951), 3; *CDSP*, III:13 (May 12, 1951), 37; Stanishevs'kyi, p. 148.

16. Iu. Stanishevskii, "V Poiskakh Novovo," *Sovetskaia Muzyka*, No. 4 (1960), 99; John Percival, "A Check List of Soviet Ballets, 1959–60," *Ballet Annual* (1962), 128.

17. M. Rittikh, "Poslednyi Bal," *Sovetskaia Muzyka*, No. 10 (1962), 81.

18. Viktorina Kriger, " 'Marusia Boguslavka,' " *Izvestiia* (June 26, 1951).

19. "Nagrady Artistam Baleta," *Pravda* (December 7, 1954).

20. "Gazetnoe Obozrenie," *Teatr*, No. 2 (1958), 151; S. Zviagina, "Chernoe Zoloto," *Izvestiia* (November 16, 1960). The Donbass is a large area in the Don River basin, noted for its coal fields.

21. Stanishevs'kyi, *Ukrains'kyi Radians'kyi Balet*, p. 167.

22. Ibid., p. 169.

23. Ibid., pp. 152–153.

24. "Pervyi Belorusskii Balet 'Solovei' " *Sovetskaia Muzyka*, No. 11 (1939), 75.

25. S. Riauzov and I. Belorusets, "Iubileinye Torzhestva v Belorussii," *Sovetskaia Muzyka*, No. 3 (1959), 155.

26. Vladimir Seduro, "Belorussian Theater of Opera and Ballet," Unpublished manuscript, Columbia University Archives, p. 50; G. Nisnevich, *Belaruskaia Narodnaia Pesnia i Muzychnai Dramaturgi Natsyial'nykh Oper i Baletau* (Minsk), p. 39.

27. I. Belorusets, "Svet i Teni," *Sovetskaia Muzyka*, No. 6 (1963), 66–67. Gogol's *Viy* is a novel in which a witch seduces a seminarian. One scene in a church depicts a wild and weird orgy of devils and ghosts.

28. "Gosti Iz Minska. Gastroli Belorusskogo Bol'shogo Teatra Opery i Baleta," *Pravda* (January 29, 1964).

29. A. Ladygina, "V Poiskakh Novykh Putei," *Teatr*, No. 10 (1963), 30.

30. "Muzykal'noe Iskusstvo Belorussii," *Izvestiia* (January 29, 1964); M. Teroganian, "Slovo o Librettistam," *Teatr*, No. 7 (1964), 13.

31. Surits, *Vsë o Baleta*, p. 95.

32. Iu. Gaudrimas, "Novyi Litovskii Balet," *Sovetskaia Muzyka*, No. 12 (1957), 77; M. Ignat'eva, "Po-delevomu o Prazdnichnom. Spektakli Litovskogo Teatra Opery i Baleta

na Vsesoiuznom Festivale," *Teatr,* No. 3 (1958), 76; "Litovskii balet—'Audrone,'" *Izvestiia* (July 3, 1957), 3.

33. J. Pozera, "The Rising Dawn," *Tiesa* (January 29, 1953), 3; *CDSP,* I:4 (March 7, 1953), 40.

34. Ibid., 40.

35. Alg. Ziuraitis and J. Pozera, "On the Path of Cultural Cooperation. Première of the New Ballet *On the Sea Shore,*" *Tiesa* (May 26, 1953); *CDSP,* v:23 (July 18, 1953), 47–48.

36. Ibid., 47.

37. George Brants, *Latviešu Balets* (Riga, 1937), p. 13; Zeglovsky, p. 46.

38. Renate Behrman, "The Latvian Ballet," *Dancing Times* (October, 1937), 13.

39. Marina Semenova, "Dekada Latyshskogo Iskusstva I Literatury. Balet 'Laima' i 'Sakta Svobody,'" *Izvestiia* (December 22, 1955); also "'Laima'—Dekada Latyshskogo Iskusstva I Literatury," *Izvestiia* (December 26, 1955).

40. Ibid.

41. Maiia Plisetskaia, "Dekada Latyshskogo Iskusstva i Literatury. 'Sakta Svobody,'" *Pravda* (December 23, 1955).

42. Surits, *Vsë o Balete,* p. 124.

43. Anna Klas, "Balet E. Kappa 'Kalevipoeg'" *Sovetskaia Muzyka,* No. 6 (1949), 47. Libretto is in Frangopulo and Entelis, pp. 115–116.

44. Frangopulo and Entelis, pp. 40–42.

45. Svetlana Ivanova, "Iag-Mort," *Teatr,* No. 7 (1962), 131.

46. Aram Khachaturian, "Obrazy Narodnovo Eposa," *Pravda* (August 23, 1956); see also "Sampo," *Pravda* (August 22, 1959).

47. A. Kirtoka and M. Manilov, *Moldavskii Gosudarstvennyi Teatr Opery I Baleta* (Kishinev, 1960), p. 34; G. Shantyr', "Rozhdenie Moldavskogo Baleta, Balet L. Kogana 'Sëstry,'" *Sovetskaia Muzyka,* No. 6 (1959), 115–118.

48. D. Rabinovich, "Moldavskie Opery i Balety," *Sovetskaia Muzyka,* No. 8 (1960), 110–118; Kirtoka, p. 41.

49. Richard Pipes, *The Formation of the Soviet Union, Communism and Nationalism, 1917–1923* (Cambridge, 1954), pp. 178–179.

50. Ibid., pp. 76–77.

51. A. Mlodik, "Tamara Khanum," *Teatr,* No. 10 (1939), 133–136; N. Zeleransky, "People's Actress," *Soviet Woman,* No. 1 (1947), 42–45; Vasilii Makarov, "Tamara Khanum" in Yuri Slonimsky, ed., *Soviet Ballet* (New York, 1947), pp. 157–160; Langston Hughes, "Tamara Khanum," *Theatre Arts Monthly,* XVIII (November, 1934), 832–834; Iurii Shirokii, *Tamara Khanum* (Moscow, 1941).

52. Georg Goian, "Natsional'nyi Balet," *Teatral'nyi Al'manakh* I, 3 (Moscow, 1946), 64; M. Ashrafi, "Strana Tsvetushchei Muzykal'noi Kul'tury," *Sovetskaia Muzyka,* Nos. 10–11 (1938), 73.

53. T. Sadykov, "Muzykal'naia Zhizn' Uzbekistana," *Sovetskaia Muzyka,* No. 11 (1939), 32.

Notes

54. "Dekada Uzbekskogo Iskusstva," *Sovetskaia Muzyka,* No. 2 (1959), 203.

55. Sh. Rashidov, "Vyshe Uroven' Muzykal'noi Kul'tury," *Pravda* (July 10, 1951).

56. "O Merakh Pod'ema Sel'skogo Khoziaistva v Poslevoennyi Period," Plenum TsK VKPb (February, 1947); in *KPSS,* III, 511.

57. R. Struchkova and A. Lapauri, "Novyi Uzbekskii Balet," *Pravda* (August 10, 1952); I. Karelova, "Novyi Uzbekskii Balet," *Sovetskaia Muzyka,* No. 10 (1952), 58–63.

58. N. Vladimirov, p. 23.

59. Komitet Po Delam Iskusstv, *Dve Rozy. Balet v 4 Aktakh* (Moscow, 1941), pp. 10–14.

60. N. Vudkevich and M. Muravi, "Novoe v Muzykal'noi Zhizn' Tadzhikstana," *Izvestiia* (December 26, 1954).

61. Tatyana Berezantseva, "Leili and Mejnun," *Soviet Woman,* No. 7 (1960), 22. M. Vol'berg, "Leili i Medzhnun," *Sovetskaia Muzyka,* No. 6 (1949), 40–43.

62. N. L'vov, *Kirgizskii Teatr. Ocherk Istorii* (Moscow, 1953), p. 75.

63. Nikolai Urzhumsky, "The Women of the Celestial Mountains," *Soviet Woman,* No. 1 (1956), 27.

64. Ibid; also E. Lutskaia, "Biubiusara Beishenalieva," *Teatr,* No. 2 (1959), 72–76; "Talanty Kirgizii," *Sovetskii Soiuz,* No. 10 (1958), 8–17.

65. Libretto is in L'vov, pp. 146–148; see also "Balet 'Cholpon,' " *Pravda* (October 18, 1958).

66. L'vov, p. 112. Libretto in Frangopulo and Entelis, pp. 66–67.

67. L. Lavrovskii, "Zasluzhennyi Uspekh," *Izvestiia* (June 2, 1944).

68. T. Shantyr', "Gornaia Byl'," *Sovetskaia Muzyka,* No. 3 (1960), 100.

69. N. Gudaidullin, "Novyi Bashkirskii Balet," *Sovetskaia Muzyka,* No. 9 (1963), 60.

70. Igor Moiseyev, "Folk Dance," in Slonimsky, *Soviet Ballet,* p. 135.

71. Ol'ga Lepeshinskaia, "Iskusstvo Blagoukhaiushchei Svezhesti," *Izvestiia* (December 17, 1958).

72. "Entuziast Kazakhskoi Khoreografii," *Teatr,* No. 9 (1959), 159; "Kazakhskii Teatr," *Teatral'naia Entsiklopediia,* II, 1054.

73. "Gastroli Bol'shogo Teatra v Respublikakh Zakavkaz'ia," *Izvestiia* (October 12, 1958); see also "Teatry Na Tselinnykh Zemliakh Rossiskoi Federatsii i Kazakhstani," *Teatr,* No. 4 (1955), 147.

74. Frangopulo and Entelis, pp. 131–133. Sometimes the ballet is entitled *Veselyi Obmanshchik.*

75. "Dekada Iskusstva i Literatury v Moskve," *Teatral'naia Entsiklopediia,* II, 351.

76. Iogann Al'tman, "Vozrozhdennoi Narod, Vozrozhdennoe Iskusstvo," *Teatr,* No. 11 (1940), 21.

77. N. Vinogradov, "Krasavitsa Angara," *Pravda* (November 29, 1959).

78. E. Maksimova, "Buriatskie Spektakli v Moskve," *Sovetskaia Muzyka,* No. 2 (1960), 112.

79. R. Farkhadova, "Pervaia Azerbaidzhanskaia Balerina," *Sovetskaia Muzyka,* No. 1 (1964), 59–63.

80. Z. Bagirov, "Novyi Azerbaidzhanskii Balet, 'Giulshen.' " *Pravda* (April 10, 1951);

I. Sviridova, "Obrazy Nashikh Sovremennikov v Balete; Novyi Azerbaidzhanskii Balet 'Giul'shen,'" *Sovetskaia Muzyka*, No. 6 (1951), 49–54.

81. D. Shostakovich, "Novyi Azerbaidzhanskii Balet," *Pravda* (December 18, 1952).

82. V. Vinogradov, "Vdoknovennoe Proizvedenie," *Pravda* (May 27, 1959).

83. "Gruzinskii Teatr," *Teatral'naia Entsiklopediia*, II, 201.

84. S. L. Ginsburg, "Muzykal'nyi Teatr Gruzinskogo Naroda," *Iskusstvo i zhizn'*, No. 9 (1938), 21; Goian, 68; Iris Morley, *Soviet Ballet* (London, 1945), p. 18; P. Khuchua, "Sovetskaia Opera i Balet," in *Gruzinskaia Muzykal'naia Kul'tura. Sbornik Statei.* A. Tsulukidze, ed. (Moscow, 1957), pp. 212–213.

85. V. Chabukiani, "Dramaticheskii Obraz v Balete," *Rabochii i Teatr*, No. 11 (1937), 25.

86. A. Gosberg, " 'Serdtse Gor,'—Balet A. Balanchivadze," *Sovetskaia Muzyka*, No. 8 (1938), 63; Joan Lawson, "The Heart of the Hills," *Dancing Times* (July, 1939), 389–392.

87. Vera Krasovskaia, *Vakhtang Chabukiani* (Moscow, 1956), p. 119. Italics mine.

88. Ak. Khoravo, " 'Gorda,' Novyi Gruzinskii Balet," *Izvestiia* (May 6, 1950), 3; N. Shumskaia, "Gruzinskii Teatr na Dekade," *Sovetskaia Muzyka*, No. 6 (1958), 139.

89. Krasovskaia, p. 140; see also V. Krasovskaia, "Iskusstvo Sluzhit Miru," *Sovetskaia Kul'tura* (July 7, 1953).

90. "Theatre," *News (Trud)* (November 1, 1953), 31.

91. Pipes, pp. 208–210, 229–233; "Dashnaktsutiun," *Bol'shaia Sovetskaia Entsiklopediia*, xx (1930 ed.), 530.

92. M. Berko, "Balet 'Sona,' " *Sovetskaia Muzyka*, No. 6 (1958), 147.

93. Goian, pp. 65–66.

94. G. Tigranov, *Armianskii Muzykal'nyi Teatr. Ocherki i Materialy.* Tom II (Erevan, 1960), 297–298.

95. Slonimskii, *Sovetskii Balet*, pp. 256–257.

96. Frangopulo and Entelis, pp. 244–248.

97. Surits, *Vsë o Balete*, p. 355.

98. N. Peiko, " 'Marmar.' Novyi Armianskii Balet," *Sovetskaia Muzyka*, No. 6 (1957), 69. Tigranov, pp. 307–308.

99. Harry Schwartz, *Russia's Soviet Economy* (Englewood Cliffs, 1954), p. 646.

100. G. Tigranov, "Balet 'Sevan' G. Egiazariana," *Sovetskaia Muzyka*, No. 7 (1956), 18.

CHAPTER SEVEN

1. L. Halevy, quoted in Skal'kovskii.

2. "At the Top of the Ladder," *London Times* (February 2, 1959).

3. "Soviet Minister of Culture Bows to Official Criticism," *Baltimore Sun* (June 21, 1963); "Plenum Tsentral'nogo Komiteta KPSS. Rech' Tovarishcha E. A. Furtsevoi," *Pravda* (June 21, 1963).

4. I. N. Ananov, *Ministerstva v SSSR* (Moscow, 1960), pp. 97–98, 145; S. S. Studenikin, V. A. Vlasov, and I. I. Evtikhiev, *Sovetshkoe Administrativnoe Pravo* (Moscow, 1950), pp. 404–405; I. M. Kozlov, *Sovetskoe administrativnoe pravo* (Moscow, 1964), pp. 204–207;

Notes

William Benton, *This Is the Challenge. The Benton Reports of 1956–1958 on the Nature of the Soviet Threat* (New York, 1958), p. 71.

5. "V Ministerstve Kul'tury SSSR," *Sovetskaia Muzyka*, No. 3 (1958), 159; "V Ministerstve Kul'tury SSSR, O Merakh po Dalneishemu Razvitiu Sovetskogo Baletnogo Iskusstva," *Teatr*, No. 2 (1958), 155–156.

6. Morley, *Soviet Ballet*, pp. 54–55. Narkomindel was the People's Commissariat for Foreign Affairs.

7. Irving R. Levine, "Khrushchev's Prettiest Propaganda," *This Week Magazine* (April 19, 1959), 12. Levine reported that the Bolshoi had a budget of $12,000,000 a year, while the Metropolitan Opera had $6,000,000.

8. Yuri Slonimsky, "Talent and the Ballet," *Atlantic Monthly*, ccv (June, 1960), 103; Kahn, p. 151.

9. G. Z. J. Bereday, Wm. W. Brickman, Gerald H. Read, *The Changing Soviet School. The Comparative Education Society Field Study of the U.S.S.R.* (Cambridge, 1960), p. 371.

10. "Imperatorskiia Teatral'nyia Uchilishcha," *Ezhegodnik Imperatorskikh Teatrov. Sezon 1890–1891 gg.* (St. Petersburg, 1892), pp. 253–260.

11. Schwezoff, p. 128.

12. N. Viaz'min, "Kustari ot Baleta. Chastnye Baletnye Shkoly Dolzhny Byt' Likvidirovany," *Rabochii i Teatr*, No. 43 (1929), 3.

13. Schwezoff, p. 175.

14. E. Bocharnikova and O. Martynova, *Moskovskoe Khoreograficheskoe Uchilishche. Kratkii Istoricheskii Ocherk* (Moscow, 1954), p. 92.

15. "Novyi Kurs Gosbaletnogo Uchilishcha," *Zhizn' Iskusstva* (Sept. 8, 1929), 13; "V Baletnom Uchilishche," *Zhizn' Iskusstva* (July 7, 1929), 16.

16. "Moskovskoe Khoreograficheskoe Uchilishche," in *Teatral'naia Entsiklopediia*, iii, 975.

17. P. Shchipunov, ed., *Leningradskoe Gosudarstvennoe Khoreograficheskoe Uchilishche* (Leningrad, 1940), p. 7.

18. Bocharnikova and Martynova, pp. 99–100.

19. See Gorchakov, pp. 32–39; see also Kostetskii, pp. 91–93.

20. Bocharnikova and Martynova, p. 104.

21. W. G. Raffé, "Ballet Training in the U.S.S.R.," *Dancing Times*, (February, 1936), 646. His information was taken from a translated Soviet document: "Education Program. Choreographic Technicum and Semeletka."

22. Shchipunov, p. 10.

23. Ibid., p. 11.

24. Ibid., p. 13.

25. Bocharnikova and Martynova, pp. 107–109.

26. Ibid., p. 111.

27. Shchipunov, p. 14.

28. Bocharnikova and Martynova, pp. 116–117.

375

29. M. Dolgopolov, "The Oldest Ballet School," *Dancing Times*, (April, 1944), 308.

30. Bocharnikova and Martynova, p. 120.

31. A. Belosel'skii, "Molodye Kadry Baleta," *Teatr*, No. 9 (1950), 87.

32. Bocharnikova and Martynova, pp. 131–132.

33. "Podgotovka Artistov Baletnogo Teatra," *Teatr*, No. 12 (1952), 150.

34. Bocharnikova and Martynova, pp. 126–127.

35. "GITIS," *Teatral'naia Entsiklopediia*, I, 1178–80; see also Matvei Gorbunov and A. Gershkovich, "The Teaching of the Theatrical Arts," in Douglas Grant, ed., *The Humanities in Soviet Higher Education* (Toronto, 1960), pp. 67–68.

36. *Programma Kursa "Rezhissura i Masterstvo Aktera,"* (Moscow, 1954), p. 3.

37. M. Alexeyev, "Academic Degree for Ballerina," *Soviet Woman* (June, 1956), 43.

38. [E.] Chesnokov, "Podgotovka Baletnykh Kadrov," *Rabochii i Teatr*, No. 26 (1934), 2.

39. Jean Battey, "A Special, Privileged World. How the Kirov Ballet School, 'The Hothouse of Russian Ballet,' Nurtures Its Future Dance Artists," *Dance Magazine*, xxxv (October, 1961), 34.

40. Bocharnikova and Martynova, p. 138.

41. "Moscow Cheers American Girl in Ballet Role," *New York Times* (May 31, 1960).

42. Shchipunov, p. 6.

43. Sam Russell, "Backstage with a Bol'shoi Ballerina," *Soviet Woman* (July, 1958), 13.

44. "Nureyev," *London Observer* (May 27, 1962), 24.

45. Irving R. Levine, *Main Street U.S.S.R.* (Garden City, 1959), p. 318.

46. Jean Battey, p. 36.

47. "Top Ballerina in U.S.S.R. Wins State Pension," *The Christian Science Monitor* (April 8, 1960). On January 1, 1961, new rubles were introduced and the old ones were exchanged at the rate of 10 to 1.

48. *S. Hurok Presents* (New York, 1953), p. 15.

49. Romanovsky-Krassinsky, p. 167.

50. James H. Meisel and Edward S. Kozera, *Materials for the Study of the Soviet System. State and Party Constitutions, Laws, Decrees, Decisions, and Official Statements of Leaders in Translation*, 2nd ed., (Ann Arbor, 1953), p. 352.

51. Slonimskii, *Sovetskii Balet*, p. 312.

52. *Pravda* (April 2, 1962).

53. "K Novym Vysotam Iskusstva," *Izvestiia* (February 19, 1965), 4.

54. Peter Grose, "25 Soviet Intellectuals Oppose Any Elevation of Stalin's Status," *New York Times* (March 21, 1966); "25 Soviet Intellectuals Warn Party on Stalin," *Washington Post* (March 19, 1966); Eric Bourne, "Intellectual Protest Gains in U.S.S.R.," *The Christian Science Monitor* (March 28, 1966).

55. Shchipunov, p. 41.

56. Ibid., p. 20.

57. Sally Hammond, "Daily Closeup," *New York Post* (April 16, 1959).

58. Sam Russell, p. 13.

Notes

59. "Khrushchev and Molotov Vote in Soviet Election," *New York Times* (June 13, 1966).

60. Urzhumsky, 27.

61. Romanovsky-Krassinsky, p. 217.

62. Jelagin, p. 121.

63. Tamara Karsavina, *Theatre Street*, p. 267.

64. "The All-Russian Theatrical Society," *Soviet Literature*, No. 4 (1952), 182–183. See also "Vserossiiskoe Teatral'noe Obshchestvo," *Teatral'naia Entsiklopediia*, I, 1038–39.

65. "Zarubezhnyi Konsul'tatsii VTO," *Teatr*, No. 1 (1956), 183.

66. "Moskva," *Teatr*, No. 4 (1952), 156–157; "Oblastnye Teatry Obmenivaiutsia Opytom," *Teatr*, No. 9 (1952), 148.

67. "Diskussii 'Iskusstvo Baletmeistera,'" *Sovetskaia Muzyka*, No. 6 (1955), 156.

68. "Dom Rabotnikov Iskusstv v Novom Sezone," *Teatr*, No. 9 (1952), 151; "Moskva," *Teatr*, No. 8 (1952), 157–158; "V Universitetakh Marksizma-Leninizma," *Teatr*, No. 9 (1952), 145; "Politicheskoe Prosveshchenie Akterov," *Teatr*, No. 7 (1952), 149.

69. "Plenum TsK Soiuza Rabotnikov Iskusstv," *Teatr*, No. 2 (1953), 146.

70. "Tsentral'nyi Dom Rabotnikov Iskusstv," *Teatr*, No. 2 (1956), 171.

71. Gerd Ruge, "Report from Moscow. Composer's Dilemma," *Survey*, No. 37 (July–September, 1961), 43.

72. "V Soiuze Kompozitorov," *Sovetskaia Muzyka*, No. 4 (1956), 203; "V. Soiuze Kompozitorov," *Sovetskaia Muzyka*, No. 7 (1956), 156.

73. "V Soiuze Kompozitorov," *Sovetskaia Muzyka*, No. 10 (1956), 156.

74. "Veliki Dokument epokh. O Nedostatkakh Partiinoi Raboty i Merakh Likvidatsii Trotskistkikh i Inykh Dvurushnikov," *Sovetskaia Muzyka*, No. 4 (1937), 9.

75. Igor Boelza, "Music in Wartime. Plenum of the Union of Soviet Composers in Moscow," *International Literature*, No. 6 (1944), 73. The ubiquitous Lepeshinskaya also complained once at a meeting of various art workers that the management of the Bolshoi had not always been inclined to heed the people's wishes in planning its repertoire, and it had not been willing to accept criticism from below. She also blamed playwrights for lagging behind life; see "Den' Nashei Rodiny. Za Dal'neishii Rastsvet Sovetskoi Literatury i Iskusstva," *Pravda* (December 7, 1952).

76. Ruge, p. 44.

77. A. G. Lashin, *Kul'turno-Vospitatel'naia Deiatel'nost' Sovetskogo Gosudarstva* (Moscow, 1955), p. 40.

78. Short biographies of these people appear in the following volumes of *Teatral'naia Entsiklopediia*: Messerer, III, 804–805; Struchkova, IV, 1116–17; Zakharov, II, 760–761; Golovkina, II, 41; Golovanov, II, 37.

79. E. Andreeva, "Gazeta Bol'shogo Teatra," *Sovetskaia Muzyka*, No. 2 (1953), 104–105. This paper is not available in the United States.

80. "Pod Znakom Kritiki i Samokritiki," *Teatr*, No. 1 (1953), 142.

81. *Teatr*, No. 2 (1952), 156–157.

82. "Pod Znakom . . .," *Teatr*, No. 1 (1953), 144.

83. A. Chirkov, "V Partiinoi Organizatsii Teatra," *Iskusstvo i Zhizn'* (July, 1938), 11.

84. "Smelee Razvertyvat' Kritiku v Tvorcheskikh Organizatsiakh," *Pravda* (January 6, 1954).

85. A. Makarov, K. Shatilov, N. Zubovskii, "Chto Meshaet Rostu Molodykh Darovanii?" *Pravda* (February 25, 1955).

86. "Muzhestvo Talanta," *Izvestiia* (April 1, 1962). The predominance of the name Ninel becomes more understandable if it is spelled backwards.

87. "Posle Togo Kak Vystupili 'Izvestiia' Muzhestvo Talanta," *Izvestiia* (June 16, 1962), 3.

88. G. Mogilevskaya and B. Pokrovsky, "The House We Live In," *Soviet Woman*, No. 7 (1960), 15.

89. Olga Racster, *The Master of the Russian Ballet. The Memoirs of Cav. Enrico Cecchetti* (London, 1922), p. 64.

90. "Teatr Narodnogo Tvorchestva," *Teatr i Dramaturgiia* (May, 1936), 249.

91. "Samodeiatel'nost' Teatral'naia v SSSR," *Teatral'naia Entsiklopediia*, IV, 828–829.

92. Yuri Slonimsky, *Atlantic Monthly*, CCV, 104.

93. "Miscellany-Music," *News (Trud)* (February 16, 1954), 31.

94. Priscilla Johnson, *Khrushchev and the Arts 1962–1964*, p. 230.

95. Celia Gordon, "Palaces for Children and Workers," *Soviet Woman*, No. 5 (1961), p. 25. The author does not specify whether old or new rubles.

96. "Dom Narodnogo Tvorchestva," *Teatral'naia Entsiklopediia*, II, 477.

97. *Tri Siuzhetnykh Tantsa*. Repertuar Khudozhestvennoi Samodeiatel'nosti No. 22 (Moscow, 1962), p. 72.

98. "Narodnyi Teatr," *Teatral'naia Entsiklopediia*, III, 1055–56.

99. "Needleworker and Ballerina," *Soviet Woman*, No. 12 (1963), 31.

100. "When Evening Comes," *Soviet Woman*, No. 2 (1952), 20–21.

101. T. Shatskaia, "Eto Prekrasno," *Uchitel'skaia Gazeta* (April 8, 1965), 4.

102. No title; pictures and subheading only, No. 7 (1964), 152.

103. "In Brief," *Soviet Literature*, No. 4 (1963), 177.

104. Yuri Slonimsky, "Inside the Bolshoi Ballet," in Yuri Slonimsky et al., *The Bolshoi Ballet Story* (New York, 1960), p. 103; also Evnika Svetlanova, "Terpsichore in a Metal Plant," *Soviet Life* (December, 1967), 9–13.

105. Mikhail Dolgopolov, "Balet 'Kamennyi Tsvetok' na Stsene Dvortsa Kul'tury," *Izvestiia* (May 15, 1953).

106. E. Ol'khovich and V. Zemlemerov, "V Narodnykh Teatrakh Leningrada," *Sovetskaia Muzyka*, No. 11 (1963), 103–104.

107. "Vechera Nasha Strana Slaviala Pokoritelei Kosmosa," *Sovetskaia Kul'tura* (April 13, 1965).

108. "Khronika Teatral'noi Zhizn," *Teatr*, No. 11 (1950), 116.

109. "Dlia Delegatov Kongressa," *Teatr*, No. 10 (1962), 170.

110. R. Petrushanskaya, "In Memory of Hiroshima," *Soviet Woman,* No. 8 (1963), 34.

111. M. Korolev, "Pamiati Khirosimy," *Pravda* (June 22, 1962).

112. A. Sukontsev, "Rejoinder: 'Superphosphate' Dance" *Pravda* (March 7, 1965), p. 6. Translated in *CDSP* XVII:10 (March 31, 1965), 33.

113. Vitale Fokine, trans., and Anatole Chujoy, ed., *Fokine Memoirs of a Ballet Master* (Boston, 1961), 60–63.

114. Klara Zetkin, *Reminiscences of Lenin* (London, 1929), p. 15.

115. V. Eaving, "The Ballet in the U.S.S.R.," *Soviet Travel,* No. 5 (1932), 35.

116. Viktorina Kriger, *Moi Zapiski. Teatral'nye Memuary* (Moscow and Leningrad, 1930), p. 113.

117. "The World and the Theatre," *Theatre Arts,* CCXLII (July, 1940), 464.

118. W. G. Raffé, "Modern Ballet in the Soviet Union," *Dancing Times* (August, 1937), 545.

119. Sam Russell, p. 45.

120. Nina Babochkina, "Bol'shoi in the U.S.," *USSR* (September, 1962), 51.

121. "V neskol'ko Strok," *Sovetskaia Muzyka,* No. 5 (1951), 133.

122. "Tol'ko Fakty," *Teatr,* No. 4 (1959), 132.

123. Georgii Khubov, "Bol'shoi Kontsert—Novyi Tsvetnoi Muzykal'nyi Film," *Pravda* (November 20, 1951).

124. "Smotr Narodnogo Talanta," *Pravda* (November 1, 1956), 1.

125. "Pesnia Bratstva," *Teatral'naia Zhizn',* No. 4 (1965), 5.

126. William O. Douglas, "Soviet Colonialism—Product of Terror," *Look,* XIX (December 13, 1955), 38.

127. Nina Tsepyuk, "Uzbekistan," *Dance and Dancers,* IV (November, 1953), 13.

128. Nikolai Elizov, "The Uzbek Dance," *News (Trud),* No. 17 (September 1, 1955), 31.

129. "Iskusstvo, Rozhdennoe Oktiabrem," *Pravda* (October 26, 1958).

130. *Moiseyev Dance Company,* Program of United States Tour, 1965 (New York, 1965), unpaged.

131. Kytasty, p. 29.

132. Olkhovsky, p. 72.

CHAPTER EIGHT

1. Bourman, pp. 131–132.

2. "Ansambliu—Zvanie Akademicheskogo," *Pravda* (January 18, 1965).

3. Slonimskii, *Sovetskii Balet,* p. 271.

4. "Miscellany," *News (Trud)* (January 1, 1954), 32.

5. "Iskusstvo, Pokoriaiushchee Mir," *Izvestiia* (July 29, 1962).

6. "Tantsy Mira," *Izvestiia* (February 3, 1962); also "Ansambl' Narodnogo Tantsa SSSR," *Teatral'naia Entsiklopediia,* I, 226.

7. V. Iakovlev, "Rasshiriat' Kul'turnye Sviazi Mezhdu Narodami," *Izvestiia* (April 29, 1955).

8. "Fingerprints Out, Russian Ballet In," *Dance News* (November, 1957).

9. "Tickets in Great Demand for First Moiseyev New York Season," *Dance News* (April, 1958).

10. *Moiseyev Dance Company*, Program, 1965 Tour.

11. "Moiseyev Glows in Report on U.S.," *New York Times* (January 19, 1959).

12. "Moiseyev Is Censured by Soviets for Unqualified Praise of U.S.," *New York Times* (April 16, 1959).

13. Igor Moiseyev, "Searching, Planning, Dreaming," *Soviet Literature,* No. 7 (1962), 156.

14. "Berëzka," *Teatral'naia Entsiklopediia,* I, 546–547.

15. "The 'Beryozka' Ensemble in Scandinavia," *News (Trud)* (December 15, 1951), 28.

16. Professor Y. Keldysh, "Beryozka Dancers," *Soviet Woman,* No. 1 (1955), 36.

17. "Ansambl' Pesni i Pliaski Sovetski Armii," *Teatral'naia Entsiklopediia,* I, 226.

18. Dmitry Andreyev, "Soviet Army Song and Dance Ensemble," *News (Trud)* (August 16, 1956), 17.

19. Col. G. Filippov, "Soldaty v Puti," *Pravda* (February 23, 1964).

20. L. Sedin, "Moral Charlatanry," Book Review of *Ideology and Co-Existence* (New York, 1959), in *New Times,* No. 27 (1960), 29.

21. This point is discussed by Françoise Reiss, "L'Esthétique du Ballet Sovietique," *Revue Esthétique,* XI (1958), 196.

22. Joan Lawson, "Pages from the History of Russian Ballet," *Dancing Times* (March, 1941), 336.

23. Vera Krasovskaia, *Russkii Baletnyi Teatr. Ot Voznikoveniia do Serediny XIX Veka* (Leningrad, 1958), pp. 246–247.

24. Ibid., p. 247.

25. V. Krasovskaia, *Russkii Baletnyi Teatr. Vtoroi Poloviny XIX Veka* (Moscow, 1963), p. 102.

26. Ibid., pp. 101–102.

27. Slonimskii, "Torzhestvo Russkogo Baleta," *Iskusstvo i Zhizn',* No. 5 (1938), 11.

28. Frances R. Grant, "The Russian Ballet," *Art and Archeology,* XIII (February, 1922), 73; "Adolf Bolm," *Dance News* (May, 1951).

29. Romanovsky-Krassinsky, p. 111.

30. Romola Nijinsky, *Nijinsky* (New York, 1934), p. 175.

31. Ibid., pp. 176–180.

32. Serge Lifar, *Serge Diaghilev. His Life, His Work, His Legend* (New York, 1940), p. 197.

33. Chudnovskii, p. 61.

34. Kriger, *Moi Zapiski,* p. 101.

35. *New York Journal of Commerce and Commercial Review* (November 19, 1921), 7.

36. *New York Herald* (November 21, 1921), 8; see also Grena Bennett, "Doll Shop Ballet at Criterion Treat in Music and Dance," *New York American* (December 22, 1921), 7.

37. Chudnovskii, p. 74.

Notes

38. Irma Duncan, pp. 287, 293.

39. V. Iving, "Spektakl' V. Maiia," *Sovremennyi Teatr* (June 3, 1928), 447.

40. Vsesoiuznoe Obshchestvo Kul'turnoi Sviazi s Zagranitsei.

41. Iu. B., "Valeska Gert Tantsuet," *Rabochii i Teatr*, No. 11 (1929), 7.

42. Zeglovsky, p. 55.

43. Tatiana Vecheslova, "Vmeste s Chabukiani," *Teatr*, No. 10 (1963), 79.

44. Rockwell Graham, "Harbingers of the New Russia," *American Dancer* (February, 1934), 6.

45. André Levinson, "La Soirée de Danse d'Asaf et Sulamith Messerer du Ballet de Moscow," clipping in Asaf Messerer File, New York Public Library, Dance Collection; also André Levinson, "Un Nouveau Nijinski?" *Camoedia* (March 18, 1933); L. Franc Scheuer, "Messerer in Paris," *Dancing Times* (May, 1933), 134.

46. Leandre Vaillat, *Ballets de l'Opéra de Paris* (Paris, 1943), p. 103.

47. L. Franc Scheuer, "Semenova in 'Giselle.' Our Paris Letter," *Dancing Times* (February, 1936), 637.

48. Emmanuel Eisenberg, "Diagnosis of the Dance," *New Theatre* (July–August, 1934), 24; Grace Wylie, "Dance Convention," *New Theatre*, 29.

49. Margaret Myers, "The Dance in Moscow," *New Theatre* (October, 1934), 25; L. Dal Negro, "Return from Moscow," *New Theatre* (December, 1934), 27.

50. Pauline Koner, "Russia Dances," *New Theatre* (October, 1936), 23.

51. "Paulina Koner," *Rabochii i Teatr*, No. 3 (1935), 21.

52. Dhimah, "I Dance for Moscow," *New Theatre* (October, 1935), 24–25; Chen-I-Wan, "American Dancers in Moscow," *New Theatre* (August, 1935), 21.

53. Galina Ulanova, "Nad Kartoi Mira," *Pravda* (January 2, 1962).

54. I. Martinov, "Avstriiskie Vpechatleniia," *Sovetskaia Muzyka*, No. 1 (1951), 77–83.

55. Beryl de Zoete, "Maggio Musicale, 1951," *Ballet*, II (September, 1951), 19.

56. "Soviet Performers in Italy," *Izvestiia* (August 1–2, 1951), *CDSP* III:32 (September 22, 1951), 31–32.

57. Galina Ulanova, "Our Tour of Italy," *News (Trud)* (July, 1951), 26–29.

58. "Romeo i Dzul'etta v Italii," *Sovetskaia Muzyka*, No. 10 (1955), 151–152.

59. "Soviet Dancers in London," *Dancing Times* (December, 1953), 137; "Red Dancers in Pink Condition," *Dance News* (December, 1953).

60. J. L. "More Russian Visitors," *Dancing Times* (December, 1954), 149.

61. Joan Lawson, "The Soviet Dancers," *Dancing Times* (January, 1955), 219; "Angliiskie Vpechatleniia i Vstrechi," *Teatr*, No. 4 (1955), 158.

62. Francis Coleman, "Canadian Dateline," *Dance Magazine*, XXVIII (June, 1954), 78.

63. Galina Ulanova, "Why I Did Not Dance in Paris," *News (Trud)* (June 16, 1954), 24; also *Izvestiia* (May 12 and 16, 1954).

64. "Protesty Frantsuzskoi Obshchestvennosti Protiv Zapreshcheniia Vystuplenii Sovetskikh Artistov," *Izvestiia* (May 20, 1954).

65. Natalia Dudinskaia, "V Parizhe i Berline," *Pravda* (July 25, 1954); "Privytie v Berlin Gruppy Artistov Sovetskogo Baleta," *Izvestiia* (May 10, 1954).

66. Kurt Peters, "Russian Dancers in Berlin," *Dancing Times* (July, 1954), 607.

67. *Keesings Archives* (July 23–30, 1955), #14330.

68. Olga Lepeshinakaya, "We Should Meet," *News (Trud)* (September 16, 1955), 18.

69. "Report of the Central Committee of the Communist Party of the Soviet Union to the 20th Party Congress," *Pravda* (February 15, 1956); Leo Gruliow, ed., *Current Soviet Policies II. The Documentary Record of the 20th Communist Party Congress and Its Aftermath* (New York, 1957), 36.

70. E. Surits, "Prava li Frantsuzskaia Kritika," *Teatr*, No. 11 (1956), 81.

71. "De Valois, Webster Return from Moscow: Exchange Set," *Dance News* (May, 1956).

72. "A Foul Provocation," *Pravda* (September 1, 1956), 4, in *CDSP*, VIII:35 (October 10, 1956), 19–20. Cultural exchanges by Russian dancers have produced a number of incidents of arrest. In 1926, a group of ballet dancers in Singapore had an argument with their entrepreneur over salaries and ended by being arrested as strikers; see R. [sic], "Arest Russkogo Baleta," *Zhizn' Iskusstva* (July 27, 1926), 20. In 1958, Olga Lepeshinskaya was accused of shoplifting while on tour at the Brussels World's Fair. She was defended by her administrators, who affirmed that she would not have needed to steal because she was already one of the richest women in Russia; reported by Howard Taubman, "Shoplifting Laid to Soviet Ballerina," *New York Times* (June 29, 1958), and "Soviet Ballerina Scoffs at Accusation of Theft," *New York Times* (June 30, 1958). The following year in New York, Gennadi P. Lvov, an accordianist with the Moiseyev company, was accused of taking twenty-three ties, five pairs of socks, a handbag, and a brassiere from Macy's; "Thrifty Russian Upsets Macy's but Store Drops Charge of Theft," *New York Times* (June 2, 1959).

73. "V Redaktsiiu Gazety 'Izvestiia,'" *Izvestiia* (September 21, 1956).

74. *Ballet Annual*, XII, 1958 (London, 1957), 24.

75. Ekaterina Sheveleva, "Nashi Angliiskie Druz'ia," *Trud* (November 1, 1956).

76. *Ballet Annual*, 1958, 24.

77. "K Gastroliam Angliiskoi Baletnoi Truppy 'Sedlers Uells,'" *Izvestiia* (November 18, 1956).

78. V. Laikin, "Biditel'nost'—Nashe Oruzhie," *Komsomolskaia Pravda* (September 15, 1960).

79. "Balet," *Bol'shaia Entsiklopediia*, IV, 126.

80. Well explained by Selma Jeanne Cohen, "Avant-Garde Choreography," *Dance Magazine*, XXXVI (June, 1962), 23.

81. John Fizer, "The Problem of the Unconscious in the Creative Process As Treated by Soviet Aesthetics," *The Journal of Aesthetics and Art Criticism*, XXI (Summer, 1963), 399–406; also V. M. Friche, "Freidizm i Iskusstvo," in *Problemy Iskusstvovedenia. Sbornik Statei po Voprosam Sotsiologii Iskusstva i Literatura*, 2nd ed. (Moscow, 1931), 48–60.

82. A. Fadeev, "O Literaturnoi Kritike," *Bol'shevik*, No. 13 (1947), 27.

83. P. P. Bondarenko and M. Kh. Rabinovich, "Nauchno Soveshchanie po Voprosam

Notes

Ideologicheskoi Bor'by s Sovremennym Freidizmom," *Voprosy Filosofii,* No. 2 (1959), 164–165.

84. B. Asaf'ev, "Za Novuiu Muzykal'nuiu Estetiku, za Sotsialisticheskii Realizm. Na S"ezd Sovetskikh Kompozitorov," *Sovetskaia Muzyka,* No. 2 (1948), 17.

85. V. Krasovskaia, "Razlozhenie Baletnogo Iskusstva na Zapade," *Teatr,* No. 10 (1950), 101. Similarly uncomplimentary remarks accusing the West of allowing mysticism and eroticism in their ballets were made in 1949 by S. Solodovnikov, director of the Bolshoi Theatre, who complained of the depravity and "formalistic decadent tendencies" manifested in the Sadler's Wells production of *Rake's Progress* and *Hamlet;* see "The Composer and Theater," *Sovetskaya Muzyka,* No. 4 (1949), in *CDSP,* 1:28 (August 9, 1949), 16.

86. Ibid., pp. 100–105. As Krasovskaia says, all of these authors have produced works which were used as the basic ideas for ballets in the West, either before or after her article. Proust's *Remembrance of Things Past* is reflected in the Tudor ballet *Dim Lustre;* Freudian themes were used in the Tudor ballets *Undertow* and *Pillar of Fire,* among others; one of the most direct uses of a Sartrean theme was in the ballet *Sonate à Trois* based upon Sartre's *Huis Clos,* as well as another ballet, *The Maids,* based upon Sartre's introduction to a play by Jean Genêt. Leslie Hurry designed the set for *Swan Lake* and *Hamlet* and Dali designed the ones for *Sentimental Colloquy, Mad Tristan, El Café de Chinitas, Labyrinthe,* and *Bacchanale,* among other examples of surrealist scenery. See C. W. Beaumont, *Ballet Design Past and Present* (New York, 1946), pp. 199, 212, 213.

87. Krasovskaia, p. 101.

88. Jean Laurent and Julie Sazonova, "*Serge Lifar. Renovateur du Ballet Français* (Paris, 1960), p. 91.

89. Viktorina Kriger, "When Will the Ballerina Begin to Dance," *Dance News* (October, 1958); translation of article in *Sovetskaia Kul'tura* (July 10, 1958).

90. M. Gabovitch, "Brillante Maitrise du Ballet Français," *Études Sovietiques* (July, 1958), 17.

91. *Fundamentals of Marxism-Leninism,* pp. 48–49.

92. "Music: The Bolshoi Ballet in Brussels," *New York Times* (June 23, 1958).

93. "Ban on Bolshoi Ballet," *London Times* (March 31, 1958).

94. "Text of Joint Communique of U.S. and Soviet Union on Cultural Exchanges," *New York Times* (January 28, 1958).

95. "Text of Khrushchev Debate with Skouras during the Luncheon at Film Studio," *New York Times* (September 20, 1959), © 1959 by the New York Times Company. Reprinted by permission.

96. M. Kharlamov and O. Vadeyev, eds., *Face to Face. The Story of N. S. Khrushchev's Visit to the U.S.A.* September 15–27, 1959; printed in U.S.S.R.

97. "Summary of the Dinner Debate between U.S. Union Leaders and Khrushchev," *New York Times* (September 22, 1959).

98. "Ballet Theatre Left Unsure of Heralded Soviet Tour," *Dance News* (June, 1960).

99. "Ballet Theatre May Still Dance in Soviet Union," *Dance News* (September, 1960).

100. Eugene Palatsky, "In Russia with American Ballet Theatre," *Dance Magazine,* XXXIV (December, 1960), p. 28.

101. "Dancing Murder," *Variety* (December, 1950); clipping in Ballet Theatre Folder, Dance Collection, New York Public Library.

102. Louis Bromfield, "Fall River Legend," *Theatre Arts,* CCL (June–July, 1948), 30.

103. N. Roslavleva, "Amerikanskii Teatr Baleta," *Muzykal'naia Zhizn'* (October, 1960), Ballet Theatre Folder, Dance Collection, New York Public Library.

104. E. Lutskaya, "American Ballet," *Culture and Life,* No. 13 (1960), 38.

105. Roslavleva, op. cit., and "Na Spektakliakh Amerikanskogo Baleta," *Leningradskaia Pravda* (October 12, 1960).

106. "Nureyev," *London Observer* (May 27, 1962).

107. "Dance," *Time Magazine,* LXXXV (April 16, 1965), 51B.

108. Arnold Haskell, "L'affaire Nureyev," *Dancing Times* (March, 1963), 336; Marie-Françoise Christout, "Presstime," *Dance Magazine,* XXXVII (March, 1963), 82.

109. "Richter Cancels Recitals in Athens over Nureyev," *New York Times* (August 28, 1963).

110. A. H. Franks, "Leningrad State Kirov Ballet," *Dancing Times* (July, 1961), 601.

111. Richard C. Wald, "Red Ballet Dancers Waltz in on Dentists in Britain," *New York Herald Tribune* (September 6, 1961).

112. M. Gabovich, "Baleta-iskusstvo Angliiskogo," *Sovetskaia Kul'tura* (July 16, 1961).

113. "Ballet: Bolshoi Stages U.S. Premiere of 'Spartacus,'" *New York Times* (September 13, 1962).

114. "Bolshoi, in Shift, Cancels 3 'Spartacus' Showings," *New York Times* (September 18, 1962).

115. *N'iu-Iuork Siti Balet. Gastroli v SSSR* (Moscow, 1962), Program of Soviet performance.

116. "How Moscow Press Received N.Y.C. Ballet," *Dance News* (November, 1962), 12.

117. "Shock Waves in Moscow," *Time,* LXXX (October 12, 1962), 57.

118. Boris Lvov-Anokhin, "Balanchine's Ballet in Moscow," *Soviet Literature,* No. 3 (1963), 165.

119. David Miller, "Moscow Critic Finds 'Vulgarity' in N.Y. Ballet," *New York Herald Tribune* (October 20, 1962).

120. "How Moscow Press . . .," 12.

121. Mikhail Chudnovsky, "New York City Ballet As I See It," *Dance Magazine,* XXVII (January, 1963), p. 39.

122. "Balanchine Talks to Russia about His Artistic Creed," *Dance News* (December, 1962), from the October issue of *Sovetskii Artist.*

123. Natalia Roslavleva, "A Lively Controversy on New York City Ballet Soviet Season," *Dancing Times* (January, 1963), 229.

124. "Soviet Ballerina Asks Experimental Theater," *Washington Post* (January 2, 1963).

Notes

125. Ernest B. Furgurson, "Leningrad 'Eggheads' Defy Party," *Baltimore Sun* (March 19, 1963).

126. "Vysokaia Ideinost' i Khudozhestvennoe Masterstvo—Velikaia Sila Sovetskoi Literatury i Iskusstva," *Pravda* (March 10, 1963).

127. Natalia Roslavleva, "The Most American. Russian Opinions about the Joffrey Ballet," *Dancing Times* (March, 1964), 311.

128. Ibid.

129. Nikolai Elyash, "American Ballet," *USSR* (June, 1964), 56–57.

130. N. Dudinskaia, "Baletnaia Amerika," *Sovetskaia Kul'tura* (January 26, 1965). The patron referred to was Rebecca Harkness. The Joffrey Company has since revived and has become attached to the New York City Center. The Harkness Ballet was formed after the split and has also become a successful company.

131. "Tvorit' Dlia Naroda, vo Imia Kommunizma. Rech' Sekretaria TsK KPSS L. F. Il'icheva," *Pravda* (December 22, 1962).

132. S. Iutkevich, "Golub' Mira Priletaet v Pekin," *Teatr*, No. 4 (1951), 99–106.

133. Mary Grace Swift, "Ballet in Communist China," *Dance Magazine* (November, 1967), 61–65.

134. "Hail the Victories of Mao Tse-tung's Line on Literature and Art," *Peking Review* (June 30, 1967), 34.

135. "Chairman Mao's Line for Literature and Art Is the Line for Revolutionary Literature and Art Throughout the World," *Peking Review* (January 1, 1967), 25.

136. Mary Skeaping, "Ballet in China. Peking Ballet School," *Dancing Times* (April, 1961), 412. David Ellis, "Notes on the Bolshoi School and Its Influence in the East," *Dancing Times* (February, 1958), 220.

137. Frederick Barghoorn, *The Soviet Cultural Offensive. The Role of Cultural Diplomacy in Soviet Foreign Policy* (Princeton, 1960), p. 208.

138. Mikhail Dolgopolov, "Masters of Indian Art in Moscow," *News (Trud)* (September 16, 1954), 26.

139. Nikolai Mikhailov, "Cultural Contacts with India," *News (Trud)* (March 1, 1956), 13.

140. Vladimir Preobrazhenskii, "Balet Kambodzhi," *Pravda* (August 3, 1965).

141. *Pravda* (August 8, 1964).

142. Olga Lepeshinskaya, "Japanese Impressions," *Soviet Woman*, No. 3 (1958), 39–41; see also L. Kudrevatykh, "Triumf Sovetskogo Baleta," *Pravda* (September 20, 1957).

143. "Pis'mo Iaponskoi Baleriny," *Teatr*, No. 4 (1956), 187; Muraichi Horie, "Japanese-Soviet Friendship," *Culture and Life*, No. 3 (1957), 44.

144. I. Sheiko, "They Met in Moscow," *Soviet Woman*, No. 12 (1962), 15.

145. Susanna Zvyagina, "The Other End of the World," *New Times*, No. 51 (1959), 30.

146. "Uspekh Armianskikh Tantsorov," *Izvestiia* (January 17, 1965).

147. "V Kaire, Beirute i Damaske," *Teatr*, No. 2 (1956), 178–179.

148. "U.S.S.R. Minister of Culture N. Mikhailov on Cultural Relations with the United Arab Republic, *New Times*, No. 17 (1958), 13.

149. In these years, Soviet teachers began to spread their activity in diverse spots of the globe. By 1961, such teachers were reported working in Japan, the United Arab Republic, Belgium, Mongolian People's Republic, and East Germany. Yuri Kondratov, "The 'Secret' of the Soviet Ballet," *Culture and Life,* No. 2 (1961), 42.

150. V. Duganov and L. Duganova, "Uchilishche v Drevnikh Piramid," *Sovetskaia Kul'tura* (May 25, 1965).

151. *Sovetskii Soiuz,* No. 8 (1961), front cover.

152. "Pervoe Vystuplenie," *Pravda* (August 9, 1947).

153. Bezil Devidson, "Kul'tura Novoi Afriki," *Sovetskaia Kul'tura* (July 29, 1965).

154. Irina Kirillova, "Ballet at the Moscow Festival," *Dancing Times* (December, 1957), 117.

155. "Laureaty Konkursov Venskogo Festivalia Molodezhi," *Sovetskaia Muzyka,* No. 9 (1959), 201.

156. "Vdoknovliaiushchii Primer, Zametki o Vsemirnom Festivale Demokraticheskoi Molodezhi 1949 Goda," *Teatr,* No. 11 (1949), 26.

157. Ibid., 27.

158. Ibid., 29.

159. S. Levit, *Sovetskaia Muzyka v Bor'be za Mir* (Moscow, 1957), p. 131.

160. Maiia Plisetskaia, "Neugasimoe Flamia. Zametki Uchastniki III Vsemirnogo Festivalia Molodezhi," *Teatr,* No. 11 (1951), 99.

161. Ibid., 99.

162. "V Muzykal'noi i Teatral'noi Sektsiakh VOKS," *Sovetskaia Muzyka,* No. 10 (1951), 107.

163. Ibid., 107.

164. Levit, p. 166.

165. "Konkurs Baleta." *Izvestiia* (May 20, 1964).

166. *Programme of the Communist Party of the Soviet Union.* Adopted by the 22nd Congress of the C.P.S.U. October 31, 1961 (Moscow, 1961), p. 119.

167. Emily Coleman, "Russia's Best," *Newsweek,* LIII (April 13, 1959), 116.

CHAPTER NINE

1. "At the Top of My Voice," *International Literature* No. 4–5 (1940), 172–176.

2. Paléologue, I, 213.

3. *Soviet Foreign Propaganda* (Princeton, 1964), pp. 67, 226.

4. See p. 301.

INDEX

Index

Index

Index

Calmette, Gaston, 251
Cambodia, Royal Ballet of, 277, 295
Cassela, Alfredo, 113
Castro, Raoul, 245
Catherine II (Empress of Russia), 10
Cechetti, Enrico, 250
Céline, Louis F, 263
Censorship, 15–16, 79–80, 292–293 (see also Repertoire Index)
Central Executive Committee *(VTsIK)*, 70, 101
Central House of Workers of Art, 224
Central Theatre Committee *(Tsentroteatr)*, 32
Cézanne, Paul, 264
Chabukiani, Vakhtang Mikhailovich, 121, 160, 193, 196, 217, 220, 229, 253–254, 305–307, 309–311
Chagall, Marc, 39, 94
Chaliapin, Fyodor, 21, 33, 287
Chamber Ballet, 67, 69
Chamberlain, Neville, 68
Changa, Yevgeny Ianovich, 304
Cheka, 222
Chekrygin, Alexander Ivanovich, 308
Chen, Eugen, 253
Chen, Sylvia, 253
Chernetskaya, 114
Chernyshevsky, N. G., 22
Chervinsky, N., 310
Chesnakov, V., 307
Chiang Kai-shek, 72, 253
Children's Song and Dance Ensemble, 231
Chinese ballet, 275–276
Chinese folk dance, 281–282
Chopin, Frédéric, 49, 174, 301
Choreographic Institutes
    General, 70, 207–218
    School of Alexei Mikhailovich, 7
    Imperial schools, 8, 10, 12–13, 67, 208
    Leningrad State Academic Vaganova Choreographic Institute, 8, 97, 186, 208–209, 213–214, 217
    Moscow Academic Choreographic Institute of the Bolshoi Theatre, 117, 208–210, 212–213, 215, 217

Lunacharsky State Institute of Theatrical Art (GITIS), 216, 227
Chowdhry, Tara, 276
Chulaki, Mikhail Ivanovich, 114, 130, 137, 189, 259–260, 312–313
Clemenceau, Georges, 251
Cocteau, Jean, 264
Commissariat of Enlightenment, 32, 40, 48, 54–55, 58
Committee on Affairs of the Arts, 101, 127–128, 159–160, 173, 182, 204, 225
Communist Manifesto, The, 36, 99–100
Communist Party
    Cell in Theatres, 131, 226–230, 291
    Central Committee, 41, 43, 101, 126–127, 150, 205
        Agitation and Propaganda Department, 205, 182
        Ideological Commission, 151
    Congresses
        8th, 33, 34
        10th, 54
        12th, 61
        15th, 78
        19th, 205, 227
        20th, 149, 258
        22nd, 205
Comédie Française, 257
Comintern, 255
"Confusion instead of Music," 103, 128, 294
Constructivism, 39–40, 43, 62, 66, 68, 92
"Cossack Song about Stalin, The," 106
Cossacks, 36, 40, 104–105, 115–116, 199
    Don, 36, 106
    Kuban, 106–107, 109–110, 294
    Terek, 106
Council of People's Commissars, 31–32, 37, 70, 101, 185, 220
"Cried the Grey Cuckoo," 168
Cubism, 39, 41

Dadashev, S., 307
Dadishkiliani, Otar Mikhailovich, 309
Dali, Salvador, 264
Daniel, Yuri, 151, 221
Danilova, Alexandra, 27, 50

Index

Index

Index